WOMAN *Critiqued*

REBECCA L. COPELAND, editor

WOMAN *Critiqued*

TRANSLATED

ESSAYS ON

JAPANESE WOMEN'S

WRITING

UNIVERSITY OF HAWAI'I PRESS

Honolulu

11   10   09   08   07   06   6   5   4   3   2   1

Library of Congress Cataloging-in-Publication Data
Woman critiqued : translated essays on Japanese
women's writing / Rebecca L. Copeland, editor.
p.   cm.
Includes bibliographical references and index.
ISBN-13: 978-0-8248-2958-2 (hardcover : alk. paper)
ISBN-10: 0-8248-2958-1 (hardcover : alk. paper)
ISBN-13: 978-0-8248-3038-0 (pbk. : alk. paper)
ISBN-10: 0-8248-3038-5 (pbk. : alk. paper)
1. Japanese literature—Women authors—History and
criticism.   2. Japanese literature—20th century—
History and criticism.   3. Women authors,
Japanese—20th century.   I. Copeland, Rebecca L.
PL725.W66 2006
895.6'0992870904—dc22   2005025329

Title page illustration: Meiko Ando, *Forest Dance,*
2000.

University of Hawai'i Press books are printed on
acid-free paper and meet the guidelines for perma-
nence and durability of the Council on Library
Resources.

Designed by Richard Hendel
Printed by Sheridan Books, Inc.

CONTENTS

*I don't wish not to be a woman, but I'd certainly like
to be a woman whose sense of purpose comes from within.*
—Uno Chiyo, "A Genius of Imitation"

"Just once I would like to read a work by a woman writer without being reminded of her sex." I have heard this comment from time to time ever since I began the study of the Japanese woman writer Uno Chiyo in the early 1980s. At first the remark came from senior scholars in the field. More recently I have heard the same from students. The statement is clearly motivated by a desire to treat all writers fairly, neutrally, equally—as artists. Implicit to the statement as well is a wish to get beyond delimiting frameworks, to depoliticize readings, and to "open" texts to new interpretations. Before we cross the threshold into an aesthetically pure realm of reading, however, greater attention still needs to be paid to the fact that few women writers over the course of the last century have been allowed to write without being reminded of their sex. One can well imagine that the woman writer who is read as a woman writer might herself think on occasion, "Just once I would like to write a work without being reminded of my sex." But it is not really one's own sex that one would like to get beyond, surely, but the way that sex has been scripted, the expectations that surround it, the "assumptions in which [it is] drenched." [1]

A variety of factors inspired this volume. Western-language scholarship on Japanese literature has been engaged in the revisionist work of recovering lost or marginalized women writers since the late 1970s. The fruits of this labor have resulted in translations and biographies that have enriched our understanding of these women's creative energies and of Japanese literature as a whole. The last fifteen years have seen conferences, panels, and symposia dedicated to exploring the link between gender and discursive practices in Japan. A number of these have culminated in proceedings and publications that have increased interest in women's writing and the dynamics of gendered discourses in Japanese literature. This volume complements this work and furthers the field by offering readers more of the contexts in and against which women have written in twentieth-century Japan.

The work of Western-language scholars on Japanese women's literature has provided those who do not read Japanese with an important window onto an aspect of Japanese culture long ignored by mainstream media and academics. In this regard as well it has been of immense value. But what of the way women have been received and read *in* Japan? How, as my students frequently ask, did *Japanese* readers read the Japanese women writers we study in class? In its collective mission of providing translations of critical essays, this book advances our understanding of the way women writers have been received in Japan over the course of the twentieth century and expands our understanding of the role of gender and writing within a Japanese cultural context.

Translations of Japanese literary criticism have increased over the last decades as well. Thanks to the work of Aileen Gatten, Nicholas Teele, Mark Harbison, Earl Miner, David Chibbett, and others, we have multivolume translations of the literary histories of scholars such as Konishi Jin'ichi and Katō Shūichi. Subsequently we have been treated to translations of works by critics with a more modern focus. Brett de Bary translated and edited Karatani Kōjin's incisive *The Origins of Modern Japanese Literature* in 1993. Paul Anderer followed in 1995 with translations from Kobayashi Hideo's prewar works. Michele Marra brought out a collection of essays in 1999 under the rubric of modern Japanese aesthetics, introducing English readers to the artistic considerations underpinning much of the subsequent literary production in Japan. In 2001 Michael Bourdaghs translated Kamei Hideo's *Transformations of Sensibility: The Phenomenology of Meiji Literature,* an incisive study by a renowned scholar of Meiji (1868–1912) literature. More recently James Fujii has edited a collection of translations of Maeda Ai's essays, thus bringing the work of this prominent literary critic to an English readership. *Woman Critiqued* takes its cue from these precursors. Rather than focusing on the work of a single critic, this study concentrates on the way a variety of critics, writers, and scholars—male and female, prominent and obscure—have critiqued, constructed, and confronted the concept of "the writing woman" in Japan.

Volume Arrangement

Given that the subject under discussion in this volume is literature, readers will find the essays herein brimming with the names of authors, editors, publishers, and awards and the titles of stories, books, and journals. Even for those familiar with twentieth-century Japanese literature, the barrage of names may be daunting. In an effort to provide essential context for the translations, to identify the names introduced, and to keep endnotes to a minimum, the works are arranged into chapters preceded by introductions that supply information for appreciating the texts under consideration. In addition, the glossary at the end of this volume provides brief introductions of the names that appear in the essays; contributors are identified by their initials.

This volume offers a variety of snapshots from different eras and perspectives so as to exemplify the complexities of the reception that awaited the "writing woman." Not every era, sector, or aspect of women's writing in the twentieth century could be represented. To assist the English-language readers wanting to delve deeper, I have appended a bibliography that includes the works cited in this volume, as well as a list of recommended further readings for those wishing to continue the exploration of modern Japanese women's writing.

Acknowledgments

As a book is being written, ideas grow and transform with the progress of the project—often to the point where the end version looks little like the earlier imagined. In a single-author work, this kind of creative development is not unduly demanding. But with collaborative volumes the challenges change with the responsibilities. It is generally easier for an author to communicate her own inchoate ideas to herself than it is to try to articulate them to a wide assortment of collaborators. She can impose deadlines on herself and then move them at will without elaborate apology. She can issue directives to herself and then change her mind. But to behave this way with a collaborative work taxes the patience and the loyalties of one's contributors. I am guilty of testing my collaborators. And I consider myself extremely fortunate that all have remained steadfast in their dedication to this project. I owe all my collaborators a great debt of gratitude. They proved themselves to be receptive, creative, enthusiastic, and punctual (for the most part).

I am especially beholden to Jan Bardsley and Janine Beichman, who were always there at the other end of an e-mail message to offer advice, encouragement, and emotional support. This project would not have been possible without them. Eiji Sekine and Maryellen Toman Mori were especially helpful in recommending texts to translate and works to include in the bibliography. Although they are not contributors to this volume, I am also grateful to Livia Monnet for her constant kindnesses, to Janice Brown for her understanding, and to my colleague Nancy Berg for all the drafts she read.

Additionally I would like to thank Pamela Kelley at the University of Hawai'i Press, who did not flinch when she saw the size of the first draft, and to Bojana Ristich, who managed the copyediting with amazing efficiency. For that matter, a special thanks must go to the anonymous reviewers who were so careful in reading that unwieldy first draft and offered thoughtful and constructive comments. While I may seem to be overly critical of "critics" in the following chapters, the success of our field depends on the selfless and largely unnoticed dedication of critics like these.

NOTES

1. Rich, *On Lies, Secrets, and Silence,* p. 34.

A CENTURY OF READING
WOMEN'S WRITING IN JAPAN
An Introduction
Rebecca L. Copeland

No male writer has written primarily or even largely for women, or with the sense of women's criticism as a consideration when he chooses his materials, his themes, his language. But to a lesser or greater extent, every woman writer has written for men, even when, like Virginia Woolf, she was supposed to be addressing women.
—Adrienne Rich

In her story "Godaidō" (The Temple Godai), published posthumously in 1896, Tazawa Inabune depicted the way literary criticism directed and inhibited women's written expression: "These women writers are certainly pitiful creatures. Whenever they allow themselves to describe even a little of their own thoughts, they are immediately derided as hussies. Fearing just this sort of reaction, they avoid writing what they really want to, both hoping to be praised as feminine and lacking the courage to go against public opinion."[1]

Inabune knew of what she spoke. A year earlier she had been the target of a harsh critical review when one of her stories featured a young woman who refused an arranged marriage. After deriding the author for portraying a flapper *(hasuha musume)* instead of a properly modest woman, one critic charged that it "was not clear where the portrait of [the heroine] ended and the author's began."[2] Inabune died before she could respond to this criticism. But critical readings that sought to establish a particular model for women's expressions continued to flourish. Nearly a century later, in her 1983 essay on women and language, writer and critic Tomioka Taeko noted the way expectations of the male critic—or, more accurately perhaps, those who write in "men's language"—have continued to exert influence on the female literary voice:

Men who use "men's language" are responsible for establishing the reputations of female writers. Unconsciously, women express themselves in a manner "for men." Writing "for men" takes the form of fitting into the category of "things women write" rather than writing with "men's language." Whether conscious or unconscious, there is a use of "women's language" which caters to the reviews written in "men's language." A "female-school" poet or a "feminine-style" fiction writer does not invite male hostility since they do not challenge "men's language."[3]

These observations of the impact criticism has had in defining and confining literary expression affirm the assessment American poet and essayist Adrienne Rich leveled against the North American male-dominated literary establishment of the 1970s, cited above in the epigraph.[4] Rich's comment in turn echoes the struggles to which Virginia Woolf alluded much earlier in her battle to overcome the pressures of the "Angel in the House," whose whispered admonitions in the ear of the author as she sat, pen in hand, threatened to silence the author's creative impulses: "Be sympathetic, be tender; flatter; deceive, use all the arts and wiles of our sex. Never let anyone guess that you have a mind of your own. Above all, be pure!"[5]

In order appropriately to appreciate the textual depths, subterfuges, strategies, omissions, and choices—or lack thereof—confronting the modern woman writer in Japan, readers must consider the kind of criticisms and expectations that she has faced. We must listen to the admonitions that have been whispered in her ear and pay attention to the way she has herself responded to them. What did it mean to be a woman writer in twentieth-century Japan? How was she defined and how did this definition confine her artistic sphere? Western-language scholarship on Japan has addressed these questions over the last thirty years—with careful analysis of women's writing, grounded in Japanese literary history and laced with Western literary criticism. This volume builds on existing scholarship by offering English-language readers access to a number of the critical sources that Western scholars have used in their studies. The essays translated herein represent some of the more salient critiques that have been directed at women writers, on the one hand, and the way women writers have reacted to them, on the other. Whereas not meant to be a complete or exhaustive coverage of all aspects or genres identified with women's literary endeavors in the twentieth century, the essays in this volume provide, in their aggregate, an understanding of the evaluative systems under which women writers have worked.

Over the course of the twentieth century, but particularly in the earlier half, many critics used the term *joryū sakka* to describe the "woman writer."[6] With no clear evaluative nuances, the phrase was intuitive and applicable to any writer who happened to be female. Not all critics have been as comfortable with such inattention to the consequences of the labeling. "Why is there a specific literary category entitled 'women's writing,' when there is no such defined category for male writers?" Hasegawa Izumi asked in 1976. The answer that he then provided is illuminating: "Inherent in the word 'writer' is the implication that the sex of the writer is male, while the word 'literature' similarly implies that which is written by men."[7] Hasegawa's statement makes it clear that literature was by definition a male enterprise, occupation, and privilege. Women were barred from it, not necessarily out of any malicious attempt at exclusivity but because they were—at least in the minds of those who had the power to make such claims—biologically, emotionally, and/or socially incapable of achieving the objectivity necessary to write superior works that pursued the expression of higher truths.

By the early 1980s, with the development of a conscious feminist approach to literary analysis in Japan, these assumptions of inherent difference and the limits they imposed were subjected to rigorous scrutiny. In conjunction with an increasing interest in challenging the traditional parameters of a women's literature and of a literary criticism that was, as Takahara Eiri noted in 1999, "saturated with the thinking of the adult male," critics began to treat male-authored texts to new, feminist readings.[8] In their playful yet pointed critique of canonical male writers, *Danryū bungakuron* (On men's literature, 1992), Ueno Chizuko, Ogura Chikako, and Tomioka Taeko not only hold men to the same gender-based criticism women have received over the centuries, but they also open these male-authored texts to new interpretive strategies. In many respects their discussion of "men's literature" brings this volume full circle. An anthology that begins with men critiquing "women's literature" ends with women critiquing men writers *as men*. This is not to suggest that essentialization is any less objectionable when directed against those traditionally in positions of power. But the intentional self-consciousness of the critique lays bare the implications of the practice.

This volume is divided into six chapters organized under headings that encapsulate the general character of the subsequent essays. The chapters follow one another more or less chronologically, with some gaps as well as overlaps in both the time covered and the concepts explored. The organization of the essays should not imply an ideological progression. Rather, what readers will find is the way the same arguments continue to insert themselves into the critical discourse of the day. The terminology and the rigidity of the arguments may transform with time. But at the core the attitudes enshrined remain the same. Regardless of shifts in historical circumstances and in critical voices, as long as the woman writer remains a "woman writer," the insistence on her inherent "womanliness," her imitative nature, her physicality, and her vanity remains constant. Concomitant with this constancy is the essentialization of "woman" as an unproblematic category. Female critics and writers are equally accountable to charges of essentialization, with claims that only a woman writer can create a "real" female character, for example. But the defensiveness of their position is perhaps understandable when we consider another constant in these essays, and that is the perceived right of men to determine when, where, and how a woman should write.

The women writers represented in this volume, therefore, are constantly being reminded that they are *women* writers and are put in the position of needing to write either in accord with or opposition to prevailing (male) attitudes about what that means. The organization of the essays into thematic divisions clarifies how the discussion of women writers has been framed by certain assumptions and how women have repeatedly tried to intervene by playing with, undercutting, or attempting to exceed these assumptions. Each section is preceded by an introduction written by American, Australian, and Japanese scholars of modern Japanese women's literature. The introductions contextualize the translated essays historically and draw out for remark aspects of the essays that warrant particular scrutiny or explication.

The Feminine Critique

Chapter 1 of this volume, "The Feminine Critique," includes four essays that range from 1898 to 1938 and introduce readers to the more prominent criticisms confronting would-be women writers in the early twentieth century. Not prepared to discourage women from writing altogether, critics were mindful of trying to find the form and approach that would most appropriately reveal a woman's strengths. Kunikida Doppo, writing in 1898, urges women to devote themselves to translation. Not requiring excessive amounts of uninterrupted time, imagination, or diverse experiences—which women do not have—translation, in Doppo's estimation, offers women a satisfying outlet for their creative energies. Others find the poetic form—emblematic of the suggestively insubstantial beauty of past tradition—most suitable to women. What is notable in early discussions of women's writing is the recurring insistence that it serve as a feminine complement to the more masculine undertaking of "serious" writing. A woman must not strive to write "like a man," the literary establishment, or *bundan,* asserted.[9] Rather, she should mine that within her that best presents her innate "womanliness," or *onnarashisa.*[10]

The characterization of "womanliness" was keyed to and exacerbated by social mores and restrictions. Believed to be the intellectually weaker of the sexes, the late-nineteenth-century woman was denied equal access to education. Predictably, she therefore had a more difficult time availing herself of contemporary intellectual discourses and by necessity resorted to a language of metaphor and emotion, which consequently only confirmed assumptions that she was incapable of anything but such language. Restricted by traditional codes of behavior from interacting with others beyond her own social ken, she was not permitted a broader exposure to contemporary social and political concerns and as a consequence focused her attention on that with which she did have contact. Thus she was assumed incapable of writing of anything else. Social reality influenced literary production, which led to critical assumptions. Assumptions coalesced into orthodoxy, which in turn restricted literary production.

Because critics shared a collective understanding of the primacy of this "womanliness," there was no need to subject it to scrutiny or attempt to define it. Women were to be womanly because they were women. And to be womanly meant to be first and foremost gentle. Gentleness gave rise to other subsidiary qualities such as modesty, altruism, and devotion to home and family and made the woman particularly susceptible to emotion and sensitive to beauty. As poet and essayist Yosano Akiko pointedly observed in 1921, women who did not recognize their inherent natures as women were deemed unwomanly and subject to repudiation. "No matter which or how many superb qualities a woman might have, if she lacks one thing—womanliness—her value as a human being is taken as zero."[11] A 1908 roundtable discussion among Oguri Fūyō and four other male writers in the journal *Shinchō* (New currents), also included in chapter 1, underscores the devastating effect of this "zero" status. If a woman writer lacks "womanliness," these critics state, they will not read her works. For a writer to be left unread (but not apparently uncriticized) is ultimately to be "nothing," a silence, a blank, zero.

Since the onset of the Meiji period, male reformers had encouraged women's literary activities. Hoping to inspire a revival of a female strain in writing, they urged the woman writer to demonstrate what was presumed to be the elegant gentility of tenth- and eleventh-century writers such as Murasaki Shikibu.[12] The women who answered the call, such as Kitada Usurai and the above-mentioned Tazawa Inabune, were known at the time as *keishū sakka,* or lady writers. They were generally of a privileged background and had been afforded an above-average education. But try as they might to write in a womanly way, they were inevitably to discover that the mere act of writing, of publishing, of pushing themselves forward, invited censure. Those who endeavored to pen "womanly" pieces were marginalized for being overly sentimental and unworthy of serious scrutiny. As the feisty critics in the 1908 *Shinchō* article observed, such writers offered little more than "housewife art" *(okusama gei):* "Women write fiction half for their own amusement—much as a retiree dabbles in tea or bonsai. A man struggles over each manuscript page. A woman writes to amuse herself."[13] But when a woman poured heart and soul into her work, when she wrote of what mattered most deeply to her, she was derided for being overly proud and forceful. Kitada Usurai, for example, had won critical admiration for her chaste and reserved character when she penned pieces with a gentle elegiac tone. "For those who have sought the Murasaki Shikibu of the Meiji period—who but she can be the one?" they had asked.[14] But once she imbued her works with a more pronounced protest over the social inequities she saw about her—particularly as concerned women—the same critics who had lauded her cried foul. "If you have the leisure to criticize us with that fancy writing brush of yours, then your time would be better served sewing dust cloths."[15] A *modern* Murasaki, Meiji women writers discovered, was an impossible ideal. "Emulate the Murasaki Shikibu of old," they were encouraged, "and not the Shikibu of the back alleys."[16] The ensuing humiliation this derision provoked was enough to force the timid writer back into the private recesses of her home, where she was to remain, as the term *keishū* connoted, "a talented lady of the inner chamber."

The first two decades of the twentieth century saw the emergence of a new kind of woman writer. Having benefited from the universal educational system and the leveling of class distinctions, she was not as averse to taking risks and facing scrutiny. Disinterested in conforming to traditional marriage arrangements, many women writers at the time flouted social expectation and used the ensuing notoriety as the subject matter of their subsequent fiction. Marked by sex but not by class, women writers from the 1900s on were largely referred to as *joryū sakka*. The change of terminology, however, did not diminish the insistence that women follow the same writing program that had been outlined for their predecessors. Indeed, if anything, by the second decade of the century "woman writer" as a concept had become codified by the male-dominated literary establishment. Joan Ericson points out in her incisive study, "The Origins of the Concept of 'Women's Literature,'" that the confluence in the 1920s of increased female literacy, mass-circulation journals for women, a leveling of social classes, and the beginning of national imperialism gave rise to the notion that *joryū bungaku,* or women's literature, was less a category and more a style:

> A market niche that mirrored the sex-segregated world of higher education and gender-specific conventions of composition—employing, principally, a written-as-spoken, rather than a self-consciously intellectual voice—came to be styled "women's literature." Such broad characterizations of style cut across gender lines of both writers and readers. But the conventions were codified, even as anomalies were allowed. Those women, or those works by women, that failed to meet these expectations were treated as "masculine" exceptions.[17]

The codification of "women's writing" as style in the 1920s did little to clarify its contours. Women from all walks of life, with all manner of educational backgrounds and political or social interests, were believed to share quintessential and irrefutable feminine qualities that were manifest in their subsequent literary productions. With the exception of those "masculine" few—typically acknowledged as Miyamoto Yuriko, Hirabayashi Taiko, and a handful of others[18]—who were able to somehow transcend or overcome their female "weaknesses," these qualities seeped seemingly unconsciously into a woman's writing, as Kawabata Yasunari observed in his 1934 critique:

> I rather enjoy reading works written by women writers. Even when the work is artistically weak, or perhaps especially when it is, I can sense how difficult it is to be a woman. I may say this because I am a man, but women's works are somehow direct. They are raw. Although many people say that women writers are reluctant to tell the truth, and that they hide it with embellishments, regardless of how experienced the writer is, or how inexperienced, women writers inevitably reveal their true selves. Even though she may not notice it herself, she is bared naked by her work. No matter how exquisitely she tries to costume herself with her writing, she is as unclothed as the emperor revealed in the fairy tale "The Emperor's New Clothes." I cannot help but think that the hearts of women are this way by nature. To put it bluntly, women's works are stimulating to the senses. They have an honest body.[19]

Kawabata's reference to a true self, the inevitability of self-exposure, and masquerade are topics that will be taken up below, as they resurface in the essays collected in chapters 2 and 3 of this volume, "The Essential Woman Writer" and "The Narcissistic Woman Writer." Here it is worth noting the essential sensitivity and inherent naturalness that are applied to women and their writing, for these are qualities that would become both the strength and the scourge of women's expression during the war years.

The Essential Woman Writer

If the 1920s saw the crystallization of "women's writing" as a concept, the subsequent war years ensured its indoctrination. War activates gender distinctions that in moments of peace are open to contestation. Agitation for equal rights is set aside out of respect for greater national (read patriarchal) interests. Feminist agendas become luxuries. Men and women pull together in the spirit of unification and strength, and the essentialization of male-female gender roles is not only intensified, but it is also justified. Writers—whether male or female—could no longer write only for their own selfish interests—be they personal amusement or basic survival. Writing now had to serve the good of the nation. Women on the "home front" were galvanized to rein in their excessive passions, overcome their scandalous proclivities, and put their inherent compassion to work in penning stories that, in the words of naval commander Tashiro Kei, would soothe the hearts of wives and families and "encourage the brave martial spirits of soldiers at the front."[20] Even women who went overseas to report from the battlefronts were expected to pack along with them their innate sensitivities and unadorned emotions, which they could then marshal to write evocative and moving pieces about the courageous Japanese soldier and the industrious colonists.

The postwar period brought with it numerous political advancements for women—most important the right to vote. Women found increased access to education and greater opportunities in the workplace. Women writers who had made their name before the war returned to the writing arena with greater creative vigor as more and more new women, the products of political and educational changes, began to write. The appearance of these new writers was seemingly so sudden and so vibrant that many male writers felt threatened. But as Setouchi Harumi notes in her 1962 essay—an observation Tomioka Taeko will echo in her 1986 piece—in reality the scene was not awash with women. "The number of women writers was few and far between when compared to men, accounting for less than 1 percent. Because writing men far outnumber women, the activity of two or three women writers always seems strikingly conspicuous."[21]

This "conspicuousness" of the writing woman invited a renewed consideration of the terms under which she was evaluated. Special journal issues were organized around the topic of "the woman writer." Roundtables were convened and questionnaires dispatched—all in an effort to analyze the relevance of current literary practices. Numerous critics, as Joan Ericson shows, advocated an immediate cessation of separation by gender.[22] There was a sense that women writers had been "coddled" by these gendered considerations. They were entitled to separate awards and were frequently allowed space in journals simply because they were women. For too long they had been allowed to depend on their sexuality and the public curiosity it provoked and were thus competing unfairly with men. It was time for women to "overcome" their sex and become genuine writers in the real sense.

The three essays in chapter 2 reveal that though critics were now aware of the implications of gendered critiques, attitudes toward women's writing remained largely unchanged. If anything, the notion of the "woman writer" that had evolved over the last few decades had grown so deeply rooted in critical consciousness that it was viewed less as a social construct and more an irrefutable fact. On the one hand, women were being asked to "transcend" their (female) natures and join the ranks of real (male) writers. On the other, critics such as Okuno Takeo and Akiyama Shun were encouraging women to celebrate their uniquely female attributes. These assumed attributes—sensitivity, raw honesty, bodily presence—were ushered forth as antidotes to the depersonalization of postwar modernity. Women were still the complement to men. But now they became not just *essentialized* by a modern literary tradition that favored men, but also essential to it. Through women's writing, as Akiyama Shun notes, men can return to their own lost childhoods—to imaginary womb-like realms where they are protected against, in Shibusawa Tatsuhiko's words "the severity of the intellect."[23] Okuno Takeo takes the proposition even further by suggesting that not only do women invite male readers into other worlds, but also the world of their writing is inherently the source of Japanese literature itself:

> Naturalism and the "I" novel are said to be based on lofty concepts that include revelations of reality, pursuit of truth, literary dedication, the literary expression of honest accounts of real life, yearning for sincerity, resistance to authority, restlessness, and transgression. However, these literary forms derive primarily from highly feminine attributes such as passivity, whinging, envy, laments of personal unhappiness, residual affection for jilting lovers, voyeurism, and gossipy chatter. Being rugged students from the provinces, the Naturalist writers deluded themselves that they were free of feminine influence.[24]

Assigning the novel to the realm of the female is of course a backhanded compliment. Because the Japanese novel could not resist negative feminine impulses, it was unable to evolve along the lines of modern masculinist principles into a format of intellectual merit. Or in Jan Bardsley's words, "Assuming that women were congenitally incapable of connecting the novel and politics themselves . . . Okuno imagines women domesticating the novel, making it women's work in much the same way as they attend to cooking, housework, and child rearing. The ease with which this transition occurred causes Okuno to wonder if the novel, as it had developed in Japan, had not always been a feminine form; domestic in the double sense of uniquely Japanese and essentially the province of women."

The Narcissistic Woman Writer

One of the themes around which discussions of women writers was often organized was that of narcissism. A glance back at the 1908 roundtable discussion between Oguri Fūyō and his peers reminds us of the acute discomfort the writing woman provoked in her male readers. Her audacity in presuming her works would measure up alongside a man's invited comparison to performers, mimics, and monkeys. "How would it be if they did not put on airs? If they behaved like the women they are—revealing their true thoughts, observations, and worries (should they have any) honestly?"[25] But what were a woman's "true thoughts" supposed to be if not those that men assumed they should be? Women had learned that they could not write about themselves or about collective female experiences without resorting to codified notions of the feminine. Otherwise, their portraits would be jarring. Like the female impersonator, women writers had to learn to represent themselves as they had been portrayed by men for centuries. Their efforts compelled Yosano Akiko to remark in 1909 that the female characters women writers produced were "lies" *(uso no onna)* meant to seduce a male reader.[26] But even when the woman writer listened to the murmured entreaties of the "Angel in the House" and suppressed the passions and brilliance that stirred within her in an effort to satisfy critical expectation, she ran the risk of inviting censure by the very process of writing, of inserting herself into the public eye. For as Setouchi Harumi suggests, "the very act of writing—of presenting one's work to the world—is in and of itself an act of male aggression."[27] Yukiko Tanaka has observed that the woman writer, while compelled to engage in "an act of self-assertion," finds herself "the antithesis of the selfless submission prescribed by Japanese culture."[28] Moreover, as Setouchi Harumi continues, a woman who writes is ultimately a woman who, it would seem, has exposed her "innermost shame to scrutiny."[29] With that in mind, one has to have what it takes to strip in broad daylight. The very act of self-presentation undermines moderation, modesty, and femininity. A woman writer cannot by definition therefore really be womanly *(onnarashii)*. Once again we confront the double bind.

As Tomoko Aoyama and Barbara Hartley observe in their contribution in chapter 3, it is this "violation of cultural prescription that makes women writers susceptible to condemnatory charges of narcissism." And yet, although women writers are derided for being self-centered and presumptuous, certain critics, like Mishima Yukio, denied women the capacity to engage in the narcissistic process that he regards as a necessary condition for literary creativity. Whereas selfishness may be feminine, self-consciousness is "utterly masculine" and "presupposes the separation of mind and body," a talent that women lack. Or, again to quote Shibusawa Tatsuhiko, "It is less difficult for a camel to pass through the eye of a needle than for a woman to separate from her own self and regard herself objectively."[30] In other words, when the woman beholds her reflection in the mirror—veiled, rouged, or masked—she sees not herself (an insubstantial phantom at best) but the image of that which men desire.

Uno Chiyo, in her oft-cited autobiographical essay, "A Genius of Imitation" (Mohō no tensai, 1936), for example, acknowledges the way she self-consciously (if not subversively) refashioned herself to meet and retain the gaze of whatever man was in a position to give her what she desired—be it money, literary recognition, or companionship. On the one hand, her essay poignantly reveals the toll on women writers who feel obliged to submit to editorial expectations and then feel inauthentic when they do: imitators, performers, wives. Highly conscious of the expectations surrounding them, these women were not allowed to author their own texts—if "author" means to have authoritative control over their own writing—and in a sense were little more than the embodiment of what the male critic desired. On the other, she shows the coy strategies a woman writer might employ in negotiating that narrow but provocative space between expectation and feelings of authenticity.

The woman writer as a result has been constantly aware of a point of fissure in her creative enterprises—a fissure that opened between the artist she felt herself to be and what she needed to project in order to survive. The necessity of a literary persona, and the feelings of fissure that then ensue, are certainly not phenomena limited only to women writers. The mere act of exposing one's personal work to public scrutiny requires bravado from any artist and results in varying degrees of masking and posturing. For the woman writer, however, the mask required was not necessarily one of her own making. It was too often a one-size-fits-all kind of apparel that all women had to wear, while men could choose among many. Moreover, the masks men were allowed were not as deeply fraught with sexual implications—with the threat to their chastity should they let the mask slip.

"How ludicrous it is that I act like a wife in my career as a writer," Uno Chiyo's "genius" complains. "I feel helpless even now, wondering how much longer I'll continue this imitating. When I think about it, I get terribly discouraged, even in my proudest moments. . . . I am thirty-eight years old, I've been writing for twelve years, and I don't know who I really am."[31] Transgressing daughter, sensational writer, or gentle wife, she is aware of the costuming she is required to don in order to secure access to print. She is also aware that the body behind the clothing, the face behind the mask—the raw flesh that Kawabata Yasunari and other men believed they perceived—was itself a fabrication.

The tension that arose from this point of fissure gave many a woman writer the energy she needed to fuel her creative enterprises. Whereas the subterfuges she felt forced to employ—the costumes and the masks—produced feelings of inauthenticity in some, they also provided a shiver of pleasure over the success of the charade. It was in this moment of fabrication, this subtle deception, that

many women writers of this era found a subversive—if entirely unintentional—
retaliation.

The Resisting Woman Writer

Published critiques and cultural conventions were not the only means to
containing a woman's literary creativity and easing her into her mask. Women
writers also learned about writing from reading works that were held up as
exemplary, the recipients of literary accolades. Works by men. Of course, in
the early twentieth century, women writers were enjoined to write like their
Heian forebears. Japanese women writers had an illustrious history to draw
on, after all—a history that was not only recognized but also—with the modern period—canonized. Although postwar women writers would find in their
ancient foremothers sources of strength and symbols of resistance, for their
nineteenth-century counterparts the success of their literary foremothers, as discussed above, was often more burden than encouragement.

Modern women learned to write by modeling men—not by echoing icons
of past feminine brilliance. "My Mr. Strindberg, my Mr. Chekhov, and my
Mr. Schnitzler," Uno Chiyo's "genius" intones.[32] Earlier "the genius" had noted
her desire to coopt the literary strategies of Takayama Chogyū and Satomi Ton
and to borrow the glasses of her writer husband, Ozaki Shirō. Not only did
female writers contrive to emulate their male peers, but female readers also
found themselves drawn to the female characters populating male-authored
texts.

Much is made in the essays under discussion, therefore, of the way members
of one sex craft characters of the opposite sex. Men are said to reach the pinnacle of their careers when they are able to create a credible female character. But
who, after all, has been responsible for determining the success of this creation
if not men? Male critics decided—despite Kobayashi Hideo's evaluation to the
contrary—that Kawabata Yasunari's female characters were not only believable,
but that they also revealed the truth of womanness more accurately than even a
woman herself. Women readers thus sought to internalize the images they found
in his works. As Takahashi Takako noted in her 1978 discussion with Tsushima
Yūko, "When women read his literature, they put on that female image like a
mask . . . and read it. I suppose a woman typically reads Kawabata's literature as
if she were the object of a man's gaze. Women have a surface that men look at,
you know?"[33] As the conversation continues, Takahashi describes the impact
this mask had on her: "When I was young, I felt that way when I read. When
I read a work written by a man that depicted a woman based on its author's

analysis of female psychology, I would think, oh, this is how a woman is. And I would read on, completely accepting his analysis. But after I started writing novels and gradually began to be able to express myself as a subject, what male authors had taught me about women and I'd accepted as truth, I came to feel was somehow false."[34]

Echoing these observations in 1984, the writer Saegusa Kazuko suggested that the process of internalizing the mask was so subtle as to be hardly noticeable: "I came this far in my work without being very conscious about being a woman, and after reflecting on the true meaning of woman, I even thought that it would be quite detrimental to my writing if I worked with an awareness of being a woman. . . . However, as I made a conscious effort to think and write about women, it gradually became clear as to how much I had adjusted myself to fit men's ideas and men's ways of thinking."[35]

Notably, it is through the process of writing—of self-creation—that women came to recognize the presence of the mask they were wearing. In turn, it was through writing that they expressed their frustrations at its imposition. By the 1970s, Japanese women were admitting—loudly—that the female characters depicted in male-authored texts were hardly credible and the expectations placed on women hardly tenable. As Joan Ericson notes in her introduction to chapter 4, "The Resisting Woman Writer": "By the mid-1970s, a cohort of college-educated women writers had reached a critical mass and explored a wide variety of approaches in fiction that, on the whole, could be considered more intellectual or ironic than those of earlier popular women writers. Many in this younger generation won the most prestigious literary prizes, thereby securing visibility and interest among an increasingly well-educated readership."

Educated, enfranchised, and bolstered by what Ericson describes as "shifting global debates on women in advanced industrial societies," these women were in a position to criticize as "public intellectuals" the effects of gender-based expectations on social, legal, and literary issues. Their writing offered a conduit to resistance. Whereas earlier women writers, like Uno Chiyo, had been more subtle in their protests, using subterfuges that were most successful when they were overlooked, the figures of resistance created by Takahashi, Tsushima, and other writers of their generation were overt.[36] They openly challenged the images of feminine nature that had been encouraged by critics since the turn of the century. Paramount among these targeted images was, as scholar and critic Nakayama Kazuko suggested in 1986, "the myth of motherhood" and of woman as inherently nurturing.[37]

What had been more intrinsic to the definition of woman than her biology and her assumed imperative to "mother"? Beyond biology, there was the social expectation that made the role of bearing and raising children a woman's sole raison d'être. But as Nakayama argued, not only was this "myth of motherhood" a male construction that "shows itself in the male wish to return to the womb, the root of life," it was also fundamentally the most problematic male paradigm of its kind—and the one to which women writers continued to return.[38] Ohba Minako, Kōno Taeko, Tsushima Yūko, Takahashi Takako, and others challenged the myth of motherhood by indulging in extreme examples of "maternal animosity."[39] Creating female characters that kill, maim, or otherwise injure children, they violently disrupted expectations of an inherent "gentleness." In pushing beyond the "normal" parameters of a "maternal nature," these writers opened avenues to new human relationships that exceeded the sexual—or certainly the heterosexual. What would seem to be a terrifyingly negative treatment of the maternal engendered new ways of affirming female strength. Or to cite Nakayama, "a new maternal which differs from the maternal myth heretofore held by men who wished to return to the womb."[40]

Sharalyn Orbaugh in her 1996 essay, "The Body in Contemporary Japanese Women's Fiction," noted three strategies for writing against patriarchal paradigms. The first is descriptive. The woman writer "*describe*[s] the current configurations of power, exposing the harm done through them." The second is to "*invert the hierarchy of value*, to valorize the object/passive side of the equation." And the third is to "*reverse the gender coding* of the hierarchical power roles. Instead of being silent, women can speak; instead of being the objects of others' gaze, they can use their eyes; instead of being killed, they can kill; instead of being dominated, they can dominate."[41] Of these different strategies, Orbaugh observed, the configuration of the hierarchies remains constant. That is, the hierarchical value of the binaries may be inverted, but the binaries themselves—male/female; dominator/dominated; voiced/unvoiced, etc.—remain intact.

Just as strategies for reading and writing women's texts have changed, so too have the critics of these texts. Women themselves have moved to the forefront of literary criticism and are no longer limited by their sex to what and whom they critique. The change has been gradual, encouraged by postwar advances in educational and social opportunities for women and, according to scholars like Chieko Ariga, is still far from allowing women an equal share of the pie.[42] Nevertheless, the changes are significant. In 1890 Wakamatsu Shizuko and Koganei Kimiko, the translators Kunikida Doppo heralded, refrained from commenting on contemporary Japanese literature (by their male peers) when responding to a survey designed to assess the views of current women writers. Whereas both were themselves receiving favorable evaluations (from men) for their creative writing and translations, they demurred from returning the favor on the basis that they were women. Their modesty was contagious. The survey had to be abandoned when other women writers declined to participate—citing illness, inconvenience, or lack of opinion. But with education and increased encouragement, women began to participate more readily in the critical evaluation of their literary peers. Miyamoto Yuriko, for example, is one of the first to have achieved recognition for her essays on both women's writing and canonical male writers, such as Natsume Sōseki. Her achievements as a critic were subsequently exceeded by those of Itagaki Naoko, who, while also contributing significantly to Sōseki scholarship, was, in Tomoko Aoyama's words, a pioneer in "foregrounding the otherwise overlooked writing of women in the early and mid-Shōwa period. She published critiques on the work of Hayashi Fumiko and Hirabayashi Taiko, in addition to an overview of women's writing in modern Japan entitled *Meiji Shōwa Taishō no joryū bungaku* (Women's writing in Meiji, Taishō, and Shōwa, 1967)."[43] Unlike Miyamoto and her reticent predecessors, Itagaki was a scholar and not herself a writer. Clearly ahead of her time in her focus on women's writing as a category worthy of serious intellectual inquiry, she nevertheless was not able to escape the pull of a phallocentric approach to literary critique. Women's writing, lacking the breadth and intellectual dynamism she ascribed to "great literature" written by men, had still not, in her estimation, reached its full potential. She summarizes the state of women's writing to date as follows:

The works of women writers are conceptually simple. While their greatest asset is clearly their feminine sensibilities, it is this very factor that prevents their work from qualifying as great literature. We have seen growing numbers of university graduates among women who write, and there will no doubt continue to be an increase in the numbers of women writers and the quality of their work. The purpose of this current journal issue is to consider the limitations that have operated on women up until this point in order to provide a reference point for writers in the future. For, above all, women lack the ability to view the big picture. Thus their ability for objective composition and for detailed observation is limited, and they lack the insight to identify issues in the world around them. It is rare to find a woman with the ability to pursue a topic with intellectual persistence, rather than from an artless, superficial perspective. Scrutiny of the work of women writers reveals a dearth of understanding of creativity or associated issues. And while they may be capable of psychological analysis, few have the control or the discipline to follow this through. Nevertheless, the strong demand for femininity in literature means that the market is flooded with writing by women.

It should be noted, however, that the very best of these writers have opened territory unavailable to men. And their works are of the highest quality.[44]

Women Writers and Alternative Critiques

The opened territory to which Itagaki refers inspired the experimentation of the 1970s and 1980s by writers such as Tsushima and Takahashi, as noted above. This experimentation, in turn, led to a trend among critics and writers to move beyond the restrictive limits of binaries. Amanda Seaman, in introducing the ramifications of these "alternative" critiques, states that "the critics . . . argue for a new form of literary (and by extension social) analysis that can overcome the shortcomings of masculine readings of women and their literature by considering that literature on its own terms, uncovering its unique history, and freeing women and their writing from the confines of patriarchy and its heterosexual presuppositions." Mizuta Noriko, for example, in her essay on "trans/gender/lation" offers a critical "bisexuality" as a new strategy for freeing reading discourses from the either/or of male/female and original/imitative. Mizuta's creative use of terms like "bisexualism" reveals the new stages to which she and her colleagues have taken feminist literary criticism in Japan. Not only do these critics challenge the binaries of gender, but they also challenge the imposition of elitist evaluations, thus opening the gates of the literary kingdom to a more diverse and popular variety of writing. Saitō Minako, for example, invites the "serious" consideration of the popular by introducing us to the importance of "girl culture" in spawning "women's writing." Girl culture, like the strength in women's voices, has remained an undercurrent—ignored and hidden but provocatively powerful. "If one-tenth of the effort these critics devoted to their serious study of the 'intertextuality' in Murakami Haruki's works had been dedicated to the study of Banana's intertextual context, they would have detected a history of girl culture that has been running as an undercurrent throughout modern history."[45] Takahara Eiri takes us beyond sex by turning us *all* into girls. "I am not referring here only to real girls, for it is not necessary to be an actual girl; rather we need to be *like* a girl. In order to highlight this point, I intend to refer to the texts under discussion as 'girl consciousness' literature." The reader position that Takahara advocates is one that disrupts the rigidity of conventional gender categories. The position of a girl—a peripheral position yet untainted by strict gender codes—"discredits adult thinking and is implicitly critical of adult thoughtlessness and insensitivity."[46] By opening the binaries, Takahara allows the play of a much more creative reading. In the process, a writer like Kawabata Yasunari becomes not just a man who understands women better than they do themselves, but a man with a "girl's consciousness." Here he is no different than certain women writers. Finally, in her poetic essay, "For a Gentle Castration," Matsuura Rieko liberates us from our gendered bodies altogether.

A Literary Coda: Women Writers Critiquing Men

This volume opens with a chapter that includes a spirited discussion by men critiquing women writers. It concludes with a similarly spirited discussion by women critiquing men. The parallels between the two are striking. As has been noted, both lapse into moments of condescension and essentialism. The difference lies in the positions of the critics relative to the subject they are critiquing. The male critics in the early twentieth century were presiding over the center, maintaining the borders of the *bundan,* and ensuring the peripheral nature of those on the outside. Female critics, even in the late twentieth century, are still on the outside, and it is this outsider position that makes their flip assessments of male writers particularly antagonistic. Relishing their rebellious stance, Ueno Chizuko urges other female critics to join the fray: "We have cast the first stone of feminist criticism into the pond of literature. If the subsequent ripples provoke more experiments of greater variety and depth, we will have achieved our goal."[47]

Women writers and poets such as Tomioka Taeko and Kōra Rumiko remain active in keeping feminist critical discourses at the surface of the literary pond. They have been joined by dynamic and outspoken women scholar-critics—for example, Watanabe Sumiko, Nakayama Kazuko, Tanaka Miyoko, Komashaku Kimi, Egusa Mitsuko, Seki Reiko, Yonaha Keiko, Kitada Sachie. The number of women with appointments as literature scholars in Japanese universities, whereas still lagging behind that for men, continues to grow, as does their interest in proclaiming themselves feminist scholars of "women's studies." The field is now so vibrant and diverse that it is impossible to name all the important contributors, let alone feature examples of criticism from each. Among them, surely the most notable is the aforementioned Mizuta Noriko, whose work on gender and literature—here represented by the essay on "Trans/gender/lation"— has made a significant contribution to pushing feminist literary criticism into the mainstream.

NOTES

1. Tazawa, "Godaidō," p. 263. As cited in Copeland, *Lost Leaves,* p. 45.
2. Gotō, "Keishū shōsetsu wo yomu," p. 31.

3. Tomioka, "'Onna no kotoba' to 'kuni no kotoba,'" p. 93. As translated by Joan E. Ericson in chapter 4 below.

4. Rich, *On Lies, Secrets, and Silence,* pp. 37–38.

5. Woolf, "Professions for Women," p. 285. "Professions for Women" is based on a speech Woolf delivered before a branch of the National Society for Women's Service on January 21, 1931. In the speech she introduced her encounters with the Angel of the House by noting the way she interfered with Woolf's first review of a man's book. The Angel did not find it appropriate for a young woman to criticize the work of a man.

6. *Joryū sakka* translates literally to "woman-style writer." For more on this expression, refer to Joan E. Ericson's essay in this volume and to her "The Origins of the Concept of 'Women's Literature.'"

7. Hasegawa, "Gendai joryū bungaku no yōsō," pp. 7–8. As translated by Tomoko Aoyama and Barbara Hartley in chapter 3 below.

8. Takahara, "Shōjogata ishiki: Jiyū to kōman," p. 9. As translated by Tomoko Aoyama and Barbara Hartley in chapter 5 below.

9. The term *bundan* was used initially to describe male writers and critics of the Meiji and early Taishō periods who belonged to an exclusive Tokyo coterie. Eventually it came to refer to a broader establishment of writers and incorporate a greater sense of canonicity. *Bundan* writers, almost exclusively male, were those who sat on editorial and prize committees; who were in positions to advance or mentor the careers of other writers; and who, in their capacity as critics, determined who was or was not a member of the *bundan.* For more on the *bundan* and the impact it had on women's writing, see Ariga, "Dephallicizing Women in *Ryūkyō shinshi.*"

10. As Laurel Rasplica Rodd points out in her translation of Yosano Akiko's essay in this volume *onnarashisa* is not just *being* womanly but also *acting* womanly.

11. Yosano, "'Onnarashisa' to wa nani ka," pp. 335–336. As translated by Laurel Rasplica Rodd in chapter 1 below.

12. The presumed chasteness of Murasaki Shikibu et al. is notable. Contemporary Izumi Shikibu was known for her liaisons with several prominent men, Sei Shōnagon was thought to be something of a flirt, and Murasaki herself was nicknamed "Miss Japanese Chronicles" because of her ostentatious bookishness. It is interesting that in seeking precursors and models for Meiji women writers, critics would reach far back into the Heian era (794–1185) while ignoring those of the more recent Tokugawa era (1600–1868). Atsuko Sakaki suggests a political motive: "Women's literature from the Tokugawa period has been conveniently forgotten in order to invent the notion of women's liberation in modern Japan, and to uncritically and ahistorically bridge Heian court culture of the tenth to the eleventh centuries (epitomized by Murasaki Shikibu . . .) and modern capitalist culture" ("Sliding Door," p. 4).

13. Oguri et al., "Joryū sakkaron," p. 10. As translated by Rebecca L. Copeland in chapter 1 below.

14. Cited in Copeland, *Lost Leaves,* p. 36.

15. Ibid., p. 40.

16. Such was Ishibashi Shian's 1888 advice to Miyake Kaho, whose debut piece suggested too direct a knowledge of the underclass. See ibid., p. 89.

17. Ericson, "The Origins of the Concept of 'Women's Literature,'" p. 103.

18. See, for example, Ozaki, "Japanese Women Novelists Today," or Nakamura, "Hayashi Fumiko ron," p. 95.

19. Kawabata, "Joryū sakka," p. 240–242. As translated by Kathryn Pierce and Mika Endo in chapter 1 below.

20. Preface to Yoshiya, *Joryū sakka jikkasen.*

21. Setouchi, "Joryū sakka ni naru jōken," p. 21. As translated by Rebecca L. Copeland in chapter 2 below.

22. Ericson, "The Origins of the Concept of 'Women's Literature,'" p. 93.

23. Shibusawa, "Okamoto Kanoko aruiwa onna no narushishizumu," p. 313. As translated by Tomoko Aoyama and Barbara Hartley in chapter 3 below.

24. Okuno, "Shōsetsu wa honshitsuteki ni josei no mono ka?" pp. 12–13. As translated by Barbara Hartley in chapter 2 below.

25. Oguri et al., "Joryū sakkaron," p. 11.

26. Cited in Seki, *Ane no chikara,* p. 247.

27. Setouchi, "Joryū sakka ni naru jōken," p. 22.

28. Yukiko Tanaka, introduction to *This Kind of Woman,* p. ix.

29. Setouchi, "Joryū sakka ni naru jōken," pp. 25–26.

30. Shibusawa, "Okamoto Kanoko aruiwa no narushishizumu," p. 310.

31. Uno, "A Genius of Imitation," p. 196.

32. Ibid.

33. Takahashi and Tsushima, "Onna no sei to otoko no me," p. 5. As translated by Maryellen Toman Mori in chapter 4 below.

34. Ibid., p. 6.

35. This quote is taken from the article by Nakayama Kazuko that is translated by Joan E. Ericson and Yoshiko Nagaoka in chapter 4 of this volume. For the original source, see "Onna ga watakushi shōsetsu wo kaku toki" (When women write confessional literature), in Saegusa, *Sayōnara okoto no jidai,* pp. 128–132.

36. In my essay, "The Made-Up Author," I discuss the way Uno succeeded in convincing male critics of her *onnarashisa* while at the same time subverting social expectations: "In order to become a writer in a man's world, Uno had to don a mask of femininity, and it was a mask she had to learn to change as befitted the moment—now devoted wife, now elegant flapper. . . . Ironically then, by concealing her true female self to avoid charges of 'masculinity,' she creates a face for herself which is in essence a 'male' construct in that it is a reflection of a male-defined femininity" (p. 15).

37. Nakayama, "Joryū bungaku to sono ishiki henkaku no shudai." As translated by Joan E. Ericson and Yoshiko Nagaoka in chapter 4 below.

38. Ibid., p. 38.

39. Adrienne Hurley notes that Ohba is the romanization the author herself prefers (over the more conventional "Ōba"). I am here following the precedent set by Hurley. See Hurley, "Demons, Transnational Subjects, and the Fiction of Ohba Minako," p. 102n6.

40. Nakayama, "Joryū bungaku to sono ishiki henkaku no shudai," p. 41.

41. Orbaugh, "The Body in Contemporary Japanese Women's Fiction," p. 123. Italics in the original.

42. See Chieko Ariga, "Text versus Commentary."

43. Unpublished letter to the editor.
44. Itagaki, "Shōwa no joryū sakka." Translated by Barbara Hartley (unpublished).
45. Saitō, "Yoshimoto Banana shōjo karuchā no suimyaku," p. 86. As translated by Eiji Sekine in chapter 5 below.
46. Takahara, "Shōjogata ishiki: Jiyū to kōman," p. 7.
47. Ueno, "Ishi wo nageru," p. 434.

I

THE FEMININE CRITIQUE
"Womanliness" and the Woman Writer
Rebecca L. Copeland

On a spring day in 1908, five Japanese male writers sat down to a *zadankai*, or roundtable discussion. The *zadankai* was quickly becoming a favored format in Japanese journalism because it allowed critics and other experts to share their thoughts on current concerns in a casual and interactive manner.[1] Organized by the journal *Shinchō* (New currents) under the title "Conversations in a Room," this particular roundtable had been meeting monthly since January of that year. The panelists were the same each time: Oguri Fūyō, Yanagawa Shun'yō, Tokuda Shūkō (also known as Chikamatsu Shūkō), Ikuta Chōkō, and Mayama Seika. All five were regular contributors to *Shinchō*, offering prose fiction, critical and personal essays, and dramatic works, in addition to musings on the current literary scene. With each meeting the assigned topic for consideration changed. Issues addressed included "The Writer and the Family," "The Writer and Society," "The Critic and the Critique," and "Desire and Art: A Search for Harmony." In May 1908 the subject was "The Woman Writer."

By 1908 the woman writer had become a popular topic of discussion. Most critics, publishers, and journal editors conceded that contributions from "the woman writer" added color and diversity to the offerings regularly provided by male authors. In the mid-1880s, when male educators and writers began actively soliciting women's writing, they clamored for works that would provide an intimate glimpse into the *true* heart of a woman. The moral imperative that confronted women writers was meant to be instructive. Through their writing they would lead men to a more favorable appreciation of the female heart.[2] Moreover, they would provide other less fortunate women with a steadfast model to follow. In so doing, the woman writer would contribute to the lofty goal of elevating Japanese civilization overall.

Many believed that the woman's literary enterprise, like that for her male contemporaries, was to be didactic and serve not just personal interests, but also the welfare of the state. How best to serve the state was a matter open to interpretation. The writer Kunikida Doppo, for example, while encouraging women to pursue their interests in letters, felt that their talents were best utilized in translation. He made his pronouncement at a time when a significant number of young women were studying in academies founded by foreign missionaries. Chauvinists criticized these women and their teachers for the emphasis placed on foreign languages, claiming that it provided the young women no appreciable skills for dealing with the "real world" (that is, the domestic world). To the contrary, Doppo argued, these skills could be appropriately applied to translation, the product of which would have a direct impact on improving Japan. With statements that, as Judy Wakabayashi notes, belittled translation more than the woman writer, Doppo contended that the mechanical nature of translation made it a perfect occupation for a woman, who had to keep her eye constantly on the household, because she could pick a translation up or put it down at any time without losing momentum.

Women translators were not unheard of in this period, and, as previously noted in the introduction, Doppo listed two of the better known: Wakamatsu Shizuko and Koganei Kimiko. Even so, translation did not become, as he had recommended, a replacement for women's creative writing. Recognizing women's persistence, the five *Shinchō* panelists noted their wish that women confine their literary energies to poetry. Men were not the only ones to suggest that women had a particular affinity for poetry. As educator Miwata Masako observes in her brief essay—also included in this chapter—poetry is an art that allows women to indulge in their "natural" emotionalism. Just as Doppo denies translation original creativity, Miwata limits poetry to an interpretation of the intangible. Both critics see in their respective genres a service to the nation. For Miwata it is the potential of poetry to represent and encourage moral truth. Because women "instinctually possess poetic thought," they have the potential to "elevate national morality."

Despite early efforts to channel female creative energies into moral missions, the *Shinchō* panelists made it clear that women were not cooperating. The dialogue that follows is interesting for a number of reasons. In the first place, it represents a synthesis of the early attitudes toward the writing woman, underscoring the fundamental biases that writing women faced at the turn of the century and the turmoil that ensued when they failed to conform to expectations. Second, it suggests that above all a woman writer should aspire to "womanliness," that vague notion of female essence discussed in the introduction to this volume. Third, the discussion points out what becomes of women writers who do not adhere to expectation.

As is clear from the names scattered throughout the *Shinchō* conversation—Hasegawa Shigure, Ōtsuka Kusuoko, Okada Yachiyo, Yosano Akiko, and others

—"women writers" were many and varied, ranging from playwrights to poets. But the five writers participating in this informal literary conversation were not interested in celebrating the diversity of their female peers. Rather, they were more concerned with venting their frustration over the fact that contemporary women writers were not conforming to their notions of what a woman writer should be. In short, these men were concerned that women writers were not behaving like "women writers."

The writers under discussion either wrote critically of male behavior—particularly of a man's prerogative to indulge in extramarital affairs—or they wrote of wives who similarly indulged in passionate desires. Hasegawa Shigure, for example, then a playwright of modern kabuki, created dramas that featured strong and self-certain women who rose up against the crushing weight of patriarchal pressure. Ōtsuka Kusuoko wrote of upper-class married women who uninhibitedly gave voice to their libidinal desires for younger men. And Yosano Akiko, earlier celebrated for her poems of brilliant passion, had taken to imbuing her works with a more decidedly "political" flavor.[3]

Since her debut in the modern era, the woman writer had been expected to adhere to an almost impossible standard: be bold enough to rise to the challenge of achieving her own creative voice while at the same time remain true to her innate feminine nature and "womanliness." In sum, the woman writer was not to let her imagination soar beyond the parameters of her narrow base of knowledge but should turn what were believed to be her uniquely acute observatory skills upon what she knew best—namely, herself, her family, and in particular her children. Writing of this sort, while of course never comparing to a male writer's more robust intellectualism and social breadth, would offer an important counterweight by providing readers what men could not. And this complement was what the Shinchō critics found most valuable in writing by women. Most offensive, therefore, was the woman writer who refused to recognize her inherent difference and attempted to "copy" men. What need did the literary realm have for a woman's poor imitation when there were men aplenty to provide the real thing?

The woman writer was caught in the proverbial double bind. On the one hand, should she write sentimental poems, as the Shinchō critics encouraged, she would be politely acknowledged as a pretty addition to the masculine lineup— a splash of red against the gray.[4] But no one would take her seriously. Her literary efforts would amount to no more than what these critics termed "housewife art." On the other hand, if she dared to be experimental, to test her limits, and wring from herself works that mattered most to her, critics—by their own admission—*would not bother to read her writing.* They would critique, therefore, not her actual work but the *image* that she presented. And this image would be held up for criticism as pretentious, imitative, and—perhaps worse—unchaste. That the men who participated in this roundtable discussion were in a position to advance (or impede) women's careers makes their admission even more troubling.[5]

The writer Tamura Toshiko, who made her debut shortly after the *Shinchō* discussion was published, described the toll this double bind exerted on creative women in her brief story "A Woman Writer" (Onna sakusha, 1913). She depicts a woman who, after laboring unsuccessfully over the writing of a particular passage, is chastised by her husband, himself a writer. "Women are no good, wasting a hundred pages in order to write ten or twenty pages, and spending ten or fifteen days only for that. You must think you're a great writer."[6] His challenge echoes the *Shinchō* critics' comment that "men write in the face of great pain." A man writes to eat, to survive. "He doesn't write—as women do—for vanity, for some shallow claim to fame." The woman writer (with the exception of the beloved Higuchi Ichiyō)—protected by father, brothers, or a husband—had no need to suffer for her art. Her writing, it was believed, was born of leisure and a selfish desire for attention. To be successful a woman had to learn to write *like a woman*. The title of Tamura Toshiko's poignant piece, "A Woman Writer," points this out. Is the woman a writer? Is the writer a woman? Or does it really matter since critics were apparently less interested in the product than they were in the image of the one producing it. In fact, Tamura's title suggests that it is neither the woman nor the writer that matters but rather the writing of "woman."

Yosano Akiko, whose 1921 essay, "What Is 'Womanliness'?", is included in this chapter, refused to acquiesce to conventional wisdom when it came to gender bias. She was perfectly serious about her art and determined to live a life that was true to her own sense of direction—womanly or otherwise. Her innovative experiments with traditional Japanese poetic forms established her as a leader in the revitalization of Japanese verse, and her contributions to the fledgling journal *Seitō* (Bluestocking) marked her as a principal player in the early-twentieth-century feminist movement. With clever argumentative rhetoric Akiko takes the *Shinchō* critics and others of their persuasion to task for their uncomplicated insistence on "womanliness" as a measure of a woman. Her essay challenges critics to move beyond their essentialized notions and to recognize their attitudes for the tyranny that they impose. Elements reputed to be indispensable to women should in fact be indispensable to everyone. If womanliness, she asks, is defined as love, refinement, and modesty, then would it not be appropriate to expect all humans to aspire to these qualities? The only distinction between the sexes, she would suggest, is biological. But just because women have the capacity to give birth does not mean they should be defined by or confined to this capacity. A woman without children, she asserts, is no less womanly than a man without offspring is unmanly.

Akiko returns to the subject the *Shinchō* critics elided. It is social pressure and social impediments that determine attitudes toward women and by extension women's writing. Because women are expected to marry and to devote themselves to marriage, husband, and household, they have less opportunity to write. But all the more reason to encourage those who do. Rather than deride their works as "housewife art," she suggests the critics celebrate the fact that such women have managed to squeeze out a little time and energy to devote to creative writing. Moreover, because women have fewer opportunities to move beyond the sphere of the home, they should not be criticized when they try to broaden their horizons or stretch their intellectual curiosity. Their efforts should be applauded. And rather than selfishly claiming all regions beyond the home as the purview of men, their male colleagues should do what they can to remove the impediments women face.

Kobayashi Hideo, in his 1938 essay, "Women Writers," acknowledges the importance of expanding a woman's social sphere. Furthermore, he shares Yosano Akiko's frustration with the segregation of women from the universality of humanity, thus questioning the very saliency of the category "woman writer." A writer, according to Kobayashi, transcends his or her physical and social state and, in the process of creating art, relinquishes his/her hold on humanity. Kobayashi assumes an absolute in art that all writers share regardless of sex and presumably nationality. Writing may bear the mark of a writer's sex—much as it does a writer's nationality. That is, the language used and other aspects of the text will reveal it to be of male or female authorship. But in reading a literary masterpiece—a true masterpiece—the reader is not conscious of the existence of the author. The author and his/her sex are translucent. The term "woman writer" is therefore oxymoronic. For if the writer foregrounds her sex, she is unable to achieve the transcendence Kobayashi declares as a requirement of excellent writing.

But having suggested that art, real art, is "not written in such a way as to make us mindful of the author's sex," Kobayashi undercuts his own position by suggesting that a man's creation of a female character will differ from that of a woman's creation of a male character. Moreover, the difference is evaluative. Men can construct successful female characters, he argues, whereas women cannot achieve the same with male characters.

In his concise but cogent critique of Kawabata Yasunari's *Yukiguni* (Snow country), Kobayashi suggests that the author's female characters are little more than reflections of the author's own male desires. That is, the male author reaches his pinnacle of success when he is able to use the female characters as a creative Other through which he can mirror his own masculine self. Women writers—as Kobayashi notes in a near echo of the *Shinchō* critics' argument— are not yet able to create successful male characters. But rather than suggesting that this represents the woman writer's immaturity in her art, Kobayashi concedes that it may be that she is simply not as interested in—or, in his words, as inherently "afraid of"—men as men are of women. More likely the case is that, as Victoria Vernon notes in her study *Daughters of the Moon*, women writers at the time had not yet achieved a level—socially, politically, or artistically— where they *could* posit male characters as the Other. And so, unlike Kawabata and his phantom females, they could not create male characters that were mere reflections of their own egos or conduits to their essential desires. That type of characterization would come later.

In citing Kawabata's own essay on the topic, Kobayashi suggested that the kind of characters contemporary women writers depicted and the stories they created lead to a naïve, unintentional self-exposure. Regardless of how the woman writer clothed her works—whether feminine drag or masculine imitation—she inevitably ended up revealing her own naked self. Hence the perils in place for the woman writer of the era. She could not escape the category of woman writer—even in essays by critics who challenged the logic of the category.

NOTES

1. A roundtable discussion is by its very essence informal. The five men participating in the 1908 roundtable were free to blurt out whatever came to mind without calculation or caution. On the one hand, we should take their criticisms with a grain of salt. On the other, we can see in the very casualness of their utterances the degree to which certain ideas were so ingrained that they did not need to be defended or explained. Among these was the assurance that all five participants understood intuitively what was meant by "womanliness," or *onnarashisa*.

2. For more on this moral imperative, see Iwamoto Yoshiharu's thoughts on the matter as presented in Copeland, *Lost Leaves*, p. 42.

3. Akiko's new-style poem "Beloved Do Not Die" (Kimi shinitamō koto nakare), written out of concern for her younger brother, who had been sent to the Russo-Japanese War, was construed by critics as an antiwar attack on not only the Japanese government, but also the emperor himself. For more on the debates that ensued, see Beichman, "Yosano Akiko," p. 210.

4. The term commonly used to refer to this "red against the gray" phenomenon is *kōitten*. Literally rendered as "one drop of red," the phrase is more colloquially translated as "the only woman in the group." See Saitō Minako's analysis of this phenomenon of gender asymmetry, which still exists today, in *Kōitten ron*.

5. Of particular note in this group of writers was Ikuta Chōkō, the driving force behind a salon for women's writing and an early mentor to the founders of the feminist journal *Seitō*. He, more so than the others in this discussion, was in a direct position to advance women's literary careers.

6. In Yukiko Tanaka, *To Live and to Write,* p. 14.

| | | On Women and Translation

KUNIKIDA DOPPO

When a young woman wrote to me recently seeking advice on how to fulfill her desire to become a novelist, I promptly urged her to devote herself to translation rather than trying to produce novels.[1] This is a view I have long entertained and have advocated in the past in the *Women's News [Fujin shinpō]* magazine. Here I would like to elaborate on my position, spelling out several reasons for this.

Some people are of the irrational view that it is highly presumptuous for women to be involved in literature. I must say that, first, such claims are out of step with the times and, second, comments of that ilk are made by people who misunderstand and deride women. Naturally, then, this opinion merits no heed, yet I believe that even proponents of this untenable notion will find in the occupation of translation something that should meet with their approbation to a certain extent.

When I refer here to translating, by no means am I limiting this to the translation of serious literature. I include not only works on politics, economics, and religion, but also any and every kind of pragmatic text. Generally speaking, not a great deal of translation is being done in Japan as of yet, and when it comes to women translators in particular, the only examples are the late Wakamatsu Shizuko and also Koganei Kimiko. So far I have not heard of any women translating works on politics and law or religion and ethics.

Yet it would be far from accurate to say that Japanese women receive no language training. In particular, Christian mission schools, which attach special importance to the education of girls, and other similar girls' schools seem to devote the bulk of their curriculum to languages, so by no means could one say that women do not receive any training in languages. Past experience shows

TRANSLATED BY JUDY WAKABAYASHI. From Kunikida Doppo, "Joshi to hon'yaku no koto" (Women and translation), *Kunikida Doppo zenshū* (The collected works of Kunikida Doppo), vol. 1 (Gakushū ken'yūsha, 1965), pp. 364–366. The essay was originally published in *Katei zasshi* (Household journal) 2 (23) (February 15, 1898). JW

All notes by the translators will be marked by their initials.

1. During the Edo period, the limited number of translations that did occur were mainly carried out by *tsūji* (translators-cum-interpreters), a hereditary occupation not open to women. Nor did women have the educational opportunities to become scholars of Dutch Learning (i.e., *Western Learning*), the only other avenue to translation work in Edo times. In the subsequent Meiji period the profession of translator became open to all comers, but in the late nineteenth century translations were still being produced by a relative few, nearly all of whom were men. JW

that the good students merely end up acting as interpreters for missionaries, while the others leave the schoolyard behind them and get married, and before you know it, many can no longer understand a single foreign reading book, and their five or seven years of study turn out to be of no use at all. Recently this has given rise to the view that it is futile to teach girls languages—an argument that sounds reasonable enough yet is actually quite misguided.

Today, when progress and opening Japan up to the outside world are regarded as matters of national policy, language study by girls is far from a waste of time, and their skills should certainly be put to full use so that women can forge our nation's destiny along with men. And the end to which these skills can be put is translation.

Naturally, translating is by no means an easy task. Although it goes without saying that in terms of difficulty it stands no comparison with the writing of original works, if one is proficient in English, French, or German and writes well in Japanese, one can be regarded as having the basic qualifications necessary. When it comes to writing serious literature, even the fine nuances of each and every word and phrase cannot be overlooked, and it calls for a certain attendant inspiration, so it is not something that can be tackled easily even by men. Nevertheless, some women, such as Mrs. Wakamatsu Shizuko and Mrs. Koganei Kimiko, have been remarkably successful even at writing, reaching heights difficult for even men to achieve. When it comes to works on childrearing and housekeeping, where men are no match for women—and even with topics such as politics and economics, which are regarded as the province of male learning—if women acquire a measure of knowledge on these topics, then in no way will they experience in translating such texts the difficulties encountered in writing original works. Furthermore, in view of the situation facing Japan today, women can undoubtedly make a greater contribution to the progress of our civilization by translating eminent Western writers than by producing their own second-rate works.[2] Given that current writing purporting to be original consists for the most part of adaptations of works by great Western writers, for women to exert themselves in translation pure and simple would undoubtedly be far more valuable than their achievements interpreting for missionaries.

For the present, let me limit the discussion to the translation of pure literature. Writing original works calls for powers of observation, past experience,

2. In Meiji Japan translations of works introducing Western knowledge and genres were of such importance as to almost eclipse original writing, so Doppo's suggestion that women devote themselves to translating is less contentious than it might seem. Rather than a belittling of women, if anything his essay reveals a belittling of translation, despite its importance in Meiji Japan. *JW*

inspiration, sustained periods of time, and occasional travel. Sometimes it also requires one to live alone, and without talent it is impossible. Given their circumstances, it is certainly not something that can be expected of a large number of women. Things are very different, however, when it comes to translating, as it differs in nature from writing. Since translation is a mechanical process, it can be done in one's spare moments, and in terms of outcome it should not matter greatly if one translates a chapter today and a section tomorrow. There is no need to await the muse nor, on losing inspiration, to throw down one's pen and bemoan the fact that one's creative juices have run dry. As long as one pours one's energies into this task and is resolved to devote oneself to it, then in due course the great works of the day can be translated. Whereas writers already have confidence in their work and hence find it unbecoming to submit their writing to acquaintances for correction, with translations there is no such compunction about having one's betters in such matters correct one's wording. When the late Morita Shiken was translating Hugo's story "Hubert," he had difficulty with the final passage and sought advice from prominent figures in the literary world, an incident related in *The Citizen's Friend [Kokumin no tomo]* at the time, and people actually speak of this as a heartwarming episode. In view of all these factors, women's translating endeavors would not, first, interfere with married life—in fact, they can consult with their husbands and benefit greatly from their advice. Second, translating does not interfere with having children, since women can engage in translation in their leisure hours. Third, it requires neither powers of observation nor travel; all they need is to sit in a room with a dictionary and the source text on their desk. As for the outcome, this is obvious if we look at *Shingakushi* or the many other translations by Mrs. Koganei Kimiko, or at *Shōkōshi* [Little Lord Fauntleroy] and other translations by Mrs. Wakamatsu Shizuko.[3] Miss Higuchi Ichiyō is an exception as far as writing is concerned, and though quite a few other women calling themselves novelists have appeared on the scene, it is highly doubtful whether they have had as much influence on belles lettres as the two women translators above.

Quite apart from the question of its potential impact, engaging in translation will bring women much pleasure, precisely because it does involve such strenuous effort. Above all, the translators themselves would derive many benefits from this occupation.

I have heard that quite a few American women are involved in translating French, German, and Russian works. Instead of bemoaning the fact that there is little that Japanese women can do for the public good, those with such aspira-

3. *Shingaku shi* is apparently a story by the German writer Paul Heyse, but the original title has not been identified. *JW*

tions should take up this task. People learning languages should devote some of their efforts to this end and prepare themselves in advance. Rather than contemplating writing their own works, women with a literary bent should for the time being give due consideration to translation, and as long as they plan accordingly, it is no difficult matter. If aspiring to this while still at school, women would not need to regard their language skills as a bother, nor lament the wasting away of their talents. On the contrary, these skills would be surprisingly effective in benefiting present-day Japan and leading our nation further along the path to progress and civilization.

When I answered this young woman along these lines, she pressed me further, saying she already had a certain facility in writing Japanese but almost no grounding in foreign languages, and it would involve several years' preparation if she now wished to take up translation. I replied that even National Readers contain a number of beautiful stories whose translation one might well show a neighbor, yet it would not take years to reach that level, and translating a famous work by the time one is thirty and has a husband and children would by no means be out of the question.[4] Miss Ichiyō was single and Mrs. Koganei is the wife of Professor Koganei, while the late Wakamatsu Shizuko was married to Iwamoto Yoshiharu. If, like them, one has completed one's education and is not yet gray of hair, I would not consider it too late to translate a famous work one loves reading.

||| Women and Poetic Thought

MIWATA MASAKO

It is not easy to answer the question "What is poetry?" Are all works in alternating five and seven syllable units poetry? No. Is everything that has rhyme and can be recited aloud poetry? Not always. In my opinion, such works may have the form of poetry but not necessarily its spirit.

Is it then impossible to say what poetry is? Ah, how could that be? I define poetry as the voice of nature. Nature is deep and mysterious and impossible to fathom, and so scientists, outside of explaining its surface phenomena, do not yet comprehend its true reality. Try breaking off a blossoming branch and gazing

4. The National Reader was a series of American language primers used widely in Japanese schools from 1883 to 1913. *JW*

TRANSLATED BY JANINE BEICHMAN. From Miwata Masako, "Shisō to joshi" (Women and poetic thought), in *Kōtō saienbunshū* (Essays for higher school women), compiled by Fujinami Shimako (Bungaku dōshi kai, 1903), pp. 98–100.

at it intently. It has mystery in exactly the same way as the deep blue sky. One who in addition to this flower's colors knows the intensity of poetry is well able to hear the voice of nature.

The difference between men and women in mental terms is that men are usually rich in reason and women in emotion. Therefore, men always rely on reason and have definite views, while women depend on feelings and so fall into superstition easily. In this way, the one goes no further than knowledge of the externals of creation, and the other tends to attain a deep realization of inward being. It is the difference between the coldness of only looking at something and the deepness of sensing its heart.

Explaining tangible things is the forte of prose, while interpreting intangible things can only be done in poetry. Thus, as explained above, we may say that metaphorically men are prosaical and women are poetical. Truly it is only because people have tears and feelings that the world can escape the law of the jungle, that old and young can band together, rich and poor cooperate, and both the harmony of the family and the peace of society can be preserved. Thus in seeking out the origin of tears and the source of feeling, everything goes back to nature alone. If you doubt this, then go inquire of the traveler who rests from his weariness under the cherry blossoms or the hermit who gazes on the moon from his humble cottage.

Even though it is true that women instinctually possess poetic thought, I do not ask them to write poems. I only pray that they will not stop at using this talent in their family life to build a happy home but that they will also go on to water the aridness and blandness of the world and elevate national morality.

Nature is the parent of poetry. Seeing the spring flowers and autumn leaves, poetry sings of beauty; seeing people flourish and decay, it sings of truth; and thinking of the principle that goodness lives on and evil perishes, it urges goodness on us all. Truly it may be called the life of our life. There is nothing as precious or beneficial.

And yet people have their weaknesses. Some, viewing human life as transitory, grieve that they are alive and wish for death. Others, swept away by the autumn moon and the spring sunlight, choose to pursue only clouds and water. With *sake* as their friend, they think only of the artistic life and never bother with human affairs at all. Such as these take poetic thought to an extreme and are incapable of moderation. How can we call them true poets?

In calling for women to apply poetic thought to their lives, I am by no means asking that they change into such dissonant writers and artists. All I say is that even if they do not get so far as composing what is commonly called poetry, then as citizens of a nation and wives in homes, they should live a high-minded and refined life. To be faithful to your husband is like the constancy of an evergreen tree; to set an example for your children is like the virtue of spring sunlight. If you hope to become a woman who walks the path of nature in all these ways, then nurture what I call poetic thought. As Confucius said, "If you do not learn poetry, I have nothing to say to you."

||| On Women Writers

OGURI FŪYŌ, YANAGAWA SHUN'YŌ, TOKUDA SHŪKŌ,

IKUTA CHŌKŌ, AND MAYAMA SEIKA

Women Writers Who Forget Themselves

If women too are human beings, then they have every right to do what human beings do.[5] There is no reason they should be prevented from writing prose fiction. But if they are to write, they should write well. Now, expecting a skillful piece of writing from a woman writer is something of a tall order, we realize. At least, it would seem to be so judging from our experience. Setting aside the question of differences between men and women, let us assume that there are circumstances unique to each that cannot be ignored. We believe, therefore, that in all cases it is natural and moreover appropriate for women to preserve that within themselves that distinguishes them as womanly.[6] By womanly we are not referring simply to a woman's cleverness at detail or her taste for elegance. Rather, whether she is strong, shrewd, violent, cynical, or even ill-tempered, so long as she is strong, shrewd, violent, cynical, and ill-tempered in a womanly way, we have no objections. However, when we con-

TRANSLATED BY REBECCA L. COPELAND. From Oguri Fūyō et al., "Joryū sakkaron" (On women writers), Shinchō (New currents), May 1908: 6–11. This essay represents a collective effort. Who exactly was responsible for the writing is unclear, as are the participants represented in the "conversation" midway through the essay. The translator would like to thank Professor Yasuyuki Ogikubo of Kokugakuin University for his assistance with this translation.

5. The phrase "if women too are human beings" is startling in its abruptness. Most likely the authors are referring to contemporary debates that in advocating for equal treatment of women testified to their equal status as human beings. Although no specific article is cited by the authors, Fukuzawa Yukichi wrote a number of essays asserting female humanity. See, for example, "On Japanese Women, Part 2," p. 50. RLC

6. I have underlined words in the translation that appear in katakana in the original and are used to represent English words. RLC

sider those creatures known today as women writers, we are dismayed to find there's not a womanly writer in the bunch. Never mind whether or not they write well. Their lack of womanliness is so irritating, we do not read their works. We have no interest in even trying to do so.

Perhaps we should refrain from naming names. But, no, since these writers are so unwomanly, we do not need to treat them with the respect due a lady. If we start with Ōtsuka Kusuoko, Okada Yachiyo, and Itō Masako, the list could go on to include Masaoka Akiko and Hasegawa Shigure—every last one of them as unwomanly as the next! We would like to say that they only imitate men, but in fact they imitate men's baser aspects. This behavior is truly regrettable.

Our wish for women writers is that they take henceforth as their guiding principle the preservation of that within themselves that is most womanly and that they adapt themselves to this womanliness and write accordingly. If women were to do so, their works would satisfy just those very elements that men's works cannot.

Furthermore, when we compare prose to poetry, we note that women were the ones originally more inclined toward the latter. Women are well suited to poetry. Thus, when a woman decides to pursue letters, we would prefer that she first write poetry. However, if she wishes to write prose, we cannot force her to refrain. But we would nevertheless be grateful if she would write prose that resembles poetry. At the very least, we hope that she favor lyrical writing. Even within the prose genres, it is preferable for all writers to rely as much as possible on personal emotion when creating characterizations or charting the flow of events, so as to avoid an artificial ponderousness. This we wish as well from women writers. When it comes to observations, isn't it true that men and women observe things differently? You can't possibly deny that there are certain things that only women would notice or that women are more attuned to minute detail in their observations. To cite a familiar example, when it comes to matters related to children, women display a far greater interest than men. Moreover, their opportunities for such observations are abundant. This example is but one of many. There is a plethora of other situations as well where women have greater access to observation than men. Thus, it is far more preferable for women to develop what is most appropriate for them and in so doing, unfurl their innate womanly strengths. This is what we wish for women writers.

While we are on the topic, sentimental writing has come under harsh criticism of late. But in fact we like sentimentalism. When you consider the bigger picture, sentimental works are absolutely essential. Moreover, when it comes to sentimental writing, it is essentially a woman's territory.

Because we have not spent much time reading recent works by women, we cannot offer a critical assessment of any particular writer. We will refrain from discussing the women writers of the past, such as Murasaki Shikibu or Izumi Shikibu. But in recent times no woman writer has surpassed <u>Higuchi Ichiyō</u>. It would seem that Ichiyō is the only woman writer to occupy a seat in the literary echelon these days. How we long to see a talented writer emerge from among today's women writers. Works by Ichiyō and others of her generation may differ when it comes to a perspective on life and the selection of subject matter. But overall, works by women writers are <u>typified by a gentle moderation and a minute attention to detail.</u> Because we need a literature of moderation, we need women writers. And yet women writers these days, even though they are women and should observe moderation, are more and more apt to select <u>wild topics</u> and <u>resort to bizarre characterizations</u> after the fashion of Izumi Kyōka. They forget their innate qualities as women writers, and they make the mistake of rebelling against their essence. Of course, Ichiyō also tended toward far-fetched subjects, and her observations were original. But she had a quality that was possible only in a woman and that could not possibly be imitated by men. When women writers imitate men, it is always a disaster. Women writers have unique talents that men cannot approximate. It is best for them to develop their uniqueness without trying to imitate men. Having said as much, it may seem that we are disparaging women's writing and demanding that they stick to fairy tales, which are quite removed from the realistic trend of the times. But this is not our intent. What we want is for women writers to pursue tenaciously that which distinguishes them as women.

It seems there are an exceedingly large number of those who aspire to become women writers. But the reason that so few go on to become successful, as do men, is to be found, we believe, in our social context. When women are girls, they have ample time to read. They even have time to write, and their enthusiasm for the art begins to grow. But, as soon as they marry, they cannot continue. Compared to men, it is <u>very important for women to marry</u>. Moreover, <u>marriage is far more constraining for women than it is for men.</u> Once married, it is a woman's responsibility to care for the household. A man may receive a wife in marriage, but a woman receives, in addition to a husband, all the household obligations. And once she has children, she neglects her reading and writing and sets aside her pen and paper. We don't know how it is with the wealthy, but in the normal household a woman can hardly help but worry about housework. Shouldering the burdensome responsibility of maintaining a family while saddled with the tiresome work of the household, even if she tries to steal a moment or two to write, she won't be able to produce superior work, and gradually her opportunities to write will dwindle even further. Here lies one of the most important reasons women writers cannot succeed.

Then there are the differences between the way men and women writers create fictional characters. When women writers depict a female character, they do so with attention to even the finest detail—much more so than would a man. But the male characters that they create are hopelessly unsatisfactory. They cannot manage even a superficial reflection of the most mundane, commonplace moment in a man's life. In comparison, the female characters that men produce are far more successful than the male characters women writers concoct. This is due to the fact that whereas women have the freedom to invest themselves in the portraitures of female characters, they hardly have any opportunity at all to observe or interact with men. On the other hand, men have occasion to study women. Whereas a man may decide to initiate a relationship with a woman, it would be extremely rash for a woman to do the same. But then again, these women who write literature nowadays are more than apt to engage in the most outrageous acts. We don't suppose women are bold enough to opt for the kind of "bald description" that is now part and parcel of the Naturalist style. But even if they did, we're not sure we would bother reading what they'd written. From an emotional point of view, we must say that we find writing by women that reveals this kind of animalistic instinct bizarre indeed.

We do not expect men and women to produce identical works. When you get right down to it, women's writing is not particularly essential. But even so they should be encouraged to participate in the literary world in some measure, and their participation should provide what is moderate and feminine and nothing more.

Belittling Women Writers [A Dialogue]

A: Women are no better than monkeys. They are adept at imitation. When they write fiction, they cannot help but imitate others.

B: Yes, I quite agree. Ōtsuka Kusuoko and Hasegawa Shigure are especially quick to imitate others. When Kyōka is in fashion, they imitate him. When Sōseki is the rage, they imitate him.

A: Kunikida Doppo has an essay entitled "Women and Beasts." In it he notes that women are not birds; they're monkeys. They are monkeys who only imitate humans. Their works of prose are not even remotely interesting, and, what's more, they are difficult to decipher. This is true for other countries too. In England, Eliot is a famous woman writer, but I can't read her because her style is so convoluted that even when I manage to get through it, I can't understand it! *Adam Bede* is more comprehensible than her other works and is considered her masterpiece. But even so, I don't understand it. She spreads about her superficial knowledge, going on about things she clearly does not understand. In a certain journal, Hasegawa Shigure wrote a critique of Plato and Maupassant, discussing them in the very same essay. I suppose because both names are written in the same katakana script, she figured they were from the same era. How ridiculous.

B: In England as well women writers imitate the carnality they see in men's texts.

A: Yes, and in Germany it is now the fashion for women to copy Nietzsche!

B: Women lack originality. And such is the case when they write fiction. They're complete imitators! Monkeys imitate humans. And like them, women enjoy imitative activities. Superficial women are presumptuous enough to assume they have the originality required to write fiction. They should confine themselves to copying in music or in the dramatic arts, which would be far more appropriate.

A: That they proudly proclaim themselves "women writers" as soon as they've patched together a prose piece based on imitation is the height of absurdity.

B: Women have no close contact with society at large. They should write honestly about life as they see it. But because they immediately set into writing with such conceit—as if they were experts about it all—it turns my stomach just to look at their drivel! The late Kitada Usurai was a case in point. She wrote about debonair rakes going off to the Yoshiwara to buy prostitutes. Compared to her, Ichiyō is by far superior. She wrote sincerely about what she had herself observed.

A: The *Tosa Diary* begins: "I intend to produce one of those diaries men are said to write."[7] Women today are doing exactly the same, are they not?

At any rate, there is no reason to believe that women will ever best men. They should try doing what men do only after they stop menstruating. Women are the ones, after all, whose sodden bodies seep with excess.

B: That's going a bit too far, don't you think?

A: But it's true. Women absorb what men ejaculate.

B: In a journal survey women writers responded to questions about their favorite novelists by listing Izumi Kyōka and noting that they could not stand to read the "foul breathed" works of the young Naturalist writers. What impudence! Woman—with her long monkey coat growing in hair by hair, posing for all the world as if she and she alone had mastered the affairs of the world—

7. Ki no Tsurayuki (ca. 872–945), a prominent male poet and statesman, wrote *Tosa nikki* (Tosa diary, ca. 935) using a female persona. See footnote 17 below. I am using the translation provided by Miyake, *The Tosa Diary*, p. 41. RLC

she speaks and writes with such appalling superficiality. No man could come close to her impertinence.

A: Women like this may not be "foul breathed," but from a man's perspective, they emit an offensive body odor. At the very least their hair pomade stinks.

B: In sum, the works women writers produce, with the exception of Higuchi Ichiyō, are simply imitations of men. They may blend their efforts together well, but they do not succeed in approaching authenticity. That Japanese poetry is unable to escape the confines of tradition, even now, is due to the fact that the Fujiwara era was dominated by the woman's hand. If men had been more involved, the art would be more developed now. It would be progressive. And the foolishness of the *New Collection of Old and New Poetry* *[Shinkokinshū]* and such would have been averted.[8]

A: Among women writers today, my favorite is Okada Yachiyo. Kunikida Haruko is also good. Ōtsuka Kusuoko and Hasegawa Shigure are so offensive, they are not fit to mention.

B: Yes, I agree. Whatever they end up doing, it's nothing but "housewife art." As long as they stick to their housework, all is well. But when they act high and mighty like some kind of expert, then there is nothing more disgusting.

A: Interesting that you should use the word "disgusting." I agree. I find the word extremely pertinent to expressing my own reaction to these women writers. And by the same token, I particularly regret Yosano Akiko trying her hand at prose. She of all people should defend her position and apply herself to poetry to the bitter end.

When a woman gets on a train, she can barely take her seat before some man stands up to offer her his. What kind of view of life does she have?

B: It's illogical! They say women are scrupulous and discriminating, but based on my own observations, I find there is no writer more slipshod than a woman. She may be perfectly scrupulous and discriminating when it comes to sitting at home knitting and keeping track of her pin money. But when it comes to art, a woman simply does not possess the power necessary for careful preparation. Given the state of things today, she'd be better off closing up shop. So long as Japan has its representative in Higuchi Ichiyō, that's enough. If a woman has time to write, she ought to invest her energies in fixing her husband a tasty morsel to snack on.

At any rate, the stories they write while they're rushing here and there

---

8. *Shinkokinshū* (New collection of old and new poetry) was compiled in 1205 by Fujiwara Teika and other poets. It was considered heterodox at the time of its compilation, and its creative liberty with tradition ran counter to the tastes of many utilitarian Meiji critics. *RLC*

with gift packs of money or boxes of sweets are just worthless. A man writes to eat. To live—he writes for his very survival. He doesn't write—as women do—for vanity, for some shallow claim to fame. The difference is stark.

A: Women write fiction half for their own amusement—much as a retiree dabbles in tea or bonsai. A man struggles over each manuscript page. A woman writes to amuse herself.

B: Men write in the face of great pain. Surely there is no greater pain than the pain a man endures as he writes in an effort to survive.

A: The ailing Kunikida Doppo proffered his own theory on women and beasts. Recently, his wife came to him while he was on his sickbed and tried to appeal to him. "You know, I've grown so used to you that even if you screamed your 'women are beasts' theory at me, I wouldn't feel a thing." "If you had feelings, you'd escape the realm of beasts," Doppo countered. "It's precisely because you feel nothing that you're a beast." And his wife Haruko is actually a very gentle person. I'd like to show him Shigure or Kusuoko!

B: In short, it's impossible for women to write exceptional works of fiction.

A: They ought to stick to washing out their underwear!

Don't Put on Airs

And so women writers continue to plod along. But there's not one among them equal to Higuchi Ichiyō. One feature of women writers today really invites our ire. And if we're to state what it is, then we'd have to say that it's because so many of them are show-offs! Well, regardless of whether there are many or not—they all show off! We never had the opportunity to speak to Higuchi Ichiyō personally, but it would seem she was not a show-off. Her works all seem to speak from her own inner self. Even when you compare her life—or what we've heard of it—with her writing, you cannot help but come to the same conclusion. But no woman writer today has inherited anything from the late Higuchi Ichiyō—not even her bad habits. We hesitate to publicize their names here, but among the women writers we know, all make an effort to put on airs—especially in regard to contemporary morals. Costumes and customs are open to individual taste, and one cannot criticize another's preferences. For example, there are those who insist on splash-patterned cloth from Kurume, whereas others demand Chichibu stripes. To each his own. Similarly, there is one woman writer who always has her hair done up in a reverse ginko coiffure. She wears a quality collar on her kimono and a fashionable apron draped loosely. Could she be the wife of an artist? Perhaps that of an art school student? Or maybe she is married to a shopkeeper? Who can tell from the appearance she affects? Are we not to conclude that she is imitating the late Higuchi Ichiyō? At any rate, we can't help but feel she's trying to affect the look of a downtown girl—which is inappropriate given her situation. Really, she wants to look so worldly. It's absurd! Women are by nature performers. It's no surprise that the fiction they concoct is itself pretentious. Putting on airs is nothing short of lying. How would it be if they did not put on airs? If they behaved like the women they are—revealing their true thoughts, observations, and worries (should they have any) honestly? Is there no woman writer today who will do this? We want to hear a real woman's voice, sounded by that woman herself! We have no use for a woman who croaks out an imitation of a man's voice. How would it be for a woman to raise her own poignant voice? At any rate, if we can't achieve as much, works of today's women writers, regardless of how well they are written, will never amount to more than the diversion of artificial flowers.

We'll say it again—as we've said it before—we want women to wrench from deep within themselves their innermost selves. And that is why these writers who take up social issues in journals like the *Literary Arts Club (Bungei kurabu)*, who pretend to be familiar with the goings-on in the teahouses and bordellos or who act like they are conversant with the wives of the newest actors and know all about the world of the theater—they just set our teeth on edge!

What we want to say to women writers is nothing more than what we've already written here. But we'll say it again; listen: Don't put on airs!

| | | What Is "Womanliness"?

YOSANO AKIKO

Buddhism taught the Japanese "the swift impermanence of this world" from early times, and we also learned very early the Confucian teaching "Make yourself new from day to day."[9] However, these ideas were interpreted only through the pessimistic lens (the view that this world is one of suffering) of

TRANSLATED BY LAUREL RASPLICA RODD. From Yosano Akiko, " 'Onnarashisa' to wa nani ka" (What is 'womanliness')? in *Yosano Akiko hyōron*, ed. Kano Masanao and Kōuchi Nobuko (Iwanami, 1985), pp. 334–345. Originally published in *Fujin kurabu* (Women's club), February 1921.

9. Impermanence is the first of the "three insights" *(sanmai)*, Buddhist conceptions about this world that must be realized to achieve nirvana: all is impermanent, all is sorrowful, and all is devoid of self. "Make yourself new from day to day. Each day renew" is from the Chinese Confucian classic *The Great Learning (Da xue)*. LRR

Hinayana Buddhism, and Japanese were unable to accept the optimistic Mahayana Buddhism in which the teaching "All dharmas are in constant flux" is precisely what is constant about human beings.[10] In modern times, thanks to imported art and scholarship, we've come into contact with the ideas of unceasing change and evolution, but we see people who are inclined to curse modern life and who try to maintain moldy old conventions and customs. These people only look backwards and are reluctant to face up to contemporary reality; furthermore, they are cowardly about considering the future. I think such people are found both among the conservatives and among the false progressives.

What disgusts me is that these people frequently include in their denunciations of "women's androgynization" attacks on the movement for the liberation of women, which is one of the critical women's concerns of modern times.[11] This is because they maintain the fixed belief that we must establish a single pattern of behavior, a single rule for human life—and at the same time they hold prejudicial and biased views that are antipathetic to women's human evolution. For this reason they deliberately use hateful language, on the one hand welcoming new influential threats to women and on the other hand disrupting the wise judgment of society with innumerable nasty arguments that attempt to vanquish the proponents of the movement to liberate women.

| | | These people say, for example, that it is not good for women to receive the same education as men or for women to have access to the same range of jobs as men because women will lose the beautiful quality of "womanliness"

10. "Lesser Vehicle," or Hinayana, Buddhism represents, according to its adherents, the original, pure teachings as they were taught by the Buddha. Its doctrines focus on escape from the suffering-ridden cycle of rebirths through one's own effort by renouncing the world and practicing strict discipline. From the point of view of Mahayana Buddhism, Hinayana is the "Lesser Vehicle" because it has the practitioner's own escape from suffering as a goal, rather than that of all beings. Mahayana offers many paths to enlightenment, including approaches by which laypersons, and even evildoers and unbelievers, can achieve nirvana. Nirvana, in Mahayana teachings, means not only liberation from the cycle of rebirth and suffering, but also the realization that the Buddha nature lies immanent within one ready to be realized. Akiko is interpreting the teaching that "All dharmas are in constant flux," which usually refers to the impermanence of all the phenomena of this world, including the various aspects of human personality, as a positive endorsement of human change. *LRR*

11. The Japanese "women's liberation movement" (*joshi kaihō undō*) may be said to have begun in response to the Meiji state's attempts to define and limit the roles of women in terms of the ideals of "good wife, wise mother." For an overview of aspects of the movement and Akiko's role in it, see Nolte and Hastings, "The Meiji State's Policy toward Women," and Rodd, "Yosano Akiko and the Taishō Debate over the 'New Woman.'" *LRR*

[onnarashisa] and will become anomalous intermediate beings who are neither women nor men.[12]

I immediately want to ask them a question. What is the premise upon which their conclusions are based? In Japan, where the majority of women don't even receive a middle school education; in Japan, where women don't even have the right to become members of their own town or village councils, why is there so much flippant concern about possible consequences of equality of education with men or of equal opportunities for employment? Is it not flagrant speculation to condemn the results without even trying to give women equal freedom with men in any area?

Even more, I want to press these polemicists by asking whether ultimately womanliness, which they value more than anything else in a woman, represents a quality peculiar to women. I question this. These polemicists place what they call womanliness at the peak of a woman's character, and they make all other qualities subordinate to this one. No matter which or how many superb qualities a woman might have, if she lacks one thing—womanliness—her value as a human being is taken as zero. It appears the opinion of these disputants is that women have no independent personalities. I ask you, is womanliness ultimately the best, the highest, aspect of a woman's personality?

||| What really is the nature of this "womanliness"? In our country if a woman breaks with convention, she is criticized as lacking womanliness. If a woman enjoys herself too much, she is ridiculed as lacking womanliness. Thus it is clear that one requirement of womanliness is to stay within bounds and to behave like a docile doll. This is the case in Japan. However, in England and the United States women, without exception, break with convention. Moreover, even in our country most girl students are now stepping out of bounds—and with their shoes on.[13] In England and the United States, physical education for women became common after the war, and schoolgirls even came to wear the same uniforms and hats as schoolboys as women strove to compete in active sports. These women in the United States and England are not criticized, so it appears this womanliness that the disputants value so is not a quality sought in all human beings but only in Japanese. Can this be so?

The polemicists say that a woman loses her womanliness if she does the

12. *Onnarashisa,* which might also be translated "female-likeness," had been used to describe gender characteristics that could be either male or female in earlier centuries. Male actors performing female roles in kabuki, for example, are praised as exemplars of *onnarashisa. LRR*

13. Akiko is perhaps referring to the increasingly common "uniform" of the woman student of the era: *hakama* (divided skirt typical of samurai-class male formal attire) often worn with leather, Western-style shoes rather than the traditional footwear. *LRR*

things a man does, but can human actions be determined to be innately men's actions or women's actions? Aside from women bearing children, I can think of no other human behaviors that belong uniquely to one sex or the other.

In the *Diary of Murasaki Shikibu* we read that this unprecedentedly great woman writer feared the criticism of her fellow ladies-in-waiting. She usually pretended not to be able to write even the character for "one," and when she lectured to the empress on the Chinese poetic form, *yueh fu,* she did it secretly.[14] Misunderstood even by members of her own sex who felt women's scholarship and literary work invaded men's domain, Murasaki Shikibu feared being attacked for being impertinent, but it seems Murasaki Shikibu has never, in the past or today, been called lacking in womanliness.

Politics and the military have long been thought to be men's realms, but even in the history of Japan, we find female rulers, female politicians, female soldiers, and loyalist women of the Bakumatsu era.[15] Not only were these women not criticized for the "androgynization of women," but also Empress Jingū is worshipped as a god, and the other women are each given the respect of our nation's people and evaluated rationally.[16] In today's world there are women who are members of the Diet, governors, mayors, scholars, artists, social reformers, teachers, commentators, reporters, aviators, drivers, conductors, government and public workers, office workers, etc. Many women are active in what were formerly male spheres. In the recent world war, over 2 million British women left their homes, joined the war effort, and worked in the munitions industry.

14. In her diary, Murasaki Shikibu describes how her knowledge of Chinese became a matter of malicious gossip among the court ladies, although the empress asked Murasaki to teach her poems by the Chinese poet Po Chü-i. See Bowring, *Murasaki Shikibu,* p. 137. *LRR*

15. Although Akiko does not mention her, such lists of prominent women in Japanese history often begin with the sun goddess Amaterasu no ōmikami, the founder of the Japanese imperial family. A queen of Japan, Himiko, is mentioned in a third-century Chinese historical document. And in early Japanese recorded history there were a number of Japanese empresses who took the throne. Other well-known women in Japanese history include Hōjō Masako, mother of the first shogun, who controlled the shogunate after his death, and the woman warrior Tomoe Gozen, celebrated in the epic *Tale of the Heike.* In referring to women of the end of the shogunate, the period known as the Bakumatsu era, Akiko may have in mind women such as Yaguchi Nakako (1790–1846), Bandai Kumiko (1783–1837), and Tagami Tatsuko (1802–1867), who were well-known lecturers in the Shingaku movement. (See Robertson, "The Shingaku Woman.") *LRR*

16. The semi-mythical Empress Jingū (ca. 200–269 CE) is credited with leading troops to Kyūshū with her husband to quell a rebellion and then herself, after the death of her husband, leading Japanese forces against the Koreans she believed were fomenting the uprising. This alleged conquest opened Japan to cultural influences from the Korean Peninsula and from the Asian continent through Korea. *LRR*

As many as nine-tenths of the bullets that were used on the battlefields were manufactured by these women's hands—an unprecedented contribution. On Armistice Day, the military commander gave a speech of gratitude for women's effort to the Parliament and said that "It cannot be denied that half of the reason England was victorious was due to the women."

Thus, there is no basis for attacking women for lacking womanliness because they do things men do. If there were a historically determined, permanently frozen division of labor by sex, men would be invading women's territory when they became tailors or cooks or took jobs in laundries or spinning mills, and "men's androgynization" would become a subject of debate. We would have to criticize Ki no Tsurayuki, who wrote what is called "a woman's diary" for the same reason, accusing him of having lost his "manliness."[17] Instead he is revered as a poet and as a pioneer of our national literature.

||| These polemicists find the qualities love, refinement, and modesty in womanliness. In contrast, "unwomanliness" is said to entail callousness, cruelty, impudence, shallowness, rudeness, vulgarity, and frivolity. However, it seems to me that love, refinement, and modesty are important qualities in a man as well as a woman. These are not characteristics that should be expected only in women but are aspects of humanity that should be common to all human beings. Being endowed with these qualities does not constitute "womanliness" or "manliness" but "humanness." "Humanness" or humanity is not something that differs according to sex. If someone, whether man or woman, loses his or her humanity, that person should be criticized. Regardless, men have been forgiven such loss of humanity. It is only toward women that the charge of being "unwomanly" has been leveled. Obviously, such rebukes are biased.

There are many men in Japan who still haven't recognized this and apologized for it. Instead, they take pride in their unseemly demands for love and refinement and modesty only of women. Not only that, but they also fail to moderate their own boorish words and deeds, perpetuating the evil ways of those preening men of the past who saw themselves as larger than life.

However, one cannot think that such faults as callousness, cruelty, impudence, shallowness, rudeness, vulgarity, and frivolity should be forgiven in anyone. That men should denounce these qualities only in women is due to men's

17. The *Tosa Diary,* by Ki no Tsurayuki, is presented as the diary of a woman accompanying a provincial governor returning from Tosa to the capital (as Tsurayuki did in 934). Tsurayuki may have chosen his fictional persona in order to allow himself the freedom to write in Japanese rather than Chinese, the language usually chosen for public documents written by men during the Heian period. *LRR*

selfish desire to reduce women to a state of gutless submissiveness as sexual play-things or as cooking puppets.

| | | When we consider this it becomes clear that there is no such thing as the quality of "womanliness," which, according to these polemicists, is both the highest standard of human value and peculiar to women. What they call woman-liness is not an ideal that has the authority to govern our lives, unchanging, throughout time. It is also clear that it is not something limited to women but is instead precisely that quality of humanness with which all human beings are endowed.

The qualities that make up humanness are not limited to love and refinement and modesty. Humanness also includes creativity and discernment and other vital cultural capacities.

Every person is endowed with humanness. What most perfectly draws out the qualities of humanness is education and work. For this reason, it is impor-tant that every individual enjoy the freedom to receive a higher education and also the freedom to hold an occupation chosen by that individual from among all possible occupations.

That these polemicists nevertheless deny higher education to women and try to stubbornly defend restrictions in the area of employment is totally unjustifi-able. I cannot think that the education and employment that enrich the human-ness of a man should, on the contrary, cause a woman to lose her humanness. These people try to support their views by pointing to such traits as vulgarity or impertinence or frivolity or superficiality as being common among work-ing women, women of letters, women students, or women teachers of today. I think, on the contrary, that this view undermines their own argument. I am in sympathy in seeing a lack of the cultivated qualities of humanness in women today, but when it comes down to it, this is, after all, because women have had too little education that would polish these human qualities, and they are per-mitted too narrow a range of human occupations. Give women the same level of education as men and raise them to positions that have the same responsibilities as men. Try permitting women the freedom to take jobs where they can make use of their talents. Just try giving them the encouragement and facilities and time that have been given to men since Meiji.[18] Then we will see that Japanese

18. Among the political and social changes implemented by the Meiji government for men, at least, were the right to choice of occupation and residence, to the vote, to participation in the developing democracy, and to universal education. However, as Nolte and Hastings acknowl-edge, "The Meiji state had much more power than its predecessor, the Tokugawa shogunate, to impose the gender asymmetry that characterized the new comprehensive vision of national

women will not be inferior to the women of Europe and America in taking a dramatic step forward and displaying their latent humanity.

Boys in middle school are at their cockiest. The words and actions of women today that are seen as crude or frivolous may be attributed to the fact that their education, which should forge their humanness, is at such a poor level that it is not even equivalent to a male middle school graduate's. Although it is said women's occupational sphere is enlarging bit by bit, women still cannot even be elementary school principals. Just because they are women, they are made subordinates of men, sometimes worthless men, even when their own abilities are superior, and so women lose the opportunity to temper the steel of their humanity.

||| [The following sections have been abbreviated.]

These polemicists also argue that it is only women who can bear and raise children. Consequently, for them a major aspect of womanliness is motherhood. They object to the movement for women's liberation because, they believe, it encourages the loss of motherliness, and "new women" avoid motherhood.

I wish to correct this view by pointing out that the ability to become a mother is not the whole of "womanliness."

While only women can become pregnant, women do not monopolize reproduction. Pregnancy requires male cooperation, and it also takes both a mother's and a father's love and wisdom and effort to raise and to educate children. Because "fatherliness" has been neglected, motherliness has been overemphasized, and reproductive life is mistakenly believed to be the responsibility of women only. But to become the parent of a human being is a human behavior common to men and women and a grave responsibility for both men and women. . . .

Still, I remind these polemicists that not all humans are going to become parents. . . . And if women are seen to lose their womanliness by not having children, then men must lose their manliness. . . .

When women have been liberated from the word "womanliness," they will have been awakened to their humanity and will no longer be reproductive or cooking puppets. They will be humans and no longer dolls. . . .

We need not fear being called "unwomanly." The thing women must fear most today—the thing any human being must fear—is to be called "unhuman," lacking in humanity.

---

development in Japan," and in some ways women were even more restricted in this period than in the past ("The Meiji State's Policy toward Women," pp. 152–153). *LRR*

Women Writers

KOBAYASHI HIDEO

According to Lermontov, because a woman will employ the most creative logic to elude her own biases, she is extraordinarily difficult to persuade.[19]
To give a simple illustration, ordinary logic would proceed in this way: "That
man is in love with me, but I have a husband, so I must not fall in love with him."
But a woman would seem to be different, Lermontov says. Her mind works,
instead, in this way: "I should not fall in love with that man because I have a
husband. But that man is in love with me, therefore. . . ." And he posits that it
is what comes after this "therefore" that needs special attention.

Nowhere, however, does Lermontov suggest that a man is better able to control himself in a love triangle than a woman. Given that they are both already
on the verge of ruining their lives, to say that the man's way of thinking follows
normal logic while the woman's logic is creative would be like a feeble attempt
at a joke. And then we have a writer like Chekhov, who, despite being Russian
as well, is so self-possessed it is unnerving; he would not even condescend to
offer maxims about "women." Chekhov once wrote in a letter, for example: "I

TRANSLATED BY KATHRYN PIERCE AND MIKA ENDO. From Kobayashi Hideo, "Joryū
sakka," in *Kindai bungaku shisō taikei 29 Kobayashi Hideo shū* (Major collection of modern literary
thought, vol. 29: The Kobayashi Hideo collection), ed. Yoshimoto Takaaki (Chikuma shobō,
1977), pp. 46–50. The piece was written in November 1937. Originally published in *Shinjoen*
(Garden of new women), January 1938: 140–143. The translators would like to acknowledge
Dr. Matthew Königsberg of Freie Universität Berlin and Professor Hiroyoshi Noto, Senior Lecturer in Japanese Language and Director of the Japanese Language Program at the University
of Chicago, for the assistance they kindly provided in completing this translation.

19. Mikhail Yurievich Lermontov (1814–1841) was a Russian poet and novelist who died at
the age of twenty-seven in a duel. Kobayashi is borrowing from Lermontov's best-known novel,
A Hero of Our Time (1840–1841). This is almost a direct quotation from the fourteenth chapter
of the fifth section of the book, "The Third Extract from Pechorin's Diary: Princess Mary." The
journal entry for June 22 reads in part as follows:

> There is nothing more paradoxical than the female mind; it is difficult to convince a
> woman of anything; they have to be led into convincing themselves. The order of proofs
> by which they demolish their prejudices is most original; to learn their dialectic it is nec-
> essary to overthrow in your own mind every scholastic rule of logic. For example the
> usual way:
> "This man loves me, but I am married; therefore I must not love him."
> The woman's way:
> "I must not love him, because I am married; but he loves me — therefore . . ." (*A Hero of
> Our Time*, pp. 266–267). KP

despise men who praise women as much as I despise those who disparage them. Whether they are men or women is not of the slightest importance."

Certainly one cannot deny that humankind is divided into males and females. But in the realm of literature, what is called genuine literature is created neither by the hand of a man nor by the hand of a woman. Of course, in a literal sense, if it was not written by a man, it must have been written by a woman; but acknowledged masterpieces throughout history have not been written in a style that creates an awareness of the author's sex. In the end, in order to write first-rate literature, it evidently requires Chekhov's kind of reckless audacity. As a writer, one's own sex must not enter into the work. The soul of a writer, or to put it differently, the soul of a true poet is evidently something elusive and indefinable that can only be firmly grasped by those that have abandoned their own human nature. The melancholy that permeates Chekhov's literature and that pierces through the hearts of readers indeed comes from that elusive, indefinable *something* grasped by someone who knows what it means to abandon one's human nature.

At least this is the way I see it. And it is because of this simple, transparent way of thinking that I cannot help but be confused when I come across a term like "woman writer." Whatever this so-called "woman writer" may be, she is certainly not a writer; from the perspective of literary theory, the term is all but meaningless. Yet actually the term "woman writer" is used everywhere, and the women who call themselves "women writers," as well as those who are called this by others, are in fact producing works. What are we to make of this? Would it not also be appropriate to then use the term "man writer" for men who write, as well as have self-proclaimed "men writers"? When I try to follow such logic, I get lost. Perhaps it is because I am not blessed with the audacity to abandon my human nature, like Chekhov.

Of course, Lermontov's ideas are not particularly remarkable. I do not like men who spout clichés about the general nature of women. In my experience, the more a man knows about women, the more averse he is to making generalizations such as "women are like this. . . ." Yet I understand the desire in Lermontov to dredge up these truisms about women. That is, I can sympathize with those feelings that men have toward women. But perhaps it would be better to express those pompous truisms more straightforwardly, which might be done in the following way. These are the words of a certain male writer, whose name I have forgotten. He says: "No matter how nonsensical his ideas may be, if a man really forces them on a woman, she will eventually wind up accepting them. On the other hand, if a woman tries to force her opinion on a man, he will wind up wanting to kill her." I don't know if all women would wind up accepting the ideas forced on them, but I can well understand the man who would want to kill the forceful woman, and that is the point I'm trying to make. In one extreme case, another male writer says: "If there is a husband out there who has never once thought of killing his wife, I would like to meet that man." Fortunately, I have never once thought of killing my wife, but I have often thought that I would like to strangle certain women.

I'm afraid my discussion has gotten a bit bloody, but what I really want to say—although the quick-witted women among you may already know this—is that perceptive men, without exception, harbor a kind of terror of women in the depths of their hearts. "Terror" isn't quite the right word for it, but I can't seem to find a better one. In any case, every man feels, somewhere, in the depths of his being, that he is no match for a woman. It is not so much something he feels, but rather something he senses by some primitive instinct. While women themselves may also say that they are no match for men, they say this merely as a conditioned response,[20] and men can sense deep down that they are being taken too lightly by women. For a woman who has not yet had experience with a man, however, this is something that cannot be understood. Likewise, a man who has not yet had experience with a woman hasn't the slightest notion that he harbors an instinctive fear of females deep in his heart.

Men who are domineering husbands and who say things like "You just don't know how men work" are outside of this discussion because such men are not in the habit of examining human feelings. I cannot help but think that for self-aware writers, on the other hand, the desire to spout truisms about women comes from the deep-seated consciousness of their fear of women. It is this self-awareness that must be emphasized as a true instinct, but it becomes vacuous because it is twisted into petty truisms. It seems that men in whom this instinct is strong will become, if not a woman hater, then a woman worshipper.

Kawabata Yasunari is a contemporary author who has one of the most visible feminist tendencies.[21] His work teaches us that the various popular interpretations of what constitutes "a man," although they would appear to be correct, are in fact mistaken, and similarly he shows us that masculine images presented in movies and popular novels are nothing more than lies. His work shows us the true, subtle workings of a man's heart. Yet there may be some readers who take issue with this assessment. They may do so because Kawabata's painstaking de-

20. Kobayashi here means that women are simply saying they cannot compare to men because it is what they have always heard and socially what they have been programmed to say. In other words, theirs is a socially conditioned automatic response and not something that women really believe. *KP*

21. The term "feminist," a foreign loan word, was used with frequency at the time to describe a man who, through his behavior, showed that he thought that women should be respected and esteemed. *KP*

pictions are almost exclusively of women and the subtlety of a woman's heart. However, in thinking this, readers have actually been tricked by the author. Kawabata by no means describes women as they exist in the real world. The women Kawabata depicts and the women depicted by Tokuda Shūsei are of a completely different kind.[22] For example, in Kawabata's recent masterpiece, *Snow Country,* what kind of snow country geisha does he describe?[23] The beauty of that geisha is in truth nothing more than the beauty that the author himself desires, and it is the author's skill as a writer that fools us into believing that such a woman could actually exist. That is, the beauty of the female protagonist is beauty as seen through the author's male heart, and women could never actually have such an image of their own sex. A woman writer would certainly be unable to write this portrayal of the geisha. Kawabata often says, "Men are by nature boring; every one of them thinks in the same way, says the same things." Somehow, it seems that exceptionally wise men have this tendency for monotony. Paradoxically, the discovery of the inanity of a woman is what attracts an intelligent man. I'm afraid women will not be happy at all to hear such things, but I feel that this tendency in men cannot be changed by any means. This tendency in men cannot be simply dismissed with the superficial explanation that it is a vestige of male chauvinistic customs.

Today, unlike in times past, the woman's sphere in society has expanded drastically. Not only in literature, but in a variety of intellectual pursuits, women have come to exercise their intellectual abilities in the same capacity as men. This is an encouraging trend, and men should do whatever they can to ensure that they do not obstruct women's advancement. I am not at all interested in the question of whether women have the same intellectual capacity as men. I would say, rather, that I find the issue trivial. We live in an unsophisticated society, where newspapers create a furor when a woman obtains a doctoral degree in the natural sciences; there should be no necessity to concern oneself with such questions. Rather than spending time worrying over such matters, women ought to be advancing into male professions.

But to write literature is altogether different. Here it is not just a question

22. In much of his fiction, Tokuda Shūsei (1871–1943) takes up issues such as "women's rights and the emergence of the new independent woman" (see Torrance, "Translator's Introduction," p. 4). His women are modern and independent; he creates female characters with whom his readers, both male and female, would have been able to sympathize and understand. Kawabata's women, on the other hand, seem at first to be realistic, lifelike characters, but as Kobayashi points out, they are merely aesthetic ideals. *KP*

23. It is important to note that although *Snow Country* was begun in 1934 and serialized sporadically until 1937, Kawabata did not finish it—in the form it takes today—until 1947. At the time, *Snow Country* was hailed as a masterpiece by critics, including Kobayashi himself. *KP*

of daring. Businessmen who have placed all their ambitions in their work, or women who dream of advancing humankind by expanding women's rights, are not likely to be distracted by the subtle workings of the human heart as it negotiates between the sexes. No one who remains unconcerned with these feelings can be called a true writer. Therefore, the attraction that men feel for the foolishness of women is, purely and simply, an issue only in the realm of literature. It cannot be helped if women who do not understand literature find this displeasing. And it would follow that this person known as "a woman writer" is also attracted to some sort of idiocy in a man that men themselves do not clearly understand. Or so it would seem.

It may sound as if writers spend their time engaged in a particular kind of amusement. To prove that this is not the case, one need only ask whether the attraction of men and women for each other's foolishness is not in fact the basis of true love. Considering that love affairs have been a rich source of material in literature from time immemorial, this theme of so-called love is of great importance to writers. After all, there is nothing other than love that allows a man to awaken to what is most masculine in himself and a woman to encounter that which makes her most feminine. Moreover, the self-discovery that men and women reach through love is a process with manifold difficulties, but to skip this onerous self-awakening while still attempting to approach the true nature of human character is impossible. There is no shortcut to this grand image of humanity, at least not for writers; the only way to approach it is to start with this hard-won self-understanding and move closer step by step.

Writers often say that if you can create a credible female character, you have matured as an artist. By the same token, if the writer is a woman, then we should say she has likewise matured as an artist when she can create a credible male character. However, women writers apparently do not seem to be troubled by this point.[24] Not only Kawabata, but also all male authors take pains with their depictions of female characters, but women writers do not seem to take as much trouble in their portrayal of male characters. Or perhaps it is that they do not feel the need to go to such pains to portray them. Why this should be the case is unclear to me. At any rate, I don't think that something like this can be explained by simply stating that women writers are less developed than their male counterparts. It may instead be because women are not nearly as afraid of men as men are of women!

In closing, I would like to cite from a critical essay that Kawabata wrote earlier, as I concur with the views he expressed therein.

24. In this essay, Kobayashi critiques the use of the term "women writers" as meaningless, but at this point he begins to use the term himself without problematizing it. *KP*

I rather enjoy reading works written by women writers. Even when the work is artistically weak, or perhaps especially when it is, I can sense how difficult it is to be a woman. I may say this because I am a man, but women's works are somehow direct. They are raw. Although many people say that women writers are reluctant to tell the truth, and that they hide it with embellishments, regardless of how experienced the writer is, or how inexperienced, women writers inevitably reveal their true selves. Even though she may not notice it herself, she is bared naked by her work. No matter how exquisitely she tries to costume herself with her writing, she is as unclothed as the emperor revealed in the fairy tale "The Emperor's New Clothes." I cannot help but think that the hearts of women are this way by nature. To put it bluntly, women's works are stimulating to the senses. They have an honest body. The stories this month are all maudlin. If we say that this is the naivety of literature, it means nothing, but if we say it is the naivety of women, then it becomes invaluable. For example, love stories written by inexperienced women writers inevitably have a heroine who is clearly being deceived by men. Female writers rarely hide women's weak spots. However, because the works are mawkish, one may be led to conclude that female writers have deeper feelings than men. But exactly the opposite is true. Contrary to expectation, even Uno Chiyo and Hayashi Fumiko, distinguished as being particularly lyrical, write works that are emotionally flat. As for the others, most are emotionally poorer than we might have imagined. From a look at women's writing in general, the idea that women's feelings are intricate and refined is nothing more than a masculine fantasy. In addition to being meager to begin with, the emotions in their works tend to wither, to harden. And there are more than a few works that portray men as insipid. It seems that women writers should be fearful of aging."[25]

Thus, a worshipper of women is much more dangerous to women writers than a woman hater, as is obvious from these words.

ashi does not give the source for this quotation, it can be found in Kawa-

2

THE ESSENTIAL WOMAN WRITER
Jan Bardsley

In chapter 1, we saw how Kobayashi Hideo expressed his dislike for the term "woman writer," arguing that gifted writers are precisely "those who know what it means to abandon their human nature." The three essays in this chapter continue the discussion by considering the woman writer as just that—a *woman* writer. That this remains a topic in the 1960s and 1970s shows the uneasy relationship the words continue to have to each other, as if one should still be surprised to find "woman" and "writer" paired in the same conversation. A sense of competition is at work here too—a tug-of-war over which of these oddly paired words ultimately trumps the other. Perhaps she is not a *woman* writer, after all, but a woman *writer*. If we resolve the competition altogether by simply saying that "she is a writer," then does the man as well as the woman disappear from our newly neutered discussion? In their essays here, critics Akiyama Shun, Okuno Takeo, and Setouchi Harumi confront the rivalry, each refereeing the same match in different ways.

Relatively close in age, our critics took higher education in Tokyo and built their careers in the capital. All experienced the devastation of the long Pacific War and its defeat yet were fortunate to lead long, productive public lives after 1945. Akiyama Shun (b. 1930) was born in Tokyo, studied French at Waseda University, and became a professor of literature at Tokyo University of Agriculture and Technology and at Musashino University. His prolific work established his reputation as a literary critic, and he gave advice to budding authors; in the introduction to chapter 4, "The Resisting Woman Writer," however, we learn why Saegusa Kazuko (1929–2003) decided that as a woman wanting to break into the literary world, she must refuse to follow his advice. Still active in his seventies, Akiyama contributes regularly to intellectual journals such as *Shinchō*. Okuno Takeo (1926–1997), who was also born in Tokyo, studied the sciences at Tokyo Institute of Technology before turning his attention to literature. Considered one of postwar Japan's most influential literary critics, Okuno wrote widely on women's literature and played a role in advocating for the acceptance of many young women authors, although, as we shall see, with some conditions in mind.[1] Our last referee, Setouchi Harumi (b. 1922), as one who was inevitably understood as a *woman* writer and whose personal life too departed from feminine codes, deserves a longer introduction before she moves into the ring. Setouchi was born in Tokushima City on the island of Shikoku and majored in native studies at Tokyo Women's College. After graduation, Setouchi dutifully married the man whom her parents had selected; followed him to China, where he took up a post assigned by Japan's Foreign Affairs Ministry; and bore one child, a daughter, in the turbulent climate of the late war years. Returning to Japan in 1946, Setouchi soon left her husband and daughter, initially to pursue a love affair in Kyoto and then a lifelong career in writing. A prolific author, especially of novels and biographies, Setouchi won the Tamura Toshiko Prize in 1961 and the Women Writers' Prize in 1963; in light of her 1962 essay, "Requirements for Becoming a Woman Writer," protesting the category of woman writer, it seems ironic that she was awarded and accepted this prize. In 1973, she became a Tendai Buddhist nun, changing her name to Jakuchō. Unlike Akiyama and Okuno, Setouchi was not always on good terms with others in the literary world. She could not publish in any major journal for five years after writing a 1957 short story ("Kashin"; The Stamen) that used the Japanese word for womb rather than a more common euphemism. She was excoriated by male critics as a "*womb* writer" or the producer of "*womb* literature." Perhaps the experience of being shoved to the silent margins during these years motivated Setouchi's affinity with the notorious, outspoken women of Meiji Japan and her decision to produce biographies of eight of them.[2]

Penning her essay in 1962, Setouchi Harumi finds herself battling the same constraints that we saw Yosano Akiko condemning in 1921. She wants to referee the match from outside the ring but finds the same old barriers forcing her inside, into a fight that men have defined. Yet Setouchi, as a woman living in postwar Japan, enjoys far more privileges than did Yosano. She has the right to vote, to join political organizations, to speak in public on political issues, and to run for office. She can sue for divorce (and in Setouchi's case, she did). Abortion and contraception are available, although oral contraceptives will not be legalized until the advent of Viagra in the 1990s. According to the strictly legal terms in place in Japan in 1962, Setouchi has the right to equal treatment with men in all family matters, in the workplace, in education, and in the political life of the country. Nevertheless, many of the conditions that prompted Yosano Akiko in 1921 to dispute discrimination against women incite Setouchi's anger in 1962 as well. Indeed, the very freedoms and the possibility for radical change embodied in the new constitution, the Labor Standards Act, and other laws inspired a forceful and conservative reaction in postwar Japan. Whereas new laws pushed toward gender-neutral policies and expanded opportunities for women to enjoy equality with men, postwar *practices* pushed right back with vigorous, even illegal, defenses of separate roles for women and men.[3] As the three essays here show, the same kind of battling over gender occurred in postwar discussions of literature: increasing opportunities for women to publish motivated a reaction against thinking of writing as a gender-neutral occupation and to denigrating what women wrote as not quite "real" literature. In looking at such discussions, we cannot help but notice that gender arises as an issue only when women's careers are at stake. Indeed, it is women who are gendered, women who must be *women* writers, and women who must create from their sexed bodies, while men, at least as critics Akiyama and Okuno conceive of them, are ultimately allowed to soar in the transcendent space of the intellect as writers, achieving that freedom from their human nature idealized by Kobayashi.

In her 1962 essay, Setouchi Harumi proves to be the most sensitive of all three of our critics to the tension evident in using "woman writer" as a single descriptive term. In her view, this assumption rigs the match from the start. Setouchi argues that it would be comical to list her occupation as a woman writer on either tax papers or a hotel registry. While she forgets that gender would be marked in other boxes on both kinds of forms, Setouchi does show that "woman" need not always be attached to "writer" in identifying women who write professionally, especially when an issue of substance is concerned, such as whether or not she can pay a bill. This argument paves the way for Setouchi to make her reader question why at any time and in any forum a woman writer must be described as such rather than simply as a writer. Using this logic, Setouchi calls attention to society's different expectations of the man and the woman who work as authors. The assumption that a writer is also a man is so well entrenched that the term "man writer" appears foolishly redundant. The word "writer" is also sufficiently elastic to include men writing in diverse forms of fiction and nonfiction. Such elasticity does not extend, however, to including the woman who writes; she threatens to stretch the word "writer" to its breaking point. Even modifying "writer" with the addition of "woman," as Setouchi's list of "ten requirements needed to become a woman writer" shows, it is still a stretch for any woman to achieve.

Setouchi explains her list, directing bitterness to the society that unreasonably expects so much from the woman author and to herself for having leapt through the hoops of such expectations. Her ten requirements for becoming a woman writer place the would-be author in competition with men, other women would-be writers, and her own weakness. She identifies how the woman/writer bout is fixed from the start and how it will inevitably shape up. That is, the fighter must present herself as a woman yet should realize that to be in the ring at all is a manly act. Talented, proud, independent, and homely, the successful competitor will not leave the match for the typical women's arenas of romance, marriage, or modest self-doubt. Nor will she lose her competitive edge by showing kindness to other writers, even other women writers, or taming her ambitions by becoming a "good wife" who puts her husband first. She must move boldly in the ring, baring all, and—most important—like other professional athletes, the woman writer must have the financial wherewithal to devote herself to the game. Setouchi imagines that the woman writer who has all these qualifications can stay in the ring match after match, winning a measure of respect as a contender in the realm of "pure literature," an endeavor governed by men.

Yet Setouchi also suggests that there may be a way to win the woman/writer competition once and for all. She argues that if a woman who writes is "madly convinced of her own genius"—that is, her own *inherent* ability and desire to create—she can fight in a different match altogether. Freed from the system that produces "pure literature" and freed from the endless need to compete against herself, the genius has the power to define the game in new ways. By banishing the "woman" from the match, however, Setouchi's solution leaves the realm of romance, marriage, and, indeed, all human relationships uncontested. Only the creative talent survives. "Woman," Setouchi implies, is far too defined by patriarchal notions of relationship to be anything but a burden to the genius. Thus, oddly enough, in Setouchi's terms too, a "woman" cannot be a writer. In this yearning for transcendence to a gender-neutral space of the genius, Setouchi has something else in common with Yosano Akiko. The heroine of Akiko's 1913 autobiographical novel *To the Light (Akarumi e)* speaks of a double life as well, one in which genius enables a flight from constraints: "I dream of the life a genius leads and write as if it were my own. . . . I may be an ordinary person but I am not only that: I am an ordinary person who dreams of genius. When I write of myself without lying, this double life of necessity becomes the poem."[4]

These essays by Okuno Takeo and Akiyama Shun, both published in the 1970s, betray the same kind of discriminatory attitudes toward women's writing offered at the men's roundtable in 1908, as discussed in chapter 1. They stride up to the ring of the woman writer debate like they own the place. Given the power of men over women in public life in Japan in the 1970s, maybe indeed they do. Both Okuno and Akiyama see men as having the ultimate right to referee arguments over defining the writer, and like the 1908 discussants, they take a patronizing attitude toward women writers and readers. Yet a fear of losing ground to women is not the only anxiety operating in their essays. Of all the men cited in this book, Okuno and Akiyama make the most explicit reference to Japan's position in global politics. This reference not only changes the framework of the discussion over gender and creativity, but also threatens the ability of the Japanese man to claim rights as the ultimate referee. For if we view the issues of essentialism, mimicry, and objectivity in art at stake here through the wider lens of international hierarchies of Cold War power, we find the Japanese man almost equally displaced and disparaged as the Japanese woman. In this view, the Japanese man too is always a mimic, always trying to imitate the creative forms initiated by the (Western) artist, and ultimately in danger of being cast as an artist who can express only from his raced body.

When a giant in the form of the United States hovers around the ring, the Japanese man finds his position precarious, his claim to masculinity in need of reinforcement. The idea of the essential woman, her femaleness inseparable from her Japaneseness, must be brought to the fore. Okuno and Akiyama's essays employ this strategy with gusto. Both critics' concerns over women's writing are intertwined with laments over the "manly" power of the United States, its influence over domestic politics in Japan, and the threat its interventions pose to the masculinity of Japanese men and their creativity. At the same time and for the same reasons, Okuno and Akiyama prize Japaneseness as *embodied* by the woman writer yet as uniquely *expressed* by the (man) writer. It is the space that cannot be claimed by the West and where Japanese authenticity can be made visible. And it is a space, the men claim, that ultimately becomes the province of Japanese (men's) art.

Okuno Takeo's 1974 essay, "Is Fiction Inherently the Realm of Women?," reverses Setouchi's logic, arguing that producing fiction, especially a novel, has always been and continues to be an essentially feminine pursuit, particularly in Japan. Two observations about trends in literary production and consumption prompt Okuno's remarks. First, he notices that literature departments enroll women students in increasing numbers, that literary prizes are being awarded to women novelists, and that for readers "there is no better description of the middle-aged housewife than fan of the novel." Second, Okuno reports on the simultaneous rejection of the novel by young men, who have turned toward different modes of artistic expression. He explains the exodus of men as a response to politics. The modern novel, Okuno argues, has been integrated with the civilizing, nation-building efforts of Japanese men from the Meiji era through the early postwar years. As such, it has been based on "masculinist principles" and devoted to the virile and vigorous explication of weighty questions and abstract ideas. The continuing defeat of popular protests in the U.S.-Japan Security Treaty disputes of the 1960s caused young men to lose their belief in political action. The novel, once a proud symbol of virility, is now part and parcel of the new politics of dependency and hence rejected by young men who refuse to surrender their last shreds of masculinity to collusion.

Okuno surmises that women quickly filled the field of literature not so much because the exit of men made way for them, but because of their "instinctive intimacy" with the form itself. They were naturally suited to create fantasy and vibrant images; could narrate "realistic depictions" of "family experiences"; and perhaps, above all, possessed "abundant physical sensibilities." Weakened by their battles with the conservative establishment, the men were no match for such empowered women. Assuming that women were congenitally incapable of connecting the novel and politics themselves (and echoing references to "house-wife art" described in the 1908 roundtable), Okuno imagines women domesti-cating the novel, making it women's work in much the same way as they attend to cooking, housework, and child rearing. The ease with which this transition occurred causes Okuno to wonder if the novel, as it had developed in Japan, had not always been a feminine form—domestic in the double sense of uniquely Japanese and essentially the province of women. He recalls women's involve-ment with the classics, such as the orator of the *Kojiki*, or the *Record of Ancient Matters*, and Murasaki Shikibu's authorship of *The Tale of Genji*, but when he turns to men writers, he thinks of the feminine quality of their work (its hyste-ria, whining, moralizing, and angry outbursts). Okuno also points to Japanese male impersonations of female voices in ancient works such as the *Tosa Diary*, as well as in the novels of Dazai Osamu and Kawabata Yasunari. Although this line of thinking leads Okuno to conclude that the novel, as it has developed in Japan, is an essentially feminine form, he applauds the skill of men whose feminine voice "surpasses that of women." After all, for men to write in such fashion requires artistic skill; for women, it is merely instinctive. Okuno implies that for all their creativity, women writers are not capable of producing intel-lectually satisfying literature, and it will still fall to men of talent to turn out these works, and perhaps special awards must be established to reward them. Although Okuno's essay appears to congratulate women writers, we can see an inherent misogyny operating here and an underlying sense of alarm. He has an obvious nostalgia for the manly men and manly novels, and even womanly Japan, Okuno believes, is most artistically expressed by a Japanese man.

Writing two years later in 1976, Akiyama Shun expresses similar notions about the essential difference between women's and men's writings in his essay, "Confessions of a Women's Literature Convert." Unlike Okuno, Akiyama wel-comes these differences because he believes that it is the very uniqueness of women's writing that has the power to revive men, especially the drained and weary intellectual. In Akiyama's view, intellectuals are men engaged in cere-bral, often petty posturing. Plagued with self-doubt, such men exert themselves continuously from youth through middle age to prove themselves smarter than other men and, in the process, hunt for ever more sophisticated vocabulary and turns of phrase. This constant striving forces men to deny their early inno-cence and sense of self, notably even to the point of rejecting the language that grounded their childhoods. Ultimately, they are on a trajectory toward death, an extinction of everything that they were originally. Akiyama mentions that his own anxiety over becoming an intellectual coincided with his coming of age during the time of the defeat and its aftermath. Although Akiyama does not connect writing, masculinity, and global politics as explicitly as Okuno does, he still implies that transforming oneself into an intellectual has been a male project enmeshed with reinstating Japan as a world power. Although Akiyama casts this as a noble mission, it is ultimately a failed one, for the intellectual is always trying to be other than himself—a mimic and not the original. Even thirty years after the defeat, Akiyama finds his nation's interests tied fast to those of the United States.

The woman writer, in contrast, can never be other than who she is. As Aki-yama sees her case, *woman* always trumps writer, her essential feminine nature overcoming differences among individual women writers, rendering such dif-ferences only minor stylistic idiosyncrasies. Rather like Okuno, Akiyama casts the woman writer as maternal, alien, and mysterious; she is not an artist who must work to create but, like the mother, one who can magically produce by let-ting nature take its course. Since the result is not *other* from the woman writer, but *of* her, even a short phrase such as Mori Makiko's "sea of people" can guide the intellectual to this emotionally rich and original wellspring of woman. Al-though the intellectual, long other to himself, will sense that such a phrase is "the source of some suppressed emotion" or "something unknown" and may be "disturbed" by this, Akiyama imagines that he will finally be comforted by it. Women's writing is not read but experienced by the intellectual, who will, in turn, rediscover his childhood innocence, the unvarnished goodness of the everyday, and his Japaneseness. It is her lack of desire or ability to be any-thing other than herself and her ignorance of international politics that give the woman writer life, and it is this life, inseparable from the maternal and the Japa-nese, that can restore the intellectual. As Akiyama sees it, the emotion coursing through the woman writer's fiction, transcending the meaning of any particular word, demands nothing of the intellectual and only serves to soothe him. It is the *woman* writer who restores the writer to himself, making *him* whole again.

Who wins the bout? The *woman* writer, the woman *writer,* or the writer? Setouchi is right. The match was rigged from the start. Restrictions on women's opportunities in all spheres of public life were too powerful in the 1960s and 1970s to let the woman writer—or the woman politician or the woman scien-tist or the woman professor—clip gender from the title people perceived her to have won. The women's liberation movement of the early 1970s responded by promoting strategies that exploited rather than resisted this typing, celebrating *women*'s achievements. Critics like Okuno and Akiyama countered by recognizing women's writing while moving to contain and ultimately disenfranchise it. What these men do not want to relinquish, however, is not so much male prerogative in the literary field as Kobayashi's fiction of the genius able to transcend his human nature. If Okuno and Akiyama located women writers and readers within the social world, they would have to acknowledge the influence of gender over the creative work of both women and men. They would become "men writers." Choosing to frame their argument in essentialist terms allows them to conflate women's creativity with their female bodies while leaving the mind — and all its potential to soar past the body — to men. Or, as Mishima Yukio puts it in his 1966 essay, "On Narcissism" (see chapter 3), because the "gravitational pull of the womb" impairs the woman, her mind is "unable to separate itself and float freely away from the flesh in the manner of the man." As long as the ring never changes, the match always comes out the same. As we shall see further in this volume, however, the ring was to change. Alternative approaches by critics such as Mizuta Noriko have changed the rules, releasing the players from bouts scored merely by binaries of male-female or original-mimic.

NOTES

1. Barbara Hartley kindly provided the biographical information on critics Akiyama and Okuno.

2. Biographical information here is drawn from Copeland, "Setouchi Harumi," and Yoshida, "Setouchi Harumi."

3. For more detailed accounts of the status of women in Japan in the early postwar years, see Buckley, "Altered States"; Uno, "The Death of 'Good Wife, Wise Mother'?"; and Upham, "Unplaced Persons and Movements for Place." See also Mackie, *Feminism in Modern Japan*.

4. As translated and quoted in Beichman, *Embracing the Firebird*, p. 25.

Requirements for Becoming a Woman Writer

SETOUCHI HARUMI

How, we must first ask ourselves, do the requirements for becoming a woman writer differ from those for becoming a writer? We can assume that the public comes to recognize a given individual as a woman writer by the way she appears in print. Once she has written a piece and published it in a newspaper or magazine, the newspaper or journal, irrespective of her wishes, clearly appends the label "writer" in parentheses following her name. I have never once seen "woman writer" written on such occasions. And I dare say that no woman writer would of her own volition record "woman writer" in the blank marked "occupation" when completing an information form at a hotel registry or the tax office or such.

Before a woman is a woman, she is a human being; and by the same token, before a woman writer is a woman writer, she is a writer. How unlikely it would be to assume that before a writer were a writer, she would be a woman writer. If writers entered the public domain by virtue of their writings alone and never once appeared in the mass media in the flesh, readers would have only the names upon which to determine whether or not they were male or female. In point of fact, Harumi, the name that I use, is my legal birth name, and yet it can also be a man's name. There are times when people assume (from my name) that I am a man. For a long time I was convinced that Sasazawa Saho, the mystery writer who uses his wife's name for his pen name, was a woman. The fact that Tsuboi Sakae is a woman but Kubo Sakae is a man is something we cannot determine simply by reading their works.

Just a few years back, during the decade journalists had dubbed the "Era of Female Genius," there were a number of literary-minded young men who had struggled for years in their coterie journals to make a name for themselves.[1] Among these were a few who seriously asked themselves, "Why don't we change our pen names? Take on women's names—as a shortcut to literary notice—

TRANSLATED BY REBECCA L. COPELAND. From Setouchi Harumi, "Joryū sakka ni naru jō-ken" (Requirements for becoming a woman writer), *Shukke suru mae no watashi kaku koto* (What I wrote before I took Buddhist vows) (Kawade bunko, 1990), pp. 20–26. Originally published in *Kokubungaku kaishaku to kanshō*, special issue, *Gendai joryū sakka no himitsu* (The secrets of contemporary women writers) 27 (10) (September 1962): 96–99.

1. The "Era of Female Genius" refers to the mid-1950s, when both Ariyoshi Sawako and Sono Ayako emerged nearly simultaneously. They were so bright and their debut so feted that critics referred to them as "female geniuses." The term "era" would make it sound as if the literary world were awash in brilliant women writers. But it was only these two who were the objects of such media attention. *RLC*

and once we've entered the limelight, reveal ourselves for who we are?" In fact, there was a man at the time who published a piece under a woman's name, and it became a best seller. At any rate, these literary youth were bitterly convinced that unless they were women, they would not earn attention as writers. In reality, however, this "Era of Female Genius" was but a temporary phenomenon cooked up by a capricious mass media. Once the hoopla had abated, it was clear that the number of women writers was few and far between when compared to men, accounting for less than 1 percent. Because writing men far outnumber women, the activity of two or three women writers always seems strikingly conspicuous.

At a glance, the number of women entering other professional fields was quite noticeable after the war, and yet why is it that the number of women writers did not increase proportionately? Undoubtedly, the answer lies in the fact that the requirements for becoming a "woman writer" are far more stringent than those facing a "writer." I shall here enumerate what these requirements are.

Be a Woman

If one had the confidence that one could survive without ever exposing one's real self to media scrutiny, then this point would be moot. But I doubt there is a writer alive today who can avoid having at least one photograph appear in print. If one aspires to become not just a "writer" but a "woman writer," then one simply must be a woman even if it requires a sex change.

Be Manly

To be a woman but to have a manly spirit is something of a contradiction. Nevertheless, possessing just this contradiction is another requirement for becoming a woman writer. For no matter how one capitalizes on one's woman(ness), even if one expresses oneself in feminine styles that could only be achieved by a woman, if one is not masculine at heart, one cannot write. A woman who is delicate and womanly at heart can never become a woman writer. She may look like a woman writer at first glance, but if at heart she is womanly, then she will not have what it takes to hold her own. The very act of writing—of presenting one's work to the world—is in and of itself an act of male aggression.

Be Homely

When Kurahashi Yumiko's works first began to receive attention, Hirano Ken wrote that he was curious as to whether or not she was a beauty. His comments sparked considerable debate. For a critic of Hirano Ken's standing to reveal such concern over a woman writer's physical appearance threatened to lead to the hasty conclusion that to be a woman writer one must be beautiful—a tragic conclusion, indeed. A woman who is beautiful by nature has ample opportunity to be flattered by men. It is highly unlikely, therefore, that she would consider giving herself to a dull, physically taxing profession like writing, a profession that would require her unstinting patience.

It often happens that while one is struggling to become a writer, one ends up entangled in love affairs with the young men in one's coterie. At times one finds oneself involved with the writer one depends on as a mentor. One imagines mining these incidents for the sources of one's masterpiece, and while one is determined to base one's writing on real experience, before one knows it, one's heart has been wrested away by passion or matters of the heart. One's dreams are hijacked and one finds oneself estranged from one's writing.

Far better to have the tenacity of an ugly woman! Her determination uncompromised, she is much more likely to accomplish her goals. Along these lines, Kikuda Ippu recollects that once the writer Hayashi Fumiko joined a group of male writers and spent a week with them, even sleeping bundled up together with them, and not one of them was even conscious of her as a woman because she was so homely.

Be Talented

When it comes to art, perseverance alone is not enough to bring success. Being blessed with natural talent is by far the most important requirement, and yet it is quite rare that an individual can discern this talent in his- or herself. This is because when cleverness or genius first make their appearance, they quite frequently strike people as being the exact opposite of what they are. Take, for example, two writers who join the same coterie magazine simultaneously. The one who bursts on the scene with an apparent abundance of ability will quickly falter, whereas the one who seems at first unable to excel at anything but failure and who earns nothing but his colleagues' laughter will in the end give flower to a talent with such vibrant force that it would seem strong enough to topple a wall of stone. The latter is the one who ends up with all the laurels. Such examples are many. Something to consider in this regard is the fact that women appear to be cleverer than men. When they first begin, their writing brushes seem to virtually burst with promise. But the rate of men who eventually hit it big is much higher. The reason why the number of women writers still does not exceed men is found herein.

Where talent is concerned, there are both prodigies and late bloomers, making it difficult to discern true ability. If you are told that you have no talent, you should not be too quick to lament your fate. But at the same time, you have to be suspicious of those who think that they occasionally receive revelations from above announcing their genius because this may well be a sign of schizophrenia. Especially among women there is a tendency to want to interpret these situations according to their own convenience.

Be Egotistical

To become a writer, rather than tentatively, timidly presenting oneself in one's texts as some petty little creature, one must be willing to disclose oneself with great bravado. Otherwise, one's efforts will amount to nothing. Generally, women are believed to be the vainer of the sexes. But men far exceed women in the intensity of their vanity.

Among men there are any number who will go for twenty to thirty years without being recognized but who will continue writing, waiting for the day they finally make it—all the while turning an innocent face to those who murmur about them behind their backs, whispering about how they'd be better off if they just gave up. But they won't give up. They continue writing with the hopes that one day they'll become a writer. What else supports them but a fierce ego? But women lack such tenacity. They are quick to give up. Because marriage offers women an easy escape, many turn to it as a way to avoid their feelings of defeat. Women need to decide beforehand that they have a pride that will not be bested by any man.

Be Jealous

Because this quality is inherent to all women, it may seem unnecessary deliberately to itemize it here. And yet jealousy is an essential qualification without which one simply cannot write. When I went to the Soviet Union and spoke to the women writers there, I was shocked when I heard them say that they harbored absolutely no jealousy for the success of their friends in the same profession. I find it difficult to accept such cool pronouncements—especially from writers, of all people, who are supposed to harbor more likes and dislikes, more evil passions, than others. If one lacks jealousy, then one ends up sniveling and bowing in all directions, offering a "Congratulations on your success" here and a "Best wishes for your masterpiece" there. How on earth can one apply oneself to one's own work? A jealous spirit is the source of energy that fuels one's own creativity.

Have What It Takes to Be a Bad Wife

I suppose there are women writers who have proper married lives and run a household. Well yes, there are Sono [Ayako], Harada [Yasuko], Yamazaki [Toyoko], and most recently Kurahashi [Yumiko]—a small enough number to count easily on one's fingers.[2] But just by putting her own fame before her husband, doesn't a woman merit the name of a "bad wife"? Women who have husbands who make few demands and women who are divorced—if we count up the numbers, we will see how important having what it takes to be a bad wife is to the requirements for becoming a woman writer. And it would be premature to conclude that the future will be any different for the younger generation of postwar writers, of which a number conform to the character of good wife. These younger writers may not divorce and disclose their discord to the world, but they must calculate each time they are patient and self-sacrificing to their husbands. A woman who desires from the bottom of her heart to be a good wife—how can she possibly become a writer?

Have the Nerve to Strip

When Okamoto Kanoko announced her intention to become a writer, her husband, Ippei, said, "You'll need the nerve to strip naked and spread eagle yourself in the middle of Nihonbashi." Because the two of them tended toward this kind of exaggerated expression, his assessment is somewhat over the top! But even with the exception of autobiographical stories, when you write, you expose your innermost shame to scrutiny. With that in mind, one has to have what it takes to strip in broad daylight.

Have Property

Advice of Nagai Kafū and Virginia Woolf aside, when one must write to eat, one cannot truly be a writer. Today there are a number of important women writers in Japan, but, starting at the very bottom of an impoverished life, they left their true life's work undone because their fame became their property. Without property—that is, an inheritance from one's parents, a wealthy husband, or one's own life savings—one cannot devote oneself to one's art.

2. "Female Genius" Sono Ayako (b. 1931) married the writer Miura Shumon (b. 1926) in 1953. Harada Yasuko (b. 1928) married newspaper journalist Sasaki Yoshio in 1951. Yamazaki Toyoko (b. 1924) married *Mainichi* newspaper arts editor and painter Sugimoto Kikuo (1921–1992) in 1961. Kurahashi Yumiko married Kumagai Tomihiro, with NHK Broadcasting, in 1964. *RLC*

Woolf offers that a woman writer must have "a room of one's own." Entering her room and locking the door, she comes face to face with her own solitude. Regardless of her husband, her children, her lover, in her room, alone, with the door locked, she has contact with no one else. Those who aspire to become a woman writer frequently turn back because they fear this solitude. Even if a woman lives up to all the other requirements, if she fails at this last one, she will never become a woman writer.

The above are the requirements that occurred to me for becoming a woman writer in the literary realm. If one aspires to become a woman writer but is not concerned about entering the realm of pure literature, one needs only one qualification—and that is to be madly convinced of one's own genius.

| | | Is Fiction Inherently the Realm of Women?

OKUNO TAKEO

When we look at literature in Japan today in 1974, there are clear signs that women have a growing monopoly on the literary arts, particularly the novel. Nogami Yaeko is nearly ninety and, along with Mushanokōji Saneatsu, the most senior literary figure in Japan. Nevertheless, having been awarded the Order of Culture, she continues to work consistently and maintain a literary output that defies her age. Shimamoto Hisae, also in her eighties, completed *The Aristocracy [Kizoku]* while working on the epic novel *The Long Flow [Chōryū]*. Beginning in 1971 with the late Hirabayashi Taiko's receipt of the Imperial Award of the Japanese Academy of Art, older women writers have recently been showered with literary accolades. Uno Chiyo received the Japan Art Academy Award, while Sata Ineko won the Noma Prize, the most prestigious award for serious literature. A contemporary translation of *The Tale of Genji* has been published by Enchi Fumiko. Shibaki Yoshiko and Ōhara Tomie, two long-established and gifted artists, quietly maintain a steady regime of literary production with no sign of fatigue or fading interest. Two years ago Ariyoshi Sawako became the focus of huge public interest with *The Twilight Years [Kōkotsu no hito]*, a best seller of unprecedented proportions. Many other writers have developed their own styles and become leaders in their respective fields,

TRANSLATED BY BARBARA HARTLEY. From Okuno Takeo, "Shōsetsu wa honshitsuteki ni ? (Is fiction inherently the realm of women?), *Joryū sakka ron* (On women inmeisha, 1974), pp. 9–15.

DSLEY

including Sono Ayako, Setouchi Harumi, Kōno Taeko, Satō Aiko, Hiraiwa Yumie, Togawa Masako, Kurahashi Yumiko, Ohba Minako, and Kanai Mieko. Yamazaki Toyoko has reemerged defiant following allegations of plagiarism that threatened to end her career. Poets such as Tomioka Taeko and Yoshiyuki Rie have also published highly original novels. Notable among recent releases from Shinchōsha Publishers is Takahashi Takako's *To the Edge of the Sky [Sora no hate made]*. Two Shinchōsha newcomers, Tsushima Yūko and Saegusa Kazuko, have also impressed with *The House Where Living Things Gather [Ikimono no atsumaru ie]* and *A Diffuse Reflection [Ranhansha]* respectively. Women such as Gō Shizuko and Yamamoto Michiko appear to be monopolizing the Akutagawa Prize. Accolades have been heaped upon newcomer Miyao Tomiko and her debut novel, *The Oar [Kai]*, awarded the Dazai Osamu Prize, while Moto Kukiko, the author of *The Weight of Travel [Tabi no omosa]*, has revealed a previously hidden identity. Even in the field of criticism, where women struggle for recognition, talented newcomers such as Tanaka Miyoko have emerged, with Takenishi Hiroko's biography, *Izumi Shikibu*, taking the Hirabayashi Taiko Prize. In nonfiction too there are a number of new writers, including Ishimure Michiko, Yamazaki Tomoko, and Kirishima Yōko.

It is evident from the random collection of names listed here that the activity of women writers demands our attention. In terms of both the number of emerging writers and level of activity, women far outclass men in their novelistic endeavors. When we named distinctive and promising new novelists in the past, attention centered on young student writers such as Ishihara Shintarō, Ōe Kenzaburō, and Fukuda Shōji (also known as Shōji Kaoru). However, we no longer see the emergence of such virile young representatives of a new age still in their teens or early twenties. There are several emerging middle-aged male authors with experience of the war, including some of relatively advanced years. Mori Atsushi, for example, is notable for making his debut at sixty. The work of these men is grounded in ideas and ideology. However, their writing fails to impress in comparison with the firmly wrought, finely crafted, and carefully constructed narratives based on everyday experience written by women writers intimately familiar with the classics. Although they are still a minority, we have also seen the advent of young avant garde women novelists, such as Kanai Mieko, Tsushima Yūko, and Shima Sachiko. But the novel appears to have lost its power to attract the new generation of young men. These young men might join the underground theater movement; write and sing rock or folk; read and draw comics; or direct their artistic talents to pop art, design, and dance. But although they become pugnacious student activists, grow their hair, adopt curious attire, or satisfy their exhibitionist needs with various hippy-like behaviors, they appear to have no interest in the novel. While some young women may also feel this way, many remain attracted to the novel and feel an instinctive affiliation with this form of expression. And, of course, there is no better way to describe the middle-aged housewife than to call her a fan of the novel.

Gesaku was an entertainment prose genre of the Tokugawa era. Since this genre was directed toward the socially "unenlightened"—namely, women and children—it was regarded as unsuitable for respectable samurai males. However, the introduction of ideas from the West led to the notion that literature, and in particular the novel, had great cultural, artistic, and social value. Young men from outlying parts of Japan, consumed with desire to build a new nation, embraced literature and the novel as the most important means available to civilize the premodern, induce self-respect and a sense of humanity, and conduct authentic social inquiry. In spite of the social changes that occurred in the intervening years, from the introduction of Western thought in the Meiji period until about the time of the U.S.-Japan Security Treaty disputes in 1960, the novel remained the most valued, all-encompassing literary genre. It was the jewel in the crown of the arts, respected as a masculine field of endeavor that enabled writers to address, all in one work, truly significant issues such as ideology, religion, politics, revolution, social issues, and human progress. There is clearly a close relationship between politics and literature. Thus, both writers and readers in Japan have used the word "novel" to refer to the work of artists of the stature of Dostoevsky, Tolstoy, Balzac, Stendhal, Thomas Mann, and Sartre. It was the pivot of culture, an expression of cutting-edge ideology. These days, however, young men have lost their respect for this form of art and no longer aspire to novelistic endeavors. For in spite of long hair and other signs of the feminization of young men, it would appear that, as in Tokugawa times, the novel is again the province of women. In fact there is every indication that young men are embarrassed even to acknowledge the visionary possibilities of the novel, let alone actually write one. While the humanities faculties in universities are dominated by young women, young men are apparently mortified at the thought of entering this field or of showing any commitment to the novel. This, of course, does not preclude the possibility that the novel may become like other feminized domains. For while cooking, sewing, beauty, housework, child care, and education are seen as women's work, it is men who are the famed specialists and professionals in these fields.

It may not be the case elsewhere, but we can see in retrospect that since the time of the *Record of Ancient Matters [Kojiki]* it has been women in Japan who have told traditional tales and written and read diaries. For example, it is said that Hieda no Are, the imperial orator featured in the *Record of Ancient Matters* prologue, performed his art in the style of an old woman reciting a tale. Ki no Tsurayuki, the author of the first diary to appear in *kana*, *The Tosa Diary*, was a man. He nevertheless assumed the persona of a woman, declaring that he intended to "produce one of those diaries men are said to write."[3] Examples such as these confirm the perception that women are both better able to write without inhibition about the everyday and more adept at expressing romance and emotion.

Beginning with Murasaki Shikibu and the world's first novel, *The Tale of Genji*, it was the woman's hand that led to the flowering of Heian period literature, with its focus on sensory experience and psychological detail. Since then, the idea of the novel as a feminine form has prevailed in Japan. Thus, while Edo period *gesaku* writers may have been men, they wrote about women and love for an audience of women.

Dazai Osamu was a novelist of the postwar period. In his short story, "Womankind" [Jorui], he noted what he believed to be the incomprehensibility of women, claiming that the categories of human and ape were inadequate. Dazai argued that since women could not be included in the former, a separate category of "woman" was required. Nevertheless, many of Dazai's better works, such as "The School Girl" [Joseito], "Chiyojo," "Skin and Heart" [Hifu to kokoro], "Crickets" [Kirigirisu], "Waiting" [Matsu], "Villon's Wife" [Viyon no tsuma], and *The Setting Sun [Shayō]*, are those in which the author takes on the persona of a woman and writes in the first-person feminine.

Incomprehensible though he found women, Dazai understood that if he was to express adequately the psychology of detailed, nuanced feelings and recreate freely the tenor of everyday life, then he could do so only as a woman. This assumption of the woman's persona was something he held in common with the *Tosa Diary*'s Ki no Tsurayuki. And so, even if we are reluctant to accept that the novel is a form of expression fundamentally suited to women, the experience of these two writers suggests that we should at the very least concede that it is a genre with limited connection to the political or the intellectual. We can therefore argue that it belongs to the realm of women. This is certainly how things have developed in Japan.

Since Meiji times the modern Japanese novel has in reality been a fundamentally feminine form. Naturalism and the "I" novel are said to be based on lofty concepts that include revelations of reality, pursuit of truth, literary dedication, the lyrical expression of honest accounts of real life, yearning for sincerity, resistance to authority, restlessness, and transgression. However, these literary forms derive primarily from highly feminine attributes such as passivity, whinging, envy, laments of personal unhappiness, residual affection for jilting lovers,

3. Translation by Lynne K. Miyake, based on the Helen McCullough translation. See Miyake, "*The Tosa Diary*," p. 41, and McCullough, "Tosa Nikki." *BH*

voyeurism, and gossipy chatter. Being rugged students from the provinces, the Naturalist writers deluded themselves that they were free of feminine influence. However, in the deeds and laments of Ushimatsu, the protagonist of *The Broken Commandment [Hakai]*, and even more so in the lingering attachment found in *The Quilt [Futon]*, there is a sense of depression, clinging sentimentalism, suspicion, and envy, all of which are characteristic of women. In fact, these elements are found in the works of a number of writers of this school, including [Tokuda] Shūsei, [Masamune] Hakuchō, and [Chikamatsu] Shūkō.

Even the father of the modern novel, Futabatei Shimei, had concerns that the pursuit of literature was a questionable career for a man. Fearing that he himself would be feminized by the project, he abandoned work on *The Floating Clouds [Ukigumo]*, with its struggling, effeminate protagonist Utsumi Bunzō. There are feminine traits too in the ornate writing of the Ken'yūsha members such as [Ozaki] Kōyō and [Izumi] Kyōka. Even Sōseki's "The Tower of London" [Rondon tō] and *Grass on the Wayside [Michikusa]* feature a distinctly female sense of hysteria. Both [Nagai] Kafū and [Tanizaki] Jun'ichirō sought to devote themselves to feminine sensibilities, while there are few overtly masculine traits to be found in Arishima Takeo. We might be tempted to regard Mushanokōji Saneatsu and Shiga Naoya, both from the White Birch Society, as masculine, with Naoya's works particularly featuring the stereotypical, tyrannical head of the house. However, there are actually few masculine traits in the emotional, moralizing, hysterical outbursts of anger in which the characters in these works indulge. Although Naoya structured his writing around a framework of patriarchal values, Akutagawa rejected the egotistical, arrogant family tyrant, choosing to devote himself instead to the representation of the weak and feminine protagonist. This strategy was adopted by other writers who achieved prominence in the mid-1930s, including Takami Jun, Dazai Osamu, and Itō Sei.

Today, there are no longer writers such as Tanizaki Jun'ichirō, Murō Saisei, or Kawabata Yasunari who dedicate themselves completely to the mystique of the feminine and whose lifework is devoted to expressing the beauty thereof. In other words, male writers who specialize in the art of the feminine to a degree surpassing that of any woman are a thing of the past.

During the war and into the postwar era Japan was governed by masculinist principles. This was natural during the war. However, even in postwar times there was a focus on male-centered issues, including social reform, the introduction of democracy, commitment to the political process, the position of individuals within organizations, and economic reform. Thus the motifs featured in novels were those linked to masculinity and men in public life, such as political activity, intellectual enterprise, adventure, and revolution. These issues scaffolded the details of literary works and were expressed in a variety of nuanced psychological sensibilities, everyday settings, and fantasy scenarios.

However, it is clear that these male principles have collapsed. This collapse took place in the time between the disturbances arising from the 1960 renewal of the U.S.-Japan Security Treaty and the student unrest in universities at the end of the sixties and early seventies. There is no longer a belief in ideals such as revolution, politics, war, ethics, or the progress of mankind. Patriarchal morals have also long lost their authority. The adventures of economic growth and technological advancement have been negatively judged as mere social pollutants. All that remains in the absence of structures to support a new novel based on masculinist principles is a vague sense of the end of intellectualism.

In this setting male writers find themselves in a wretched plight. Having no masculinist principles upon which to base their work, they are reduced to merely writing psychological novels of the everyday based on fantasy and the senses. The more ambitious and committed they are, the more serious their dilemma concerning how and what to write.

Women are essentially much better equipped to deal with the physical and the sensual and have more finely tuned sensibilities than men. Therefore, their capacity to write fantasy and to create images is far more striking and vibrant. In an age when all taboos have been cast aside, the freedom and unrestrained development of women writers knows no bounds. They effortlessly navigate a course through a veritable flood of images almost to the point of flagrancy. No man is their equal.

However, women have been endowed with the gift of narrating tales since times long past. And today too, while male writers, debilitated by their battle for survival in the face of a hopeless future, writhe in agony at their inability to speak, an endless source of inspiration wells up within women. The sole concern of women in their ascendancy is about which of the many possibilities available they will choose to write.

As I see it, women writers are possessed of an unassailable strength. I once believed that they lacked the critical capacity to abandon self, be objective, or to caricature; the ability to be ironic; or the ability to produce the facetious wit that was a feature of *gesaku*. However, the achievements of writers such as Kurahashi Yumiko, Kōno Taeko, and Tsushima Yūko have confirmed the emergence of the aware and intelligent woman writer. It is clear that in the near future women will dominate the novel in Japan. Women today possess abundant physical sensibilities, a capacity for fantasy, the ability to provide realistic depictions based on family experiences, and the power to tell tales. They also have the capacity for irony and satire. Today we have prizes for women writers. However, before too long we may need to introduce literary awards for male writers, if only to acknowledge the rarity value of this commodity. All evidence would point to the mainstream novel in Japan becoming the territory of women. Perhaps this development was only to be expected.

| | | Confessions of a Women's Literature Convert

AKIYAMA SHUN

The other afternoon, feeling relaxed after a few drinks, I set off for a bar with a young friend. As we came to the train station, a wave of humanity surged in full view before us. I suddenly remembered something I had read by Mori Makiko and realized that this must be what she had in mind when she wrote about "a sea of people."

I don't remember where I first read the term. Perhaps it was in her short novel, *The Yellow Prostitute [Kiiroi shōfu]*. Regardless, it was a work of great style with perfectly chosen, unadorned language. I recall that the expression "sea of people" shone forth from the page the instant I read it. In the context of Mori's writing the term had a modernist yet outdated air. It was like something found in an old toy box: a symbol of vague uncertainty and a source of suppressed emotion. In short, I found it unsettling.

Recalling the phrase the other day, I also remembered that I had often used the expression as a child. We would say things like: "Don't go that way! There's a huge sea of people in the lantern procession." But for some reason I had forgotten the term, using words like "crowd" or "assembly" instead.

There were a number of reasons for this. First, I aspired to be something of an intellectual and had obviously discarded real, everyday words for the sort of abstract language used in written texts. I had obviously deluded myself that all

TRANSLATED BY BARBARA HARTLEY. From Akiyama Shun, "Joryū bungaku no tōwaku" (Confessions of a women's literature convert), *Kokubungaku kaishaku to kyōzai no kenkyū*, July 1976: 14–17.

The original title of Akiyama's essay translates literally as "The Dilemma (or Perplexities) of Women's Literature." Such an English title, however, gives the impression that it is the texts themselves that are the source of the writer's dilemma, but Akiyama's discussion makes it clear that it is his biased reading of these texts that has been the cause of the difficulties. Further, the article reveals that the author repents of his previous opinion and now advocates for the writing of women. The title given above was chosen both as encapsulating this general position and, although not a direct translation, as being reflective of the original Japanese title. *BH*

I needed to do to be a great thinker was to replace the everyday words of my childhood with the language of the classroom blackboard.

Reason number two: The change in my own language was indirectly related to postwar society's ongoing process of urbanization. In my petty cleverness I seemed to find it more fitting to use a word like "crowd" when discussing these modern trends and developments.

When I began my career, I believed that everyday language was unsuited to my professional endeavors. I expected writers of critical essays to use intellectual discourse, especially the compound expressions translated more or less directly from European languages during the rapid social changes of the last seventy or eighty years. Although in that context simple expressions like "a sea of people" seemed out of place, I am still uncertain precisely why I began using the term "crowd." Perhaps I was impressed because the word was associated with specialist expressions such as "crowd psychology" (although I'm sure that I drew on my childhood image of "a sea of people" when assigning meaning to this term). All this relates to the definition of an intellectual, a topic concerning which there is seemingly no end of debate.

Nonetheless, while the term "sea of people" struck me as odd when I first read it in Mori's work, it has since become increasingly familiar. Her novel has cleared the word of odium and revived its use for me.

The impact of women's literature on me has been very similar. Initially, I found it extremely discomforting. But gradually this very discomfort revealed afresh, one by one, forgotten elements of the Japanese mind. And once again I became free to make use of these elements, which were now illuminated before me.

But for a long time women's literature made me ill at ease. I simply did not understand it. For instance, when I first came across Higuchi Ichiyō's "Troubled Waters" [Nigorie] and "Child's Play" [Takekurabe], I just could not comprehend why these works were so highly regarded. So I was relieved to discover that, at the height of his career, Masamune Hakuchō had questioned the value of Ichiyō's work, denouncing it as tedious. Later, I was puzzled to read in his *Essays on Writers [Sakkaron]* that this tiresome old man had actually declared her the genius of the Meiji era.

Ichiyō's fiction failed to resonate with a young man desperately seeking an intellectual status that eluded him. In my arrogance I thought her novels nothing more than the fiction of a mere girl. It seemed to a boy growing up in the shadow of defeat that there could be nothing of consequence in a peacetime tale of trial and tribulation. As a result, I dismissed accounts of her devotion to literature while destitute as meaningless. Now, of course, I understand my error and realize that she did indeed suffer the most severe hardship. But at the time I had no clue as to why she was so admired by the likes of Mori Ōgai. I was even contemptible enough to wonder how the great man with the moustache could be so gullible.

For, you see, in those days I had no notion of the value of the novel in Japanese literary history. Trying to fathom this was like beating my head against a wall. I finally decided, therefore, that I would never understand the value of prewar literature and that I should just hold my peace. The scar of these times still remains.

My biggest blunder was Ichiyō—the *tour de force* writer among women. Try as I might, I could only say that there was a purity and lyricism to her work that made it rather delightful. I found nothing else of value. I believed that her work had no intellectual edge and was concerned that her mind lacked the ability to probe any depths. However, even as I thought this, I had a vague premonition that someday I myself would be derided for my own inadequacies. I could almost hear the jibes: "What a callow youth you are."

I should also confess that, in addition to not understanding women's writing, I found females (women, if you like) somehow alien. They seemed to be different sorts of creatures leading different sorts of lives.

Women lack the aura of death and have few nihilistic tendencies, an impression that may well be due to my inexperience. Nevertheless, it seems to me that they put too much into life and desire life too much. Odd though it sounds, women persist and survive even when it seems inhuman to do so, premising their existence on an affirmation of life. In terms of the desire to live, men, by comparison, are essentially weak.

But age is a funny thing. Now, in the second half of my life, I demand less of myself and have begun to see the appeal of women's literature. I have been gently convinced by Uno Chiyo's *Ohan* and Kōda Aya's *Younger Brother [Otōto]*, in addition to works by Setouchi Harumi and Kōno Taeko. I was forced to read the first two works, but as I did so, I soon became aware that never before had reading fiction given me such peace.

I believe that the essence of women's writing is the capacity to plumb emotional depths, allowing us to sympathize with and think kindly of the most heinous deeds. Consuming us as they do, these emotions are, in fact, our karma. And here we find a distinct difference. A man overcome by emotion in the course of the trials of life will feign death. In other words, he is driven to crime. A woman, however, will never feign death but tenaciously cling to life, regardless. Ultimately, however intelligent a woman writer may be, above all else she has this emotional depth. Her intelligence, nevertheless, can trace the pattern of her emotion and provide it with a sense of logic.

Emotion begins when the self is relinquished. A woman standing erect, ramrod straight like a television personality, has no light or shade and, therefore, gives no sense of emotion. However, emotion will flow when she allows her body to yield and bend.

Reading women's writing, we become aware of these matters. We begin to understand the power of emotional refraction. First there is the relinquished self, bending low and casting a deep shadow. From this deep shadow an emotional incline emerges, whereupon an infinite array of feelings fight for recognition, as if sustaining themselves on nothing other than the nuance of shadows. We only enter a world of breathtaking fiction when, through this infinite and finely wrought array, the writer gives meaning to the foundation of humanity, to our feelings, and to our real world existence. Thus fiction gives meaning to the terrain of our lives.

My words here fail adequately to describe the processes at work in women's writing, for I lack the necessary emotional intensity. But in the depths of their work I find a base that might sustain me, a base that, like a mother's womb, is an affirmation of the reality of life. For just like the expression "sea of people," the writing of women distills my thinking, derides my pathetic cleverness, and strips away my conceptual disguise, my intellectual costume. And I once again slowly understand the profound meaning of being Japanese.

As I read *Ohan*, I remembered that I had once been deeply moved by a popular song without even understanding the words. So you can see the sort of person I am.

3

THE NARCISSISTIC WOMAN WRITER

Tomoko Aoyama and Barbara Hartley

Chapter 1 of this volume saw a coterie of critics active in the nascent modern literary community accuse women who wrote of a "lack of womanliness." So outraged were these critics by this alleged lack that they refused to read the work of women writers of the time. Members of this coterie would undoubtedly have been shocked had they read Setouchi Harumi's later declaration, featured in chapter 2, that the writing woman must be manly and immodest. The position taken by these male commentators confirms Yukiko Tanaka's belief that the woman who writes performs "an act of self-assertion" that marks her as the "antithesis of the selfless submission prescribed [for women] by Japanese culture."[1] It is precisely this violation of cultural prescription that makes women writers susceptible to condemnatory charges of narcissism.[2] The narcissistic woman writer is one who, to borrow a phrase used above by Rebecca Copeland, refuses to be merely "a splash of red against the gray" of the masculine literary community and who demands recognition in her own right. Twentieth-century society may appear to acquiesce to the demands of growing numbers of these "narcissistic" women writers, the archetype for whom is undoubtedly the inimitable Okamoto Kanoko. Nevertheless, as woman critic Tanaka Miyoko notes in her essay translated here, women ultimately pay a high price for asserting their identities in this manner.

According to Maryellen Toman Mori, clinical narcissism is characterized by "self-absorption, grandiose delusions, exhibitionism, oral aggressiveness, and blurred ego boundaries."[3] In literary discourse, however, the term is used less precisely, often denoting a variety of cultural or mythological categories, many of which are gender-specific. Flamboyance in the male writer may elicit charges of egotism and self-indulgence. But when the writer is female, the attention to self necessitated by the very act of writing invites accusations of deviation from or perversion of the discursive feminine norm. In other words, the "narcissism" of the woman writer often implies the sense of pathological deficit inherent in the clinical use of the term.

The following collection of translations consists of five brief commentaries on narcissism, women, and writing published between 1966 and 1976. Not surprisingly, given this historical context, each work is based on a male-female binary, although the authors provide various interpretations of the significance of this divide. The translations are an extract from Mishima Yukio's "On Narcissism" (Narushishizumu ron); "Contemporary Women's Literature" (Gendai joryū bungaku no yōsō), an article written by literary critic Hasegawa Izumi in response to the Mishima text; Tanaka Miyoko's "Narcissism, Cynicism, and the Writing of Women" (Hyōgen ni miru narushishizumu to shinishizumu); Hara Shirō's "Nakedness and Decoration in Women's Writing" (Buntai ni okeru ratai to sōshoku); and Shibusawa Tatsuhiko's homage to the literature of Okamoto Kanoko, "Women, Narcissism, and Okamoto Kanoko" (Okamoto Kanoko aruiwa onna no narushishizumu).

It is perhaps to be expected that as one of the great observers of feminine performativity, Mishima Yukio would have an interest in the issue of women and narcissism. Like the other essays featured in this chapter, the extract given here from the author's "On Narcissism" focuses very much on women's bodies, with the claim that a woman's body operates against the logical functioning of her mind. According to Mishima, this logical function and narcissism are part of one and the same process. He questions whether a woman, who sees a made-up face rather than her real face in the mirror, can be said to be narcissistic or, by extension, logical. While the author does not refer directly to the woman writer, the widespread response to Mishima's theories among members of the literary community, including Hasegawa's essay, certainly indicates that the former's ideas were interpreted by colleagues as relevant to women and literature. The author expands at length on what he claims to be the absence of a mind-body separation in women and the dominating presence of the body in women's intellectual activity, arguing that while men reason only with the intellect, the reasoning processes of women are subject to the "gravitational pull" of the womb and the sex organs. Invoking the troubling essentialism referred to in a number of commentaries in this collection, the text unambiguously confirms Jan Bardsley's observation in chapter 2 that it is "women who are gendered, women who must be *women* writers, and women who must create from their sexed bodies."

Notably and quite symbolically, Mishima's essay, which also included a section on narcissism and men (omitted here), was first published in *Fujin kōron* (Women's review), a widely circulated women's magazine. The surface tone is one of jocular familiarity, and it is easy to imagine the magazine readership being entertained by the great writer's authoritative announcements and clever repartee. Playing both to his audience and what might be regarded as a desire to establish masculine ascendancy, the author presents his argument in a climaxing series of "logical" maneuvers, concluding, with a theatrical flourish, that there is obviously "no such thing as [intellectual] narcissism in women."

Mishima's logic conforms to classic gender discourse in that the claim is made that women are fundamentally and essentially different from men. However, in some places the text reads against itself to question contradictorily the masculine form of narcissism being valorized. In spite of the suggestion here that women's sexed bodies prevent their engaging in creative production, it might be noted that on other occasions Mishima was not averse to commenting on the writing of women in a highly complimentary manner. He gave lavish praise to Enchi Fumiko; was an admirer of Mori Mari; and, as noted in Shibusawa's essay translated here, commended elements of Okamoto Kanoko's writing. In the "On Narcissism" essay too, there are suggestions of a subterranean attraction to and admiration for "woman," the very entity whose processes the author sets out to establish as lacking in relation to men. Sections of the essay reveal a not uncommon patriarchal envy of women, including incredulousness at what the writer perceives to be the feminine capacity for happiness. Thus like any number of texts that appear to establish the ascendancy of the male, this extract ultimately reveals the tenuous nature of that claim.

Hasegawa Izumi's essay commences as a direct response to Mishima's essay, a clear indication of the receptiveness of the literary community to the latter's ideas on the subject of narcissism. However, where Mishima's text was circulated in the popular women's press, Hasegawa's was the lead article in a special 1976 edition devoted to women's writing published by the influential literary magazine *Kokubungaku kaishaku to kanshō* (Japanese literature: Appreciation and interpretation). It should be pointed out that the publication of the three remaining essays in this set actually preceded that of the Hasegawa article. However, given its evident genealogical association with Mishima's essay, it seems appropriate to locate this translation directly following "On Narcissism." Hasegawa's discussion enthusiastically applies Mishima's theories to "academic" discourse on modern women's literature. Particular attention is paid to Setouchi Harumi's essay "Requirements for Becoming a Woman Writer," featured in chapter 2, and works by Ariyoshi Sawako, Hagiwara Yōko, and Kurahashi Yumiko.

Born in 1918, Hasegawa was a critic of considerable influence throughout the last half of the twentieth century, and his position might be expected to reflect the patriarchal discourses of the literary establishment at the time the essay was written. However, as is the case with Mishima, the response of this critic to the writing woman and the writing of women is clearly marked by ambivalence. Acquiescing with Mishima's notion that literary production can be the province only of the masculine eye, Hasegawa argues that the writing successes of women such as Ariyoshi, Hagiwara, and Kurahashi are the result of their possessing this all-powerful "male eye." With the essentialist claim that the successful woman writer views the world as a male, Hasegawa confirms the long-standing institution, directly alluded to by Mishima, of man as viewer and woman as viewed. He thus locates himself in a tradition of scopic privilege common to male thinkers and artists in both Japan and the West. However, having aligned himself with this tradition, Hasegawa is also eager to identify uniquely feminine elements—that is, elements that are unlikely to appear in the work of male writers—in the work of the women writers discussed. He is particularly fascinated by those aspects of Ariyoshi Sawako's texts that relate to childbirth. Like Mishima before him, Hasegawa finds it difficult to disguise his envy for what he appears to regard as privileges enjoyed only by women. He marvels over the nature of the bond between mother and child, which he notes is completely denied to a man and his lover and which, he maintains, biologically "takes priority over the relationship between the male father and child." Yet in spite of the essentialist assumptions upon which his argument is based, Hasegawa ultimately acknowledges both the genius of the specific women writers he discusses and the capacity of emerging women writers generally to compete on equal terms with men.

Tanaka Miyoko's discussion on narcissism and cynicism begins by noting the importance of the fact that the Narcissus of the Greek myth was a man rather than a woman. This fact was also cited as evidence supporting Mishima's theory that women are unable to detach from their bodies or engage in intellectual endeavor. However, Tanaka uses Narcissus' biological sex as a starting point from which to argue the unreasonableness of critics, including Mishima, who would judge women's putative inability to observe their physical selves as lack. Referring directly to the latter's claim, Tanaka concedes an association between women and makeup, citing the work of Uno Chiyo as an example. She notes that in a society in which women are judged inevitably by physical appearance and bodily form, makeup is often the only recourse to social acceptance. Moreover, she argues that women who do successfully meet this demand are in fact demonstrating an intellectual skill since the made-up face is ultimately as much a work of art as any masculine creation.

Tanaka cites the account of the queen from the Snow White tale and her anger when denied the status of most beautiful woman in the land as an analogy for the awakening of all women from narcissism and self-adoration. She further asserts that this awakening results in an outward direction of rage in the form of cynicism. Thus, to Tanaka, women have two equally unpalatable options. The first is acquiescence with social demands by engaging in the self-mutilation of physical narcissism. The second is refusal to conform to the social script by engaging instead in the cynical mutilation of others. The latter is a tactic that

Tanaka claims is increasingly resorted to by young women writers who resist social demands. While she notes that detached cynicism can achieve literary effect, Tanaka argues that the tragedy for these writers is that they resort to cynicism as a result of the desperate desire to avoid self-mutilation. Thus their writing can only ever be second rate.

Tanaka, a prominent Mishima scholar, argues a similar position to the novelist. There is a crucial difference, however, in that Mishima claims to reveal characteristics of the essential woman as defined by "nature." Tanaka, on the contrary, is very much aware of the manner in which both cynicism and narcissism are functions of the discursive restrictions that operate on women.

In "Nakedness and Decoration in Women's Writing" Hara Shirō notes "the widely held view that women writers have a strong tendency toward narcissism." He draws an analogy between women's decorating their bodies with the cosmetic devices demanded by social convention and the facility with which women decorate their texts with fantasy and other literary strategies. However, Hara also notes that any decorative narcissistic element in women's texts is balanced by a tendency toward nakedness—that is, the "completely uninhibited revelation of the naked body." This state, Hara argues, is in fact a variant of narcissism. The critic goes on to suggest that texts written from this perspective are written "with the full force of the body" and have a strong impact on the reader.

The Hara text is significant for the readings it provides of the works of a number of prominent women writers. While the analysis notes the connection between the work of each writer and narcissism, it nevertheless rejects the usual negative stance adopted by critics making this claim. On the contrary, Hara is adamant that the capacity for narcissism is something that enhances the text production of the woman writer. The essay is further noteworthy for the writer's careful attempt to distance himself from a hierarchical male-female binary. However, in the conclusion (omitted here) Hara reverts to an essentialist, although not necessarily hierarchical, gender paradigm in which women's writing represents "time" while men's writing represents "space."

In the final commentary, Shibusawa Tatsuhiko's discussion of the work of Okamoto Kanoko, the writer advocates greater recognition of Kanoko's contribution to twentieth-century literature in Japan. Shibusawa, who achieved prominence as the translator of the works of the Marquis de Sade, argues that Kanoko's work is grounded in a powerful and all-encompassing strain of narcissism. Overtly declaring himself a defender of Kanoko against those who would dismiss her work as the baroque expression of excess femininity, the critic argues that it is precisely this narcissistic excess that gives Kanoko a literary lineage as significant as that of Tanizaki Jun'ichirō.

Shibusawa's discussion is noteworthy for the position taken toward Kanoko's being a woman writer. While, unlike Hara, this critic makes no conscious attempt to destabilize the female-male binary, he ultimately argues that women are ascendant in this pair. The opening of the essay, with its reference to the "recidivist self-centeredness that is the narcissism of women," creates the expectation of a negative judgment against the narcissistic woman and her writing. However, Shibusawa ultimately valorizes this tendency in women, concluding that Kanoko's "unique and liberated fictional world" is actually a function of her extreme narcissism.

Each of the five essays featured in this set of translations was published during a decade that saw a new type of postwar educated woman writer emerge as a force in the Japanese literary community. As noted in Okuno Takeo's 1974 discussion of women's dominance of the novel (featured above in this compendium), few of these new artists conformed to the highly prescriptive definition of "woman writer" that had previously operated. The appearance of these noncompliant writing women generated alarm and resistance among conservative factions in the world of Japanese letters. Fearful of the challenge to the order of things presented by the overt assertiveness and independence of the new generation of women, more traditional elements sometimes responded with attempts to denigrate those women who violated previously inviolable social codes by asserting their writing identity. Nevertheless, as a number of the discussions presented here demonstrate, social changes in postwar Japan made it increasingly difficult for discourses that had previously operated, and that defined women who asserted themselves through acts of writing as "narcissistic," to remain ascendant.

In conclusion, it might be noted that the recent wave of feminist scholarship in Japanese literature has seen a renewal of interest in the issue of narcissism, particularly in terms of deconstructing the binary assumptions of earlier critics. Examples include Takahara Eiri's detailed analysis of the conscious construct of self-love in the writings of Kurahashi Yumiko and Mori Mari,[4] Urushida Kazuyo's dissent from the view of Okamoto Kanoko as narcissism impersonated,[5] and Maryellen Toman Mori's reading of Kanoko through Paul Zweig's affirmation of narcissism as "an anti-authoritarian discourse of non-conformity."[6] The interest of these writers indicates that while essays of the era translated here may belong to the history of women in modern Japanese literature, the issue of narcissism itself is one that is likely to remain significant in discussions of women's writing in the future. Indeed, given the number and stature of the writers who have contributed to the debate, it would appear that some knowledge of the discourses surrounding the issue is essential for a full understanding of women writers in Japanese modernity.

NOTES

1. Y. Tanaka, Introduction," p. ix.

2. It is interesting to note that charges of narcissism are not confined to comments about woman as object. Saegusa Kazuko discusses the manner in which some women writers define their own subjectivity in terms of narcissism, demonstrating a "tendency toward narcissism in their self-representation and self-expression." Saegusa, "The Narcissism of Female Representation and the Professional Writer," p. 18.

3. Mori, "The Splendor of Self-Exaltation," p. 99.

4. See chapters 7 and 8 of Takahara, *Shōjo ryōiki*. The introduction to this book is translated in chapter 5 below.

5. Urushida Kazuyo, "Konton mibun (Okamoto Kanoko) wo yomu," in Egusa and Urushida, *Onna ga yomu nihon kindai bungaku,* p. 101. Urushida questions the kind of impressionistic criticism of Kanoko's literature as represented by the essay of Kamei Katsuichirō (p. 88), the essay mentioned by Shibusawa. She also criticizes the general tendency to relate Kanoko's female protagonists directly and automatically to the author's narcissism (p. 117).

6. Mori, "The Splendor of Self-Exaltation," p. 100.

On Narcissism

MISHIMA YUKIO

A woman lingers before a mirror, putting the finishing touches to her face. She then dresses and adds accessories and, *voilà*, after a last careful look to check the result, finally makes an appearance. We call this a woman's narcissism and assume it to be her second nature. However, does the woman before the mirror really see an image of her own face? Can we say that she actually views her own true self? I can't really tell. It would seem, however, that nature is quite concerned to ensure that women do not see their true faces. And while this vigilance might surprise, we can only assume that nature has good reason to act in this way.

Self-consciousness is utterly masculine, presupposing, as it does, the separation of mind and body. The mind detaches itself and drifts away from the body. Then, from the point to which it has wandered, this same mind performs the feat of regarding itself objectively, while also objectively viewing its own flesh. This feat, of course, may not always be successful. However, it would seem useful to define self-consciousness as the curious tendency of the mind to try to accomplish such a performance.

The mind of the woman, however, is inhibited by the gravitational pull of the womb. It is thus unable to separate itself and float freely away from the flesh in the manner of the man. The actions of the upper part of the male anatomy— namely, the head and the mind—are performed independently of the sex organs in the lower part. It would appear that women, however, like the reptiles of ancient times, have brains in both the upper and lower parts of their bodies.

Although I use the term "brain," there are in fact two centers that control the mind of the woman. One is indeed the anatomical brain. The other, however, is the womb. These two work intimately together. The woman's mind is unable to divest itself of the flesh because it is subject to the constant pull of both the brain and the womb. We know that the word "hysteria" derives from a word meaning "womb." Put simply, we might think of the male mind as structured like a circle around a single point, while a woman's mind is oval in shape, featuring two points of focus.

Thus it is apparent that the female mind returns to and resides in existence. The male mind, however, is located in nonexistence. That which we call consciousness of the self is a form of pure thought associated with nonexistence.

TRANSLATED BY TOMOKO AOYAMA AND BARBARA HARTLEY. From Mishima Yukio, "Narushishizumu ron" (On Narcissism), *Mishima Yukio zenshū* 32 (Shinchōsha, 1973), pp. 375–389. Originally published in *Fujin kōron*, July 1966.

It is the most uncorrupted of all thought and that which is closest to a state of nonexistence.

Women's minds, of course, may think in ways that appear to engage the conscious self. However, their thinking lacks any capacity for self-reproduction. This is the process of the conscious self infinitely propagating itself, like two mirrors that dazzle by creating never-ending images of each other. Given that it fails to absorb the thinker truly, we might call the thinking of women "pseudo self-consciousness." The element that *appears* to be the conscious self in women actually has a safety valve—namely, the physical presence of the womb. Therefore it is impossible for a woman to plunge headlong, brake disengaged, into a state of self-consciousness in the manner of a man. (Strangely, when this happens, it is as if the reckless vehicle of the male conscious self plummets into what is actually a sea of its own self-consciousness.)

We may now begin to understand the reluctance of nature to permit women to see their true faces. It is clearly a matter of biological necessity and the need to ensure that women commit to their child-bearing responsibilities. It would lead to the extinction of the human race were the women who have such intimate and ongoing relationships with their mirrors to throw themselves completely into these mirrors and self-destruct. Since men do not fall pregnant, this is not an issue for them. Narcissus, obsessed by the beauty of his own reflection seen in water, plunged into that water and drowned. That he was a man, and not a woman, is evidence of the wisdom of the ancient Greeks. For Narcissus must, of necessity, be a man.

We have now generally confirmed the fact that women do not see their own image in the mirror. And since it would clearly be a misuse of the word narcissism to apply it to a fascination with something that is not a self-image, it is obvious that there can be no such thing as narcissism in women.

2

I have pointed out that nature appears to be at pains to persuade women not to see their faces. "Face," of course, is used here in the psychological rather than physical sense. Perhaps I go too far in rashly asserting that the woman before the mirror is able to infer the psychological face from the physical face. It may not be possible to draw an analogy so easily between the exterior and interior face or to make a direct connection between the face in the mirror and the inner self.

It is well known that women are notoriously inept at talking about themselves. Even the most distinguished woman will rarely give the impression of having an accurate self-image. No matter what she may have endured or what worldly wisdom she may have acquired, a woman is generally blind in matters relating to herself, displaying an inescapable stupidity that adheres to her like lint to a coat back. The more intellectual she is, the more morbid both her conceit and her inferiority complex are likely to be. Her reasoning is clouded and her logic obtuse, lacking any spring of lucid thought. I have no idea why this might be. However, this is the reason that I detest arguing with women so.

It may well be that what we call logic is, in fact, the logic of the male rather than a universal human attribute. The autonomy of male logic resides in nothing more than the fact that the male psyche is able to separate itself from the body and, therefore, from a state of being. I have argued that the inherent lack of objectivity that is a feature of women's logic, if we can even use such a term, is inevitably tied to a state of being through the unique structure of the feminine psyche. Without a division between mind and body there can be no objectivity and, hence, no capacity for self-criticism. As a result, women are unable to engage in considered criticism of others, since the sole criterion for this process is the ability to critique one's self. The blind spot that afflicts women is their perpetual inability to critique themselves and the associated tendency to criticize others unjustly.

Women say of each other, " 'A' may think she is wonderful, but what a stupid woman she really is!" This criticism is invalid, however, unless the speaker too is aware of her own stupidity. But no woman will ever admit to being stupid. She might say, "I'm so stupid." But what she actually means is, "Unreasonable people like you may think I'm stupid, but this is not the case." Women say to men, "My eyes are so small, aren't they?" However, only a brave man would respond in the affirmative. And should a woman lament the shape of her flat nose, it would be equally dangerous for a man to try to comfort her by responding, "But it's much more charming than a pointy one."

You may have noted that I have made a gradual shift here from the inner to the outer face of the woman, for I believe that there is no defining line between the two. There is a huge difference between a man's declaring himself to be stupid, on the one hand, and ugly, on the other. In the case of a woman, however, any difference is so slight as to be almost negligible. Self-mockery in men is generally informed by irony and criticism—that is, elements of the conscious self. A woman's declaration of stupidity, however, involves a deliberate blurring of subjectivity as a result of ambivalence concerning who is making the judgment. While she may claim the judgment as her own, in reality she is assigning the negative assessment of herself to "unreasonable people like you." On the contrary, when a man says, "All right, I'm stupid," he has in fact arrived at this position by exercising his own powers of judgment. He furthermore feels a clear sense of pride that the decision has been made of his own accord.

We should also consider the statement, "I'm not good-looking." When a woman says this, we see an almost identical example of the deliberate blurring of subjectivity that occurs when she claims to be stupid. However, when a man declares that he is not handsome, uncomfortable though this may be, the subjectivity of the judgment clearly resides completely in an invisible and independent third person. For from an early age men must learn the bitter wisdom, through the training of the conscious self, that the beauty or otherwise of one's face or appearance is essentially a social value judged only by others. Men develop complexes of inferiority or superiority early in life by experiencing the objective judgment of comparison. It is true that, like a girl, even a man will become aware of his own charm upon being loved for the first time by a woman. However, this will never lead to a direct relationship between his outer and inner selves, no matter how such an experience might inspire or pervert the latter.

When a man looks into the mirror, he clearly views his own face, his uncorrupted external appearance. A woman viewing her image is subject to the workings of a complex and captivating imaginative process. This process invokes a connection not only between the inner and outer selves, but also with a second made-up exterior. While a man may shave, he has no need for makeup. For it is only when viewing the unadulterated facial exterior, and when the subject of the gaze is the uncorrupted conscious self, that narcissism, the love that appears in the myth of Narcissus, is possible. . . .

4

. . . Men are secreted away behind concealed values while women are forced into public view. This is apparent in modes of attire. Men dress in dark, uniform outfits, no longer adorned in suits of gorgeous armor, for it is women who are now slaves to myriad fashions, increasingly covering less of their bodies. The concept of women's narcissism seems to have been adapted from that of men. It is clear, however, that if women had been granted the usual sort of physical narcissism, the rules relating to the conscious self could not have come into play. It was therefore necessary to devise a different method for the woman narcissist. Thus the advent of makeup. For makeup is the sole factor that can rescue the usual sort of physical narcissism from the comic. The widespread practice among women of the second method, the application of makeup, is compensation for their lack of awareness of the conscious self. Through the process of applying powder and lipstick, thus transforming themselves into something beautiful, women insist on the wholesale corruption of physical narcissism.

Whether a woman is beautiful or ugly, she will spend an eternity before the mirror making herself up. Yet people will never laugh or say that she is ugly. For it is not a question of the objectivity of the conscious self, nor is it merely that she wants to make herself beautiful. If the ugly woman looks more beautiful with makeup than without, it is merely because this is what society demands. Both women and society in general, however, confine the praise of women to physical appearance, for men do not want women to invade their jealously protected territory of spiritual-intellectual narcissism. Thus men have opened up and passed to women the hellish anxiety of physical narcissism that once belonged to ancient men.

It seems unlikely, however, that this realm passed on to women has actually generated anxiety. Women in front of the mirror clearly look happy, although it is a complete and utter mystery to men why someone would be so overjoyed by the application of makeup. Since narcissism and happiness are mutually exclusive, the emotion felt by these women must be something else, something indefinable. For while "happiness" is the concept that is most difficult for men to understand, it is the most feminine concept of all.

| | | Contemporary Women's Literature

HASEGAWA IZUMI

In an essay entitled "On Narcissism" Mishima Yukio outlines his forthright views on the difference between men and women. Mishima, who had a complex and highly insightful view of sex, points to the existence of men and women as a biological given, a natural phenomenon. It is for this reason, he argues, that we use terms such as "the opposite sex." In the essay Mishima explains his position on narcissism and consciousness of self while also theorizing the "natural" difference between men and women.

Narcissus, the mythological character who drowned after being captivated by the reflection of his own beauty, was a man. He was not a woman. Noting that the concept of narcissism derives from the fact that Narcissus was a man, Mishima reasons that narcissism cannot therefore exist in a woman. Mishima maintains that while Narcissus was able to view the image of his own face, a woman is incapable of confronting her own natural image.

Mishima's theory is grounded in his belief that only men are capable of the mind-body dichotomy and that without this ability it is impossible to be conscious of one's self. Consciousness of self, he argues, demands the mental acrobatics that permit the subject to separate mind and body and thereby consider its

TRANSLATED BY TOMOKO AOYAMA AND BARBARA HARTLEY. From Hasegawa Izumi, "Gendai joryū bungaku no yōsō" (Contemporary women's literature), *Kokubungaku kaishaku to kanshō*, September 1976: 6–14.

own mental state objectively while also contemplating the body. To Mishima, the essence of masculinity is associated with this ability—that is, with the consciousness of self.

What, then, is the basis of femininity? Mishima characterizes women as follows: "The mind of the woman . . . is inhibited by the gravitational pull of the womb. It is thus unable to separate itself and float freely away from the flesh in the manner of the man. The actions of the upper part of the male anatomy— namely, the head and the mind—are performed independently of the sex organs in the lower part. It would appear that women, however, like the reptiles of ancient times, have brains in both the upper and lower parts of their bodies." This difference results in a formulaic dualism whereby the woman's essence is related to existence while the male essence transcends the necessity to exist. In other words, the male essence is best understood as grounded in "nonexistence." The attribute most closely associated with this "nonexistence" is consciousness of self, regarded as the mental state most removed from the workings of the body. Consciousness of self is thus the purest quality of the male.

The woman's capacity to attain consciousness of self is inhibited by the bodily functions associated with her womb. Therefore, unlike the man, she is denied the "never-ending images" generated by two mirrors. The mirror into which the woman gazes reflects a subject with no consciousness of self. On the other hand, the mirror into which the man gazes is the objective mirror of the conscious self. The mirror of the former operates only to facilitate makeup and transformation. The latter is the mirror of the self without disguise. Narcissism, of course, resides in the latter.

It is useful to consider how these matters are related to the difference between men and women in general and between men writers and women writers in particular. Why, for instance, is there a specific literary category entitled "women's writing" when there is no defined category for the writing of men? Surely there is no need to distinguish between the genders of creative subjects unless there are significant differences between the creative methods of men and women associated with the different lives of each.

The construction of a special literary category for women writers, and the absence of such for men, is related to Mishima's theories presented above. Inherent in the word "writer" is the implication that the sex of the writer is male. The word "literature" similarly implies that which is written by men.

The purpose of literature is to seek out literary truth through fiction. Although fiction is the nonexistent, the construction of fiction does not merely imply the creation of a pack of lies, for fiction is associated with objectivity and the pursuit of literary truth. Objectivity implies the consciousness of self, which, as we have seen, is based on the separation of body and mind. The ability to enact this separation is a masculine attribute. Narcissus was a man. Since the purpose of literature is essentially related to masculine attributes, it is also related to narcissism. This is why we have no need for expressions such as "men's writing" or "men's literature."

Fiction is nonexistence. However, fiction charged with the subjective fails to reveal literary truths. The subjective has no relation to consciousness of self; on the contrary, it derives from an inability to become conscious of one's self or from a false consciousness of self, a state that merely mimics self-consciousness. This inadequate, false, or quasi consciousness of self is a product of the spirit or mind unable to divest itself of the body. Thus it is characteristic of women. In the same way that Narcissus was not a woman, the literary process is essentially exclusive of women. Women have no connection with Narcissus. The existence of terms such as "women's writing" and "women's literature" is similarly evidence of the chasm between women and accepted literary practice.

Setouchi Harumi has written an essay entitled "Requirements for Becoming a Woman Writer" [*Kokubungaku kaishaku to kanshō*, September 1962]. Here she lists ten conditions as follows: being a woman, being masculine, being not overly good-looking, having natural talent, having a strong ego, having the capacity for strong jealousy, having the potential to become a bad wife, having the courage to reveal one's inner self, having property, and having the mental toughness to endure loneliness.

These ten conditions provide very interesting reading. The first two conditions—namely, being a woman and being masculine—appear to be somewhat contradictory. A woman writer is naturally a woman. We have already pointed out that the term "male writer" is something of a tautology. Thus Setouchi's highlighting the issue of masculinity is significant only because the writer is not a man, a fundamental point that yet again confirms the essentially masculine nature of literature.

The remaining conditions are various secondary specifics of this masculine literary essence. Two important points are "having the potential to become a bad wife" and "having the mental toughness to endure loneliness." The bad wife is the obverse of the good wife and wise mother. The family is a social unit, the purpose of which is to allow a man and his wife to raise children. This unit is based on the union of a man and a woman. The bad wife is one who divests herself of the restraints and restrictions of the family in order to be free. Leaving aside the issue of children, this freedom demands that a woman cease to treat her husband as such. This is not the same as a bad woman, whose target, while it may be a man, is not necessarily her husband. The bad wife is one who consciously rejects her husband's standards.

Self-reliance leads to the perfection of the ego, which must be tenacious in solitude. To some extent egotism is a writer's dogma. But women under the patronage of men such as their husbands know no solitude. The essential identifying feature of a woman is dependency. Since only the masculine spirit has the capacity to endure isolation, women must suppress their dependent tendencies if they wish to compete with men. Experiencing solitude will enable a woman to be more like a man and thus enhance her capacity to write.

Hana is the protagonist of Ariyoshi Sawako's novel, *The River Ki [Ki no kawa]*. Prior to the birth of her children she visits Jison'in Temple to dedicate breast shapes that she has fashioned from white crepe. The sex of the woman is unequivocally invoked in this gesture, for giving birth is a privilege available only to women. Men are unable to give birth. Therefore, the true feeling of being bound by blood to a child is something only women understand. Regardless of the depth of love that binds them, a man and a woman are ultimately strangers with no blood connection. It is a function of the sexuality of men and women that the incontestable relationship of the female mother to her child, joined as these two are by blood, takes priority over the relationship between the male father and child. Tomoko, the young protagonist of another of Ariyoshi's works, *Incense and Flowers [Kōge]*, is confronted by the physical image of her mother's thighs, spread in the throes of giving birth to her new brother. With the heightened sensibility of a young girl, Tomoko is overwhelmed by an awareness of her own self as a woman. While these incidents undoubtedly highlight the sexuality of women, the writer who expresses this as literature can only do so through the eye of a man.

Exactly what process is at work here? While "being a woman" is clearly a state available only to women, it is not an absolutely necessary condition to write about "being a woman." The emergence of the masculine eye in the woman writer confirms the fundamentals of the literary process. We must remember that in narcissism there is no cosmetic. It is purely the reflection of realism, of things as they are. For women, however, the mirror is inevitably associated with the cosmetic.

Hagiwara Yōko's *The House of Nettles [Irakusa no ie]* is the frank revelation of a dysfunctional family based on the life of the writer's poet father, Hagiwara Sakutarō. Shimako, the promiscuous first wife of the protagonist, Naitō Yōnosuke, elopes with a student. Futaba, the daughter of Shimako and Yōnosuke, is constantly mistreated by her grandmother, Katsu, who is also Yōnosuke's mother. While the old woman harangues Nobuko, her son and heir's adored new wife, whom she accuses of being "evil" and "promiscuous," it is Futaba toward whom the full force of her venom is directed. The grandmother accuses the girl of being like that "shameful daughter-in-law" and taunts her with being ugly and having "the face of a gargoyle." She cruelly ridicules Futaba's made-up face, telling the girl that "with those painted lips of yours you look like a black sow in heat."

At one point in the novel Futaba, the object of this vile abuse, is persuaded by a friend, Ranko, to make up her face. At first Ranko, who is three years older than Futaba, has a sisterly relationship with the younger girl. Futaba provides an account of the incident as follows: "Ranko wanted me to put on some makeup, but the very sound of the word made me think of Katsu's abuse. 'Just look at your ugly self in the mirror,' I could hear her scream. At first I felt embarrassed, but Ranko wouldn't take no for an answer. She even showed me how to do my face with her own makeup. 'Look at that,' she cried. 'Who would have thought you would look so beautiful?' I blushed to the tips of my ears and secretly tried to steal a peek at myself in the mirror." Ranko declares that she lives for love and proceeds to tell Futaba that she plans to take Yōnosuke as her lover. Eventually, she even steals Futaba's lover, Yasuo, the younger brother of Nobuko, whose child she conceives.

The work features another memorable woman, Yōnosuke's beautiful younger sister, Reiko. In *The Heavenly Flower [Tenjō no hana]*, the work depicting Miyoshi Tatsuji's tragic love affair, Reiko is the beautiful woman who brings about the catastrophe. However, *The House of Nettles* transcends the dimensions of *The Heavenly Flower*, with the masculine eye at its most perceptive in the former.

It should be noted that although Yōnosuke is the eldest son and legal head of the household, he is totally incapable of assuming this role. "Literature will be the ruin of this family," declares the eldest daughter's military officer husband. Unable to grasp the power to which he is entitled, Yōnosuke becomes a completely impotent patriarch. The only occasion in which he manages to assert his authority is on his deathbed, when he refuses to disown Futaba or have her name removed from the family register. Power in the Naitō family is in the grip of Yōnosuke's mother, Katsu, who openly tramples on the rights of other members of the family. Her mistreatment of Nobuko, Yōnosuke's second wife, eventually drives the latter from the house, while her cruel taunts concerning the appearance of her granddaughter, the child of Yōnosuke's first wife, border on the inhuman.

Katsu's attitude is evident in her refusal to allow Nobuko, whom she regards as unclean, to wash her underwear in the basin used by the matriarch for her own clothes and those of her son. In this sham display of cleanliness, Katsu reveals herself as the family member who relentlessly controls the operations of the household.

In *The House of Nettles*, Hagiwara Yōko gives an account of the manner in which the family in wartime Japan was an omnipotent microcosm of the wider society. She reveals the different natures of men and women, rawly exposing and laying naked their different lives for all to see. Hagiwara's focus is the monstrous power that supports the family system and the desperate struggle for individual expression within that oppressive atmosphere. The pain of the woman judged as ugly, the impact of her lost virginity, her ignorance and naivety, her rouging the lips of her dead child—these and other fragments are overlain with issues of sexuality and human nature, gradually creating a detailed and finely wrought literary structure that affects the reader powerfully.

As mentioned previously, Hagiwara's novel is based on real life, and it is easy to deduce whom each character represents. However, *The House of Nettles* is not simply a *roman à clef*, for the characterization of the novel obviously complies with the conventions of fiction, particularly regarding the formation of characters that are overt, almost stereotypical, fictional categories. In this depiction of the old-style family, for instance, Naitō Yōnosuke, the character based on Hagiwara Sakutarō, is presented as a powerless head of household with respect to both his first and second wives. This weakness is a metaphor for a family system in decay. Unable to sustain a relationship with either wife, his position in relation to his mother further demonstrates his inability to assert himself as a man. Each of these elements contributes to the protagonist as a constructed character, the product of a fictional imagination. It is also interesting to note that the novel never delves into Yōnosuke's inner character. Although he is a poet, the protagonist is constructed with complete disregard for either internal psychology or objective behavior, such as his literary activities. In fact, the reader can build an understanding of this token head of the family as a superfluous being of no use to a country at war only from the reactions of other members of the Naitō household, particularly Katsu. Yōnosuke's significance as a social being is limited to the conceited and arbitrary observations of the vibrant, uninhibited Ranko and the comments of the students and teachers of Futaba's school. It is clear from the responses of these characters that *The House of Nettles'* Naitō Yōnosuke is a tragic and benighted man in spite of his ostensible fame as a poet and man of letters. I would suggest that the failure to address the internal workings of the protagonist is a conscious decision on the part of the author in order to limit the structural boundaries of the work.

Futaba is the character around whom the novel revolves, and her construction is another superb example of a deliberately typed character. Hagiwara skillfully calculates the impact on the young woman's psychology of being forced to endure her grandmother's constant taunt of "ugly bitch," especially the manner in which this determines her reaction to men and her family. Even during sexual intercourse with the gambler Oka, who lures Futaba into losing her virginity, her grandmother's refrain, indelibly inscribed onto the girl's body, remains fixed in her heart. Belief in her own ugliness has arisen not from any objective judgment. Rather it is the result of ongoing humiliation by her grandmother, whose abuse of the girl is part of the old woman's need to maintain her vice-like grip on power in the family. Part of the novel's special interest lies in the consistent manner in which these women are depicted. Juxtaposed against Futaba is Katsu's daughter, the divinely beautiful Reiko. Reiko's beauty makes her complicit in her mother's power regime and the seizure of family authority. The contrast between the beautiful and the ugly is yet another example of the deliberate presentation of types.

Katsu continually demands that Futaba confront her ugliness in the mirror. However, Futaba lacks the courage to view her own image until she agrees to Ranko's demand to make up her face. Viewing one's image transformed by makeup is associated with fictional or false satisfaction. Since the pure element of narcissistic fiction is lost, this is a complete remove from viewing one's unadulterated image in the pristine water mirror of male narcissism. Nevertheless, Hagiwara Yōko's *The House of Nettles* qualifies in both content and structure as literature of the conscious self based on the separation of flesh from spirit. This effect is achieved by the premise forced on the pivotal female character—namely, her alleged ugliness—which would normally be a fatal attribute for a woman. Thus we can consider the work a very masculine text. This is in spite of the fact that the author provides only a limited representation of Yōnosuke, the male protagonist who should be the center of family activity, focusing instead on the details of the women who move in and out of his orbit.

Kurahashi Yumiko's essay "About Incest" [Insesuto ni tsuite] discusses the notion of incest as a fictional crime, free of guilt. She argues that as long as different sexes exist, from the point of view of mere biology the notion of sexual relations with a member of one's family is something that has no value judgment. It is neither good nor evil. However, a shift from the macrocosm of the biological, through the prescription of human ethics, to the microcosm of the sociological results in incest's being marked as a despicable crime. Kurahashi argues that whether human freedom can transcend the ethical and social prescriptions constructed by humanity in the progressive context of history is an issue for literature rather than the social sciences. Indeed, her own novels, such as *The Adventures of Sumiyakist Q [Sumiyakisuto Q no bōken]* and *The Bridge of Dreams [Yume no ukihashi]*, explore extremities where the limits of human freedom soar uninhibited by socially constructed boundaries.

In "Partei" [Parutai] we see a corporeal dimension being given to the complete rejection of "onto [Fr. *honte*, shame] (existence)." As Kurahashi explains in her essay entitled "My Method of Writing Fiction" [Watashi no shōsetsu sahō], she chooses technical forms designed to suggest a clear indication of masculinity or femininity with respect to consciousness of self. These forms include, to borrow the writer's own words, "giving form to the meaning of the world by building an illusionary castle" and "delving into the 'I.'" In addition, Kurahashi strives to create the nonexistent world one might look at before leaping and to discover the authentically fake.

The opening of the short story "Partei" sees a character referred to only as "you," a member of an avant garde political party and lover of the protagonist, "I," arguing that "joining the Partei means that everything you do with your individual life, including of course matters of love, must be subordinated to the Partei's principles." "I" is thus persuaded to commit herself unreservedly to every extreme of existence, breaking away from "onto" in a process of ever-increasing restraint of self. In the end, however, the protagonist discards her Partei membership.

In this text there is no connection between the mind and the womb. On the contrary, the work is an example of the mechanism that symbolizes the masculine in the woman writer. Kurahashi Yumiko might well modify her technical approach in the future. However, her macro viewpoint is likely to remain unchanged.

While it may not have been the case in the time of *The Tale of Genji,* women in modern society, for all its inadequacies, have to some extent been liberated from the constraints traditionally regarded as women's work, including home duties and child care. Increasingly today women are able to become "writers" rather than merely being confined to the production of "women's literature," with all the ideological restrictions inherent in that term. Given the social restraints and the lingering feudal residue of the Meiji era, the lot of women in that era was charged with a dispiriting pathos. This is evident from the examples of Higuchi Ichiyō and her colleagues. However, there have been marked improvements since this time so that many women now write under conditions that permit them to compete as serious writers addressing the fundamental issues of literature.

However, the fact remains that women writers face an arduous path to recognition. No longer can they rely on the old style of patronage that operated, for instance, in both journalistic and social circles and that supported women merely on account of their being women. They must now compete solely on the merit of their work. We discussed in detail the two primary conditions proposed by Setouchi Harumi in her "Requirements for Becoming a Woman Writer." The remaining criteria provide an insightful, if emotional, account of other likely difficulties faced by women who wish to write.

More than ever before, writers today are evaluated on the quality of their work regardless of sex. As we made clear at the beginning of this discussion,

Narcissus was a man, narcissism is a male function, and literature is essentially born of narcissistic processes. If we permit terms such as "women writers" and "women's literature," we must remember that these "women writers" cannot possibly write without such fundamentally masculine functions as narcissism. Literary production that occurs in the absence of these functions may result in texts that will be lauded in the short term. However, such texts will not endure nor be acknowledged by readers of the future.

| | | Narcissism, Cynicism, and the Writing of Women

TANAKA MIYOKO

Since both narcissism and cynicism appear to be merely complexes outside the control of the individual, I find little appeal as a woman in discussing either as a feature of women's literature.

We are all undoubtedly subject to a variety of complexes that we should at least try to order, tame, or corral into some manageable form when expressing ourselves. "Narcissism," however, is one of those words thrown about recklessly with little thought for its real meaning. The self-love that all of us feel, common or garden egoism, even doggedly blind self-obsession—each wants to be identified as narcissism.

We must remember that the Narcissus of the Greek myth, from which the word "narcissism" is derived, was a beautiful young man. He was definitely not a woman, a point that should be fixed clearly in our minds when assigning meaning to the word.

Why did Narcissus need to be a man? Mishima Yukio argued that it was necessary for Narcissus to possess both absolute beauty and the absolute critical capacity to discern that beauty. Claiming that women lacked the latter, Mishima believed that women possessed neither the capacity for self-consciousness nor self-criticism. Therefore, he concluded, it was impossible for Narcissus to be a woman. While Mishima asserted that women had an intimate relationship with their mirrors, he questioned whether a woman fascinated by her made-up face could be labeled narcissistic. He argued instead that the made-up face was not a real face but merely an illusion created from the base of the self-confessed imperfection of the real face's raw material.

Perhaps Mishima was right to associate the kind of narcissism seen in women

TRANSLATED BY TOMOKO AOYAMA. From Tanaka Miyoko, "Hyōgen ni miru narushishizumu to shinishizumu" (Narcissism, cynicism, and the writing of women), *Kokubungaku kaishaku to kyōzai no kenkyū*, July 1976: 88–92.

with the idea of makeup. Uno Chiyo's writing is a typical example. We can see this in the following extracts, although similar passages can be found in various other places in her recent autobiographical work, *The Sound of Rain [Ame no oto]*. Uno writes:

> Occasionally, the past would appear and then fade away. Perhaps it was the virtue of Jizō that eased my pain, transforming it into something sweet and beautiful.
>
> If misfortune occurred, I immediately wiped it from my mind without thinking about it. I would completely forget it. Secretly, however, I knew that this philosophy of life was proof of my being a cowardly weakling.
>
> I did my best to forget as quickly as possible even those things that, had I not been devoid of all pride, would have caused me immense distress.
>
> Strange though it may seem, I really liked having a problem and working steadily to solve it.

Dependence on makeup would appear to contradict a desire for self-awareness and the pursuit of truth. In fact, it does the very opposite in that it is motivated by an urge to escape the truth, conceal the truth, and deceive the self and others. The essence of Uno's protagonist is the desire to become rather than to be. The narrator is not without knowledge of her real face or the truth; nor does she lack pride or self-respect. However, loathing what she believes to be the absence of beauty in herself, she is compelled by an acute self-awareness and pride to seek salvation in makeup. In this sense Uno's novel deals with the fierce battle between the real and made-up face, between fact and illusion.

Of course, though a woman may try to flee the truth, there can be no guarantee that the day will not come when she will be forced to dispense with these trappings. This is the fate of Kaoru, the protagonist of Nakazato Tsuneko's work, *Chains [Kusari]*, as follows:

> For many years Kaoru had endured the burden of living with self-deceit. But there seemed absolutely no reason to do so any longer. A divorce was a divorce, whatever the reason. Who else but herself did she want to know or understand? It was sad that after so many years she had been unable to come to terms with what was expected of her. Kaoru had been constantly tormented by feelings of deep guilt and fear ever since her husband began living outside the family. For some years she had gazed fixedly at her injured life, as if to cut off its decaying roots. Her chest was tight; even water made her nauseous. She tried to walk in the shade, for the warm sun made her flushed and dizzy. . . . The empty, insincere hours had been unbearable. As if brutally skinning herself, she peeled away the outer layer of her body, satu-

rated as it was with the smell of the family rather than an independent being. The cool fresh air felt pleasant as it blew across her exposed breasts and legs.

In this passage, a woman who has spent much of her life as a housewife and mother abandons everything to live independently. Thus she must gradually remove her makeup and move toward the narcissism of the male.

Clearly narcissism is a self-complacent, self-replicating consciousness based on a division of mind and body and a split between viewer and viewed. Narcissus was punished for valuing absolutely the imperative relationship between self and self in a manner that obliterated the external world. It is clear, though, that the narcissistic experience is essentially the prototype of eroticism, for we all ultimately yearn for the illusion of a self reflected in the Other. Since such a desire can only be fantasy, we might question the need for a woman to confront her physical body and argue instead that it is surely acceptable for her to be captivated by the reflected image of the self transformed by makeup. We must also concede that what a woman admires in this instance is not her flesh, but her skills of metamorphosis. In other words, she is captivated by her intellect or mind.

It is rare that any value is given to the invisible, intangible entity that is the mind or intellect of the woman. Certainly society has never directly acknowledged such an entity, assessing women instead in terms of the visible beauty of the flesh. Women who engage in the act of writing must be able to take the invisible and transform it into something that can be seen, creating the body as illusion in the process. While there is an expectation of a distinct division between the beautiful woman as illusion and the mind that creates this image, the self-intoxicating abilities of the woman writer permit an unfettered merger of the two.

There was once a queen who believed she was the most beautiful woman in the world. To the question, "Mirror, mirror, on the wall, who is the fairest of them all?" the answer always came, "Your Majesty is the fairest in the land." One day, however, the mirror replied, "Your stepdaughter is now fairest, and you are but second to her." It is well known that upon hearing these words, the queen was completely and utterly *beside* herself with rage. This, I believe, is not merely a children's tale of an eccentric queen, but a metaphor for the awakening of all women from narcissism. The mirror's reply rent the queen's world with an earth-shattering gash. The brutal penetration of the "Other" through this gash led to an awakening of the queen's conscious self. For the first time, her interest focused on a woman other than herself, a woman whom she had no choice but to attack.

Cynicism may well be a method of making such an attack. The generation of an intense sense of the conscious self is uncharacteristic of women. It therefore results in a woman's being no longer able to sustain her narcissistic self-intoxication. At this point her wounded pride emits an aura of cynicism toward the world. We might note, then, that narcissism and cynicism are two sides of the same coin. For while narcissism is a solipsistic interest in the conscious self, cynicism is the conscious self rejected by one's own self, which then turns toward the outer world. The woman who fails to find satisfaction in the passive offering of the self as object seeks then to (re)create an active and positive self. In this way she must make the transition from physical to intellectual narcissism. However, what is intellectual narcissism for a woman? Having drifted into this invisible, intangible world, there will ultimately be nothing definite to seize upon in an infinite gloom of ambiguity.

It is clearly less offensive, both to the woman herself and to those around her, for a woman to say she is clever rather than beautiful. The woman who entitles her book *Clever Women Can Cook [Sōmei na onna wa ryōri ga umai]* is ingenuous enough to publicize unashamedly her talents through the medium of a tangible substance such as food.[1]

However, the wise and intelligent woman can fail to inspire confidence precisely because of her intelligence and thus fall into the trap of self-mutilation. It is then that her feelings of depression and entrapment give rise to cynicism. This cynicism, sadistically directed outwards in a distorted, suppressed form, is rife among the new intelligentsia of women writers. The editor requested that I provide specific examples. Although I could easily put forward four or five names, I would rather limit myself to generalizations, for I am sure that readers will recognize my own intentions as rather cynical.

We might say that cynicism is no more than the mere reversal of pride and vanity. If this is the case, then cynicism in a writer is proof of that writer's inability to be released from an ego that should be subordinate to the writing itself or to be free from an attachment to the self. In this sense, such writing can never be better than second class. Those who thoroughly and completely seek to pursue the conscious self should be able to free themselves from the incomplete state that is cynicism. They will pass through the tunnel of the ego and, of necessity, into the open space beyond.

In spite of its limitations, literary cynicism can have a Wildean or Baudelaire-like appeal when used as an intentional art or device rather than an uncontrolled expression of the writer's raw emotion. This presents difficulties for women. Cynicism as art must invoke reader sympathy and not antagonism or distaste.

---

1. *Clever Women Can Cook* is the title of the best-selling cookery book written by Kirishima Yōko (b. 1937) and published in 1976. *TA*

One characteristic of sympathy is detachment. This is a passive state in which a degree of pride is maintained by keeping a certain distance from an object. The prerequisite for detachment is a critical mind. Such a mind rarely gives rise to the overt physical or emotional activity, such as feminine malice or spite, that results from a direct relationship with the object.

Like narcissism, then, cynicism is ultimately inaccessible to women, who, with their characteristic lack of self-criticism, are unable to attain true objectivity or a fair and disinterested viewpoint in relation to self and Other. This is not particularly regrettable, however, for cynicism is not highly regarded in literature, something we might understand through a consideration of the etymology of the word.

According to the *Kōjien* dictionary, cynicism can mean either the view of the Cynics or an attitude that generally disregards convention and derides commonly held moral views. The word "Cynic" is explained as follows: A school of Greek philosophers founded by Antisthenes, a pupil of Socrates who believed that happiness derived from moral living and that morality could be attained through the use of individual will to control desire, regardless of external conditions. The Cynic ideal was a simple, natural, and selfless life. In order to achieve this, the Cynic dismissed social convention and condemned cultural artifice. Cynicism, therefore, often denotes an attitude that consciously disregards the traditions of vanity and social life.

It is evident that, at least in its original if not derivative forms, cynicism was a variety of philosophy that expounded both an ideal and practical view of life. In the modern context, only a hippy would reject civilization for nature and the impoverished life of a beggar. It is highly doubtful that any woman writer would adopt such an extreme position.

In later times, cynics became meaner and less agreeable. Oscar Wilde, for example, had this to say in *De Profundis:* "And delightful as cynicism is from its intellectual side, now that it has left the Tub for the Club, it never can be more than the perfect philosophy for a man who has no soul. It has its social value, and to an artist all modes of expression are interesting, but in itself it is a poor affair, for to the true cynic nothing is ever revealed."

It is well known that Diogenes, the disciple of Antisthenes, was called the philosopher of the tub. One day, when he was passing time in his tub enjoying the sun, he was visited by Alexander the Great. Diogenes famously requested the king to stand out of the way of the sun. However, as Wilde has pointed out, once the Cynics left the tub, so to speak, and entered the club, they lost their souls.

The club in question represents what we might regard as the epitome of unproductive cultural life. In this sense, cynicism has degenerated into an accessory of the intelligentsia. Availing themselves of the material benefits of a society, cynics now nonetheless seek to satisfy their egotistic vanity by deriding the conventions and morals of that same society. Cynicism deprives the self of creative power. It nevertheless induces a drug-like effect that gives the illusion of standing on top of the world by belittling and criticizing everything except the self. It is little wonder, then, that the gifted but powerless woman should jump at this.

||| Nakedness and Decoration in Women's Writing

HARA SHIRŌ

I

When I was first given the title "Nakedness and Decoration in Women's Writing," it seemed interesting and exciting. Reasonable though it may sound, however, I soon realized that it is quite an ambiguous topic and even impossible to write about. Although I regretted so eagerly accepting the subject, I felt there was some value in trying to analyze the impracticalities involved and will conduct my discussion accordingly.

I have no fixed understanding of "women's literature" and have in fact tried to resist the tendency to discuss this topic as a single category. Similarly with "women poets," the value of the poem has nothing to do with whether the author is a woman or a man. Women writers today display unprecedented individuality and potential, enjoying prominence in a variety of literary genres, including traditional *tanka* and *haiku,* modern poetry, and fiction. This makes the idea of a standard category require even greater caution. However, in the activities of writers and poets we can recognize some kind of common element, some special characteristics of any given age: *Zeitgeist* if you like. Thus in any era there will be common literary forms adhered to by groups or schools. It similarly seems logical that there will also be common characteristics intrinsic to and shared by women writers.

Each age has a characteristic style, as opposed to the individual style of a particular author. The common style in any given age is an amalgamation of elements of that age in addition to elements of the styles of individual authors. Thus communal styles can be regarded as the product of both temporal setting

TRANSLATED BY TOMOKO AOYAMA. From Hara Shirō, "Buntai ni okeru ratai to sōshoku" (Nakedness and decoration in women's writing), *Kokubungaku kaishaku to kyōzai no kenkyū,* July 1976: 98–104.

and individuality. In order to elucidate this common style we must be prepared to transcend sweeping generalizations or instinct, focusing instead on clear evidence. What might appear to be the personal characteristics of a poet or writer may in fact merely be a modification of elements visible in other writers of the same period. In other words, ostensibly individual style can actually be an intentional or unintentional variation of a common characteristic. Perhaps there are conscious or unconscious influences operating on writers of the same period with the same inclination. Or perhaps the common style of any period is the sum of individual elements. In either case, personal style both constitutes and is constituted by the superpersonal.

These apparently conflicting ideas are not necessarily contradictory. However, in order to ensure that works by women are regarded as "literature" we must avoid a preconceived notion of "women's literature." We can concede the existence of "women's literature" only if it is experiential and *a posteriori,* with clearly identifiable elements common to other women writers of the age. These common elements are those that remain evident as characteristics of women's literature following the erasure of commonalities of the era, such as contemporaneousness, urbanity, or regionality.

Consideration of these fundamental issues seems to render the subject of "Nakedness and Decoration in Women's Writing" a little absurd. Thus if we wish to argue that these elements represent aspects of women's literature, we must explain the process by means of which we arrive at this position. At least this is my belief and my first reason for being reluctant to write on this topic.

My second reason relates to the often-cited fact that many women write from the body, focusing on the emotions and sensibilities of daily life rather than abstract matters. Although it may not be the case in recent years, I have certainly found this in my reading of the autobiographical or *shishōsetsu* works of prewar writers such as Hayashi Fumiko, Hirabayashi Taiko, Sata Ineko, and Tsuboi Sakae.

There is also the widely held view that women writers have strong tendencies towards narcissism, manifested in their need to apply makeup. Women, we are told, conceal, beautify, and decorate the naked skin and believe themselves to be the fictional image so created. (This tendency is evident also in the works of more recent writers who adroitly combine elements of fact and fantasy.) This has definitely been my impression of such highly idiosyncratic works as the prewar writing of Okamoto Kanoko, the pre- and postwar work of Uno Chiyo, and the postwar material of Mori Mari.

The tendency to reveal the naked body may appear to be in opposition to a tendency to decorate, especially if we consider each as representative of a type of writer. However, on closer consideration we see that both can be found in varying degrees in the work of the same author in a manner that is not necessarily contradictory. We might go so far as to say that the harmonious coexistence, or even the organic and inevitable coalescence, of "nakedness" and "decoration" is the defining characteristic of women's literature. For it can be argued that the completely uninhibited revelation of the naked body, whereby the subject can rely only on intuition and sensory awareness, is in itself a form of decoration and essentially a variety of narcissism. Similarly can we not say that erotically bewitching decoration is, in fact, a form of bare skin or nakedness? When we talk about self or nature, there are two versions: the raw or primary and the secondary or literary. However, these are so much a natural and unassuming part of each other in women's literature that it is impossible to distinguish between them. This is an infinitely free and homogenous blending. It is in no way related to the many paradoxes in those extremes of "nakedness" that, although they might resemble "decoration," actually expose the everyday, concrete elements that permeate the abstract and conceptual.

In any case this may be nothing more than a notional and intuitive impression. For when we talk about writing with the body or the "nakedness" of the author, we invoke a metaphor denoting the power of the passion and emotion of the writer. These ideas assume meaning only when contrasted with the overtly "decorative." Furthermore, there is no expression that is not decorative, and all literature is, in one way or another, a departure from "nakedness" and fact. Thus different impressions are all relative. Texts that have an impact on the reader, including "decorative" texts, are those that are written with the full force of the body of the writer.

From this perspective the topic "nakedness and decoration" would appear to be not only without substance, but, provocative though it may sound, also without any quality that would make it exclusive to women writers.

2

The only woman who hated Maria was an old woman, a neighbor, who believed that Maria knew about the abnormal sex life of her daughter. She would glare, long and hard, with a face that said, "You think you're so grand, but what depths you've sunk to." But Maria, who had sunk nowhere at all, still felt affection for the old woman. One day, her neighbor almost stepped on an insect. The old woman leapt up, limbs jutting from her baggy clothes and the hem of her underclothes, gaping mouth screaming, and horizontal wrinkles showing beneath her flattened nose. The sight called up a vivid picture to Maria of the neighbor as a little girl kicking taws about in a dark, back alley. "What a noisy old woman you are. I'm not making fun of your daughter, you know," Maria thought to herself. For Maria had not one jot of elitism, or anything as offensive, within her. She was shocked, at first, when she saw the other women walking noisily down the corridor in their pink or white slips. But she soon became used to this world. She would fondly watch the women, looking like figures from a poster of Kafū's *It Happened One Night [Aru yo no dekigoto]*, swapping jokes with the tinplate workman wiping his body at the washstand.

The passage above is a brief excerpt from Mori Mari's short story, "Crazy Maria" [Kichigai Maria]. I do not quote this passage in support of the unique style for which the author is known. The passage gives an account of assorted aspects of the writer's daily life and, as such, barely qualifies as fiction. While it provides an example of unembellished, bold, and direct self-expression, it is also replete with the narcissistic rapture of decoration. In fact, it offers a prime example of the fusion of "nakedness" and "decoration" and the difficulty in distinguishing between the conscious and the unconscious or between fiction and fact. The rhythm and flow of the passage erase all contradiction and bring the seemingly conflicting elements to a perfect harmony in a manner that rejects further stylistic analysis. Furthermore, the total obsession with self somehow evokes the Romanesque, so that the reader finds the same pleasure in the writer's self-absorbed meanderings as in a tale of old. Here again we see the erasure of the contradiction between self-obsession and self-liberation, concerning which Kawamura Jirō has offered an insightful comment.

Kawamura argues that the defining characteristics of the woman writer are storytelling skills and narcissism. He further claims that while there may appear to be a contradiction between the abandonment of self apparent in the former and obsession with the self inherent in the latter, these attributes are, in fact, not incompatible in the writing of women. Both are a manifestation of an identical psychology, so that "abandoning oneself to the narrative flow and being absorbed by an image of the self are one and the same act, so long as these share the same kind of sincere, earnest, and totally absorbed gesture." In other words, "illuminated by the sensuous and erotic light emitted by the world of direct emotion *an sich*, in itself, narrative becomes confession and confession becomes narrative" *(Modern Women's Literature [Gendai no joryū bungaku]*, Mainichi Shinbunsha, vol. 2, *Commentary [Kaisetsu]*).

Indeed, if we follow Kawamura's analysis, "nakedness" and "decoration" can be regarded as the same kind of psychological phenomena. They are identical acts in terms of emotional immediacy. As I argued previously, Hayashi

Fumiko's *Diary of a Vagabond [Hōrōki]* clearly represents "nakedness" with its frank and bold physicality, while the works of Okamoto Kanoko feature a rich rococo "decoration," criticized in the past as unnecessary "padding." Yet both may be regarded as one and the same act and, in Kawamura's words, as "the victory of emotional immediacy." Furthermore, not only are "nakedness and decoration" united by an ultimate logic, both are also evident covertly and overtly throughout the works of both writers. It is only from an overall impression of each writer that we can identify the dominance of one or the other element. The coexistence (be it unconscious on the part of the writer) of these two elements is a feature that has been handed to writers of later generations, in spite of differences in attributes, propensities, and techniques.

> That year there had already been several November snowfalls and other clear signs that we could expect a bitter winter. I had been helping my husband, who worked as a photographer, late at night in a basement room of the Art Building. Exhausted, I went out into the corridor when a door opened and a tall woman emerged, her coat a fiery blaze of color. I felt as though a ghost had appeared, come toward me, and possessed me as she was about to pass. Immediately I knew that this must be the Virginia I had heard about. She spoke to me, realizing as she must have that an Asian woman standing in the corridor at this hour of the night could only be the wife of my husband, Tomihiro.

The passage is taken from Kurahashi Yumiko's *Virginia* (1970). Kurahashi is known for her metaphysical novels, a form unusual among women writers. The conviction of the writer is summed up in her claim in the afterword of *A Dark Journey [Kurai tabi]* that she "liberates fiction from the fallacy of realism, which purports to depict the world as it is." Therefore, readers may be puzzled at my claim that there is a luxuriant narcissism in her work. From the time of "Partei," the work that brought her to public attention, Kurahashi's writing has consistently displayed a chic and stylish form reminiscent of literature in translation. She also has an even and dispassionate fluency of style. The issue of realism notwithstanding, Kurahashi's writing can be considered decorative, adorned by ideology and intellect, decorated by her very rejection of accepted forms of decoration. Although her stylistic homogeneity can lead to a loss of rhythm and monotony, it also provides an opportunity for her to demonstrate her cynical and incisive intellect.

With respect to narcissism, hers is the kind that rejects vulgarity or, as she explains in the long introductory section of *Virginia*, a narcissism that indulges itself in small doses of cathartic and masochistic pain and pleasure. She writes as follows. "The restrictions of time, length, and audience inherent in writing, or at least the writing of prose, invoke both the pain and pleasure of undertaking mental exercise in a confined space. It is rather like the physical contraction required before one jumps. If there were no commercial restrictions or style demands, the exercise benefits involved would probably ensure that the 'job' of writing was not necessarily bad for the health." In this passage it is the writing itself, rather than the meaning, that is subject to a narcissism that rejects vulgarity. The fact that writing such as this fits naturally into her fiction is not because she is the author of intellectual novels, but because her writing is grounded in emotion and held together by the pathos of pleasure.

Although it is tempting to digress to provide proof and to analyze these claims, it is beyond my brief to do so here. Let's move, instead, to the next passage:

> My aunt was in hospital. It was an obstetrics and gynecology facility where the building housing the records office was being demolished to enable the construction of a new building in a neighboring lot. I left the ward and found myself in a dark corridor, like a brothel, with a tap at one end. Beside the tap was a staircase with a wide landing, like stairs in a school. The smell of disinfectant hung heavy in the air. Jars of all sizes were lined up on the stairs, leaving just enough room for walking. Inside these jars were mysterious solid shapes, although there was no doubt that they were human body parts and organs, quietly sinking in formalin. I stood at the end of the corridor, my feet paralyzed, unable to make my way down the stairs.

The passage is a seemingly unexceptional account taken from Kanai Mieko's *A Life of Love [Ai no seikatsu]*. The work of prewar and wartime writers before her carried the heavy weight of experience, which saw them depict the self as entity. However, Kanai, who was born in November 1947, has no notion whatsoever of war. To her, self can be nothing but a false entity, while both "love" and "life" represent no more than an uncertain, fluid consciousness. This is apparent in the novel's opening sentence, which reads, "I already have no clear memory of where yesterday ended." Having seen the young man with whom she is sharing a restaurant table eating spaghetti, the protagonist is reminded of roundworms, then of a school sick bay, and finally of making the hospital visit to her aunt.

Kanai's depiction of memory might be mistaken for realism; however there is a distinct difference in that the imagery is fundamentally light and dry. The existence of objects is due only to their respective weight in the flow of consciousness of the first-person protagonist, and the writer permits only that consciousness, rather than the objects themselves, to narrate. The reference to the "brothel," a place that the writer is unlikely to have experienced, would be a metaphoric blunder in conventional realism. But in this passage it has the desired effect.

This innovative device, however, can also be regarded as a highly conscious manifestation of the intrinsic nature of the woman writer. Women writers have demonstrated a strong ability to draw the world of the extraordinary and its objects into the everyday and to narrate themselves (at least through their protagonists and narrators) rather than abrogating the responsibility for narration to the objects in their fiction.

Both Kurahashi and Kanai may seem to be talented new writers free from the concept or "tradition" of "women's literature." Nevertheless, characteristics common to other women writers are evident also in their writing. I have already discussed the issue of "nakedness and decoration" in the context of Kurahashi's writing. Similarly, if we agree that the notion of "decoration" can include technical awareness, then Kanai's writing can also be considered a kind of stylish and measured decoration. Furthermore, we should acknowledge that both writers present "nakedness" in a secondary, literary sense. Of course, the starting point of these writers is an aversion to either desperate, intuitive "nakedness" or decadent, intoxicated "decoration." We can therefore say that their writing simultaneously has and does not have "nakedness and decoration." In the sense that they have these, we can bestow on them the honor of being "women writers"; in the sense that they do not have these, we find proof of their innovation.

I should point out, however, that great literature is never produced only by technical consciousness. Neither is it the mere product of innovation. It goes beyond the dimension of "nakedness and decoration" and transcends those elements usually referred to as style but which in fact comprise no more than expressive skill and rhetoric. Great literature is born of the impact of true style. This true style takes the form of a selfless creative spirit that invites the reader to return again and again and that transcends popular questions of writing technique. . . .

Women, Narcissism, and Okamoto Kanoko

SHIBUSAWA TATSUHIKO

All married men and men who engage in conventional sex have undoubtedly had firsthand experience of the recidivist self-centeredness that is the narcissism of women.

It is less difficult for a camel to pass through the eye of a needle than for a woman to separate from her own self and regard herself objectively. Among the recently increasing numbers of homosexual men there are also undoubtedly those who revel in a highly subjective form of narcissism, identical to that of women, that is closely associated with the physical body. But this is a separate issue. For my task here is to discuss the mysterious entity referred to as the woman writer. Given that she is a variety of woman, the woman writer will doubtless be subject to the same obsessive self-centeredness that afflicts all women. This is her biological fate. And since Okamoto Kanoko is also a woman, we must expect that she too will be subject to the same effect.

The point of my discussion then is this. Okamoto Kanoko may well have been overly burdened with the biological fate of all women—namely, the self-centeredness of feminine narcissism. Nevertheless, it is precisely her extreme pursuit of this that has led to the development of her unique and liberated fictional world. In this sense she is indeed an exceptional writer among women.

When men consider the work of the woman writer, they inevitably do so with a disdainful or mocking eye. I have already labeled the woman writer a "mysterious entity." In fact the expression "woman writer" is something of an oxymoron. While it may have been acceptable for women to write in Heian times, in the context of modern literature the words "woman" and "writer" are largely incompatible. Thus we have Baudelaire, notorious for the contempt in which he held the woman writer, making statements such as the following: "Today, there are growing numbers of women who dedicate themselves to literary pursuits regardless of distress to their families or lovers. Among these women it would be rare to find one not contaminated by the kind of absurd imitations of masculinity that pervert and distort the women who adopt them."

TRANSLATED BY TOMOKO AOYAMA AND BARBARA HARTLEY. From Shibusawa Tatsuhiko, "Okamoto Kanoko aruiwa onna no narushishizumu" (Women, narcissism, and Okamoto Kanoko), Hen'aiteki sakkaron (On the writers I'm partial to), pp. 310–321. This essay was first published in the appendix to The Collected Works of Okamoto Kanoko (Okamoto Kanoko zenshū, Tōjusha, 1974). The essay was subsequently published in Shibusawa, Hen'aiteki sakkaron (Seidosha, 1976). This collection was reissued by Kawade shobō shinsha in 1997, which is the edition used for this translation.

The average male is in the thrall of the same type of prejudice that afflicts Baudelaire. Therefore, we men dispense with our everyday inhibitions and rowdily rejoice when we encounter the rare woman writer who is not "contaminated by the kind of absurd imitations of masculinity that pervert and distort women" but who, instead, is armed with a sexuality or passion to rival the male intellect. Like men who commit to the adoration of an ideal woman, our appreciation of women's literature demands passion over intellect and sensuality over mind. Ishikawa Jun is one critic who lavishly showers praise on these aspects of Okamoto Kanoko's writing. However, Master Isai, as Ishikawa is known, was certainly not the first critic to adopt such an approach. In *L'Art romantique*, Baudelaire damned George Sand, whom he loathed, as in the passage cited above. Nevertheless, he gave unconditional praise to the poet Marceline Desbordes-Valmore, a passionate and sensual woman who was quite the opposite of Sand. A close examination of Kanoko's writing reveals, in fact, that the George Sand factor that Baudelaire so despised is not entirely absent. But let us leave this issue for now and proceed.

An unashamedly obvious representation of self-centered female narcissism is found in Okamoto Kanoko's memorable debut work, *The Crane Falls Sick [Tsuru wa yamiki]*. It is irrelevant whether or not the author felt any affection toward Akutagawa Ryūnosuke, the model upon whom the novel is based. However, it is obvious even to the reader unfamiliar with the novel genre that the work is a product of the completely biased observations of a woman. Evident too are Kanoko's natural gifts in her detection of the "wounds of self-complacency" behind Akutagawa's proud and intelligent face. In this sense, the odds are ultimately all stacked against the male. For while I do not have Akutagawa's ill health or delicate mental state, I cannot but feel as a male that these "wounds of self-complacency" are occasionally visible in my own face. A woman observing me would doubtless feel the same.

We might compare these "wounds of self-complacency" to the sinking feeling that follows ejaculation, which for men is the result of a surge in both the intellect and desire. Kanoko perhaps believed she could offer salvation to Akutagawa through her own Buddhist beliefs, a claim regarded as wildly presumptuous by a number of critics. However, perhaps all she desired was gently to stroke the back of a man completely drained of strength following a spiritual orgasm. If this is the basis of her literature, we must then concede that such gentleness fully compensates for the self-centeredness of her woman's narcissism. In Kanoko's literature there is something round that has the power to fill the emptiness inside a man and that, like the roundness of a woman's body, can gently enfold and protect against the severity of the intellect.

A Mother's Love [Boshi jojō] is a masterpiece set in Paris. Here, the protagonist hears the story of how the artist Pissarro forced his son to work while the young man was still a student. Appalled by behavior completely at odds with her own child-rearing beliefs, the woman comes to hate Pissarro's art. The rather shocking egocentricity of this protagonist borders on the comic. However, it well demonstrates the logic of female narcissism, which dashes ahead independently. The man is then left far behind, pleading for the woman to wait. But, of course, it is all too late.

To Kanoko, gentleness and self-centeredness appear to have been indistinguishable, something that undoubtedly made things difficult for those around her. However, her egoism merges with the power of her embrace. I began this discussion with the claim that women find it difficult to regard themselves objectively, something that Kanoko herself clearly understood. From this perspective, her early story, entitled "The Love of Kishimo" [Kishimo no ai], gives some insights into her literature. Here she writes: "All her life, Kishimo's spirit had sprung forth with the strength of wild bamboo. It was impossible for her to regard herself objectively, for she could never admit to another self within her."

Psychoanalyst Miyamoto Tadao argues that the phenomenon of having different personalities is confined mainly to women. He points out that multiple or substitute personalities are generally found in, for example, female cult leaders, mediums, psychics, or patients with hysteria. On the other hand, the literature overwhelmingly suggests that it is men who manifest split personalities or double personalities *(Doppelgänger)*. Miyamoto explains this as follows: "When the self is split, men project 'another self' outside themselves. In women, however, the self transmutes internally into 'another self.' Here we find an explanation of the difference in the creative powers of men and women."

Miyamoto's argument *(Modern Thought [Gendai shisō]*, July 1974) is very convincing and seems to be confirmed by the fact that, from my knowledge of literary history, no other modern writers have been more obsessed with the *Doppelgänger* phenomenon than Izumi Kyōka and Akutagawa Ryūnosuke.

In *The Crane Falls Sick* the protagonist, Asakawa, the Akutagawa character, "stopped at the mirror in the bathroom, stuck out his tongue, stroked his forehead, sneered, and pulled his lower eyelid down. Finally, he returned to his room with his usual composure, thinking he hadn't been seen." In Akutagawa's own "IV: Not Yet?" [Mada?] of *Cogwheels [Haguruma]*, written just before his suicide, we find this passage: "For the first time in quite a while I stood in front of a mirror and stared squarely at my own reflection. The image opposite me, of course, was smiling too. As I gazed at the mirror, I remembered my other self. This second self—what the Germans call *Doppelgänger*—was, fortunately, never visible to me."

We can safely assume that Kanoko was never touched by anxieties of the kind that plagued Akutagawa. Like Kishimo, her spirit had "sprung forth" throughout her life with "the strength of wild bamboo." Thus she too found it impossible to admit to "another self within her." Contrary to popular opinion, it seems to me that the narcissistic hell created by gazing at the mirror is the province of men. The narcissism of women, on the other hand, has no need for mirrors.

Kanoko's narcissism evokes the expansiveness of the mythical mother, which transcends the ego and spreads into a series of never-ending and all-encompassing concentric circles. Like her body, her narcissism is round. To borrow the ideas of psychoanalyst Miyamoto, rather than projecting "another self," she consumes this other self reproduced infinitely within her, so that her ego grows ever rounder and more plump. If we read the evocative extracts given below from "The Love of Kishimo," it soon becomes apparent that the author has no need for the narcissistic mirror. For her lovers and her child are the other selves she will engulf and absorb within her own self. Kanoko writes: "Kishimo finally realized that in order to retrieve her child from the hands of the Buddha, her own hands would need a much greater capacity than those of a single, individual mother." And again: "It was heart breaking to lose the child she had once clasped to her breast and loved without constraint. But she was overwhelmed with joy that the luck of being attached to all the children in the world had been bestowed upon her."

Here in "The Love of Kishimo" Kanoko already expounds the convictions, based on her own interpretation of Buddhist philosophy, to which she adhered unswervingly for the rest of her life, applying them to both her many lovers and her son.

Kanoko aptly referred to Kishimo's desire to eat children as "the violent assimilation of love." We must remember that the essence of the terrifying desire of this mythological mother, reminiscent of primeval cannibalism, is quite different from mother love in the usual meaning of the word. The George Sand element in Kanoko is perhaps related to this. I would argue that Kanoko's gentleness, which I have already discussed, is indistinguishable from the fearsome aspect of the mythological mother. For unlike popular motherhood, Kanoko's motherhood is that of the primeval mother goddess, a detailed discussion of which is given in Ishida Eiichirō's *The Mother of Momotarō [Momotarō no haha]*. Kanoko's mortality fed off a group of little male gods who persistently surrounded the great mother goddess and subordinated themselves to her love. Concerning the terrifying nature of this mother love, Kanoko had Kishimo declare to the Buddha as follows: "You used the word love when you asked me about my child. But love is far too tender a word to describe this emotion. My relationship with my child is something much more desperate. For it is surely obvious that my child is my absolute self." These words provide clear insight into the concentric circles of Kanoko's narcissistic processes, which lured the child gods around her into their ever-increasing wake. Kamei Katsuichirō called Kanoko "a river nymph," and it would be interesting to examine her work from the perspective of the relationship between women and water, as discussed, for instance, by Orikuchi Shinobu in his essay "The Water Woman" [Mizu no onna].

The absolute nature of Kanoko's narcissism operated with unchanging force throughout her life. Remarkably, it never weakened, even after her emergence as a writer of note and the publication of novels that drew the highest praise from the literary community. It is interesting to note that the very best of Kanoko's narratives objectify her narcissism rather than presenting it directly. These works, which beautifully display the crystal perfection of her talent, include "A Floral Pageant" [Hana wa tsuyoshi], "The Gorgeous Goldfish" [Kingyo ryōran], "The Old Geisha" [Rōgishō], "The House Spirit" [Karei], "The River Light" [Kawa akari], "The Apprentice Geisha" [Sūgi], and "The Gourmet" [Shokuma]. While they may not directly address the issue of narcissism, the respective motif of each work is unmistakably grounded in the writer's narcissistic processes.

In "A Guide to My Writing" [Jisaku annai], Kanoko explained the theme of "The Gorgeous Goldfish" as follows: "The woman is free to develop her own beauty and aesthetic life without self-consciousness. The man, however, although his love is doubtless sincere, is slowly perverted through a sense of inferiority. Consumed by both love and rivalry, he is driven to devote his life to the creation of beauty that surpasses that of the woman." We should take note here of the author's use of the term "sense of inferiority," for these words explicitly express Kanoko's innate worship of vitality and nobility. This is certainly a form of narcissism in women.

There are many male protagonists in Kanoko's works. Each is perverted, to use the writer's own expression, by an awareness of his "sense of inferiority" in the shadow of the brilliantly dazzling vitality and pride of the childlike heroine. These men include Kobuse from "A Floral Pageant" and Yuki from "The Old Geisha." Like Fukuichi, the protagonist of "The Gorgeous Goldfish," both feel inferior before the heroine. Similar responses are apparent in Tokunaga, the old man from "The House Spirit," Besshirō from "The Gourmet," and, although she is obviously not a man, even Kanoko, the young geisha who appears in "The Apprentice Geisha." It is no coincidence that Kanoko's novels often feature geisha, *ikebana* masters, cooking experts, craftspeople, inventors, and artists. This is because devotion to an art of some kind is essential, both for the woman to find an outlet for her vitality and pride and for the man to compete with these forces. In the predominance of characters with these backgrounds we see a reflection of the firm and powerful narcissism of the inner life of the author, who, we might note, referred to herself as "a devouring ghost, a *gaki,* of art."

Worship of vitality is a constant theme in Okamoto Kanoko's literature. She also displays an uninhibited aristocratism, which is evidence of pride in her family's status. These elements are psychologically grounded in feminine narcissism, while anthropologically they arise from mythological maternal desire, factors that I have already mentioned in my discussion.

My own preference is for those works rich with an aura of decadence, a decadence that can be interpreted as the reverse aspect of the worship of vitality. This aura is present in works such as "The Previous Life" [Kakoze], "The Bat" [Kōmori], and "The Gourmet." In fact, the manner in which this aura of decadence permeates all her works might well be because her strong sense of family honor is intimately linked to the notion of ruin.

"The Previous Life" is an unusual work featuring the heavy decadence of the popular illustrated stories of Edo times. The influence of Tanizaki Jun'ichirō is also clearly visible. It is not surprising that the work was a favorite of Mishima Yukio, for the depiction of the sadomasochistic conflict of two beautiful brothers evokes a suffocating atmosphere of suppressed youth and sexual desire. It is a finely structured text, with a particularly well-crafted ending in which the female protagonist reveals the secret of the same-sex love suicide of the brothers. Of Yukiko, the protagonist who has witnessed the sinister quarrels between the pair, Kanoko offers the following comment: "Woven into her being was a thread, both sadistic and masochistic, common to those raised in an old family, which made her both understand and envy the psychology behind the behavior she witnessed."

"The Bat" is a relatively unexceptional short story with the nostalgic air of a Tanizaki narrative. As a lover of animal tales, I was fascinated by the notion of using "a small mysterious animal, black as soot" as a symbol for nostalgia. It is evident from the works of writers such as Shiga Naoya and Kajii Motojirō that Japanese literature has a tradition of using animals to represent the life force. However, in Kanoko's work this tradition is endowed with a particularly powerful physical dimension.

"The Gourmet," which undoubtedly deserves recognition as Kanoko's masterpiece, has a setting similar to that of a work written three years earlier, "The Maiden Invited" [Yobareshi otome]. The former is a complex work with a double protagonist structure. Detailed descriptions of the acute poverty of the first protagonist's family life are presented in tandem with the activities of a secondary protagonist, the eccentric owner of a Western-style restaurant who is in the last stages of cancer. Inherent in Kanoko's cult of vitalism is an element that, although rich and gorgeous, borders on the grotesque and decadent. This element is powerfully foregrounded in "The Gourmet." Particularly memorable is the scene, strongly suggesting the irony of life, in which the face of a man is drawn on the tumor protruding from the dying patient's neck.

The novels of Kanoko are a rare species in the simplicity and refinement of the Japanese literary landscape. Hers is a literature of the baroque with the excessive decoration and luxuriant abundance of her uniquely feminine narcissism. I certainly advocate a rereading of her work and acknowledgment of the true value of her literature, which clearly has a similar lineage to the writing of Tanizaki. The baroque fictional world created by Okamoto Kanoko is supported by four pillars. These are narcissism, adoration of the life force, decadence, and aristocratism. And it is these pillars that also permit Kanoko's fictional world to maintain a rhetorical equilibrium.

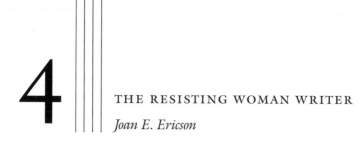

THE RESISTING WOMAN WRITER

Joan E. Ericson

In the middle of the twentieth century, most women writers of modern Japanese literature confronted critical condescension that categorized much of their work as *"joryū bungaku"* (women's literature) and that, if not explicitly disparaging, effectively segregated it from the modern canon.[1] These gender-based literary categorizations were thoroughly revised from the late 1980s, partly in response to a series of feminist critiques and partly as a result of a less-well-perceived, somewhat prior shift in the social dynamics of authorship that undermined the gendered conventions of the Japanese literary establishment *(bundan)*. This latter process is both reflected in the three articles in this chapter and also serves as the lens through which we should read them. The articles, all published in widely read intellectual journals from the late 1970s to mid-1980s, represent three distinct styles of discourse that collectively illustrate how female authors and analysts sought to break free from old gendered concepts, habits, and practices. The adoption of new terminology, best illustrated in the widespread rejection of the term *"joryū"* and its associated cultural baggage, was rooted in this earlier process, which questioned entrenched conventions and helped to recast how the works of female authors were written and read.

Women's dissatisfaction with long-standing gendered literary categories and institutional practices was twofold: the culturally dominant paradigm that privileged men restricted and excluded women writers, and the terms with which their works were evaluated failed to reflect their diverse array of literary innovations. But several far-reaching social trends enabled the dissemination of a rather disparate discourse questioning basic assumptions about female fictional characters and gendered social conventions, including those of authorship and readership. The first trend to note is generational. By the mid-1970s, a cohort of college-educated women writers had reached a critical mass and explored a wide variety of approaches in fiction that, on the whole, could be considered more intellectual or ironic than those of earlier popular women writers. Many in this younger generation won the most prestigious literary prizes, thereby securing visibility and interest among an increasingly well-educated readership. We should note, before we develop the idea at greater length below, that the presence of women, as writers and intellectuals, in the public sphere was critical in advancing this discourse. Media coverage mattered, not only because it got the alternative perspectives of women out but also because, through it, the Japanese discourse was tied to shifting global debates on women in advanced industrialized societies.

Disillusionment with the literary establishment was not generally linked to movement politics of the era, such as AMPO or Beheiren, nor even directly to the women's liberation of the early 1970s.[2] But the global cultural discourse of feminism gradually, even glacially, gained ground. Women fiction writers were among the first and, arguably, the most influential in the broader public sphere in advancing feminist and radical perspectives on oppressive social institutions and sexist practices. Women's fiction sold well and, especially among the best-known writers, boldly explored the stifling constraints of sexist conventions and the possibilities of alternative social arrangements. But it was in their role as public intellectuals that these writers were commissioned both by mass circulation magazines and self-consciously intellectual journals to write or comment on a wide range of topics; as public intellectuals, women writers often wrote about themselves and their peers and how their writing reflected the critical issues of the day. One important aspect of this public sphere is that for the writers, it was a relatively small, self-referential world. Knowing most of what had been written by whom, lately, was expected, and they engaged in a kind of common conversation that was then shared by very large numbers of the public.

The three articles in this chapter each offer critical appraisals of how women engage literature and confront the sexist literary and critical conventions. But the articles also illustrate important aspects of the shifting social dynamic of female authorship and how women have sought to explore new literary terrains. A common theme is the incompatibility between the past practices celebrated by the literary establishment and the inclinations and innovations of contemporary women writers. In a 1984 essay not included in this collection, Saegusa Kazuko recounted how she was encouraged to write confessional fiction by a number of male literati, including the critic Akiyama Shun.[3] They advised her to write in this style if she wanted to be recognized as a serious writer. Saegusa's deceptively simple response: "The reason I do not write confessional fiction, in one word, is because I am a woman." At issue was how the most celebrated of literary genres, although not explicitly barring female entrée, presumed a language and subject position antithetical to most women's experience.

The 1978 dialogue between Takahashi Takako and Tsushima Yūko, translated here by Maryellen Toman Mori, critiques the way that Japanese male authors handle female characterization, speculates on how fiction might be read differently by male and female readers, and expresses much dissatisfaction with the male arbiters of literary tastes and standards.[4] The imposition of male standards and expectations on what women write has continued to receive sharp criticism and, more recently, careful archival analysis. Seki Reiko's research clearly demonstrates the ways that Higuchi Ichiyō's male mentor, Nakarai Tōsui, edited her works to conform with expectations of how female characters should think and speak.[5] The Takahashi-Tsushima dialogue reflects many of the concerns with gendered literary practices that would dominate the debates of the next decade. Here readers should be alerted to Masao Miyoshi's perceptive indictment of such easily digestable "conversations," contributing to the decline of critical exposition and encouraging conformity.[6] However, two additional points about such dialogues should also be considered. That these two female novelists, both relatively young, would be showcased in a "serious" journal as public intellectuals demonstrates the crucial role of popular recognition in opening up venues for female perspectives, even if the title ("Female Sexuality and the Male Gaze") was selected, as I suspect, by the editors to pander in rather old-fashioned ways to prurient interests. Once these two popular authors, who were otherwise unaffiliated and quite different in their backgrounds and literary styles, were brought together by the journal (as is the publishing convention), they were free to address a range of issues, not just sexuality, and advance a far-reaching critique of sexual discrimination in both literary and social institutions.

The 1983 essay by Tomioka Taeko, a writer whose oeuvre includes poetry, novels, short stories, plays, and essays, first appeared in the mass circulation women's journal *Fujin kōron* (Women's forum). Tomioka adopts a rambling, speculative approach in addressing male critical condescension of women writers, rooting it in the gendered nature of the modern Japanese language. Her objective is to provoke readers to consider "what is to be done" to redress sexist conventions, and she employs an imaginative series of neologisms with more standard gendered linguistic categories; she also exhaustively flags her terminology with quotation marks. This was one of the first popular works to expose the bounded aspects of commonly accepted linguistic practices and indict the culturally valued disparities in which they were embedded. Connecting language with power would become a major field of analysis and debate in subsequent years, and it led to the general rejection of the term *joryū* (woman style) and its replacement by *josei* (woman/female). What is striking in this contribution is the breadth of field that a popular writer, best known for her rebellious and disturbing short stories (which secured a series of important literary prizes), should adopt in response to rather senseless male critical condescension.

She sees the language of Japanese modernity as entwined with the oppressive institutions of the nation-state and male privilege, and she presents her case in a provocative but thoroughly accessible survey that goes to great lengths to avoid intellectualizing pretensions. Employing a noticeably straightforward grammatical format, Tomioka discusses how a woman must become multilingual to operate successfully within Japanese society and learn to negotiate linguistic categories that move far beyond the familiar binary of women's language *(onna no kotoba)* and men's language *(otoko no kotoba)*.

The 1986 academic survey by Nakayama Kazuko represents a third, increasingly influential form of feminist discourse. Nakayama reviews, in a clear, authoritative style, the broad range of contemporary women's fiction, connecting it with issues in feminist perspectives in Japan and the world. Academic feminists came to play a much larger role from the mid-1980s in shaping the course of critical discourse on women writers.[7] But it is important to remember how few women occupied positions of prominence in the academy at this time. Most female academics were relegated to the margins in two-year women's institutions, and only a handful held professorships at national universities.[8] As a professor of Japanese literature at Meiji University, Nakayama brought a scholarly commitment to advancing feminist literary analysis.[9] The attention of such a senior mainstream scholar highlighted the innovation of contemporary women writers (such as Tomioka, Takahashi, and Tsushima, who appear in her essay) and also helped to validate their critical interventions as serious public intellectuals. Her essay, "The Subject of Women's Literature and the Transformation of Its Consciousness," appeared in a special issue of the flagship journal *Kokubungaku* (National literature) on *"Écriture* of the Changing Female" that marked a significant shift in academic engagement with feminist perspectives.[10] While indifference toward such approaches remains a hallmark of many of the most eminent departments of Japanese literature, the rising surge of publications and debates has made feminist academic analysis among the most influential arenas in which the works of women writers are read.

NOTES

1. *Joryū bungaku* has been translated as "female-school literature" (Lippit and Selden, *Stories by Contemporary Japanese Women Writers,* p. xiv), and "feminine-style literature" (Vernon, *Daughters of the Moon,* p. 137), but I prefer "women's literature" because it conveys some of the ambiguity that in Japanese facilitates conflation of an author's gender with a specific literary style. See Ericson, *Be a Woman,* pp. 3–15, passim.

2. AMPO is an abbreviation for Nichibei Anzen Hoshō Jūyaku Hantai Undō, the movement to protest the revision of the U.S.-Japan Security Treaty. The original treaty, which was signed in 1952 at the end of the Allied Occupation of Japan, allied Japan with the United States militarily and permitted the continued operation of U.S. military bases in Japan. The treaty was

brought up for revision several years later, and massive protests erupted over the treaty and more specifically the way then Prime Minister Kishi bulldozed the revisions through the Diet in 1960. Beheiren, another abbreviation, refers to the Peace in Vietnam Citizen's Committee, which was founded in 1965 to protest the war in Vietnam. The group is still active today in working to keep Japan from restoring its former military presence. Although women had been advocating for greater freedoms long before the postwar period, the term "women's lib" *(uman ribu)* became entrenched in the 1970s as a designation for those who were politically vocal about women's rights. *RLC*

3. "Onna ga watakushi shōsetsu wo kaku toki" (When women write confessional fiction), in Saegusa, *Sayonara otoko no jidai,* pp. 128–132.

4. Both Tsushima and Takahashi have received numerous literary awards for their fiction. A number of the novels by Tsushima, daughter of the famous novelist Dazai Osamu, have been translated into English, including *Child of Fortune* (*Chōji*, 1978) and *Woman Running in the Mountains* (*Yama wo hashiru onna,* 1980). Takahashi, whose writing career took off in the 1970s, focuses on a psychological dreamworld in her fiction. For a recent translation of five linked short stories, see Takahashi, *Lonely Woman.*

5. Seki, *Higuchi Ichiyō wo yomu,* pp. 48–51.

6. Miyoshi, *Off Center,* pp. 217–131.

7. Ueno Chizuko's *Onna wa sekai wo sukueru ka* was one of a series of widely read works by female sociologists that advanced the debates on gender and, in this case, directly addressed the place of women in literature.

8. Women were less than one-half of 1 percent of the full professors of Japanese literature at national universities in 1985, less than 10 percent of those at private universities, and 25 percent of those at two-year colleges. Government of Japan, Ministry of Education, *Gakkō kihon chōsa hōkoku sho,* pp. 178–183, 252–253.

9. For other essays by Nakayama, see the recently published Nakayama, *Nakayama Kazuko korekushon.*

10. Successive special issues of the major journals illustrated feminism's impact by the early 1990s: "Kotoba to josei" (Women and language) (*Kokubungaku kaishaku to kanshō,* July 1991); "Feminizumu no shinpuku" (Feminism's pendulum) (*Gunzō,* October 1991); "Feminizumu no kotoba: Josei bungaku" (The language of feminism: Women's literature) (*Kokubungaku: Kaishaku to kyōzai no kenkyū,* November 1992); "Dansei to iu seido" (The institution called "male") (*Nihon bungaku* [Japanese literature], November 1992); "Masei to bosei: Onna no me de bungaku wo yominaosu" (Witches and mothers: Rereading literature through women's eyes) (*Shin Nihon bungaku* [New Japanese literature], Winter 1992).

Female Sexuality and the Male Gaze

A dialogue between TAKAHASHI TAKAKO and

TSUSHIMA YŪKO

Behind the Mask

TAKAHASHI: Tsushima-san, is there a male author who you think portrays women skillfully in his fiction?

TSUSHIMA: To find someone I really admire, I'd have to go all the way back to Shakespeare. In modern times—not that the author is active now— Arishima Takeo's novel, *A Certain Woman*, comes to mind.[1] I think that's well done. When you read a contemporary piece of literature you understand even the fine points, so it's hard to think of a current author whose work I can praise unconditionally. Well, Furui Yoshikichi, for instance, portrays women . . .

TAKAHASHI: Mr. Furui? His female characters aren't real women. They're attractive images of women, but from a female perspective, they're not women. They're pseudo women. Still, I agree they're attractive.[2]

TSUSHIMA: I understand what effect Mr. Furui is trying to create in his depictions of women. I understand it, but as images of real women, I'm not so sure his female characters are convincing. I don't think his vision comes through to the reader.

TRANSLATED BY MARYELLEN TOMAN MORI. From Takahashi Takako and Tsushima Yūko, "Onna no sei to otoko no me" (Female sexuality and the male gaze), *Waseda bungaku* 30 (11) (November 1978): 4–14.

1. *A Certain Woman* (*Aru onna*, 1919; tr. 1978) concerns a beautiful woman whose passionate nature causes her to defy social conventions of all kinds. She enjoys a brief period of happiness during an intense love affair, but she and her lover are ostracized for their scandalous behavior. She becomes increasingly reckless, cruel, and unbalanced, and her life ends dismally. *MTM*

2. Here Takahashi criticizes the idealizing quality of Furui's characterizations of women, but elsewhere she has written admiringly of his literature. Both Takahashi and Furui belonged to the so-called "introverted generation" of 1970s writers, who eschewed treating social and political issues in their fiction in favor of exploring the individual human psyche. In a 1971 essay on Furui's literature Takahashi discusses his novella *Yōko* (1970; tr. 1997), which describes a man's fascination with a psychotic young woman. She writes that the reader is "apt to interpret Yōko as a woman who is merely an object of the gaze of a male protagonist who seems to be purely an organ of vision." But she adds that the man's empathetic identification with Yōko complicates the violence implicit in his constant, close scrutiny of her. See Takahashi, "Furui Yoshikichi-san no hisseki." *MTM*

TAKAHASHI: The wife in Shimao Toshio's novel, *The Sting of Death*, is well drawn.[3]

TSUSHIMA: I think so too. But—I know this is a trivial point—in that novel the representation of the woman who caused the husband's infidelity might be somewhat problematic. I don't think it spoils the work, though, so it's all right.

TAKAHASHI: Probably not many people have pointed this out, but Inoue Mitsuharu is good at depicting women. In all of his works, from a woman's viewpoint, his female characters are portrayed skillfully, especially middle-aged women. His perceptiveness about their psychology is quite deep.

In considering who represents women skillfully and who poorly, if we look at who does it poorly, the matter becomes clearer. Take Kawabata Yasunari, for example. That author is widely acknowledged for his talent at portraying women. But from a woman's perspective, those aren't real women at all. You can't exactly say that they're false. When I try to analyze this, it seems that Kawabata's female characters are insubstantial. They're like phantoms. But I think that their exteriors, as perceived through men's eyes, are meaningful. When it comes to whether a person's exterior or interior is more real, you can't say that only the interior is real; the surface has its own truth. The beauty of the women that Kawabata creates seems phantom-like to a woman, but it's female beauty as it appears to a man's eyes, so in that sense, you can't deny its validity. That kind of female image isn't peculiar to Kawabata Yasunari's fiction; it's typical of the literature of many male authors, I think.

Kawabata Yasunari's women seem to be wearing masks, and it's as if those masks are being observed through a man's eyes. But what's behind the mask isn't described at all. I'm not saying that kind of portrayal is inadequate; I think it can't be helped. There's beauty in a mask and literature is created from that kind of beauty, so that way of representation is fine as far as it goes. Maybe it's unreasonable to expect more than that of male authors.

3. Shimao Toshio (1917–1986) is best known for his stories based on his harrowing life with his wife after she suffered a mental breakdown upon discovering her husband's infidelity. *The Sting of Death* (*Shi no toge*, 1977; tr. 1985) is a collection of these stories, one of which has the same title, published together as a novel. *MTM*

TAKAHASHI: That kind of depiction of a woman isn't just a male fantasy; it's an image of a woman as she appears in a man's eyes, filtered through the man's fantasies. So it's true for a man, but for a woman, it seems that the female character's interior reality is simply missing. That doesn't diminish the literary value of a work. It's just that there's that difference between male and female authors' portrayals of women.

Even so, the overwhelming majority of Kawabata's readers are women, which must mean that when women read his literature, they put on that female image like a mask, as I've just described, and read it. I suppose a woman typically reads Kawabata's literature as if she were the object of a man's gaze. Women have a surface that men look at, you know? That exterior and Kawabata's image of woman merge, and I think that most women read Kawabata's literature from that point of view. In other words, they want to be seen as beautiful by men. If a novel is written in such a way that it makes women want to appear beautiful, when they read it, they feel pleasure. I suppose that kind of work satisfies female narcissism.

TSUSHIMA: I recognize in literature by male authors—not any one in particular but in general—the tendencies you've just described. I think they really are inevitable. A man definitely acts differently when he's with a woman from when he's with other men. He cheers up temporarily. [Laughter.] The same thing is true of women. When a woman is with other women, she's different from when she's with a man.

If we take Yoshiyuki Jun'nosuke rather than Kawabata Yasunari as an example, the majority of boys around me were avid fans of Yoshiyuki. To say that male readers feel good when they read Yoshiyuki's fiction sounds a bit strange. It's not that they feel comfortable, but I sense that they experience a kind of exhilaration. So when I read Yoshiyuki's literature, I find myself wondering if maybe he's right . . .

TAKAHASHI: That feeling of "wondering if maybe he's right." It's not as if aspects of the female mind that you hadn't known before are being revealed to you. When I was young, I felt that way when I read. When I read a work written by a man that depicted a woman based on its author's analysis of female psychology, I would think, oh, this is how a woman is. And I would read on, completely accepting his analysis. But after I started writing novels and gradually began to be able to express myself as a subject, what male authors had taught me about women and I'd accepted as truth, I came to feel was somehow false.

Take, for example, Mauriac's *Thérèse Desqueyroux,* a novel that I'd loved.[4] Recently when I read it, I feel as if it were a lie. Or rather that the author hadn't delved really deeply into a woman's heart.

But when I read novels, for example, by you, or by Ohba Minako, or by other women writers, I can really identify, in a visceral way, with their heroines—not identify intellectually, but understand them with my body.

TSUSHIMA: If you consider the matter from the opposite angle, it may make it clearer. Often it's said of women writers that they aren't good at creating male characters. Of course, I think the individual author's ability is a factor, but it's the reverse of what you were talking about. No matter what type of man a woman author portrays, male readers probably think, this isn't what a man is really like; this isn't realistic. When this struck me, I felt that unless the work itself was very powerful, it wouldn't satisfy male readers. I'm really attracted to the type of male character like Heathcliff in *Wuthering Heights*.

When I reflect on these kinds of issues in the context of my own novels, it occurs to me that the majority of men work, and there's a kind of all-male sphere that's aligned with society. Here men are bashing each other with their knowledge. Politics and the like are so-called male domains. Men don't easily make the transition to a female sphere. Even a man who says really brilliant things when he's in a male environment drops his mask completely when he's with a woman and becomes a good-for-nothing. And that's the only side of him that the woman sees. Even, for example, when a woman becomes involved in political activity, the men around her all automatically adjust their behavior to accommodate her, so it's almost impossible for her to grasp what those men are really like. I suppose the opposite is also true.

TAKAHASHI: When men are showing off their brilliance and a woman comes on the scene, she can't witness that. Because in the presence of women, men show their weaknesses, their inept sides.

TSUSHIMA: When women are with men, I think they want to put their best foot forward. They assume a manner that's aimed at pleasing men, and I think that for most women this situation is more stressful than any other.

TAKAHASHI: Trying to show a good side of themselves, right?

TSUSHIMA: Or rather than a good side, a side of themselves that generally men consider to be attractive. They tense up and try their best to show that. In a sense, it's the opposite mechanism, psychologically, of men not exposing their weaknesses. When a female author begins writ-

4. This 1927 novel by François Mauriac concerns a vibrant woman whose exasperation with her stiflingly proper married life leads her to try to poison her straitlaced husband. *MTM*

ing about parts of herself that women don't ordinarily reveal, I think that male writers are startled, and they begin to say that she writes nothing but incomprehensible things or revolting things.

TAKAHASHI: For women, the part that's suppressed by society is very large, isn't it. It's those aspects of themselves that women ordinarily conceal that women authors express in their novels, I think.

Corporeal Sensibility

TSUSHIMA: Takahashi-san, I read your novel *The Tempter,* and while reading it I was strongly reminded of Joan of Arc.[5] One image of Joan of Arc is of a maiden who's dressed like a man, riding a horse and leading an army. A young woman who, although she was from an obscure village, changed the course of French history. In everyday terms, her image is of a masculine woman. It's a very aggressive image. But from her point of view, she'd simply heard God's voice and had obeyed it—just doing whatever she was told. She wasn't at all thinking what influence her actions would have on history or the contemporary political situation. She just kept behaving as if she had no choice but to do as she was told to do. The information that Mr. Takayama compiled and presents in his book *The Execution Trial of Joan of Arc* is really fascinating.[6] For example, in the middle of the trial the Catholic bishops ordered Joan to change from trousers into a skirt, and she replied that she wouldn't change her clothes because God didn't tell her to do so. It was a very simple thing, but if she'd just done what they told her, probably her punishment would have been more lenient. But without considering such a practical matter at all, she just stubbornly repeated that she couldn't hear God telling her to do that, so she wouldn't. She was totally passive and she had no personal identity.

5. *The Tempter* (*Yūwakusha*, 1976), one of Takahashi's major novels, represents the culmination of the first phase of her literary career, devoted mainly to expressing a nihilistic view of life. It is a fictionalized version of a sensational event that occurred in Japan in 1933, in which a disaffected university student incited two female classmates to commit suicide by jumping into an active volcano crater. The novel's title refers to both the diabolical influence that the protagonist exerts over her friends and the negative impulses within her that threaten to consume her. While undergoing a police investigation for her role in the incidents, the protagonist coolly and minutely describes her mentality and actions, but she manifests no remorse for her complicity in her friends' deaths. *MTM*

6. The book to which Tsushima refers, containing data that were translated from French and compiled by Takayama Kazuhiko, was published in 1971 and has been reprinted several times since then. *MTM*

TAKAHASHI: Like a Shinto shrine medium.

TSUSHIMA: That's right. To put it in Japanese terms. But conversely, she was so passive that she was really aggressive. You can see a typically female psychological mechanism operating in that kind of behavior. Maybe if you were to peel away various outer layers from the average woman, you'd uncover this kind of psychological structure. I kept thinking of that as I was reading *The Tempter*.

TAKAHASHI: Her society's interpretation of Joan of Arc's behavior and the secret in her heart that compelled the woman to act as she did are two different things, aren't they.

TSUSHIMA: She insisted that she was simply obeying God's orders, that she was just an instrument of his will, that she had no individual identity. Even during her trial, the bishops of the day couldn't understand such naïve claims, and so in the end she was sentenced to death.

What kind of responses did *The Tempter* receive from men? When I read that novel I really feel as if it's telling my own story.

TAKAHASHI: Women readers, authors among them, told me that I'd captured their feelings exactly. That the novel seemed to be describing their own states of mind. Male readers also told me that the novel was good, but their responses seemed a bit different from the women's. They expressed the surprise of someone who's been shown something that he hadn't known and feels stunned. So even when men praise it, that aspect of their response is different. For women, the kind of world I described in the novel is nothing extraordinary.

TSUSHIMA: Sensually, it really rings true. I'm impressed by how exquisitely you evoked a woman's sensibility the way you did.

TAKAHASHI: From the way female readers responded to the novel, I realized that the mentality I depicted wasn't rare or abnormal.

It's not that male readers said they didn't understand the book, but it was as if they were shocked at the revelation of something that they hadn't been aware of. Not any specific concrete thing, but [they were] startled that women experienced things in that way. . . .

TSUSHIMA: Ultimately, I think it's a matter of human beings understanding what their abilities are. Women seem to have a relatively strong intuitive sense of how life and death are intertwined.

The heroine of that novel is constantly thinking, I don't want to live; I don't want to live, but I don't want to die; I don't want to die, but I don't want to live, either. She's a university student who's caught up in that way of thinking. I understand that mentality very well. One feels as if one is being forced to live. For instance, I often think that women have as a special trait the ability to give birth. That's the moment when life begins, but conversely, at that point the moment of death becomes visible to you. You know the expression "to minister to a dying person"? For women, childbirth is somewhat more common of the two experiences. But when it comes to the mundane aspects of caring for a dying person, the people who nurse the sick in hospitals are women, and those who make funeral arrangements are women. It's usually women who handle the physical tasks related to those occasions. Because of that, women don't think about either life or death separately, in a linear fashion. We think of them as a circuitous, amorphous whole. A woman seems to view the world as a system that she's powerless to influence, and she instinctively adapts herself to that.

TAKAHASHI: That's right. Female physiology is embedded in that universal physiology that encompasses life and death. So in a sense, women don't think of life and death as separate from each other. Men tend to think of life and death in a conceptual way. They consider them in the context of an ideological system. But women's physiology is deeply enmeshed in those. That's a difference. Tsushima-san, you're regarded as an intellectual writer, and so am I. Even so, when I think and when I write, my whole body is involved in those processes. I think this is fundamentally different from a male writer's approach.

Even when I speak in intellectual terms, I feel as though I'm formulating my thoughts with my body. When I write, it's the same way. Even when I'm expressing myself intellectually, there's a corporeal element in my intellectual formulations. When a male author says or writes the same things, there's something different about it. The feel of it. Even when men and women use the same intellectual expressions, isn't there something different about how they engage with those words? Recently I've come to sense that acutely. Until the present age, men have assumed that only the world they perceived was the real world.

TSUSHIMA: That's what I think too. It's because the overwhelming majority of literary critics also are men. For example, in the past when a woman wrote something, it was men who evaluated that, and it seems that they'd often say, "I don't get this," or "This is no good." That still happens today too, I think.

TAKAHASHI: For example, when a male critic favorably reviews a male writer's works and when he writes approvingly of a female writer's, his praise is somewhat different, depending on whether the author of the work under review is male or female. When the critic is a man, something about his view of women's literature seems to be subtly different from a woman's understanding of it. I can't pinpoint just what that is. I don't mean that the critic is incompetent; it seems like a problem that can't be helped.

TSUSHIMA: To give another example, I'm often told that I'm intellectual, but it seems that the people who say that find it difficult to understand that my intellectualism has physiological underpinnings. Conversely, they don't seem to understand that when I don't overtly convey ideas in my fiction and I write in the same vein as the postwar "Carnal School" of writers did, then they treat the work as if it were *only* a blend of sensual impressions. They don't seem to realize that works like those actually have an ideological dimension.

The Intermediate Woman

TAKAHASHI: You know how Yoshiyuki Jun'nosuke doesn't portray women as human beings? He treats them as things. So when a woman reads his literature as if she were a thing, she can enjoy it. In other words, as if she were an object. I'm not a human being who exists only as an object, but I turn myself into an object in order to read Yoshiyuki's stories. When I do so, it's pleasant to read his fiction. But the part of me that isn't an object is saying, no, it's not that way. It's saying that, but it's useless to protest. I divide myself and read his work. In order to enjoy reading Yoshiyuki's novels, this is how I read them. Likewise, in order to enjoy reading Kawabata Yasunari's novels, I read them like this. But as a complete human being, part of me wants to protest, no, it's not like that.

In his fiction, Mr. Yoshiyuki never plunges deeply into the "Other" in order to explore the nature of the mystery that she embodies. He insists on maintaining a distance between himself and a woman and enjoys viewing her from there. He enjoys her mystery. But he never approaches her as an individual human being. So as long as he writes that kind of novel, I don't suppose that he can understand a woman as a human being. But there's beauty in that kind of portrayal, so I'm not saying that it's worthless.

Mr. Yoshiyuki doesn't depict women as main characters in his works, but in the first place, he doesn't portray women as human beings. It's the difference between a man enjoying himself with a bar hostess and falling in love with an innocent woman. When he falls in love with an innocent woman, his whole self is exposed to danger. His partner also exposes herself to danger when she approaches him. I think that through that engagement of one human being with another, something true emerges. But as long as a man just fools around with bar hostesses, there's no element of danger at all. Even if there's some danger, it's probably of a different kind; it's a slapstick comedy type of danger. It's not the kind of danger that's related to some insight into human nature.

TSUSHIMA: What's inescapable is that there's a particular society, and a person is born into that particular society. Likewise, the novel too can't escape, no matter how it tries, from Japan's male-female relationship mold. So I think that the pattern that inevitably emerges in a Japanese novel is of a woman yielding and a man snatching only what he's looking for and going on his way.

TAKAHASHI: What you've just said—you and I belong to different generations, but as a member of your generation, do you feel that way?

TSUSHIMA: Yes, absolutely.

TAKAHASHI: Is that so? I asked because I thought that things were changing.

TSUSHIMA: I also thought, during my student days, that society had been transformed. But after I left the school environment and began to live in the real world, it seemed that on the surface things had changed, but people's way of thinking hadn't changed a bit.

TAKAHASHI: During my university days, I too felt that it was a totally new age. But after graduating and going out into the world, joining another family and such, I found that things were as old-fashioned as ever.

TSUSHIMA: As a student you had a sense of liberation, so afterwards, the discovery that things hadn't changed was all the more of a shock, wasn't it? Gradually I began thinking that the same thing was true of the novel, and I became very conscious of questioning why that was.

What always bothers me is the distinction made between woman as mother and woman as sex object. Men tend to consider those as completely separate from each other. It seems that when the subject of maternal instinct is brought up, it arouses a powerful, sentimental longing. But from my point of view, there's actually no such thing. I feel that it's a notion created by men. The idea of woman as sex object is just the same, I think. Surely the reality of womanhood lies between those two extremes. It's not that I'm irritated by the idea of woman as a purely sexual being, but I get irritated because that image is usually polarized against the idea of woman as a personification of maternal nurture. If a woman is only sexual, then why not try to understand her just in those terms?

TAKAHASHI: Men tend to classify real women according to their desires. But real women can't be classified that way—both aspects are intermingled. You expressed it as real women being in between the sexual and the maternal, and, Tsushima-san, you explore that intermediate zone in your fiction. I think that especially in your recent novel, *Child of Fortune*, you convey that very clearly.[7] Maybe your awareness of that won't be well understood by men. The idea that women are in an intermediate zone. I think that's one of your main themes.

TSUSHIMA: Whether you force women to personify maternal instinct or you reduce them to sex objects, it's the same thing. I want to make people a little more conscious of how much pain they cause women by doing that. To take maternal instinct as an example, if you assume, as a premise, that such a thing exists, then women shouldn't feel any resistance to having children or to raising children. Usually a woman is docile, so she goes along with the conventional wisdom. Then one day she discovers a completely different side of herself. There are moments when she really wants to murder her own children. At those times, I think the violence of that impulse drives her to the point of wondering, am I completely lacking in maternal feeling? In other words, am I not a woman? I think when women are stereotyped as sex objects, the same kind of thing happens. Women want to be understood differently, as complete human beings, so to be viewed only as a sex object is painful to them.

The Desire for Vitality

TAKAHASHI: When men read *Child of Fortune*, I wonder if they're repelled by the female menstrual cycle. That doesn't bother me. What I mainly sense is the loneliness of the woman who's driven to experience a false pregnancy. To use the word "loneliness" gives it an old-fashioned nuance, and I don't intend that. But in the midst of the free, liberated human relations of contemporary Japan, women's lives are all the lonelier; they're truly lonely. I think that you suggestively evoke that loneliness in the form of a false pregnancy. From a woman's point of view that's not especially weird. But probably men don't understand that aspect of the novel.

It's not that her desire for a child causes the false pregnancy, is it. If that were it, the work would be simplistic, and it wouldn't have a particularly contemporary significance. Because the novel is hinting that it's something different from that, it's extremely good. It's not that the heroine merely

---

7. The heroine of Tsushima's acclaimed novel, *Child of Fortune* (*Chōji*, 1978; tr. 1983), is a divorced mother who earns a modest living as a piano teacher and has a young daughter. Her job is unfulfilling, and her relationships with her family members and sexual partners lack the warmth and support that she craves. While having an affair she develops symptoms of pregnancy, but her fantasies of blissful intimacy are crushed when she discovers that her condition is imaginary. *MTM*

wants a child. Of course, maybe she does want a child, but maybe she's also yearning for her dead retarded brother, and maybe she's also yearning for something like "vitality" in this huge modern city, where human beings don't relate to each other in a human way. But to express it analytically like that distorts the whole work. To me, the imaginary pregnancy suggests the kind of void that's at the center of the woman's life. The fact that the heroine is driven to experience a false pregnancy.

But until now, Japanese women's literature has been interpreted analytically, in various ways, by men, and it seems that certain theories have become entrenched. There's some gap between men's and women's understanding of women's literature.

TSUSHIMA: If men and women, as members of opposite sexes, could write works that would emotionally appeal to each other, that would be ideal. . . .

TAKAHASHI: In that novel I feel that you yourself, whether consciously or not, are yearning for vitality. The novel's heroine is, and so are you. In this huge Japanese metropolis, where people's vitality hasn't been nurtured and has gradually drained away. That's the context of the novel, isn't it? The heroine is searching for life; she's pursuing it with her whole heart and soul.

Words That Flow like Breath

TSUSHIMA: Like the female characters in *The Tempter*, real women too grapple with the question, "Why am I alive?" and they wonder what in the world the value of their lives is. I really want men to understand this.

TAKAHASHI: Yes. Men have precise words to articulate what the meaning of their lives is. But maybe women are faithful to their intuitive understanding of their lives.

TSUSHIMA: I'd like to think so. But at some point one can't help but ask that question. Then she may respond to herself: I don't know why I'm alive, but as a way of expressing the question, I think I'll just do something. It's that kind of impulse. "Will" is a bit too strong a word for it.

TAKAHASHI: It's not that you engage in some kind of action in order to rebel against common sense, right?

TSUSHIMA: That's right. It's an attitude like this: anyway, I just want to know what it means for me to be alive. It's hard silently to accept not understanding the purpose of my life, so I'll just keep walking like this. It's that kind of feeling.

TAKAHASHI: By taking some action one tries to confirm why she's alive, but I don't know whether one can really confirm that or not. Woman is a physiological creature, so words can't help her do that. To put it a different way—so as not to create misunderstanding by using the word "physiological," then "carnal," or "sensual"—she grasps life on a deeper level, as a whole. In my case, as I said before, I use intellectual words and manage to make my point, but I always end up feeling that words are totally inadequate to express my understanding of my life.

In general, women like to chat, but those words too come from the body, and they seem to gush out inexhaustibly.

TSUSHIMA: That's right. So there's no purpose, and one isn't even at all conscious of what one is saying.

TAKAHASHI: Words emerge from the body like breathing.

TSUSHIMA: So often men discount them. Take, for example, a married couple—that familiar scene of a quarrel. The woman says something, and it's completely misunderstood by her husband—always. The man wants to do something to please his wife, so he thinks he'll go along with what she says. So when she asks, "Do you love me?" he replies, "Sure I do." Then the woman gets all the more annoyed and says, "What's that supposed to mean?" or else, "When you put it that way, it only proves that you don't love me," and they go on and on like that, at odds with each other. I think it's that difference—toward how they use language.

TAKAHASHI: I agree. A married couple's quarrel is fraught with misunderstandings, as you've just described. For any married couple, there's always a gap, so the husband feels that there's no woman who's as stupid as his own wife, and conversely, the woman thinks that there's no man as uncomprehending as her husband. I think the communication gap between man and woman is clearly exposed in that most intimate of relationships, between husband and wife. If the other person is a stranger and there's a misunderstanding between the two of you, it doesn't matter. You shrug it off and say to yourself, oh, that's not what I meant. But husband and wife, who face each other squarely, end up most acutely aware of the distance between man and woman. When verbal communication between husband and wife doesn't mesh, isn't it because they're living the truth? Isn't it because they're closing in on the truth about those fundamental differences? If it's a stranger, it doesn't matter at all. Even if there are minor verbal miscommunications, it doesn't bother you. What I said about husband and wife applies to lovers too.

Women too, in most cases, don't communicate with each other. But if two women understand each other at a certain depth, their verbal communication will be satisfying. In the realm of Japanese literature, when it comes to assessing the merits of a literary work, it's been the plight of women writers all along to feel that they're not in step with the critics. I think that probably male writers have seldom felt this way.

Various people offer critical commentaries on literature, don't they. The majority of them are male literary critics, but male authors make critical appraisals too. Their standards for evaluating literature seem somehow different from women's. I think that female authors have always felt this. But even when a male author feels that his works aren't understood by a critic because of differences in the pair's respective positions or their personalities, I think that he rarely senses those unbridgeable communication gaps that I've talked about just now. Because it's men who make authoritative pronouncements. Whether it's a literary critic or a male author, those who decide what's good and what's bad are men. Based on their judgments, certain trends take shape.

I'd been thinking these things to myself for quite a while, and when I recently discussed them with Ohba Minako, I found that she'd been thinking the same things to herself. So I've begun to feel that women writers in general are in agreement about this. Today you've voiced the same view, so I think it may be all right to say publicly that women writers share this opinion about male literary critics' evaluation of their work. I recall that Saegusa Kazuko also once said something similar.

TSUSHIMA: When I consider the times that I serve as a book reviewer for a man's work, I'm conscious from the moment I begin writing the review that I am a woman and the book's author is a man. For men, I imagine it's not like that. They seem to approach a work as one human being evaluating the work of another, although probably they're vaguely aware of the category "woman writer." But I think it would be good if the critic could take the attitude, "I'm just a man and this author is a woman, so it's natural that there will be a gap in understanding between us," and to read the work as something utterly alien to him. But in most cases the reviewer doesn't think like this.

Witches

TAKAHASHI: . . . . I happen to have taken up in my novels only shocking topics such as a woman who kidnaps a child and the like. But I think it's a mistake to understand the demonic element within women only by such extreme examples. I sense those dark impulses within myself, so I'm interested in exploring them. It's not that I've made a conscious decision to focus on the theme of human evil because I think it's important to draw attention to it. The theme has found its way into my fiction because I feel those tendencies inside myself.

TSUSHIMA: In Europe during the Middle Ages, women were called witches because their parents were drifters or foreigners or they were fatherless, or because of similar circumstances of birth, and so they weren't recognized as citizens. Conditions like those foster a desire for one's own place to live. When people live in a state of oppression, their sensitivity becomes extremely acute. And they become much more attuned than the average person to other people's sadness and suffering. So a woman like that would take beer, or any ordinary thing at all, call it a secret remedy, and offer it to people, saying, "This is medicine; if you drink it you'll recover." She realized that people are influenced by the power of suggestion. With the sensitivity of the oppressed, she knew too that human beings' illnesses are also healed through the power of suggestion. She'd perform good deeds of that sort. On the other hand, she'd see someone who looked at a glance to be happy, and she'd shrewdly perceive the hypocrisy in that. She knew how fragile that sort of happiness was, so then a kind of mean impulse would spring up in her. She'd see through to the person's most hidden, vulnerable place and realize that if she did such-and-such, the entire structure of the person's life would collapse. So she'd try poking at that place a bit—that sort of thing. Then when the person's life began to wobble, she'd say to herself, oh, it's collapsing, just as I thought. And as she continued doing those sorts of things, people would begin to say, "That woman is making secret, magic potions." And "That woman put a hex on that house and made it collapse." So as these kinds of incidents accumulated, they came to be considered proof that the woman was a witch. It's not that she did such things with a specific intention of doing evil, right?

TAKAHASHI: Her sensitivity was well honed. Women have been oppressed, so like any oppressed people, their sensitivity becomes acute. So a woman stares hard at her oppressor—maybe it's a man, maybe it's a social authority figure, maybe it's another woman—and she's able to see that person completely and clearly. She's clairvoyant, so she's able to make others happy, and she's able to destroy others simply by pricking them with the tip of a needle. I suppose she has the keen perception that develops naturally in oppressed people. And precisely because she's oppressed, her energy is tremendously suppressed. So when she acts decisively, that energy gushes forth powerfully. When people witnessed such incidents, the person responsible for them must have appeared to them like a witch. Women who behaved in that way came to be labeled "witch," but maybe the tendencies that you've described can be found within ordinary women living at the present time.

Women writers older than me were extremely socially oppressed—physically they were constrained, and internally too they were constrained by morality. Compared to those people, I probably appear to be living as quite a liberated woman, but I too feel that I'm writing from a position of being constrained. I think that you're more liberated than I, but I suppose there are areas in which you aren't.

TSUSHIMA: This is a trivial thing, but, for example, in daily life, if you're a woman writer, probably you make you own meals, you answer the phone, you do all those things for yourself. Even while you're writing a novel, part of you has to pay attention to other things. Male authors—I don't say all of them—have a woman who tends to those things. I feel as if they're using someone to take care of their menial tasks and devoting selves entirely to their writing. A person's sensibilities are shaped by her daily routine. These days I think that in that respect there's a huge difference between male and female authors.

Women as Human Beings

TAKAHASHI: When I write a novel, first I discover my heroine within me. That character is my alter ego, and while she's not identical to this self who's actually living, what she feels and thinks is just what I feel and think. The novel develops accordingly. During the writing process, I of course think about fiction-writing techniques and how to express my theme. But the work seems to unfold naturally, like a great river flowing.

TSUSHIMA: At first I wrote fiction feeling that I wanted to take as my subject human beings themselves. For me, I felt that meant women. I began to portray women, but in the context of human issues. So when I created a protagonist in order to explore a theme, that character was a woman. In the case of *Child of Fortune*, I wanted to create a situation of isolation. I think that various situations are suitable for literary treatment. For example, to describe a woman who's playing the role of a lover is fine, and a spinster's life is fine too. Any number of ordinary situations that have nothing to do with literature can be used. When one takes a close acquaintance as a model certain problems may arise, so I thought maybe I'd better take someone almost like myself. Because I could treat someone in my position as one example, a typical example, of the isolated situation in which contemporary women find themselves, I used a divorced woman.

TAKAHASHI: You speak of using a situation of "isolation" as a setting. The word is different, but, like you, I'm inspired by conditions of "unhappiness." When I think of a woman who's trapped in unhappy circumstances, my imagination catches fire and my characters start to come to life. You talked about isolation, and I think that what I'm talking about is a very similar state. I have no desire to write about a happy woman.

TSUSHIMA: Society, by and large, is a male society. I think that in most cases when a woman is happy, it's because she has very skillfully fit herself into that male society. She lives in a way that's secure.

TAKAHASHI: When one deviates from that path, one becomes isolated, right?

TSUSHIMA: Being in such a situation also helps a woman see things clearly, I think.

TAKAHASHI: People who are on the periphery see things clearly, don't they? So when you use that type of woman as your heroine, she's easy to portray. Even male authors probably aren't inclined to create a happy individual as their main character. Probably only an isolated or an unhappy character stimulates a man's imagination too. Human beings are fundamentally isolated and unhappy, and people who see the way things really are, realize that. This is the human condition, so men and women are the same in this regard, I think. I'm not sure how to express what the difference is.

TSUSHIMA: Because they're different they're drawn to each other, and through that connection each becomes an individual human. And from that interaction, novels emerge too. That's what I want to think. But there's always a social imbalance, and as long as there's an imbalance, men's literature and women's literature will be at variance with each other.

TAKAHASHI: Tsushima-san, you say that being socially oppressed makes women different from men, and that's one thing that can be said. Another is that men and women are fundamentally different in some ways, and those differences are irreconcilable. And when men impose differences on them that women feel aren't real, they can't say that. So women have suppressed themselves for a very long time.

Women's Language and the National Language

TOMIOKA TAEKO

I do not remember when it was, but I read a commentary entitled something like "A Woman Writer, Again!" by a (male) writer who had served as a judge for a literary journal's New Writer of the Year Award. One of the winners had been a woman. Not too long ago someone else wrote an anonymous newspaper article entitled "A Woman Again!" after a female poet had won the New Writer of the Year Award for a poetry journal.

There are certainly many women skilled at self-expression in the literary world. But when it comes to the total "number" of women writers, poets, and critics, it is too meager to even compare with that of men. If a few women stand out by consecutively winning an award, why do men always respond, "A woman again!" or "Another woman writer!"?

Such senseless remarks convince me not to trust those who unconsciously use the term *"joryū"* [women's style], be they men or women. The *"ryū"* of *"joryū"* means simply "style," but this term for a "women's style" conveys societal conventions [about gender]. It is interesting that before the term "woman writer" *[joryū sakka]* became popular, the expression used was *"keishū sakka"* [talented lady of the inner chamber].

"Not another woman!" Anyone can see in these words a kind of conscious presumption—no, more of an unconscious process—that "literature (so supposedly high class) is a man's domain." This kind of condescension is often used in reference to "women's" work. "Exceeding our expectations for women." "Men are also thrilled with it," etc. These kinds of expressions are used for the most part without reflection. Now, instead of "Women are no good [as writers]," they write "She does pretty well for a woman," or "She is hanging in there." That's why they say "Men are thrilled with her writing." These phrases often appear in newspapers and journals when they discuss a "woman."

The first language children learn is their "mother's language" *[haha no ko-*

TRANSLATED BY JOAN E. ERICSON AND YOSHIKO NAGAOKA. From Tomioka Taeko, " 'Onna no kotoba' to 'kuni no kotoba' " (Women's language and the national language), in *Tomioka Taeko shū* 8 (The collected works of Tomioka Taeko) (Chikuma shobō, 1999), pp. 85–97. " 'Onna no kotoba' to 'kuni no kotoba' " was originally a section in Tomioka's essay series *Fuji no koromo ni asano fusuma* (Wisteria clothing and linen quilts), which was serialized in *Fujin kōron* (Woman's forum) from January to December 1983; it appeared i[n] pp. 470–479. It was subsequently published in Tomioka Taeko, *Fuji no kor[...]* (Chūō kōron sha, 1984), pp. 107–123.

toba]. Having been raised with this language, they are then forced to learn the "national language" *[kuni no kotoba]* when they go to school. School is the mechanical system that erases the "mother's language." In other words, children make their way along the educational path from "mother's tongue" *[bogo]* to the "mother tongue" *[bokokugo]*. This trajectory also marks a transition from "women's language" *[onna no kotoba]* to "men's language" *[otoko no kotoba]*. Consequently, most people spend their lives as bilingual with "mother's language" and the "national language."

The "mother's language" is also the "regional language" *[chihō no kotoba]*, where the mother lives or hails from. However, the "national language," which you are forced to learn at school, was created at the "core" *[chūō]*. Here also is a forced bilingualism of the "provincial periphery" and the "core." The "national language" of the "core," which schools teach, towers above "natal languages" and "dialects" and extinguishes them. Those who have not attended school are embarrassed to speak in public. Those who can use only "regional language" tend to stand mute. The language one is forced to learn at school may circulate nationally, but in reality it may not be used very much. The first expression I was taught to read in elementary school (then called the school for the people) was "It bloomed, it bloomed, the cherry bloomed," but I don't think I have or ever will use that expression my whole life. People may exclaim, "The cherry bloomed, didn't it?" Or "They're really pretty, aren't they—the cherry blossoms?" But they probably don't say, "It bloomed, it bloomed, the cherry bloomed."

But people continue to learn the "national language," following the models set by the school, the nation, and the core. Before long they lose the ability to speak the other, earlier languages, which in turn causes them to grow ashamed of these ways of speaking. While the natal and peripheral languages are close to the climate and the natural features of a region and to everyday life, the school's "national language" represents knowledge or a means toward knowledge. This language has clearly become superior.

For this reason, there developed the presumption that the more education one has, the more familiar one is with language. Once, a visitor to our house asked my mother, who was born during the Meiji period and who only had three years of elementary education, "Is your husband in residence?" My mother for a second didn't know what "in residence" meant, and she answered, "Yes, he is in residence," and was laughed at for referring to her own husband in such a polite way. When I saw this, I wondered if my mother would be falsely convicted if she were mistakenly taken to court. The judicial language employed at court is based on Chinese-derived vocabulary, which is taught at school, and I knew that my mother would not know most of it. The "national language" (here I mean the "country's language," or *kokugo,* the subject taught at school) alienates and discriminates against the "mother's language" or "mother tongue."

Children first learn language from their mothers. In other words, they first learn "women's language." However, both boys and girls later are separated from "women's language." When they become adults and speak in a public place or write a document or letter for public consumption, it must be via the "national language" created in the "core." Moreover, they are required to use a national language based on "Chinese characters" and "Chinese-derived vocabulary." What uneducated ordinary people particularly fear about talking in front of people (in other words, in a public place) is that they will have problems knowing how to use "Chinese-derived vocabulary." How-to books such as *How to Prepare a Wedding Reception Speech* or *How to Write a Letter* sell very well. Also, for example, the stereotype that people from Tōhoku, the northern part of Japan, are taciturn is attributable to the fact that they become ashamed of their "regional language" since people in the "core" cannot understand the speech of these peripheral immigrants. This attitude is exactly what foreigners harbor toward the Japanese; Europeans and Americans especially claim that the Japanese are not talkers and are said to be incomprehensible mumblers who only grin and never answer clearly, yes or no. People from Tōhoku are not by nature silent, nor do Japanese, as a group, simply mumble incoherently.

The "mother's language" is meant for conversation. The "national language" that you learn at school is meant for reading and writing. Here, also, there is a tendency to make the written word superior to the spoken. Regional dialects are spoken and have not been given the status of written languages. "Women's language," like regional dialects, is not written and is subordinate to the "national language" created by men.

Regional folk entertainment is not derived from the "core" and then spread uniformly across the nation. In the same way, there is diversity from the outset in each region's language. Variety in language means variety in culture. In other words, "Japanese language" and "Japanese culture" originally had this kind of diversity. Consequently, "mother's language" is varied.

There is no strict sense of sexual distinction or gender in Japanese vocabulary. Therefore, unlike the earlier women's movement in America, there was no fervent fight against language discrimination. I considered the whole process English speakers underwent quite troublesome—having to replace "chairman," the one presiding over a meeting, with "chairperson," for example, or replacing a masculine pronoun with "he or she." The English word "poetess" is almost dead, and "poet" is used for both men and women; however, in Japan we still use "female poet" with utter indifference.

There was originally no writing system in Japan. Spoken Japanese became a written language by employing a (Chinese) script introduced from the outside. However, it was difficult to transcribe the already existent Japanese language into complicated characters that had been developed to convey foreign sounds (and of course meanings). That difficult work of transcription could be accomplished only by one segment of the elite intelligentsia. It was the nonelite and women who first simplified the phonetic symbols of Chinese characters into what is known as the *kana* syllabary. And it is said that the Japanese writing system developed due to the appearance of this phonetic syllabary. We today are indebted to this nonelite invention when we write Japanese language. However, we tend to forget that this system is a shorthand version of Chinese characters. In other words, we tend to forget that the "national language" is indebted to the nonelite and to women, who simplified Chinese characters and made them usable. Therefore, even now the convention has spread that those who know many difficult Chinese characters are intellectually superior, so much so that an adult working for a company who writes and submits this letter of resignation— "Since I am sick, I would like to quit my job," all in the *kana* with no Chinese characters—would be thought imbecilic.

Songs and tales originally appeared before there was a written language. At that time, regardless of whether one was a man or a woman, one could sing a song or recite a story. It was much later that songs, stories, and scholarship became exclusive to men through means of the written language. Furthermore, once a stratum among women was able easily to employ written language, it was only natural that women would express themselves through literary forms, just like men. Even though the "feminine-style literature" of the Heian period was the literary domain of aristocratic women, today it is not so restricted. When a critic writes, "Not another woman!" he is conveying nothing less than the widely held presumption that written expression is still a male prerogative. This is despite the fact that it was through the nonelite and women that written Japanese was freed from being recorded exclusively with Chinese characters.

Even now it is said that the nonelite, women, and youths are the ones who "destroy Japanese language" or "corrupt Japanese language." Those who deem this corruption of Japanese to be disgraceful are usually language elites. Or at least think they are. What supports the elite sensibility is their familiarity with the ancient conventions and their awareness of their knowledge and schooling concerning the classics. Using this, then, as their authority, *they* threaten the language of the nonelites.

Words possess the capacity to discriminate, depending on how they are used. In an attempt to avoid many "discriminatory words" by "rephrasing" them, the old connotation can be shifted to the new word that replaces the old. For example, even the simple verb "to help" may be "loaded." It has been a long time since *"jochū-san"* [one of the women; maid] became "Otetsudai-san" [Miss Helper] or *"otetsudai"* [helper]. However, when the simple verb "to help" *(tetsudau)* was turned into the noun *"otetsudai,"* the new word adopted the same discriminatory connotation. The simple word "help" was tainted by association with the word it replaced.

Women themselves do not realize that the common noun "woman" is also often used in a discriminatory manner. When a wife says, "My husband's got a woman," the word "woman" clearly means someone separate from the wife's social class. The wife is a woman, but she takes the position that she is a different kind of "woman" from her husband's "woman." The connotation is the same when she says, "A woman tricked my husband." The "woman" whom the wife denounces experiences more prejudice than the "maid, one of many women." The word "lover" in the phrase "he got his lover pregnant" is also certainly discriminatory, and the word "widow" [literally, "a person who is not yet dead"] can be occasionally discriminatory.

The one who utters the phrase "My husband's got a woman" versus "My husband's having an affair" clearly intends to convey different meanings. In the same way there is a distinction between saying "feminine-style writer" *[joryū sakka]* and "woman writer" *[onna no sakka]*. We often hear a wife say, "My husband's got a woman," but hardly ever "My husband's having an affair." Here there is ample sense of opprobrium by women toward the "woman." However, we cannot include this in men's discriminatory attitudes toward women.

For women, the awareness of discrimination in the word "woman" comes from an awareness of social class. However, the discriminatory attitudes that men feel toward women are based on their "sexual social class." It must be pointed out as a matter of course that the battle between the sexes is not included in the fight that men carry out for themselves among the social classes of society.

Women are aware of their sexual privilege. Concepts of "a mother's consciousness" and "the right of motherhood," where "only women can bear children," discriminate against men. Men are nearly powerless in the face of "a mother's consciousness." Men's recognition of these capacities could explain their strategy to subvert or overturn biology's rank order. Perhaps this is the reason that if men cannot deal with "mother," then their only recourse is to attack "women."

It may be partly because I have a low voice, but sometimes over the telephone I am mistaken for a man. Probably it is more because at the time I do not use "a woman's way of speaking." In other words, I assume that it is because I sound very blunt. Girls live with "mother's language" when they are young, move over to a sexless language, learn "men's language," and then, before long, are urged to live using "women's language." When "women's language" takes a privileged form, it is usually when a more polite language than is necessary is used as proof of one's high status. "Language is proof of one's national origin," and at the same time that "language is proof of one's social class." No matter how elite that social background, the fact that the language is effective only within that class means that social distinctions rely on nothing more than jargon. Elite language is essentially no different than a grifter's deceiving gab. In this sense, no matter what its class context, "women's language" also is a secret social code.

Some argue that women should use "women's language" when they speak out against sexual discrimination. But that practice could be construed as hypocritically self-serving. For a woman to use "men's language" with men is contradictory and could perpetuate sexual disparities; for a woman constantly to use "women's language" risks perpetuating its limits as a stigmatizing code. In a society controlled by "men's language," "women's language" is a kind of dialect. If it does not ingratiate itself to "men's language," there is no choice but to create an Esperanto between the way men and women speak. Men may not see a need for such an Esperanto, but women cannot help but see a radical linguistic need. This problem goes way beyond a girl's use of the male first-person *"boku."* Scholarly discourse on the relationship of power and language is all very well, but the link of language to power has been fully apparent in daily life ever since the beginning of language.

From the time that we attain the age of reason, we are required to indicate the sex for every activity. It is the same for language. A woman's signature is also socially required in language. And yet, for example, a female member of the Diet is not allowed to address the Diet assembly using "women's language." Women are forced to be bilingual both in public and in private. It is interesting that women continue to speak two different kinds of language, reflecting an awareness of both the inconvenience and the practicality; women can choose to use bilingualism to their advantage and not simply as a weakness.

When a man talks about his wife to another person, he uses *"kanai* = in the house"; *"kamisan* = my old lady"; *"nyōbō* = woman in the room"; *"uchi no yatsu* = my 'woman'"; or *"uchi no yomehan* = my bride" and except in unusual circumstances does not say *"uchi no tsuma ga* = my wife (as the agent)" or *"uchi no tsuma wa* = my wife (as the topic of the conversation)." A woman also refers to her husband as *"shujin* = master"; *"teishu* = master of the house"; *"yadoroku* = my old man"; or *"uchi no hito* = my person" and probably does not usually say *"otto wa* = the man (as the topic of conversation)" or *"otto ga* = the man (as the agent)." Which of these terms of address you use when you refer to your spouse depends on the person with whom you are speaking and the relationship you have to him/her.

In this society it is actually very difficult to reject completely the original meaning of "master" or "master of the house" in reference to one's husband. The meaning derives from a very class-based master and servant relationship. However, if you completely let up in your opposition to these terms, the reality is that the establishment of equality between husband and wife will emotionally fall apart. "My master" is "women's language," but "my man" is more Esperanto than "men's language." Although "women's language" recognizes the radicalism of demolishing control and power, one comes up against the contradiction, about which one cannot help but be conscious, of a radical conservative element found in an Esperanto between men and women. However, I would rather choose the conservatism of Esperanto. I also believe that for some time to come women need to make the same choice.

Esperanto is meant to be a neutral language. Because it is a neutral language, it eliminates the cultural signifiers that words carry. "Women's language" carries women's culture, and the language itself is women's culture. In contrast, there is no trace of women's culture in an Esperanto phrase like "my man." When women publicly use such an Esperanto, they cannot help but use it consciously and strategically.

It can be said that people who deliberately like to say and write difficult things usually like authority and power, but everything should be easy to understand with Esperanto. Just as "men's language" is difficult for women to understand, "women's language" is probably difficult for men to understand. A certain linguist wrote, wondering if women thought the same way they spoke—"Such and such, you know" [naninani na no yo]. The science of linguistics has not yet reached the "deep structure" of "women's language."

There are a relatively large number of female poets, novelists, and essayists but extremely few reviewers or critics. This paucity is because unlike songs, poems, and fiction, reviews and criticism are expressed in "men's language." If women used "women's language" for their reviews and criticism, men would not take them seriously. Therefore, women who are able to write critiques are inevitably obliged to use "men's language." If there were criticism that used "women's language," no matter how insightful or trenchant, it would be ignored by men because of the language in which it was written. This neglect guarantees social oblivion. Men rarely quote women's "thoughts" in their reviews and criticism. It is ironic that Sartre did not have to address the concept of "the first sex" in his writing, but de Beauvoir was forced to write *The Second Sex* with "men's language."

Men who critique using "men's language" are usually responsible for establishing the reputations of female writers. Unconsciously, women express themselves in a manner "for men." Writing "for men" takes the form of fitting into the category of "things women write" rather than writing with "men's language." Whether conscious or unconscious, there is a use of "women's language" that caters to the reviews written in "men's language." A "female-school" poet or a "feminine-style" fiction writer does not invite male hostility since they do not challenge "men's language." Men's praise for that which is usually written with "women's language" includes such comments as, "We can't match women" and "Men have to pay more attention to language," and is not in response to the "thought" that is found in the writing.

Yasumaru Yoshio's impressive critical biography of Deguchi Nao, the unschooled widow of a carpenter in Tanba Fukuchiyama, treats the "thoughts" of her "brushstrokes" seriously. This impoverished female had never learned to read and write, had never even written a word in her life, but suddenly began to write. Her writings are a record kept in the language she used for everyday speech. Her declaration for "making the world a better place" *[yonaoshi]* was Deguchi Nao's revolutionary manifesto. However, it was treated at the time as an act by someone "possessed" or insane. In other words, no matter how radical the thinking, the "woman's language" of a person who was raised in the provinces without knowing the "national language" was completely rejected by the hegemonic discourse. Nao's thought was transmitted only after having been translated into the "national language."

Poetry and song were not originally composed in the "national language." Moreover, the expectation that poetry and song should be read in a written form is rather recent in the long history of such compositions. However, currently, more stress is given to meaning in poetry and song rather than sound. That is because, as a matter of course, that which can be set down by means of the written word cannot thereby escape incorporating the logic of "men's language." Poetry became difficult, and for the masses, what was left over was the poetic debris of a "commodity" like the lyrics to a popular song. "Poets" became more and more elite. Even though elite poets recognize that poetry is gradually disappearing in the "works" of the "poets" like themselves, they cannot easily let go of that power. In the end, they are dragged along by the "language of the nation-state" *[kokka no kotoba]*, and ordinary people come across only the dregs of poetry.

In addition, as society becomes more controlled, language becomes more symbolic. What we have computers learn is not language but symbols. Language has spirituality, something lacking in symbols. Therefore, we expect symbols to be limitless. People who possess a large number of symbols are articulate. Symbols are the farthest thing from the spoken "mother's language" and "regional language." Such languages tolerate the unnecessary, since there is no expectation that they be written down, but symbols do not allow this. Symbols respect efficiency.

The "national language" is becoming more symbolic. Originally, the written word was no more than a convenient means to establish language. However, contemporary society, hypercontrolling, is intentionally and systematically promoting the symbolic lexicon. "Mother's language," "regional language," and "women's language" are further alienated since they oppose this symbolic language. "Youth language" *[wakamono no kotoba]*, the subculture of every society, resists these symbols with its indifference. It is always targeted as the chief instigator of disorder in elite language.

"Women's language" was almost devoid of vocabulary to talk about sex. Expressions such as *this, that,* or *down there* were euphemisms for sexual terms. Of late, with the adoption of foreign terms such as "sex" and "to have sex," these words have overtaken the inconvenience of pronouns. However, a word like "intercourse" is not "women's language." That women talk about sex sentimentally and emotionally is because that is the only possible vocabulary in "women's language." Sex was usually discussed both in "men's language" as dialect and in "men's language" as the "language of the nation-state." In other words, a secret language has been used to speak of sex, and, for the most part, even now that is the case.

The language "chosen for liberating the people" in early Meiji adopted a style, as in the documents of the Imperial Rescript of Education, a language of the nation-state that was unable to deviate from a kind of sutra-esque codification (we are relieved that we do not really understand it). Today the situation remains the same, because language completely shifted away from "mother's language" and "women's language." Just as "women's language" could not speak directly about sex, so it lacked the vocabulary for politics. Matters of politics excluded "women's language." Sex also ignored "women's language." Rather than "women's language" moving toward "politics" and "sexual matters," we have reached the stage where we need to adopt a kind of Esperanto for "women's language."

Reading material referred to as pornographic fiction also is written using "men's language." Nowadays there are women who write pornographic fiction, but the number is very low. The purpose of pornographic fiction and that kind of reading material is to create excitement in the reader (this is called lust in the "national language") through intentionally elaborating on the sections with the sexual acts. Among those who write pornographic fiction, there are those who use "women's language," but that is only as a token gesture of "women's language" as seen from a man's perspective. In the end, this kind of pornographic fiction is written for men. Since pornographic fiction for men employs the tropes of gazing on women masturbating, heterosexual intercourse, or solitary peeping Toms, it is not a style that incites women's desire. Depicting women in this way will always only be material for men's "lust."

When women must use "women's language" to express their sexuality, they feel just like a flustered patient in front of her gynecologist. The inexplicable embarrassment they feel when forced to talk about sexual diseases or symptoms without using medical terminology is mostly related to the irritation that "women's language" cannot accommodate these topics. In other words, when it comes to sex, daily speech (as contrasted with medical terminology) uses the language of pornographic fiction or similar reading material. The use of pornographic language—and the inexplicably embarrassing world that pornographic fiction reveals to us—is unavoidable. For someone formally to say "I sought sexual intercourse with that person" does not constitute pornographic fiction. Pornographic-like conventions must be used such as "He slowly moved toward the slippery, gently sloping hill, where the spring gushes forth from the marsh at the bottom of the hollow." Although this may seem to be ordinary daily language, it is definitely not. It is a kind of "men's language"; more precisely it can be called a dialect that has pidginized the "national language."

Pidgin shares with Esperanto the fact that it is nationless, but its occurrence and content are totally different. Most books categorize pidgin as a "deformed business English." We are meant to surmise that it developed out of the necessity of conducting trade and commerce. It is a language that inevitably arises between a nation that controls a colony and an indigenous people who have been colonized. Or it is the language that develops between an immigrant's language and that of the new country. Immediately after Japan lost in World War II, the English of the pan-pan girls, or hookers, was pidgin English, as was the English used by the first and second generation of Japanese who emigrated to Hawaii. Furthermore, when Africans were taken to the new continent as slaves, as a matter of course, a pidgin language arose between them and their owners. Even now, in many parts of many countries, pidgin English or pidgin French or pidgin Spanish is used.

I have pointed out that women occupy a liminal position within the Japanese language and thus have no choice but to use a kind of Esperanto to navigate between "men's language" and "women's language." My intention was to prevent "women's language" from being pidginized under the domination of the "national language." "Women's language" is the native tongue of women, and it may be inevitable that over time "things fall apart." But if women continue to have no choice but to appear in the public sphere through a manipulation of a pidginized "national language," then we can only conclude that "women's language" has been eroded and colonized. Anyone who wants to play it safe will certainly not defend "women's language." In fact, in their "speech" "progressive" women tend to cross over to either "men's language," the "national language," or a pidginized "national language," without even being aware of these shifts. Women writers who adopt these styles have only been able to extract offhanded remarks (hardly criticism) from men, such as "Women do a great job"—in other words, "Women are now skilled at using men's language."

It is deceptive to think that the "national language" differs from "women's language" or "regional languages" because it is universally shared. A common language originates organically, mothered by necessity. My point is that when speakers of "women's language" and "regional language" seek a common means through which to communicate with men and the national elite, they will have no choice but to create a kind of Esperanto. We expect women who articulate their ideas to be self-aware and to actualize these language practices. We find pleasure in knowing that an unexplored territory for expression still remains.

| | | The Subject of Women's Literature and the
Transformation of Its Consciousness

NAKAYAMA KAZUKO

In the afterword to her recent collection of essays, *Farewell to the Age of Men [Sayonara otoko no jidai]*, the author Saegusa Kazuko wrote the following:

I came this far in my work without a profound consciousness of being a woman. After reflecting on the true meaning of woman, I even thought that it would be quite detrimental to my writing if I worked with an awareness of my womanhood.

Then I gradually began to express the fact that I was a woman. This was from about ten years ago. I really don't understand the reason or the cause of this change. Actually it was as if I were responding to an exterior request, instead of its being my own problem.

TRANSLATED BY JOAN E. ERICSON AND YOSHIKO NAGAOKA. From Nakayama Kazuko, "Joryū bungaku to sono ishiki henkaku no shudai" (The subject of women's literature and the transformation of its consciousness), *Kokubungaku kaishaku to kyōzai no kenkyū* 31 (5) (May 1986): 37–43. A more recent publication of this article is "Gendai josei bungaku: Ishiki henkaku no shudai (Women's literature: The subject of the transformation of its consciousness), in Nakayama Kazuko, *Nakayama Kazuko korekushon* (The Nakayama Kazuko collection), Kanrin shobō, 2003.

However, as I made a conscious effort to think and write about women, it gradually became clear just how much I had adjusted myself to fit men's ideas and men's ways of thinking.

Saegusa Kazuko is considered a prominent theorist among the contemporary mainstay of women writers. This piece is very interesting for its discussion of the transformation of her consciousness over the past ten years. When Saegusa realized that she had been dependent on men's ideas without even being aware of it, a "fissure" arose between their ideas and her own and resulted in a "discordant sound." She relates how now that she clearly ascertains reality, she wants to discover, as she gropes her way along to the next stage, a "women's way of thinking and what one should call the basis of women's ideas."

It is this desire that has compelled her to overturn all the male paradigms that have evolved up until this point, a radical as well as a massive task. Even Simone de Beauvoir could not think about women's problems except through male principles in a world long controlled by men. It is only by groping through the dark in pursuit of a new paradigm "not yet even born" that we will discover natural "women's principles."

In the quotation above, even though Saegusa states that her awareness of femaleness began with an "exterior request," her realization is probably not unrelated to the feminist movement and feminist thought since the 1970s. From early on there were two currents of feminist thought. On the one hand, there were women who wanted to become "like men" through the expansion of women's rights, reinforced by legal and economic factors. Their position through this process was to seek equality of "the individual, without difference." Such was the thinking behind the 1980 United Nations treaty abolishing discrimination against women, which "rejected consideration of the role of sex."

The opposing view recognizes the differences between men and women. It presents the notion of protecting the qualities of women through upholding "nondiscriminatory differences" or "difference without discrimination." This latter view rapidly increased in influence in the late 1970s, espoused by the early radical feminists such as Shulamith Firestone, author of *The Dialectics of Sex*. She negated women's reproductive difference as a handicap. Believing in the infinite progress manifest in life science and technology, she advocated a society with complete equality of both sexes. Accordingly this viewpoint gradually became predominant due to the deepening understanding of the "disparity" between men and women in the real locale of women's liberation and the trend toward self-examination in relation to radical expressions of that kind of early theory.

However, there has arisen a large debate within feminist thought regarding how to problematize male and female sexual difference. Those like the

Illich feminist faction, which maximizes sexual difference, are in conflict with the young, spirited feminist anthropologist Ueno Chizuko, who recently set out her remarkable arguments. However, since I am not introducing feminist thought at this time, I will not pursue this discussion further.

Nevertheless, since they cannot be completely indifferent to these currents of modern feminism, what kind of original female paradigms do Japanese main-stream women writers adopt in the arena of their own specialty of literature? This is the problem facing us now. The topic of a male paradigm revolution is a task that would probably need to be examined in conjunction with the long process of male cultural dominance. Since we have such an enormous topic before us, let us consider a schematic ordering of the writings by modern women in order to take up the subject as concisely as possible.

The dismantling of the myth of motherhood can be considered one of the first factors instrumental in the destruction of the male paradigm. The male illusion that woman, as the child-bearing sex, symbolizes the fruitful earth goddess who is irrevocably tied to her sex, suggests a longing for the eternal maternal among men and shows itself in the male wish to return to the womb, the root of life.

However, that kind of manmade myth of motherhood encroached on woman's consciousness and continued to neglect woman's existence as an individual. The female protagonists depicted by Ohba Minako, starting with her first work, "Three Crabs" ([Sanbiki no kani], 1968), as well as in her subsequent works, "Ship-Eating Worms" ([Funakui mushi], 1969), "A Mother's Dream" ([Haha no yume], 1971), and others, portray women in the role of middle-class housewives and mothers whose self-consciousness is unconnected to husbands, children, relatives, or the friends who surround them. In other words, these are women who cannot discover fundamental meaning within these relationships. Ohba seeks to reexamine the original meaning of being involved with others. She essentially calls into question all kinds of relationships that make the task of bearing and raising children through the social system of marriage the reason for women's existence. For example, the passage in "Three Crabs"—"In the twentieth century pregnancy is not a symbol of ripeness, but a barren and destructive one"—clearly indicates a vehement rejection and hostility toward the idea of woman as maternal.

The short stories in Takahashi Takako's *The Faraway Sound of Water* (*[Kanata no mizuoto]*, 1971) convey a conspicuous fear and hostility toward the sex that gives birth. The female protagonists of these short stories all hate their female blood relatives—daughters, older and younger sisters, and other kindred women—to the point of contemplating murder. The protagonist, who during the course of her daughter's onset of menses vividly smells her own reeking menstrual body odor, keeps away from and even feels the impulse to kill her daughter, and she does so in her imagination. It is animosity and fear of a woman's "fleshy genitals," which become aroused and long for a man, instinctively moving in the direction of procreation. That the maternal sex gives birth does not mean fertility is fundamental to life; it is simply a bloody-smelling offensive thing; "you spread your thighs widely apart and give birth to innumerable potatoes," "a gigantic obscene earth." The woman who gets pregnant is nothing more than a bitch dragging along her swollen belly. Maternal love is merely "men's illusion." Prose of this kind can be seen as the extreme challenge to the maternal myth.

Takahashi Takako has said, "It is not a question of a woman embodying the devil as well as the mother, but rather of a self that is awake as opposed to one that is not awake." We can see that she has depicted women as devilish and despicable because they cannot overcome their sex and stand independently. Takahashi expresses strong irritation toward those who exist without self-awareness. It is an expression of hatred toward a sex that sinks into the physical procreative function and gives birth but that lacks a clear understanding of this world.

Saegusa Kazuko also depicts maternal animosity: "I close my eyes. I can't help but want to kill my child. It's a terrible hatred. It's a fear toward life that has taken form. For a human to give birth to a human, there's no more hideous act than this" ("Blood the Color of a Childish Singing Voice" [Osanai, utagoeiro no chi], 1968).

The unsightliness of giving birth is due to the fact that those who struggle to find meaning in life unconsciously give birth through their fleshly functions. This hatred and fear of the maternal gives birth to a full-term meaningless existence. The animosity worsens and turns into a desire to kill one's child.

Saegusa also depicts the same problem from a child's point of view. Born of a mother who did not wish to bear a child, the child curses the mother. An increasingly violent rage toward the maternal appears in such passages as "It's a murderous intent that negates all that has given birth to me" (from "The Village of the Dancing Moon" [Tsuki no tobu mura], 1979).

In a recent roundtable discussion with Tomioka Taeko and Ueno Chizuko (*Shinchō*, December 1985), Saegusa talks about how young contemporary female writers express a "man-hating" emotion through "child killing." Not only do women avoid becoming pregnant, but they also express a murderous intent toward any child. Rather than stemming from a hatred of the maternal, this intent derives from a direct hatred of men. The animosity may materialize through the killing of the child, but even if it takes that form, there is no mistaking its force in causing the maternal myth to collapse.

These authors are examples of those who attempt to shake off the male illusion of the "Sacred Mother" who accepts without limit and who nurtures in perpetuity. They attempt to contemplate from a woman's viewpoint the actually lived circumstances of women, to become free from the confinement of motherhood.

On the other hand, in opposition to this, while affirming the sex that gives birth, Tsushima Yūko depicts a new motherhood hitherto unseen. She is a writer who expresses the sense of being a woman through distinguishing characteristics of the body such as "being pregnant" or "giving birth." She portrays women as the "very flow" of life and the heirs of human life. Relations between men and women are based only on instinctive sex. By means of the body, they attain true understanding. Men as natural beings are free from the social system and established roles. They are not given a standard social role as father.

The protagonist of *Woman Running in the Mountains* (*[Yama wo hashiru onna]*, 1980) does not tell the man about their illegitimate child, which she raises on her own. The man is necessary only as the tool by which the woman becomes pregnant. He is just "along for the ride," and there is the belief that the child she conceived is her possession.

The female protagonist of "The Silent Traders" ([Danmari ichi], 1982) has left her husband and is raising their two children, but there is a scene where she assumes that the stray cat she meets in the forest is the children's father. This cat has made the female cat disgustingly pregnant and, moreover, is a father who does not know his own progeny. The female protagonist wonders, "It seems that in the case of humans, there is the understanding that a man first becomes a father when he recognizes his child at birth. But this is certainly a narrow view. Do you mean to say that a male can arbitrarily divide children into two categories, those he recognizes and those he does not? Isn't it enough for a child to choose from among suitable males when he or she chooses a father?" Viewing the stray cat that has jumped onto the veranda of her condo to forage for food, she decides she would not mind if her children chose this cat as their father.

Here too the child is a possession of the mother who bore it and refuses to seek the father's feeble acknowledgment. The male cat and the male human are treated on an equal footing; furthermore, the strange notion of the male cat being chosen over the man becomes obvious. The social role of the father is completely nonexistent.

When we come to *Child of Fortune* (1978), any room for man's intervention as a natural sexual being has disappeared: "When she had sex with Nagata, just for a brief moment she experienced the sensation of swallowing the motion of a heavenly body, and it was precisely in that instant when the heavenly body also began to move in her womb. It was the moment of impregnation, a moment of grace. Then what was there to worry about?"

The woman's physiology came into the picture with the movement of the celestial object, and for a moment she became one with the universe. Men's sexuality is unnecessary, even with this impregnation. Women's sexuality, which is symbolized in this "imaginary pregnancy," not only embodies a universe-sized life, but also something beyond the maternal—in other words, "gynogenesis."

In this way, there can be an affirmation of the maternal that itself is a source of a larger motherhood, even though excluding men. It is a new maternal, which differs from the myth heretofore held by men who wished to return to the womb.

Saegusa Kazuko posits a prostitute nature to the affirmation of women's sexuality. Up to now, it was thought that "prostitute" was a female sexual role created to satisfy men's pleasure in a male-dominated society. The usual view of "prostitution" is that it is a relationship that provides an exchange of flesh for money and represents women's subordination to men. However, here prostitution is presented as the merciful aspect of women's sexuality that gives the flesh to release men's lust and rescue them: "Men passed through her body. When she opened her body to these men, Yūko always felt a strange sensation inside, maybe even compassion, sweep over her. To Yūko, men were always of a temporary nature. Even if she had a relatively long relationship, because she saw them ultimately as temporary, she was able to receive them in a yielding way" (*Eguchimizu Station [Eguchimizu eki]*, 1981).

She is not a one-man woman. She is a woman for whom a sexual relationship is not premised on family or children. There you can find a woman's true freedom, potentialities, and pure love.

"If a woman seeks pure love, she should not bear children even though she becomes involved with a man. If she has sex with a man in order to have a child, she should not look for love," Saegusa declares in her collection of essays, *Farewell to the Age of Men*. She places the greatest potentiality for women in the nature of the prostitute, where a woman has sexual relations but does not bear children.

Women's prostitute nature shows compassion and mercy to men who exist naturally. Men who are rescued through mercy cannot be men who control and subordinate women. In this way, Saegusa presents the basis for a drastic reversal of the male-female power relationship.

As part of her new theme of depicting women's control over men, Takahashi Takako's "Doll Love" ([Ningyō ai], 1976) and "Secret Ceremony" ([Higi], 1978) are rather peculiar examples of how an older woman's discovery of the beauty of a youth leads to her love. The youth is definitely of a different sex, and there is no atmosphere of motherly love on the part of the woman in the relationship. However, with skin as white as wax, the youth is not a typical man. The older woman's love thoroughly controls this beautiful man. It is a relationship not usually found between a man and a woman.

Ohba Minako creates a reversal of typical male/female roles and power relationships between husband and wife, first in *Misty Journey* I and II (*[Kiri no tabi]*, 1980), followed by *The Singing Bird* (*[Naku tori no]*, 1985). The female protagonist, who is married, meets a playwright and has an affair with him. Deciding to return to her marriage, she behaves hysterically, and her husband feels he has no choice but to take her back. The husband is forced into the position of looking after his wife, who usually acts as she pleases. Soon thereafter he quits his company job and seems to enjoy playing maid and secretary to the female protagonist. She slacks off, writes fiction, and does nothing wifely. He plays the role of the helpmate without whom she could not exist. He seems to have reached the state of becoming little more than a common, ordinary fish. When the female protagonist rails at him, yelling, "You've bound me with the chains of freedom. You stinking flounder!" he responds as someone who has completely taken on the role of a mundane, indistinguishable being, "You stole my freedom and set me free. Yes, I'm a happy flounder." He recalls that "I guess the male, no matter how things go, has to die in order to lengthen the life of the female and children." There is a complete reversal of the power relationship of male dominance. The male is instead an entity that has sacrificed himself for the female.

This technique of overturning the position of men has further been caricatured by Tomioka Taeko, who renders the image of man insignificant. Her "Water Beast" ([Suijū], 1985) is a case in point. The middle-aged man in this short story has a respectable position as a scholar but does not understand the feelings of others. He is arrogant and indifferent and upsets people with what he says. Despite his personality, he is childlike in his desire to be praised and is very conceited. Even though completely ignorant of everything else, he thinks that if he is knowledgeable about scholarship, he will be able to appeal to women.

"It makes me laugh to hear someone like you who doesn't know anything about women say that he likes people and loves the masses," his wife says to him in cold disdain. Her husband is totally oblivious to the fact that he gets on her delicate nerves. She truly hates him. He ends up being thrown out of the house and living in his office. But on one occasion when he returns to the house to pick up some clothes, he rapes his wife. Unaware of how pitiful a sight he casts dangling a plastic shopping bag, he nonchalantly tells a female screenwriter with whom he is not particularly close, "Come see me sometime. That is, when you don't have your period."

Tomioka gave the work the title "Water Beast" because "most all the disagreeable biological emissions of man" appear unpleasantly in the slimy beast that lives in the water. This extreme, petty image of men also serves to magnify their disgusting and miserable qualities. One could say that it exudes a hatred of men. Moreover, dependable or beloved males are completely absent, resulting in the collapse of the myth of male dominance.

As men are further excluded, there seems to be an unfolding of a particular lesbian ideology and to women's attacks replacing men's—in other words we see a rise in an uncharted arena that allows the possibility of female rape. On the other hand, the female project for changing the male paradigm is still in the fledgling stage and mired in chaotic darkness. In this essay I have ended up presenting just fragments of issues in the critical thinking that appears in modern literature written by women. The biggest dilemma is the fact that women themselves have internalized a male paradigm during the long history of male dominance. According to Saegusa, women are "men come late." But rather than endeavor to be like men, the serious problem before us lies in the need to aim for the transformation of the interior through a self-cleansing of male culture.

The fundamental truth of motherhood—on which our hopes were pinned to deliver us from the modern ethos and culture that had reached a dead end— proved to be nothing more than a male illusion. However, at the same time that women take up the reform of the male paradigm, it should also be an essential subject for men. As a question of overcoming modern culture, the problem of transforming a paradigm most certainly lies before both men and women. Women have no reason to hate or exclude the men who have arrived at this kind of self-awareness. For the first time there will probably be the possibility of creating equal relations between men and women. It is only natural that contemporary writing by women should shoulder these themes.

5

WOMEN WRITERS AND
ALTERNATIVE CRITIQUES

Amanda Seaman

The four essays in this chapter are representative of the exciting trends in late-twentieth-century writing on Japanese women's literature and literature in general. Encompassing the works of internationally known scholars and writers, these pieces take the study of literature beyond the normal parameters of what is thought of as literary criticism in Japan. The authors not only integrate international discussions of critical theory into their analyses of Japanese literary and historical tropes, but also create a new language to write about their literary bodies and lives. It is significant that each author focuses on literary works or literary approaches outside the confines of *junbungaku,* or canonical literature—a fact that distinguishes these pieces from traditional literary criticism in Japan. At a glance, Mizuta Noriko's "Translation and Gender: Trans/gender/lation" is perhaps the most traditional essay in this section, yet dipping below the surface, we find that her approach to translation connects with the other selections in its exploration of women and their bodily relation to the production of literature. Saitō Minako's "Yoshimoto Banana and Girl Culture" draws upon the interdisciplinary field of cultural studies to examine the nature and importance of Yoshimoto Banana's work. Takahara Eiri's "The Consciousness of the Girl: Freedom and Arrogance" traces the genealogy of the notion of "girlishness" and argues for a new style of literary analysis based upon "girl consciousness." Finally, Matsuura Rieko's "For a Gentle Castration" radically rethinks the body and its erogenous zones as a means of overcoming the phallocentric emphasis of both literature and literary criticism.

While working from different perspectives, each of these authors challenges the traditional parameters of women's literature and a literary criticism that is, in Takahara's words, "saturated with the thinking of the adult male," reacting against and offering alternatives to the status quo. Although this is not a new endeavor, what separates these critics is their openness to other critical and creative resources (including market research and poetry) to make their arguments. In addition, all of the writers included here focus upon the themes of excess and history (its uses as well as its abuses) in their exploration of women's litera-ture. Of these authors, Mizuta Noriko is the best known outside of Japan for her work, bringing Japanese women writers to the attention of readers both in academia and beyond. Her anthology of translations with Kyoko Iriye Selden, *Japanese Women Writers*, has been used in classrooms around the world. In Japan, her work in this field has been even more prodigious, and she has produced nu-merous critical studies on Japanese women's literature, most recently *Encounters with Women's Studies* (*Joseigaku to no deai*, 2004) and *Twentieth-Century Women's Expression* (*Nijūseiki no josei hyōgen*, 2003). Her 1991 essay, "Translation and Gen-der: Trans/gender/lation," published in the literary magazine *Gunzō*, focuses on the act of translation, an act that has certainly had a profound impact on Mizuta's life. Mizuta's interest in translation is significant, as Judy Wakabayashi points out in a translator's note, because despite translation's prominent role in Japanese literature and its literary history, it has not received the kind of critical attention that it garnered during the Meiji period. Mizuta's essay, which draws heavily on Western theory, was innovative when it was published for its attempt both to place translation within a larger context of literary studies and to dis-cuss women's participation in it. As Wakabayashi notes, however, despite being published in *Gunzō*, a magazine of the literary establishment, it did not kindle significant dialogue about translation, reflecting Mizuta's own observation that translation has been overlooked by contemporary criticism.

Mizuta's essay was sparked by reading Murakami Haruki's review of a new translation of Gertrude Stein's work *Three Lives;* Murakami did not mention an earlier translation by Tomioka Taeko. That Murakami, himself a noted trans-lator of literature into Japanese, did not acknowledge the existing translation prompted Mizuta to ruminate on the significance of a retranslation that does not significantly improve, invigorate, or challenge its predecessor. As Mizuta ex-plores the theory of textual production, she notes that earlier Romantic writers had gendered the author as male, with the equation author = critic = male, while later French feminist thinkers, such as Cixous and Irigaray, offer a female-centered vision in which literary production is similar to giving birth and thus can be only a female act. Mizuta rejects both of these conceptions and offers a middle ground: translators as authors in their own right are bisexual, both female and male. Through these two statements Mizuta re-genders translation and resituates it from the periphery to the center.

What becomes crucial here is not the actual sexual orientation of the person performing the translation but the ability of the translator to find and respond to "something similar to oneself in the text of an Other and being attracted to something different that is lacking in oneself . . . penetrating into the internal territory of the Other so as to know it better." Mizuta's intention is to highlight the way the untranslatable portions of the self are made visible through translation into the Other. With this provocative reconceptualization, Mizuta liberates translation from being a mechanical task—a task often done by women—and shows how each work is a vital original text.

One of the few professional female literary critics in Japan, Saitō Minako burst onto the Japanese literary scene with her iconoclastic examination of the trope of pregnancy in modern Japanese literature. Exploring the depiction of a pregnancy (usually unplanned) in a selection of modern canonical (male-authored) works, she disrupted the common reception of the heroes of these texts. Through this work and others, Saitō has urged women to adopt new methods of reading Japanese literature as a fundamental protest against male writers, male readers, and patriarchy itself. Saitō has made her mark writing about contemporary authors, most of them women, focusing upon the issues of literary commodification and audience reception. In her collection *Idols of Literary Journalism* (*Bundan aidoru ron*, 2002), she examines the literariness of several of the most prominent and prolific writers of the late twentieth and early twenty-first centuries, including Yoshimoto Banana, whose work is addressed in the essay translated here.

Yoshimoto has been one of the most popular and contested female writers in Japan since her debut in the late 1980s, publishing a prodigious number of books, with sales in the millions of copies. This level of popularity also has subjected her to attacks from many literary critics in Japan and elsewhere, who have derided her as a mass producer of "mass" literature. Whether embracing her "innocent form of expression" or decrying the contrived artlessness of her prose and plotlines, in each case the "freshness" or novelty of Banana's work has been taken for granted—an assumption that Saitō argues is faulty.

Saitō traces this error to an inadequate appreciation of Banana's literary influences and more generally to an inadequate awareness by (male) critics of the history of "girls' literature" in Japan. While a number of writers have drawn parallels between Yoshimoto's work and the girls' *manga* (comic books) popular in the 1980s and 1990s, Saitō points out that Yoshimoto's works, unlike girls' *manga*, do not contest the traditional family structure. She argues instead that despite the inclusion of unusual characters, such as the transsexual Eriko in *Kitchen*, Yoshimoto's novels and stories are fundamentally conservative in nature in that they support and even embrace the notion of the family, whether consanguinal or affinal. In this respect, as well as in tone and plotlines, Yoshimoto's oeuvre is much more indebted to what Saitō describes as "borderless" girl novels such as *Heidi* and *Anne of Green Gables*—a literary pedigree ignored by male critics unfamiliar with this type of literature, who see Yoshimoto as an exemplar of a new way of writing or a reaction against the more sexualized female characters found in the popular literature of the "bubble economy."

Saitō also demonstrates, however, how other aspects of Yoshimoto's fiction link it to wider trends in contemporary consumer culture. With their appeal to young girls, Yoshimoto's books form part of a continuum of girl-oriented products such as "character goods" (items featuring pictures of well-known cartoon characters) or dolls. By examining Yoshimoto's sales figures and comparing her books to other items intended for immediate consumption, Saitō demonstrates how Yoshimoto's works, despite their conservative aspects, are part and parcel of the very modern consumer excess surrounding young women in Japan today.

Like Saitō, Takahara Eiri takes the concept of "the girl" and "girlishness" (shōjo) as a point of departure for literary analysis, focusing not only upon girls in literature or girls' literature per se, but upon the girl as a potential subject position for criticism itself. In the introductory essay to *The Territory of the Girl* (*Shōjo ryōiki*, 1999), a series of studies of *shōjo* in Japanese literature, Takahara explores what it means to be a *shōjo* reader, offering as a guiding principle that "it is not necessary to be an actual girl: rather, we need to be like a girl." For Takahara, the essence of the contemporary *shōjo* is her combination of freedom and arrogance, presented as a peculiarly modern phenomenon representing the two extremes of desire in the modern subject. Freedom, suggests Takahara, is not concrete—instead, it is something that can be imagined or desired; arrogance, on the other hand, is the epitome of self-satisfaction, characterized by intense narcissism. Takahara's goal, however, is not simply to explicate what comprises the consciousness of the girl, but also to use thinking like a girl as a means of literary criticism. In doing so, Takahara aims both to decenter the traditional patriarchal process of literary criticism, seen as draining the work of its fantastic, unmediated appeal and joy, and to privilege works of literature. Spanning from Nomizo Naoko's 1924 *Gardenia* to Ōhara Mariko's *Hybrid Child*, including as well Kawabata's early novels to those of Matsuura Rieko, Takahara selects those works in which the girl takes center stage, with heroines who demand more power than society allows them.

Perhaps the most striking aspect of Takahara's treatment of *shōjo* is its ecumenical scope. While Takahara believes that the traits of freedom and arrogance are manifested most fully in girls, who desire only to do the things that interest them and to be the center of attention, "girlishness" is not limited to girls—on the contrary, it is a way of being, open to women seeking to opt out of the competitive and aggressive world of the adult, and even to men who wish to reject the norms and restrictions (gender or otherwise) of everyday society. The rationale for this novel approach is historical, for Takahara finds the antecedents to the *shōjo* not in the world of women and children, but in the premodern era *chigo*, boys whose sexual favors were sought by adult priests and samurai. Unlike women and children, who were considered to be social as well as natural inferiors and thus susceptible to violence and domination, the *chigo* were able to manipulate their patrons into giving them what they wanted. Takahara suggests that the "modern girl" who emerged in the Taishō period, with her power to contest gender and sexual power relations, is the *chigo*'s successor, lending the *shōjo* an androgynous, if not asexual, quality today.

Takahara's effort to deconstruct the traditional relationship among sex, gender, and subjectivity is given a more radical, and personal, form in the final essay included here, Matsuura Rieko's "For a Gentle Castration," part of a loosely linked collection of essays by the same title originally serialized between 1984 and 1988. Addressing an unnamed lover (*anata*, or "you") who sometimes appears to be a woman and sometimes a man, Matsuura reflects upon her and her lover's bodies as sites of desire, arguing that standard sexual intercourse, far from being a source of pleasure, is defined by pain—a pain rooted in birth itself, defined by Matsuura as a "gentle rape." Matsuura thus turns her attention to the anus and the belly button as sources of pleasure—places that neither substitute for the genitals nor replace them. These orifices, together with the menstruating womb, a disruptive and chaotic organ defying the reproductive imperatives of heterosex, are the cardinal points in Matsuura's radical vision of human sexuality. She is particularly unimpressed by the heterosexual act of vaginal penetration by the penis, declaring at one point that "sex is boring. Like classical music." For Matsuura, sexuality (in life as well as in literature) instead should be woman-centered and focused upon pleasures freed from the stale conventionality of orgasm.

The oppressive nature of conventional heterosexuality, and the search for alternatives to it, are central themes in Matsuura's best-known works of fiction, *Natural Woman* (*Nachuraru ūman*, 1987) and *The Apprenticeship of Big Toe P* (*Oyayubi P no shugyō jidai*, 1993). *Natural Woman* was one of the first mainstream novels to deal with a lesbian heroine, and it gained notoriety on account of its young narrator and graphic scenes of lesbian sex. In her subsequent work, *Big Toe P*, Matsuura puts a Kafkaesque spin on sexual liberation with the tale of a young woman, Kasumi, who wakes up one day to discover that her big toe has become a penis. The rest of the novel deals with Kasumi's exploration of sex and physical pleasure, both her own and that of her partners and friends. In both novels, Matsuura works against the conventional approach to sex and romance found in earlier Japanese literature, developing characters who seek sexual satisfaction outside the "normal" parameters. In turn, Matsuura herself seeks to exceed standard hetero-normative plotlines and to create a new language for talking about sexual relations. The centerpiece of this new sexual lexicon is the anus, an organ that, "like a Klein bottle," is free from reproductive associations and free from gender identification. This liberated and liberating object is for Matsuura the embodiment of excess, a place that stands beyond the boundaries of convention and repression—a marketplace, as she calls it, offering a pleasure open to all people regardless of sex or gender.

Matsuura's challenge to hetero-normative sexuality and her search for alternatives to it are themes common to all of the essays translated in this chapter. In each of them, relationships between men and women, in particular sexual ones, are conflated, avoided altogether, or discussed only in the most nebulous terms. Matsuura's brief discussion of the male sex organ in "For a Gentle Castration" emphasizes its ungainly appearance rather than its sexual function, while the penis in her novel *Big Toe P* is emphatically freed from any association with the masculine subject. Saitō's analysis of Yoshimoto Banana calls attention to the striking lack of sexual relations in her fiction, a feature that Saitō argues grows out of a long tradition of girls', rather than women's, writing. Takahara, in turn, embraces the nonsexual girl as an avatar for literary criticism in general, offering a way to reintegrate female and children's perspectives into the critical landscape. And finally, Mizuta offers a twinning of sexuality, a doubling, as a way of resolving once and for all the power play between creation and reproduction. In each case, the critics excerpted here argue for a new form of literary (and by extension social) analysis that can overcome the shortcomings of masculine readings of women and their literature by considering that literature on its own terms, uncovering its unique history, and freeing women and their writing from the confines of patriarchy and its heterosexual presuppositions.

||| Translation and Gender

Trans/gender/lation

MIZUTA NORIKO

On coming across Murakami Haruki's review of Gertrude Stein's *Three Lives* in the February 1991 Japanese edition of *Marie Claire* magazine, I was intrigued to learn of the appearance of a new translation. Although Stein is a difficult writer who has even been described as untranslatable, Japanese readers were introduced to this first work of hers, *Three Lives*, at a relatively early date in a translation by Tomioka Taeko under the creative title *Sannin no onna* [Three women].

Stein, who had been portrayed as oft-discussed but seldom read, has become so well known in Japan that she almost merits her own fan club. This is largely attributable to Tomioka Taeko's *Sannin no onna* and to Kanaseki Hisao's translation of Stein's autobiography, *The Autobiography of Alice B. Toklas*, as *Arisu B. Tokurasu no jiden*. In fact, these translations by Tomioka and Kanaseki are themselves worthy of being regarded as masterpieces. Stein had a major influence on Tomioka Taeko's development as a writer—most notably on her literary language and expression—so *Sannin no onna* in particular is a unique work that occupies an incontrovertible position in Tomioka's "map of misreading."

When I heard of the new translation by Ochiishi Ōgasutomūn, my reaction was that the remarkable Stein revival of recent times had quite rightly also led to an attempt in Japan to present a new image of Stein and a new interpretation of *Three Lives*. Yet Murakami's review offered no insights into whether any such attempt had been made in the new translation, and he made absolutely no mention of its predecessor, Tomioka's *Sannin no onna,* an oversight I found inexplicable.[1] So I sat down and read the new translation, also entitled *Sannin*

TRANSLATED BY JUDY WAKABAYASHI. From Mizuta Noriko, "Hon'yaku to jendā: Trans/gender/lation" (Translation and Gender: Trans/gender/lation," *Gunzō* 46 (8) (August 1991): 216–223. The translator would like to thank Professor Mizuta and Professor Carol Maier for taking time from their busy schedules to read the translation of this essay and give the benefit of their comments.

1. Nowadays translation has lost its position close to the center of Japan's literary polysystem, but prominent critics' views on translation are still revealing—as are their silences on the subject. A century after Kunikida Doppo's article (see chapter 1 of this volume), this failure by a male critic to address translation issues led Mizuta to reconsider the link between translation and gender. Although Mizuta's essay appeared in a leading monthly literary magazine, it does not seem to have had much impact in the sense of "engendering" a discourse in Japan on the ties between gender and translation. *JW*

no onna. Yet not just the title, but also the style and the commentary on Stein's text more or less follow Tomioka's, and overall it provides no fresh insights into Stein to supplement those already offered by Tomioka. I was baffled, then, as to why the translator's afterword nevertheless made absolutely no mention of the existing version by Tomioka.

Such neglect of outstanding earlier translations on the part of subsequent translators and reviewers, as in the case of this retranslation of Stein's *Three Lives,* seems to me to overlook the importance of translations, a trend that has become increasingly noticeable in recent contemporary criticism. Surely it is only natural to show due respect to outstanding predecessors? These events led me to reconsider the meaning of translation in literature and its treatment in Japan.[2]

||| The fact that a translation is an original work is not only self-evident, but it also signifies that the distinction between translated and original texts is blurred—particularly if we accept the ideas of Jacques Derrida and Barbara Johnson and of Harold Bloom and Geoffrey Hartman, who regard all texts as translations of works by earlier writers. If this is true, then any text has an infinite number of antecedent translations, but in the particular case of retranslations of foreign literature, this means that at the very minimum there are two such antecedents—the author's text and any existing translation into the same language as the new version. What's more, with foreign literature it is often not so much the original itself as the translation that governs the impression of a particular work, and its reception also depends heavily on the translation.

No matter what linguistic errors one might try to uncover in existing translations, the act of setting one's hand to a new translation—for instance, tackling a fresh rendition of Kawabata Yasunari's *Yukiguni* for English readers, despite the existence of Edward Seidensticker's *Snow Country*—should be based on the premise of presenting a new portrayal of the writer (Kawabata) and an innovative perspective on the text *[Yukiguni].*

In fact Arthur Waley's translation of *Genji monogatari*—a rendition that is very free and has numerous omissions—was for a long time read in English circles as the *Genji monogatari* text *[The Tale of Genji],* conveying to English

2. Retranslations become necessary for various reasons. The language of translated works tends to date quickly; the existing translation might contain mistranslations or omissions; or advances in research might have led to new insights into the source text that were not reflected in the earlier translation. Retranslations might also be polemical in critiquing and challenging earlier translations. These new translations can reinvigorate the source text, but what bothers Mizuta here is the fact that the second translator of *Three Lives,* Ochiishi Ōgasutomūn (August Moon), fails to bring out any new aspects of Stein's work and fails to acknowledge the 1969 translation by Tomioka Taeko. JW

readers something different from and over and beyond what Japanese readers derive from *Genji monogatari*. Seidensticker's more recent translation, which is far more accurate than Waley's, is to be welcomed, yet few insights would likely be gained even if, for instance, we were to learn that Waley's *The Tale of Genji* made an impression on Virginia Woolf and we compared her writing with *Genji monogatari* and Seidensticker's translation. The *Genjis* by Arthur Waley and Edward Seidensticker are two different texts, which is why many teachers of comparative literature still use Waley's translation. For the English reading public the Japanese-language *Genji monogatari* constitutes what should be regarded as yet another version.

Although *Genji monogatari* is a highly translatable text, Waley's *The Tale of Genji* always struck me as an untranslatable original. Seidensticker's achievement lies in having tackled this myth in the English world about *The Tale of Genji*. I was of the impression that through his translation, *Genji monogatari* was reborn in its original form as a translatable text.

In fact *Genji monogatari* has been translated on numerous occasions, with several famous renditions into modern Japanese, each based on a unique portrayal. Yosano Akiko's *Genji monogatari* adopts the perspective of a woman yearning for the ideal man, while Tanizaki Jun'ichirō's *Genji* worships women. On the other hand, Enchi Fumiko's *Genji* presents a tale of female malice. There is also an inimitable new translation by Hashimoto Osamu, and there is no guarantee that Komashaku Kimi, who argued that Murasaki Shikibu was a lesbian, will not produce a contemporary rendition at some point in time.

The phenomenon of the recent Stein revival has occurred against the backdrop of a feminist reevaluation of Stein as a lesbian, and it is clear that Stein's fans today relate to, respect, and admire her more as a lesbian than as a Cubist writer. So what first sprang to mind when I heard about the new Stein translation was that perhaps it focused on aspects of Gertrude Stein as a lesbian that had not been brought to the fore in Tomioka's translation. Such an approach would be of great interest, I thought, but again I was in for a letdown.

The view that only lesbians can truly understand lesbian literature, and the exclusivism that is the flip side of this prejudice, became a factor highlighting the differences within feminist discourse. The argument that lesbian works can be translated only by lesbians or that lesbians are better able to translate such works cannot go unchallenged, immediately raising as it does questions about the appropriateness of women (men) translating works by male (female) writers. Even more fundamentally, it involves issues concerning the gender of the writer and that of readers. In turn this raises elemental questions for feminist criticism, such as whether author gender and textual gender do in fact coincide and on what basis the gender of a text is formed.

As well as questions such as whether, if we adopt the view that Murasaki Shikibu was a lesbian, the gender of the *Genji monogatari* text means that a male or heterosexual translator would be inappropriate. . . .

||| Translation is a genre with close ties to gender. In "The Task of the Translator" (1923) Walter Benjamin defined translation as a genre, and in fact the words *gender* and *genre* have the same etymology.[3] Translation has long been regarded as a female act and occupation. As with typists, translators were usually women. Translators have been regarded as mere technicians who convert someone else's writing into another language, and—just as midwives cannot call the child they deliver their own—translated texts have, in the final analysis, been regarded as the work of another. According to this view, translation is a service industry, and the service industry is an occupation to which women are naturally suited.

If translating is a feminine act, then it is writing—i.e., original creation— that constitutes a masculine act. So authorship is a masculine occupation. It was the Romantic writers who aspired to equate the author with God, in the belief that writers create their own universes from naught, drawing solely on their own personalities and the belief that the work as a universe created by this God-like writer is a unique and absolutely original text that brooks no imitation— i.e., is untranslatable. The writer-subject who aspires to the position of God-the-creator is a genius aloof from ordinary beings and signifies an individuality that defies imitation. In this way the schema whereby woman = translator = midwife exists, as opposed to that whereby man = author = God.

Before modernism and New Criticism simultaneously cast fresh light on the "critic" from different perspectives, the same could have been said about critics in place of translators. Critics were regarded as transmitters whose comments rendered a work comprehensible to readers, and they were perceived as having a parasitic relationship to the original.

3. Benjamin actually uses the expression *eine Form*, which is usually translated as "a mode" or "a form" in English translations of his text, "Die Aufgabe der Übersetzung." His *Form*, which has no relation to "genre" in either meaning or form, is a key word whose meaning in this influential German article has been much debated. Presumably Mizuta worked from a Japanese translation that renders *Form* as *janru* (genre), so this constitutes an example of the repercussions of mistranslation, or what is called a "rupture" by Rainer Nägele. It is unlikely that any direct connection with gender can be read into Benjamin's original text, but this "rupture" deriving from the Japanese translation of his article provides a platform for Mizuta to develop her ideas, and the etymological link she makes between "genre" and "gender" is valid, as is the argument she constructs on the basis of this link. In doing so, she contributes to the "afterlife" of Benjamin's text, to use his own term. See Benjamin, "The Task of the Translator," p. 16. *JW*

Aiming at the destruction and remodeling of existing culture and of established works with a unified and harmonious order and wholeness, modernism presented creative works as a lack of order, a miscellany (collage) of scattered fragments, and it thereby destroyed the notion that the original = a microcosmos connoting order and set not only the writer-subject and originality, but also the "author" on the road to extinction. On the grounds that texts always transcend the writer's creativity and individuality and are merely an attempt to reinterpret and reinvent these within the framework of tradition and cultural archetypes, New Criticism also placed authors and critics on the same plane.

In this schema, whereby author = critic as a result of a diminishing of the writer's authority and enhancement of the critic's, again the gender remains masculine, clearly because the concepts constituting tradition and cultural archetypes are the products of male-centered ideology.

Yet when a translator enters the equation and we end up with the schema author = critic = translator, the gender abruptly tilts toward the feminine. Since translation is in essence an act of transferring something to another culture, the text (i.e., tradition) runs the risk of being rendered impotent in the presence of a heterogeneous Other. What lies at the center of one culture is, through translation, displaced to a merely peripheral position in another. The translator is a bilingual, bicultural entity who belongs to neither culture or has a foot in each. In other words, the translator is not located at the center of either culture.

When in this schema or equation the author's gender becomes equivocal and moves toward the feminine, it becomes obvious that in the nature of things there is nothing in the slightest unusual about the author being of feminine gender. If we regard authors as creating a living universe from nothing, relying solely on their own individualities, then they are the very image of mothers, who bring forth life from their bodies and gain a sense of pride and joy at the cost of suffering in childbirth. I have long used the metaphor of self-birth to portray women's attempts at autobiography and the process of being born as a writer through self-expression; regarding a piece of writing as the offspring and child born from a writer is a very natural trope, and it begins to seem only proper and natural that author gender is in fact feminine.

Indeed the French feminists Julia Kristeva, Luce Irigiray, and Hélène Cixous base their feminist ideology on the premise that creation is a feminine act. Although there are differences among the feminist views of these three women, they are alike in speaking of the act of writing as not only the maternal experiences of childbirth and bonding with one's child, but also as depending on the physical experiences unique to women, particularly women's sexual feelings.

The act of creation on the part of men has a centralist orientation focusing solely on the phallus, and this produces a dictatorial and localized mini-universe system—i.e., the text—that links directly from the brain to the genitals, whereas the act of creation on the part of women is based on an infinitely great cosmic unconsciousness and libido that unfold, open out, are transposed, transformed. These feminists argue that the essence of acts of creation worthy of being deemed "feminine" lies precisely in creation as an unconscious outflow that—rather than classifying, regulating, and possessing—seeks pleasure and spreads in tune with the waves of desire, swaying, flowing, and breaking down barriers with others; crossing into new territories and embracing others; undergoing transformation. The act of creation is, they assert, inherently feminine.

In this way feminists formulate a schema whereby author = translator = woman, and they look upon both creative acts and translation as having a positive valence precisely because they are feminine. By deeming the act of creation to be feminine, they redeem feminine translation.

||| Yet the most legitimate gender for the author = critic = translator (when this schema is valid) should be that of the bisexual.[4] If the author is dethroned from the position of a god = genius who creates an untranslatable original from nothing and is relegated to the position of someone who merely misreads—i.e., revises and rewrites—earlier writers within the traditional framework (the aggregate of texts), and the text is regarded as a copy of a copy and as infinitely translatable (things that cannot be translated are not texts), and the author is neither producer nor owner of the text and no longer has any responsibility for it, vanishing or disappearing in a certain discourse, then the author takes on a new garb as critic or translator and is transformed = reincarnated, perhaps becoming active in a different culture somewhere. The author has survived as a transmitter, a transvestite, a trans/gender/lator who blurs the boundaries between self and other and transgresses into different cultures and across gender distinctions.

In "The Task of the Translator" Benjamin asserts that a translation is not a "faithful" reproduction of the original but its survival or afterlife, and that through translation the original gives itself and survives as raw essence, while undergoing transformation. This could also be depicted as the act of a father = god who orders his child to perpetuate him or that of a son who gains an identity through representing himself as his father, yet at the same time it is also a metaphor for the reproduction of life.

In fact, when in *Des Tours de Babel* (1984) Derrida discusses Benjamin's theory

---

4. Mizuta reconfigures in gender terms the tripartite classification of translation proposed in Roman Jakobson's 1959 article, "On the Linguistic Aspects of Translation." *JW*

of translation, he uses the metaphors of a rare encounter with another; the fleeting physical contact between two texts; a movement of love, sexual union, marriage, and blood ties to translate Benjamin's translated theory of translation. Derrida's theory of translation proposes that what constitutes translation is precisely a contract marriage producing a child. Translation is a seedbed, a maneuver aimed at the birth of a child, and the original develops through its progeny. The mother tongues of both the original text and the translator are transformed by the translated text = offspring.

Barbara Johnson ("Taking Fidelity Philosophically," 1985) depicts translation as a love-hate relationship with the mother. Here translation is the relationship not between father and child, but mother and daughter. By tearing at her mother in the encounter with the Other that is translation, the daughter affirms her mother as her own origins, and although resenting her mother for not providing everything necessary for dealing with the Other, she also reaffirms the close ties of love for her mother.

If in discussing translation these gender metaphors can be infinitely extended, then the metaphor most suited to translation is, I believe, that of the bisexual.

In his theory of translation Roman Jakobson classifies translation into three types: (1) intralingual changes, (2) interlingual changes, and (3) changes from language to a nonlinguistic sign system (intersemiotic translation). Although Derrida is critical of Jakobson's supposition that language has a distinct identity, with a clear unity, limits, and boundaries, if we rearticulate Jakobson's three categories in terms of gender metaphors, they throw even greater light on translation and the "task of translation" in relation to sexual differences.

If we follow along Jakobson's lines, then as well as discussing translation in terms of a male metaphor, where it is regarded as a succession from male to male (from god = the father to son), and a female metaphor, where it is viewed as female-female succession (mother to daughter), and a heterosexual metaphor that perceives translation as succession through the formation of a family resulting from the union of a man and woman and the birth of a child, there should also be a theory in which translation is regarded as an outflow of and response to a bisexual being. And translation from human beings into "sexual" entities other than human beings—for instance, animals—ought also to exist. And what about translation into cyborgs. . . ?

Finding and responding to something similar to oneself in the text of an Other and being attracted to something different that is lacking in oneself and then penetrating into the internal territory of the Other so as to know it better—both these acts constitute self-reaffirmation and a discovery of one's unknown self. The attempt to render visible the untranslatable, unexplored territory that is one's self by crossing over into the Other through translation into the Other — this is precisely an act of translation. Hence translation is nothing but a bisexual's response to a bisexual being. The return to and complete absorption in the mother entity as self-contradiction and the crossing over into another heterogeneous being to escape oneself are both attempts at self-affirmation.

||| The following is one of those common Jewish jokes. Wishing to start a new life in France, a German Jew first decides to change his name. In German it was the common name Katzmann, so he tries converting this into French. *Katz,* meaning "cat," is *chat* in French, and *mann,* meaning "person," is *l'homme,* so for his new name he adopts *Chat l'homme* — pronounced "shalom" in Hebrew! This joke — a metaphor for how the more Jewish people try to escape themselves, the more they end up back where they started — works equally well as a theory of translation.

One text that in and of itself demonstrates that the relationship author = critic = translator or original = critique = translation is a bilingual, bisexual relationship would be Joyce's *Finnegans Wake.* This text is already a conglomeration of multiple languages. Individual words have manifold meanings, etymologies, and connotations, and these evoke and negate each other, transforming the very language itself. Sentences that have neither a beginning nor an end but flow on like a river; a text that subsumes within itself the archetypal man and woman and that has the character of androgynous twins. Life, issuing forth and being transformed as it flows from antiquity to contemporary times, from its primordial sources to infinite shores and, as it transposes from dream to reality, from unconsciousness to consciousness. That text, where creation = translation, as a wake (a vigil for the dead and an awakening) that watches over its life, and death. A tale of eternal self-transformation interposed between birth, life and death, from heterogeneous to homogeneous, homogeneous to heterogeneous, homosexual to heterosexual, man to woman, woman to man. If translation is a tale of transformation (metamorphosis/metaphor), then translation into and from entities other than human beings is the very destiny of translation and the "task" it fulfills.

Yoshimoto Banana and Girl Culture

SAITŌ MINAKO

Yoshimoto Banana made her debut in 1987 with the story "Kitchen" (Kitchin), which won the Kaien Newcomer Writers Prize. It was some time, however, before the "Banana boom" exploded, and she did not become a phenomenon until 1989. Even though her collection of stories, which was published under the title *Kitchen* in January 1988, received favorable reviews, Murakami Haruki's *Norwegian Wood [Norway no mori]* ran off with the 1988 best-seller race.[5] The "Banana year" followed that, when four of her books were listed among the ten best sellers of the year, an unprecedented accomplishment. By then Banana had published five novels and one book of essays. All sold explosively: 1.3 million copies of *Kitchen;* 0.9 million copies of *Utakata/Sanctuary* [*Utakata/Sankuchuari,* published in August 1988]; 0.8 million copies of *A Presentiment* [*Kanashii yokan,* December 1988]; 1.4 million copies of *Good-bye Tsugumi* [*Tsugumi,* March 1989]; 0.7 million copies of *Asleep* [*Shirakawa yofune,* July 1989]; and 0.5 million copies of *Painappurin* [September 1989]. Occasionally a new writer will have a first book on the best-seller list. But Banana's case was exceptional. All of her books sold extremely well in a very short period of time, totaling an amazing 5.7 million copies.

Banana's reception resembled Murakami Haruki's. Both were admired equally by ordinary readers and professional critics. Not only did Banana's books sell well, but she also won a number of literary prizes. In addition to being a two-time nominee for the Akutagawa Prize, she won the Izumi Kyōka Prize *(Kitchen);* the Best Newcomer Artists Recommended by the Ministry of Education *(Utakata/Sanctuary);* and the Yamamoto Shūgorō Prize *(Good-bye Tsugumi).* Nevertheless, critical examination of Banana's works did not keep pace. Literary critics sought to understand "why Banana was so well received" yet

TRANSLATED BY EIJI SEKINE. From Saitō Minako, "Yoshimoto Banana shōjo karuchā no suimyaku" (Yoshimoto Banana and girl culture), in *Bundan aidoru ron* (Idols of literary journalism) (Iwanami shoten, 2002), pp. 60–90.

The essay by Saitō contains notes by the author herself. In the footnotes corresponding to her essay, these will be marked with the abbreviation AU for author.

5. Murakami Haruki (b. 1949) is a popular novelist. His 1979 debut novella, *Hear the Wind Sing* (tr. 1987), sets a drastically new, postmodern tone of narration—light, cool, casual, and mildly sentimental. His type of pop and colloquial narrative tone is the overwhelmingly dominant one adopted by today's generation of novelists. In *Idols of Literary Journalism,* Saitō discusses the similarity between Murakami's narrative method—casually controlled reshuffling of fragmented plot elements—and the structuring of computer games as a source of his popularity among today's generation of gamers. *ES*

failed to provide a satisfactory explanation. To leap quickly to my conclusion, I believe that for conventional literary critics, Banana was an alien from an "unknown country."

In brief, Banana criticism differs from that of other authors and their works in that it falls into three major categories: (a) conventional criticism of her works and of herself as an author (that is to say, analyses of her newness); (b) criticism of her marketability (analyses of her reception); (c) commodity criticism (analyses of her books as commercial products).

One identifying characteristic of the Banana phenomenon is found in the very fact that (b) and (c) are significant components of any critical analysis of her works. Readers are more concerned with how Banana has been read by others than they are with their own readings.

Radical Style/Conservative Story

To illustrate the first category of criticism, I offer fragments from two reviews published just prior to the Banana boom.

What impresses me the most about Banana's novels is the absence of any of the ideological unnaturalness that characterizes so many of the works of young authors today. Banana's novels are, of course, just as fictional as any other novel, but her stories are narrated with such a sense of sincerity. Both this honest style of narration and her positive outlook on "life" move readers. I feel refreshed after reading her novels. (Yasuhara Akira, *New Book Review,* April 1988)

When this author feels sad, she writes that she is sad; when she falls in love and is happy, she writes that she is happy. Everything is honest and charming. The passage that impressed me the most was the one on the beauty of an urban twilight. With no unnecessary description, Banana wrote, "It was awesome." This honesty is almost radical. It is similar to the radical way writers of girls' comics deal with the topic of pure love. It is amazing to know one can be this honest! (Kawamoto Saburō, *Sunday Mainichi,* September 4, 1988)

What amazes me is that Kawamoto would be so honest himself! At any rate, the first citation above is from a review of *Kitchen* and the second a review of *Utakata/Sanctuary.* These are typical in that they suggest Banana's popularity—like that of Haruki and Tawara Machi—derives from her shockingly novel style of writing.[6] Positive evaluations of Banana repeatedly rely on the

6. Tawara Machi (b. 1962) is a popular tanka poet. Her 1988 debut anthology of *tanka* poems, *Salad Anniversary,* sold 2 million copies by the end of that year. Respecting *tanka*'s tra-

same set of terms: refreshing, honest, straight, innocent, girls-comics-like, and so forth. . . .

The majority of Banana criticism focuses attention on the content of her stories rather than the style of her narrative. Tomioka Taeko and Asada Akira have been critical of Banana from her debut. In the *Asahi* newspaper's "Book Review," Tomioka states, "This work offers the sentimental melodrama popular with young people today. And because of this sentimentalism, her book touches the hearts of the old men in the village of the 'literary institution' " (August 29, 1988). As an experienced reader of girls' comics, Asada points out their influence on Banana's works but concludes that her novels completely lack the radicalness found in comics. Here are examples of criticism of Banana's stories:

> Banana skillfully utilizes the Ōshima Yumiko-like empty feeling shared by her story's dysfunctional family members, but she makes them develop a lukewarm pseudo-family unity and brings her story to a happy end. . . . In short, Banana betrays the girls' comics writers' effort to dismantle the institution called family. As a good little girl, she sentimentally reconstructs the institution. Old men therefore love her. She is very reactionary. (Asada Akira [interviewed], *GORO*, March 9, 1989)

> The ending of *Utakata* seems artificially tacked on and unconvincing. . . . It is just like the ending to a sentimental love story. I was disappointed. In the end, she creates a "lie" of fiction. I am not pleased either by the fact that *Utakata* as a whole is structured by following the conventional *ki-shō-ten-ketsu* order of construction.[7] I wish this author would refrain from reproducing the same "stories" we have already read over and over again. (Nishio Kanji, *Kaien*, October 1988)

It is interesting that both the New Leftist critic Asada Akira and the neo-conservative critic Nishio Kanji criticize the lukewarm quality of Banana's stories and her tendency to end them with sentimentally optimistic conclusions.

In short, Banana's style may be radical, but her stories are sentimental melodramas. In other words, Banana fans are enchanted by the expressive aspect of

---

ditional fixed format (consisting of 5-7-5-7-7 syllables), she fills it with contemporary topics expressed by casual colloquial language. Her signature poem, from which the title of the anthology is taken, reads: " 'This tastes great' you said and so/ the sixth of July—/our salad anniversary." Saitō sees in Tawara's success the most visible example of the popular literary format of the 1980s—that is, to create a fresh, new bottle for old wine. *ES*

7. *Ki-shō-ten-ketsu* refers to the traditional format in Chinese poetry of an introduction, development, turn, and conclusion. Here, the word is figuratively used to negatively value the structure of Banana's story development as something manneristic and predictable. *ES*

her stories, while anti-Banana critics are dumbfounded by their content. This summary characterizes the way Banana's novels were discovered and identified in the beginning of her career.

Yoshimoto Banana and Fancy Goods

Now let us turn to the second category of reviews, those that criticize her marketability.

If you still believe that "the cluster amaryllis is my favorite red flower," you are an outdated old foggy. Today, the trendiest red flowers are those of banana trees. ("Yoshimoto Banana is the Sei Shōnagon of the 1990s," *Weekly bunshun*, January 5, 1989)

"I never cried this loudly in my entire life" (confession of a high school girl student). Aren't these the words a man wants to hear from his girlfriend once in his lifetime? Ms. Banana Yoshimoto is the one who makes all these women cry out loud, a novelist much talked about these days. What? Haven't you heard of her? Being that ignorant, you cannot be a popular guy in the First Year of Heisei. ("Why Are Women Taken in by 'Yoshimoto Banana' These Days?" *GORO*, February 3, 1989)

. . . The titles of these articles and the magazines in which they appeared, as indicated in parentheses, are revealing. They were all carried in men's magazines and written in response to the news that a commodity called "Yoshimoto Banana" was becoming very popular among young women. According to one survey, 90 percent of Banana's female readers were in their teens and twenties. Articles like the ones cited above not only examine why Banana sells so well, but they also try to understand the character of contemporary women. This type of criticism, therefore, is driven by different methods and objectives from that written by literary critics. Honestly speaking, I often find these articles more insightful than conventional literary reviews in shedding new light on the essence of Banana's works. Reviewers in this category start their arguments from the standpoint of "I-have-no-idea-how-to-understand-Banana's-charm" and then try to study the enigma from perspectives broader than the field of literature per se.

I am most impressed by a special edition titled "Yoshimoto Banana for Grown-ups" in *Days Japan* (September 1989). Under the subtitle "Girl Studies: An Introductory Seminar," the article consists of four parts: "girl commodity studies," "girl ethnicity studies," "girl linguistics," and "girl literature." By interviewing a number of cutting-edge media creators and critics such as Fujioka Wakao (commercial film producer), Nishikawa Ryūjin (marketing planner),

Ōtsuka Eiji (critic), Itō Seikō (multimedia creator), and Akimoto Yasushi (writer), this article is full of key concepts and insightful opinions that help in understanding the Banana phenomenon.

Opening with a photograph of the popular "Rika chan" doll,[8] experts display their opinions: "Stationery goods and fancy goods are popular among young people today, and Yoshimoto Banana's popularity is similar. . . ." (Fujioka Wakao). "Banana's books are fashion items just like dresses and accessories. For girls these days, music and novels are props in a theater centered around themselves as heroines" (Nishikawa Ryūjin). "She is an old-fashioned literature lover who writes her stories with spoken language. Her project is similar to Hashimoto Osamu's translation of [the tenth-century classic] *The Pillow Book* into contemporary Japanese" (Akimoto Yasushi). "Banana creates a simulation of modern literature in an easily understandable fashion" (Ōtsuka Eiji). "As today's girls live in the fictionality of images, the Banana world quickly becomes reality to them" (Itō Seikō).

Fancy goods, accessories, contemporary translations of old novels, the simulation of modern literature—these words sound like the clichés utilized in the field of commercial advertisement. I still believe that they fit the values attached to the Banana phenomenon more appropriately than conventional literary evaluations such as "refreshing aftertaste" and "original writing style." Some literary reviews, such as the following, sound inappropriately dimwitted:

> After all, who on earth is "I"? . . . This is not a question that can be easily rectified. Yet this uncertainty is a "virtue," largely shared by the "I"s in Banana's works. In fact, her novels often depend on a privileged mystery of the self. When the protagonist declares, "I understand everything now," I believe her. But what will remain after "understanding everything"? Will it be a *mono-no-aware* [the "pathos of things"] or an emptiness of "understanding"? (Shima Hiroyuki, *Kaien,* May 1989)

> What if we consider it this way? When the narrator says, "Yeah, the place I like the best in this world is the kitchen." Behind these words I hear her mutter "that's right" and "yeah." This is a type of "yeah," not as a response to someone's words, but as an accompaniment to a statement she has made after giving the topic a lot of thought: "Yeah, well, I believe it is so and so." It is a "yeah" that is addressed to herself as self-agreement and marks a rhythm in the way she lives. (Katō Norihiro, *Shisō no kagaku,* April 1992)

8. Rika chan is a popular Barbie-type doll on the market since 1968. Distributed by the toymaker Takara, when officially romanized, the name of the doll is transcribed "Licca." *ES*

The former is a review of Banana's short story "A Traveler between Nights" [Yoru to yoru no tabibito]," while the latter is an interpretation of the beginning sentence of *Kitchen*. . . . Katō's reading looks painfully bulky to me. Content-wise, what Shima and Katō try to point out differs very little from the comments made by Ōtsuka and Akimoto. Still, when expressed as conventional criticism, they sound much duller. This impression indicates that Banana's core character-istic resists the established terms and logic of literary criticism. Such criticism still functions with Haruki's works, which allow critics to "forcefully under-stand" their texts within "literature's problematics." For these critics, Banana seems unexpectedly difficult to digest.

Is the Banana World Cobalt Literature?

Now what is Yoshimoto Banana "after all"? Compare the following two extracts:

To say that this was the first time I had cherished such a feeling toward an-other would not be an exaggeration: a pure blank emotion with no biased filter and no unnecessary confusion. With Arashi, I felt like I was just a living being.

I thought I should keep that kind of feeling only in my heart and carefully cherish it. Of course, I can no longer walk or run, but the feeling that came to me then was a treasure.

The former is an extract from Banana's *Utakata*, while the latter is a pas-sage from Kitagawa Eriko's *Beautiful Life* (2000), the novelized version of a hit TV drama starring Kimura Takuya and Tokiwa Takako. (The exact sentence as quoted above was narrated by the protagonist when the drama was shown on TV.) Both segments are monologues by the protagonists. Close similarities be-tween the two can be found in the way the sentences are constructed, the way the protagonists express their feelings, and the way they distance themselves from the stories.

The scenarios of popular TV dramas were published just as they were until the end of the 1980s. In the 1990s they began to appear in novel form. Time-wise, *Utakata* and *Beautiful Life* have different historical contexts, but their similari-ties are still conspicuous. Does this similarity indicate that new novels and novel versions of TV dramas are all copying Banana? Probably not. I rather believe that women in Banana's generation share the same generational "style" of ex-pression. As for Banana's "style," people have often talked about the influence of girls' comics. . . . I wonder why no one has thought to make the connection to "another element of girls' culture." Perhaps this is a blind spot in the history of Japanese literature, but the other element to which I am referring is the Cobalt Library, a printed version of girls' comics whose paperback novels attracted many girls in the 1980s. They are naturally a more appropriate comparison for Banana's writing style as they are products consisting only of written text, as opposed to comics, which deal with pictorial and written texts.[9]

Shūeisha's Cobalt Library started in 1976, targeting teen girl readers. With its selling point of "teen sexuality," the library first tried to establish itself in the genre of "soft porn for girls" (a genre called "junior novels"). It transformed itself in the 1980s, when a number of young women writers (such as the best-seller Himuro Saeko and others in their twenties) started to write high-school-love comedies and the like, which enjoyed a tremendous popularity among teen girls.[10] Arai Motoko deserves special mention, as she was the one to introduce a sci-fi element into Cobalt novels and also established the explicit use of the first-person pronoun *atashi*.

We were waiting for something. In this pure white room. For quite some time. Possibly, we may have been waiting from the time we were born. Suddenly, I sensed something. In a flurry, I looked up. A goddess was standing in front of me. A goddess. I don't know why I realized that it was a goddess. (Arai Motoko, *Until the Day When I Become a Cat*, 1980)

Family members, who used to be solid existences, decreased one by one, and now I am here alone. The moment when I realize that fact, everything in front of my eyes looks unreal. In the room where I was born and raised, time continues to pass, and I am the only one left. That amazes me. It's like a sci-fi world. It's the darkness in the universe. (Yoshimoto Banana, *Kitchen*, 1989)

9. An exception is found in the interview of a Cobalt writer, Kurahashi Yōko, in "Yoshimoto Banana for Grown-ups" *(Days Japan)*. The article refers to the similarity between girls' novels and Banana's works. The analysis, however, remains obscure and is unable to explain the similarities clearly. *AU*

10. The early Cobalt Library included writers such as Tomishima Takeo, Saeki Chiaki, Satō Aiko, and others. Tomishima's "Here, In the Chest of My School Uniform," in the inaugural issue, is indicative of the original aim of the series—that is, "soft porn written by middle-aged male writers." In the 1980s, "big sister writers" in their twenties, led by Himuro and others such as Tanaka Masami, Kumi Saori, and Shōmoto Non, started to dominate the series. The library was understood as printed versions of girls' comics or original stories for comic versions and formed a giant market. At its peak in the late 1980s, many first editions of its novels printed between two and four hundred thousand copies. The library has published over 2,900 books to the present. From the late 1990s on its dominant topic has turned to "boys' love," concentrating on homosexual love between young boys, with less popularity than the library had enjoyed in the 1980s. Still, boys' love stories cumulatively have sold more than 1 million copies. *AU*

Let me note that *Until the Day When I Become a Cat* was the first novel Arai wrote for the Cobalt series, and it became a mega hit, creating an unprecedented boom in girls' novels. Narration based on the first-person pronoun (*atashi* for Arai and *watashi* for Banana) and the narrator's sudden distancing from the story she is in the process of narrating are highly valued and much analyzed characteristics of Banana's writing, but they are commonly shared by Arai. Shouldn't we say that the so-called characteristics of Banana's writing are, in fact, those of different Bananas?

I found two articles discussing the connection between Yoshimoto's works and the girls' novels of the Cobalt Library: one is Shimura Yukiko's "Girls' Reading: Images of the Girl in the Novels of Orihara Mito and Yoshimoto Banana," an article that appears in an educational journal; the other is Mitsui Takayuki's "The Myth of Yoshimoto Banana" (Mitsui Takayuki and Washida Koyata, *The Myth of Yoshimoto Banana*, 1989). Based on the *Mainichi* newspaper's surveys of books favored by students between the fourth and twelfth grades, Shimura delineated a changing trend in terms of favorite authors for junior high and high school girl students. Accordingly, many girls' novels by Himuro Saeko and Arai Motoko began to make the list from around 1980. . . . From the end of the 1980s, Orihara Mito becomes the favorite author for junior high students, while Yoshimoto Banana is the favorite for high school students.

Orihara Mito has written mainly for Kōdansha's X Library Teens' Heart Series, a Cobalt Library rival. Precisely speaking, she is therefore not a Cobalt writer, but she succeeds to what had been achieved by Himuro and Arai. Shimura stresses strong similarities between Orihara's popular works *(When an Angel Comes Down, Teenager Blues, Let's Meet under the Cherry Flowers)* and Banana's popular novels *(Kitchen, Good-bye Tsugumi, NP)*. First, they are all essentially "coming-of-age stories." Second, they are all narrated by a first-person narrator. Shimura even goes so far as to claim that except for differences in the protagonists' ages, they are all essentially the same story.[11]

When Orihara and Yoshimoto started writing in late 1980s, the genre of girls' novels formed a gigantic market, as the success of the Cobalt Library had trig-

11. The narrators of Orihara's stories sound more childish than Banana's. Take, for instance, the following line: "Cancer and blood type A. Grades above average. The best skill I have is the cooking I learned from my mom" *(Teenager Blues)*. In this sense, we cannot literally say that Orihara's and Banana's novels are the same. Teen girls develop their reading by moving from Orihara's novels to Banana's. Shimura states that "the genre of the so-called youth novels and junior novels has never been seriously studied because it has been separated from both children's literature and regular literature for adults. In order to improve our literature and reading education for children, we need to pay serious attention to this in-between genre of literature." I believe this remark is important. *AU*

gered many rival publishing companies to create new libraries for teenagers.[12] In terms of content, this was the time when surreally sci-fi fantasies started to replace the originally favored topics of high school comedies and realistically written love stories. The change was probably influenced by popular computer games like Dragon Quest. This environment seems to explain why Banana was enthusiastically received by teen readers. The type of stories first developed by Himuro and pushed by Arai into a sci-fi universe were returned to the earth, so to speak, by Banana. . . .

Thematically, most of the early Banana novels consist of three key words: family, death, and solitude. The narrator/protagonist is always surrounded by the heavy shadow of death and solitude. In "Kitchen" the protagonist loses her grandmother, who was her last family member. "Full Moon," the continuation of "Kitchen," begins with the death of one of the main characters. The protagonist of "Moonlight Shadow" suffers from the death of her boyfriend. The protagonist of *Utakata* is an illegitimate child whose mother attempts suicide. "Sanctuary" unfolds with an encounter between a widow whose husband was killed in a car accident and a young man whose former girlfriend killed herself. In *A Presentiment* the protagonist, who lost her childhood memories, later realizes that her parents died when she was an infant. A beautiful cousin suffers from an incurable illness in *Good-bye Tsugumi*. All these stories seem unable to start without someone's death or at least a strong smell of death.

Most stories conclude with these lonely girl protagonists developing a light, family-like unity with the people who surround them and experiencing some modest sense of healing. This pattern of conclusion inevitably attracts criticism for its "conservativeness" and "reactionarily sentimental melodrama." Girls' comics, which developed much earlier than the Cobalt novels and Banana's stories, display incomparably radical conclusions. It seems erroneous to compare Banana's theme development with that of cutting-edge girls' comics. Don't Banana stories look more like the older stories that were pushed out of the market by girls' comics? I am thinking of the girls' novels that were popular from pre-World War II through the immediate postwar. These now extinct girls' stories stereotypically glorified the unhappiness of the girl heroines. For example, there was the story of a young girl completely bereft after the death of her parents; or the story of a girl who sells flowers on the street after her family

12. Teens libraries include Kōdansha X Library Teens' Heart, Kadokawa Sneaker Library, Fujimi Fantasia Library, Asahi Sonorama Library, and the like. A little later, libraries for elementary school children were started in 1989, including Tokuma Library Pastel Series, MOE Library Sweet Love Story, Futabasha Strawberry Library Teens' Mate, Gakken Lemon Library, and others. *AU*

falls to ruin; and the story of a girl who suffers from tuberculosis and lives in a sanatorium in Shinshū, and so on.[13]

Banana's acceptance proves the existence of a repeated pattern of marketability: to pour old wine (story's content) in a new bottle (writing style). It is the same pattern with which Tawara Machi was accepted as a colloquial *tanka* poet. The way Banana connected the new style with the old story seems to have created a shock effect stronger than Tawara's case. Isn't this why Banana could "refreshingly move" readers of two different generations — older conventional literature readers witnessing the original bottle (style) they had never before seen and the younger Cobalt literature readers tasting the old wine (story) for the first time?

Meta Messages in Pen Names and Afterwords

Here I will introduce examples of "commodity criticism," the last category of critical approaches I mentioned in the beginning of this essay. This criticism evaluates not the book's content itself, but the information surrounding the book and the values added to the book. One of the strongest added values comes from the fact that Banana is the daughter of a famous critic, Yoshimoto Takaaki. Another surprising feature is her almost jokingly bold choice of "Banana" for her pen name. Early reviews often referred to this naming. . . . Miura Masashi noted that the majority of readers are certain to conclude "[Banana] may be OK as a name for a dog or cat, but how dare one choose it for a real person" (*Sunday Mainichi*, March 13, 1988). Or, in the words of Agawa Sachiko: "How did she come to choose such an unusual name? Moreover, that she writes it in the *hiragana* syllabary is intriguing. If written in *katakana*, we could easily associate it with such images as yellow, sweet, Satchan (a girl character in a comic strip who can eat only half a banana), and so forth. With Banana in *hiragana*, we cannot tell if the author is young or old, man or woman, modern or traditional. It is curiosity over this mystery that leads us to take a look at her book" (*Classy*, October 1988).

This simple name, Banana, created a furor. The reaction may not have been comparable if it were the name of a TV personality. (Note the absurd names

13. According to Karasawa Shun'ichi's *The Counterattack of Beautiful Girls*, the peak of popularity of these stories "with unhappy girl heroines" was from 1945 to the late 1950s, a time when Japan still suffered the trauma of World War II. Their popularity was quickly replaced by girls' comics and girls' novels in translation. Karasawa notes that these girls' novels always had a message to readers in the authors' "foreword." The Cobalt afterword seems to be a variant of this format. *AU*

used by some members of Beat Takeshi's Troupe.) This proves how naïve literary journalism is. We should remember the famous haiku poet who held the same name. Banana's ancestor is none other than Bashō.[14] It is a mystery to me that no one linked her with him earlier.

To identify Banana with Bashō, however, seems absurd when we situate her name in the context of the Cobalt world, where writers have names like Ai Azumi [Indigo Azumi], Akizuki Kō [Autumn Moon Kō], Isshiki Minto [All But Mint . . .], and illustrators' names include Kobayashi Ponzu [Citrus Vinegar], Hanasaki Sakura [Flower Blooming Cherry], Momokuri Mikan [Peach-Chestnut Tangerine], and the like. Nakamura Usagi [Rabbit], a writer who has become well known these days, was originally with the Cobalt Library. The name "Yoshimoto Banana" would be very much at home in this culture.[15]

Another feature frequently discussed in Banana criticism is her use of the "afterword." Her books always include somewhat awkwardly expressed afterwords. Let me quote one (although omitted from the paperback version).

I dedicate "Kitchen" to Mr. Terada Hiroshi of Fukutake Shoten, "Full Moon" to Mr. Nemoto Masao of Fukutake Shoten, and "Moonlight Shadow" to my friend, Yoshikawa Jirō, who introduced me to Mike Oldfield's classic piece of music, from which my short story borrowed its title. I also want to happily dedicate to my father the very fact that my first book was published. I am sorry to dedicate my book in such a complex way, but I wish you would accept it. I am thankful to all of you. *(Kitchen)*

Unlike books of criticism and nonfiction, novels do not usually include an afterword. Moreover, it seems odd to include fairly private acknowledgments to her editors, friends, and family members. A passage before the lines quoted

14. Grand master of the early Edo "linked verse" poetry *haikai,* Matsuo Bashō (1644–1694) composed such an impressive number of the 5-7-5 opening triplets (called *hokku*) that he became known as the founder of haiku when it became an independent Japanese verse category in the Meiji period. He adopted his pen name, Bashō, which means banana tree, after the much beloved banana tree that had been given to him by his students. ES

15. In Cobalt novels (as well as in Banana's) heroes' names are also elaborately chosen. The heroes/narrators, with unusual names, always introduce themselves in the beginning of their stories: "My name is written with the *kanji* for bird-sea-human-fish. It is pronounced as Toriumi Ningyo. I asked my mom the reason for this absurd name when I first heard about the person named Arashi" (Yoshimoto Banana, *Utakata*); "My name is Unno [Sea Field] Momoko. Mokuzu [Seaweed] is, of course, my nickname. (What kind of crazy parents would think of a crazy name like Unno Mokuzu?) I'm their only child and will turn twenty tomorrow" (Arai Motoko, *Until the Day When I Become a Cat*). AU

above includes the stunning lines: "I have a lot of friends and acquaintances. I would dedicate to all of them my virginity . . . as a writer."

The words "joy of a professional writer," used in the afterword of *Utakata/Sanctuary*, angered Tomioka Taeko, who found in Banana a certain shamelessness when the novice writer called herself a professional in her second book. At any rate, Banana stunned the common expectations of grown-up critics. . . .

> I believe Yoshimoto Banana is epoch-making in Japanese literature when it comes to the "afterword." Nobody has written his or her afterword in such a naked, straight, and strategic fashion. . . . In her afterword, we can sense her honest thankfulness. The "complex way of dedicating" each short story to different persons indicates how much she fondly appreciates each individual connection she has with them. . . . Her afterword functions as a meta-fiction of the fictionality of her book's preceding short stories. (Kamata Tōji, "'Afterword' and 'Nostalgia,'" *Kokubungaku*, special edition, May 1991)

The reviewer claims that Banana's popularity comes from the sense of nostalgic fondness inspired by her afterword as meta-message. I find this reading interestingly insightful. However, the afterword is not original to Banana. Rather, the novels in the Cobalt Library first developed this type of afterword and its meta-fiction/meta-message. The addition of an afterword became standard in Cobalt novels around 1980 and was probably started by Himuro Saeko. Since then, the afterword evolved as more than a supplement to the novel and was established as an inevitable feature—offering space where the writer introduced her readers to her own real life episodes. It is also a message board that connects the writer with her readers. . . . Let's take a look at an afterword by Arai Motoko.

> I will never forget the time when my first book was published. Bikke distributed a number of copies to her relatives and friends. Cham negotiated with her neighborhood bookstore owner and successfully placed a number of copies of my book there. Akira moved copies of my book to a more visible location every time he went to bookstores. The bravest one was Mikiko: She tried to sell my book to a door-to-door sales person when he visited her house (I hear she was not successful, however). I truly don't know what to say. (Arai Motoko, *Until the Day when I Become a Cat*)

I truly don't know what to say. . . . Arai mentions over twenty of her friends by name in this afterword. Compared to this, Banana's is much more official and impersonal.

Banana as an Export Good

The Banana boom had a second stage in 1993, which corresponded to the translations of her novels into different languages. Translations of *Kitchen* were published in Italy, the United States, the United Kingdom, Germany, and Spain, and contracts for additional translations were negotiated with publishers from eight other countries, including France, the Netherlands, and Korea. In Japan, the 1989 Banana fever had subsided, and she was now just another popular writer. But news about Banana's popularity abroad (that she was popular not only among students majoring in Japanese literature, but also among young female workers like bank clerks and young housewives) reignited a domestic curiosity about her global acceptance. Example of Japanese reviews read:

> The catch phrase "Banana mania" proves that the way Banana is consumed abroad is similar to her reception here in Japan. In both cases, her readership accepts her as a member of a subculture. Murakami Haruki has been accepted as a representative of canonical Japanese literature and mainly attracts those with a special interest in Japanese literature. In contrast, Banana's novels seem to have been accepted as subculture texts in the States and elsewhere. (Ōtsuka Eiji, *Voice,* September 1994)

> Banana is not aware that her works are part of world literature but keenly understands her marketability. That's why she calls herself a craftsman. The market for girls' comics, by which she is heavily influenced, is tough: if one cannot sell, one will quickly be out of the market. Comics writers develop a sharp sensibility to grasp what readers want to read. Banana has the same sensibility. As the Japanese comics market has been accepted universally, Banana's global popularity basically explains the same mechanism of marketability: Her popularity in the States is parallel to Jarinko Chie's acceptance in France. (Karatani Kōjin [interviewed], *Kōkoku hihyō,* May 1993)

Both Karatani and Ōtsuka view Banana as a subculture phenomenon. Her novels were accepted as "un-Japanese" products, just as comics and computer games made in Japan were accepted worldwide. Karatani even pointed out that "what we see here is a childishness toward which the world culture has regressed."

As for American and Italian intellectuals, here are examples of their reviews.

The two most common phrases in classical Japanese literature, as well as in modern pop songs and in Yoshimoto's book, are sadness *[kanashimi]* and nostalgia *[natsukashisa]*. Translated into English, this can sound odd. . . . Perhaps "nostalgic" isn't even quite the right word for *natsukashii,* but I don't know of a better one.

Nostalgia is closely linked to that other key element of Japanese aesthetics: *mono no aware,* the pathos of things. (Ian Buruma, "Ian Buruma's Inquiries about Japan," *The Missionary and the Libertine,* 1996)

Literature for girls is expected to be rosy, but in Japan it is shadowy. Youth is not a period when one enjoys the blossom of a bud; rather, it is a time when, with resignation, one accepts maturity as an inevitable destiny. It does not stress an occidental optimism that ends with the joy of "I am alive! How happy I am!"; it consists of a quiet sigh of *"mono no aware."* (Renata Pisu, *La Republica,* July 18, 1991/*Marco Polo,* December 1993)

It is with *mono no aware* [the aesthetic of the Japanese classics] that American and Italian reviewers commonly characterize Banana! How on earth can we bridge this gap between global subculture and Japanese *mono no aware* in terms of understanding Banana? There is another element both Buruma and Pisu point out about Banana: her transgendered or androgynous quality.[16] According to them, this quality is uniquely Japanese (as seen also in Takarazuka performances).[17] Then the question will remain why such a Japanese story of *mono no aware* and cross-dressed beauties is accepted worldwide. Do women in the States and Italy read Banana just as they read Kawabata and Mishima?

To connect Banana with the concept of *mono no aware* or with Takarazuka seems to show an erroneously Orientalist reading. At the very least one should say that the extent to which these critics have read between the lines in Banana's books is excessive. What we are dealing with here is the commonality of sentimentalism that we can find almost anywhere in the world. But to make short

---

16. "Yoshimoto Banana's stories are clearly related to the androgynous teenage universe of Takarazuka and the girls' comics. The characters in *Kitchen,* a book of two short stories, include a transsexual father and a boy who dresses up in his dead girlfriend's school uniform. Yet there is nothing overtly kinky about these transformations" (Ian Buruma). "In the world of Banana's literature, sexes are mixed up, helping her to create ideally androgynous images, which are not unusual in Japan. Japanese women dream of being eternally girls and detest playing the role of a grown-up woman. They are in love with men performed on stage by women and intoxicated by the fact that on stage they can act like men. The men they can love should be sweet and kind like these *bishōnen* in the theater" (Renata Pisu). *AU*

17. Founded in 1914 in the city of Takarazuka, this girls-only revue theater became very popular after the late 1920s. Known for performances of Western revues and musicals like "Mon Paris," "West Side Story," and "Gone with the Wind," today the revue performs regularly in its own theaters in Osaka and Tokyo and still attracts large, mostly female audiences. *ES*

work of Banana by writing her off with clichéd terms like "subculture," which are constantly used in reference to girls comics, is overly facile.

I believe that Banana stories (as well as those by Himuro, Arai, and Orihara) are equipped with elements that are popular among women readers throughout the world: "girl's coming-of-age stories" are borderless. One typical example can be found in the British genre of "family romance." Burnett's *Little Lord Fauntleroy* and *The Secret Garden*, Spyri's *Heidi*, Montgomery's *Anne of Green Gables*, and Webster's *Daddy Long Legs* are stories that attracted girls all over the world. Notice that they all share common elements: the authors and protagonists are women, and the protagonists are orphans. These are elements shared also by *Kitchen*.

If the peak of the Cobalt Library's popularity was during the 1980s, what did Japanese girls read during the '60s and '70s? They read *Anne of Green Gables* (and stories that were modeled on it). *Anne of Green Gables* and *Heidi* were televised in the '70s and gained a male audience. Before then, they were products for "girls only." Of course, "girls-only products" included Alcott's *Little Women,* Porter's *Pauliana,* and even Brontë's *Wuthering Heights,* and Colette's *Blue Wheat* for older girl readers. Stories from the J-Poem series, written by Gin'iro Natsuo, Tachihara Erika, and Mitsuhashi Chikako can be added to the same list.[18] There should be quite a number of women who remember that they read some of them when they were in high school. The term "subculture" applies perfectly to this "girls-only literature" as a global subculture with implications of secondary, marginal, subterranean, inferior, and discriminated cultures.[19]

18. J-Poem is a nonestablished poetry subcategory. Saitō uses the term with double layers of meaning. It is an abbreviation of "junior poems," a category commercially used to refer to collections of sentimental poems for teenage girl readers (Gin'iro is a star poet in this sense). "J" also carries the same implications found in more established category names like J-Pop and J-*bungaku,* where "J" stands for the "Japan permeated by pop culture sensibility." J-Pop implicitly claims that the songs of this category belong to the universal global category of pop songs, with Japan's local flavors added. In the case of J-*bungaku,* "J" overlaps Japan and *jun* in *junbungaku* (pure literature), meaning that works by J-*bungaku* writers (Abe Kazushige, for instance) mix high-brow thematic elements with young protagonists associated with particular teen subculture contexts (for example, the Shibuya street culture of the 1990s). In this sense, J-Poem refers to the particular mode of Japanese consumption of girlish poetic expressions from the 1970s through the present: cute and fancy book covers, poems displayed together with pictorial texts, and books sold at fancy goods stores together with Hello Kitty goods. *ES*

19. For an older generation of readers who spent their teens before and during World War II, Yoshiya Nobuko seems to have been the cult figure of girls' culture. Her style clearly differentiated itself from other writers of the girls' novels at the time, and I believe because of it, she enjoyed tremendous support from her readers. Himuro's popular novel in long series, *Clara's*

Although *Anne of Green Gables* is separated by a hundred years from both Banana's stories and the Cobalt series, the three are almost blood relations in terms of their contents. Each contains a tomboyish protagonist who is fairly free from girlish gender-role assignments; a coming-of-age story in which the heroine develops spiritual independence through small personal incidents; a validation of friendship among girls; a heroine who is cautious about falling in love with a boy; no description of sexual acts; and, finally, an acceptance of transgendered or androgynous elements, an example of which can be seen in the Cobalt romances of the late 1990s describing love between young males. (I personally feel that these stories have weakened Cobalt literature as a genre.) These are elements globally favored by the majority of teen girl readers.

On the other hand, girls' literature also conventionally included conservative elements such as a stress on the value of family and the conformist ending, which reinforces the existing social order. *Anne of Green Gables,* for instance, once enthusiastically accepted, is now read only by a few. Banana Yoshimoto was exported in this Western historical context of girls' literature. That she is now accepted by girl readers of different countries seems to indicate that she has been read as a contemporarily revised version of Anne, with an attractively nostalgic flavor. Readers are probably filled with a sense of "yes-I-know-this-world."

An Alien from the Country of Women and Children

The way in which Banana is read differs from that of ordinary literary works. She is treated like a literary commodity or even a sort of "character good." In this sense, she is not unlike "Rika chan" or the ubiquitous "Hello Kitty." The Banana world is a world where girls may play with their dolls, a world in which they may explore the melodrama of death through childlike expressions. As long as it is a dolls' world, stories replete with death and dysfunctional families do not become threateningly real. Because she is a commodity good, information surrounding her novels, such as her pen name and her afterword, invite curiosity and speculation. Commodity criticism reviewers' understanding of Banana as a "character goods" product is relevant in this sense. Their analyses do not, however, situate her in the context associated with the Cobalt literature.[20]

White Paper, has something in common with girls' novels from abroad, as well as with Yoshiya's girls' dormitory stories. The girls' literature seems to thus form a genealogical context. *AU*

20. A computer game designer, Yonemitsu Kazunari, who studies Cobalt literature, was the one who told me, "When Banana made her debut, everybody around me said, 'Hey, this must be a Cobalt.'" All critics, including myself, who didn't realize this connection should recognize our incompetence. For more details, see Yonemitsu Kazunari, "L Literature's Origin Was in the Cobalt of Late 1980s" (*Hato yo!* May 2000). About literature for girls only, also see my essays

When I say Banana is an alien, I mean that she is like "Sally the Witch," who has crossed the border from the "country of women and children" to the "country of grown-up men."[21] Things that are ordinary in literature for girls-only (the country of women and children) can look powerfully charming for inhabitants of orthodox literature (the country of grown-up men). The girl's magic spell, "*maharik, maharita*," enchanted male intellectuals, who were clueless about who she really was. If one-tenth of the effort these critics devoted to their serious study of the "intertextuality" in Murakami Haruki's works had been dedicated to the study of Banana's intertextual context, they would have detected a history of girl culture that has been running as an undercurrent throughout modern history. Without this context, readers of Banana repeat absurdly painful misreadings and overreadings.

Haruki, Machi, and Banana are symbolic of the literary scene of the late 1980s. They are all old wine in new bottles; that is to say, their pop expressions coat their *enka*-like old lyricism.[22] Evaluations of their art clearly split into two streams, depending on the reviewer's focus. There are those who emphasize the stylistic newness and those the stories' oldness. Why was, for instance, Haruki's pop writing style (what Nejime Shōichi called "the style of a coffee house owner") so strongly supported by his readers? Satō Yoshiaki explained this phenomenon in association with a historical change in audiences' bodily sensibilities. Nineteen seventy-nine was the year Haruki published his first novel. It was also the year the pop-rock group Southern All-Stars made its debut. After analyzing the musical "styles" of Haruki's *Hear the Wind Sing [Kaze no uta wo kike]* and the Southern All-Stars' "Ellie, My Love," Satō states: "Haruki's skill is to be acknowledged for his string of hit novels. But at essence his success depends on the proliferation of pop products and the way they've been received. Haruki responded promptly to the contextual change in audience taste—that is, a change in the reception of the perceived naturalness of 'songs.'

"Usage of Girls' Literature" (*Bungakkai*, June 2000) and "A New Anatomy of L Literature" (*Hato yo!* May 2000). *AU*

21. Sally the Witch first appeared in the 1966 girls' comic book *Ribbon* as "Sanny the Witch," written by Yokoyama Mitsuteru (a popular comics writer mainly working for boys' comics). In December of the same year, it appeared as the first TV anime for girls under the title *Sally the Witch* and became an immediate hit. A series of 109 stories was broadcasted through 1968. The shows were repeatedly rerun through the mid-1980s. *ES*

22. *Enka* are traditional popular songs. Mostly love songs, they typically highlight disappointment in love. Musically, they are usually slow ballads known for their very long high-tone vibrato. Saitō's discussion of the way physical sensibilities changed from *enka* to pop culture stresses that the newness of Banana's generation was something that was perceived physically as well as emotionally. *ES*

The same can be said of the popularity of the musical group Southern All-Stars" (Satō Yoshiaki, "History of J-Pop Literature," *Creation of Twenty-First-Century Literature: Post-Literature and Trans-Literature,* 2002).

During the 1970s people's living environments changed dramatically. This is especially true for young people. Their private lives were permeated to the core by comfortable sounds and images. This increase in pleasant stimuli on the auditory and visual senses transformed the reading experiences and increased demand for new literary styles. In sum, the "body that responded to *enka*" was replaced by a "body attracted to pop." Satō claims that this change in people's "bodies" occurred around 1980, at just the time when Haruki and Southern All-Stars had made their debut. I believe Satō's point is crucial. Haruki, Machi, and Banana thus represented a new historical moment, together with the Southern All-Stars and pop female vocalist Arai Yumi (known as Yūmin).

The content of their messages, however, complicates things. Regardless of the perceived newness of their style, their stories are still sprinkled with old sentimentalism, like the maudlin lyrics of an *enka* ballad. The authors' seemingly anticonformist attitude hides their essentially pro-establishment mentality. At their stories' conclusions they have neatly reinforced the existing social order and values. Where does their messages' ambivalently conservative nature come from? I believe it reflects their readers' desire for conservative stories. They were writing at the peak of Japan's bubble economy, a time when people nakedly exhibited their sexual desire. The media created booms highlighting sexy female college students and pampered princesses from rich families. Sensuous clothes showing off every curve in the female body became popular, and at night (seemingly) sexual young women swaggered about on urban streets. Imagine locating Machi and Banana next to these women. To do so would only make you realize how purifying, heartwarming, and appeasing the former looked. They were really refreshing tonics that could give older people that secure feeling of "yes-we-still-have-this-nice-kind-of-girl."

It is true that some feminist critics regard Banana with, most often, reservations. Her evaluation in their eyes is determined by whether they view the girl-ness of the Banana world as a regression or a mutation or a sign of true change. Kanai Yoshiko claims that Banana's heroines carefully study "the despondency that descended on feminists once the 'Decade of Women' had passed."[23] These

23. The Women's Decade (or the Era of Women) is a journalistic term emphatically used in the late 1970s and 1980s. Tired of the established stereotypical woman (e.g., an office worker with no serious job assignments before marriage and a homemaker with no special skills after marriage), a new generation of women, inspired by the 1960s women's liberation movement, pursued more socially successful/visible self-expressions. New women's magazines like *Croissant* and *MORE,* which began publishing in the late 1970s, answered women's desire for more

"mothers' daughters" are, according to Kanai, keenly aware of the emptiness of their mothers' "Women's Decade" ("Reading the 'Banana Phenomenon' from Feminist Eyes," *Kokubungaku,* May 1991). Kanai's words remind me of the rapid change in popular trends. Before the popularity enjoyed by Banana's "innocent girls," idols of an older generation flaunted themselves with an air of anti-innocence.

‖ ‖   The Consciousness of the Girl

Freedom and Arrogance

TAKAHARA EIRI

I. The Need to Think as a Girl

Among my friends there is a married woman who is a writer. I once heard a man tell her that she needed to hurry up and have a child in order to develop her writing style. I remember being astounded and furious, although I couldn't think of anything to say at the time. Who gave him the right, first of all, to imply that every woman should have a child? And where did he get the idea that having a child could somehow influence a woman's writing? There was no way, without seeing her work, that he could tell a woman she should write like a mother. In fact, what right did he have to claim that any woman should be a mother?

My concern was unnecessary, however, for fortunately my friend was much more alert than I. "That's sexual harassment," she retorted. "How dare you talk

---

independent and aggressively individualistic visions of womanhood. Images of career women, who were fashion-conscious as well as sexually mature and liberated, emerged from the pages of these journals as the model of a new woman. A Martha Stewart-like homemaker with special skills for home decoration/improvement was another attractive vision of a new woman. With the collapse of the bubble economy, the woman's image in the Era of Women was replaced, according to Saitō, by the popularity of less aggressive female images, symbolically represented by Yoshimoto Banana and Tawara Machi. Although these images were seemingly conservative, they embodied a new critical energy that distanced them from their outwardly aggressive predecessors. *ES.*

TRANSLATED BY TOMOKO AOYAMA AND BARBARA HARTLEY. From Takahara Eiri, "Shōjo-gata ishiki: Jiyū to kōman" (The consciousness of the girl: Freedom and arrogance), the introduction to Takahara's *Shōjo ryōiki* (The territory of the girl) (Kokusho kankōkai, 1999), pp. 6–20. (The book discusses the works of Nomizo Naoko, Ryūtanji Yū, Kawabata Yasunari, Ozaki Midori, Murō Saisei, Inagaki Taruho, Kurahashi Yumiko, Mori Mari, Nakamori Akio, Matsuura Rieko, and Ōhara Mariko.)

to me like that? Mind your own business!" But her words had no effect, and the fellow blundered on without apology. "It's true, you know; your writing will really change." I don't know what others would have said. I wanted to cry, "But why should she change the way she writes? And who asked you to tell her to have children?" In the end, though, all I could do was mutter a few words about his speaking out of turn.

Of course this is different from the question of whether or not one should become a mother, but it is something that implicates all women. When I come across these bigots, I want to scream "Why?" to the whole world. My friend probably felt the same. However, she was accustomed to such attacks and handled the situation like an adult. I still don't understand the need for these insufferable, insensitive people. The world is a beautiful place. Why should we put up with such ugly creatures?

My response to the situation above, which demands an answer of society even before the offender, is a typically girl reaction. Thus you can see that being a girl has nothing to do with age or sex. For we are thinking like a girl when, upon meeting these insensitive brutes who symbolize every hideous trait of the adult male, we wonder where such bad taste comes from. Some might choose the label "woman," but I believe that "girl" has greater impact since it discredits adult thinking and is implicitly critical of adult thoughtlessness and insensitivity.

We might be tempted also to use the word "boy," for once long ago in Taishō times, when Orikuchi Shinobu wrote a novel about young boys' love called *The Whistle [Kuchibue],* the boy's consciousness did imply a criticism of such matters. Today, however, the youthful male spirit no longer seems to critique the world of adult men. In contemporary times, for some reason, boys set out at a very young age to take possession of a woman. This desire for ownership arises from an ingrained insensitivity, for these boys have already sensed the significance of the miniature adult male within.

In her commentary on the collected works of Nomizo Naoko, a writer to whom I will return later, Yagawa Sumiko noted: "For better or for worse, girls are both women and underaged. This gives them unlimited benefit in that they are unrestrained by the conflicting interests of the society around them. Young men are susceptible to a sense of obligation or the desire for success, advancement, and power. Girls, however, remain free from these desires precisely because they are girls. Thus they are imbued with an unsullied sense of objectivity."

Unfortunately, I lack the "unsullied sense" to which Yagawa refers, contaminated as I am by vested powers and interests. Nevertheless, there are still times, few though they may be, when I am able to think like a girl. All of which leads to my failing to understand the need for men like the one who accosted my friend.

Having said that, I should point out that I do not wish to valorize particularly the thinking of girls. The girls' viewpoint basically really only has the same potential value as adult women's thinking, adult men's thinking, the thinking of elderly people, and so on. None of these is good or bad in itself. Nor does any one call for special censure. These days, for example, you might need to think like an adult male to be given membership in an organization. (This might change in the future. It is quite possible that women's ideas might become the standard for institutional thought.) But society nowadays is so saturated with the thinking of the adult male that we cannot but question why.

If the role of the critic is to discriminate selectively and express dissent, then it is only my ability to think as a girl that qualifies me as such. As well as informing critical ability, thinking like a girl also permits the discovery of all sorts of things: "fantastic" things—things that give us a sense of pure joy, things we yearn for, and, of course, creative works of art.

In fact, I actually think that ideas and beliefs that do not arise from thinking like a girl can be unbearably brutish. Certainly, when deciding what appeals and what does not, I myself have always tried to do so as a girl. "Fantastic" is a word that is commonly used to express our joy when we come across something really appealing or interesting. Its use in this way has, in effect, been defined by girls. What I'm referring to here is no formulaic girlish fad, but a more fundamental and all-encompassing sense of beauty. Of course, a person of any age or sex can adopt such an outlook. The film director Iwai Shunji, for example, is discerning enough to draw constantly on what we might call his "girl consciousness."

In the field of literature publishers provide us with a myriad of novels and other stories, few of which have any appeal. Many, in fact, are highly insensitive and among other things impose a given set of gender stereotypes that imply that men behave in one way and women in another. Perhaps it is the base craving to dominate and oppress that I find so distasteful in these works, or perhaps it is the absence of reading pleasure. It should be noted that what I refer to here is quite different from the "appealing insensitivity" discussed in later chapters.

In any case, when deciding whether or not I like something, I try to think like a girl. Let us consider the novels of Mishima Yukio as an example. Mishima's work can be grossly sexist. However, I can forgive this to some extent, for somewhere in his writing is the highly attractive notion of "the girl who wants to become a man." Although they themselves are in no way girl-like, there are a number of other writers in this category, including Edogawa Ranpo, Kawabata Yasunari (at least in some of his novels), Inagaki Taruho, Tsukamoto Kunio, and Nakai Hideo. (I should make clear that what these writers actually had was the ability to think like a boy. However, when they were writing, this was equivalent to the modern ability to think like a girl.) Of course, Ozaki Midori and Mori Mari also fit the given criteria.

On the other hand, Murakami Ryū might have tremendous talent and the ability to think occasionally like a girl. But I want to shriek, "Stop!" at his naked desire for adult male power. Even so, his work has some value. I wouldn't give him the time of day if he were a blatantly macho writer. (I am not referring here to physique—in spite of all his body-building efforts, there was nothing macho about Mishima). I don't waste my time discussing macho writers, let alone actually reading their work.

We should also note the error of assuming that merely being a woman ensures the ability to think like a girl.[24] However, be assured that the works of each of the writers discussed in this book give full play to girls' thinking. It is my aim, in fact, to read fiction through the ability to think like a girl that is lodged somewhere in the consciousness of each of us. I am not referring here only to real girls, for it is not necessary to be an actual girl; rather we need to be *like* a girl. In order to highlight this point, I intend to refer to the texts under discussion here as "girl consciousness" literature.

II. Resistance against Talking about the Girl

In an essay entitled "The Runaway Girl in a Labyrinth" (Meikyū no naka no iede shōjo, in Honda Masuko, ed., *Shōjo ron*, Seikyūsha) Hashimoto Osamu notes the conflicting perspectives of girls and middle-aged men and the mutual misunderstanding between the two that results in a deep communication gap. Hashimoto also expresses his contempt for those who make declarations about young women based on their own narrow prejudice, distancing his own endeavors from these. His words are a sober caution to me as I embark on this discussion of the literature of the girl. However, there is nothing one can do to prevent oneself sometimes taking the consciousness of the girl, a possibility that Hashimoto appears to have dispensed with completely.

Perhaps the girl's love of the "fantastic" and her desire to resist appear juvenile to Hashimoto, who has aligned himself with what he seems to regard as a more mature path that is both just and fair. I, however, want to respond to the

---

24. Although the author Takahara is biologically male, this fact has been carefully concealed from the reader of *The Territory of the Girl*. The writer's real name, Katō Mikiya, clearly marks him as male. But his penname, Takahara Eiri, is gender neutral. The brief biographical note accompanying *The Territory of the Girl* mentions only that the author's surname is Katō, leaving out the clearly male given name. Takahara emphasizes throughout the book that what he terms the consciousness of the girl does not simply or automatically belong to the biological girl. Nevertheless, given the nature of his argument, many readers (including the present translators) believed that Takahara was a woman. This is despite the fact that at no time does he overtly assume a female persona.

presence of the girl within me. It is useful here to recall that Hashimoto himself, even while denying any affinity with the thinking of girls, commenced his literary career with *The Peach-Bottomed Girl [Momojiri musume]*, whose protagonist narrator was an adolescent girl. He is also the author of a seminal collection of critical essays on girls' comics entitled *The Tinned Pea Salad of the Maidens in Full Bloom [Hana saku otometachi no kinpira gobō]*. His ongoing interest in the accepted social processes of gender development in young men and women can also be seen in the quasi-tearjerker morality tale-cum-confessional text *Cinderella Boy, Cinderella Girl*.

So here we have it: there is a way of looking at things that we might refer to as "girl consciousness." I have it and you have it. The texts to be discussed here are informed throughout by a strong girl consciousness, and my aim is to draw on this same consciousness as I read and critique these texts. To this end, I totally reject any endeavor that responds to girls with a drooling leer. Like Hashimoto himself, I cannot stress strongly enough the crass self-centeredness and total lack of self-awareness that fuels the urges of adult men who lust after girls. There have been any number of discussions that regard the girl merely as an "Other" to be desired. This text rejects that approach. Here I seek to consider the texts being discussed as if I were a girl. Furthermore, I want to foreground the contestation of gender, which is inherent in the consciousness of the girl. For what I think of as girl consciousness effectively disrupts accepted gender norms.

The girls featured in the novels discussed here demand a masculine, adult power far in excess of what is generally permitted to young adolescent women. Especially noteworthy is the fact that, in both thought and deed, they far transcend the usual gender models. While acknowledging their female bodies, these girls refuse their assigned gender role, thus questioning the whole notion of gender itself. And although there is nothing special per se about being a girl, the ability to view the world with the eye of the girl positions the person involved outside accepted gender categories. Thus, as becomes apparent in the following discussion, girl consciousness thoroughly disrupts all accepted notions of gender and sexuality.

III. The History of Girl Consciousness as a Critique of Gender and Sexuality

While I use the term "girl consciousness," I wish to confirm once more that this mode of thinking is not confined to girls. The term is in fact a tentative convenience and thus something of a performative gesture. In other words, it is logically possible to identify the desired mode of thinking with any number of labels. As long as it is a view that valorizes the "fantastic," even when this leads to derision on the part of conventional adults, the label attached is largely irrelevant.

The manner in which I use the term "adult" is not impervious to change, while the category "child" too is merely a product of modernity. Similarly, masculinism and heterosexualism are far from being fixed, universal categories and may at some time assume different forms. However, as long as we adhere to the center-periphery model, a designated center will, of logical necessity, invoke the opposing category (although this may not be the case in the absence of the model in question).

I would like, for the time being, to define what I refer to as "girl consciousness" as a peripheral position. For it is clearly the case that, here in the time and place of Japan in 1999, thinking like a girl contests the accepted models of gender, an effect that, in 1910, would have been a function of "boy consciousness." The nature of critical consciousness in the future is unknown, for this cannot but vary according to time and place. So far, the focus has been on the consciousness of the boy or the girl, a development that would have been impossible without the emergence in modernity of the notion of individual consciousness. This boy or girl consciousness is not merely having the mind of a child. It is rather a pre-adult condition that, although it understands the significance of the adult, nevertheless stands aside from the mainstream. For it demands the suspended space of what psychologists have referred to as the "moratorium" of adolescence, a social state that, by and large, had not yet emerged in early Meiji.

Having said this, I would nonetheless argue that the origin of this consciousness in Japan might be traced back to the pre-Meiji notion of the *chigo*, a young male acolyte. In pre-Meiji times there were three gender classifications: man, woman, and *chigo*, also known as *wakashu*. *Chigo* were boys and young men (although the word also applied to older men who performed the role of this third sex) used for sexual gratification by men. Thus, although *chigo* were men, their designated role was closer to that of a woman.

It is common knowledge that sexual relations between men carried little social stigma in premodern Japan. These relations were quite different from the modern form of homosexual love that includes, or is certainly grounded in the possibility of, mutual acknowledgment of the other. Premodern Japanese male same-sex relations were grounded solely in one-sided sexual desire.

In premodern times, both women and children were defined as inferior social beings and regarded as passive objects to be violated, the sexual playthings of men. The word *nyoshoku* was used when the object of sex was a female, while the term *danshoku*, or *nanshoku*, was used for a male. Both terms implied an intractable right of violence on the part of the dominant male partner. However, *chigo*, even if they had no modern self, were doubtless well aware of the attraction they held for other men. They would thus have had the capacity to think like an object of desire. In other words, to some extent at least, they encompassed the sensibilities of both men and women. Such an entity, like the girl today, would directly contest gender/sexual power relations.

Almost all the young women protagonists in the "girl consciousness" novels discussed here have what we might call an androgynous consciousness—that is, the capacity to think as either men or women. In fact, I have deliberately chosen protagonists who, from the standard viewpoint, exercise a strange fascination. These androgynous young women are far more interesting than the usual protagonists featured in women's writing. They are also the ones upon whom readers most clearly wish to model themselves.

The passing of Tokugawa and advent of Meiji saw the rise to dominance in all aspects of Japanese politics of the Satsuma clan, connoisseurs of the aggressive expression of male same-sex relations. Thus their *danshoku* leisure pursuits too became the national vogue. Students with this inclination, called *kōha,* the hard school, engaged in a practice known as "boy hunting," as featured in Mori Ōgai's *Vita Sexualis* and Tsubouchi Shōyō's *The Characters of Modern Students [Tōsei shosei katagi].*

This is clearly a continuation of the Edo tradition of *danshoku,* a form of sexual violence, or rape, lacking mutual consent. Certainly, *danshoku* can include the ideal of reciprocal love, something often featured in accounts of love in narrative tales. However, such relationships were fundamentally grounded in the notion of nonconsensual sexual intercourse between an adult male and a boy and thus assumed a difference in age and social standing. The question of love was irrelevant, and there was no expectation of an equal balance of power.

Orikuchi Shinobu's *The Whistle* was the first modern novel to deal with the mutual love of two adolescent boys. In this unfinished work, two weak but beautiful youths, both objects of the unwanted lust of older boys, attempt a double suicide. Here, for the first time in Japanese literature, was a depiction of reciprocal passion based on a modernist sense of the narcissistic self. The novel presented both the boys' awareness of the attraction they held for the men who dominated them and the self-regard that arose from this. In other words, it depicted the aestheticism of the adolescent male. Also depicted was the anxiety of those awaiting violation, their fragility in the face of masculine brutality. These sentiments accord with what we might today refer to as "girl consciousness." They were first attributed to young men simply because women were not yet regarded as legitimate individuals.

It would appear, then, that the concept of the girl began to emerge only from late Meiji into Taishō. Before this time the word "daughter" was used to refer to a woman who was not yet a mature adult. The term "girl" suggested no positive meaning until the 1920s, following women's being seen as having their own personalities. (The New Women's Association, for instance, was founded in 1920 by identities such as Hiratsuka Raichō, Ichikawa Fusae, and Oku Mumeo.)

While there are undoubtedly exceptions, it seems that the emergence of the notion of the girl did not occur until late Taishō, when the innocence, beauty, and appeal of the boy, formerly attributed to the *chigo*, were transferred to girls. This theory is confirmed by the appearance at this time of Nomizo Naoko's *The Gardenia [Kuchinashi]*, which, as I argue in the following chapter, is the very first example of girl consciousness literature. As the practice of *danshoku* waned and boys ceased to be the object of male desire, the beautiful young girl became the symbol of self-centeredness and the fascinatingly desirable.

After World War II, this notion, which peaked in the 1980s, was reinforced through an education system grounded in American-style heterosexualism. The "fantastic," that which has unmediated appeal, is now monopolized by the girl, with the concomitant prejudice that, in order for a boy or young man to know any joy in life, his sole option is to take possession of a "pretty" girl. However, girl consciousness contests this view also. For as Yagawa correctly notes, in modern times it is often girl consciousness that immediately recognizes that something is amiss.

IV. Freedom and Arrogance

The aim of seeking out literary representations of the girl or the consciousness of the girl is related to the fact that the desire for freedom and arrogance, unique to modern times, is most effectively depicted in the person of the girl. I introduce the notions of freedom and arrogance because these concepts represent the two extremes of desire of the modern subject. It should be noted that the word "freedom" here is restricted to that which can be imagined or desired under that name. It is not concrete freedom, but freedom as it functions in the imagined text, and is thus not concerned with the issue of whether or not any individual being can actually attain freedom.

Arrogance too refers to a textual rather than a concrete notion and might well be regarded as "pride" or "honor" by modern citizens. However, these are masculine, social notions without much meaning in the consciousness of the girl, whose principal concern is her own ego. Thus, I use the word "arrogance" to indicate clearly the self-satisfaction associated with intense narcissism.

During the Taishō era, girl consciousness was manifested first among young women of the middle and privileged classes. Thus, it might be regarded as a marginal product of the excess of that age, an age in which a small group of reasonably affluent people adhered to aesthetic values that defied both the national hegemony and economic rationalism.

Being an excess product of the margins does not imply an absence of value. On the contrary, we might recall Bataille's maxim that the purpose of an economy is to permit the flagrant disposal of the excess. Whether or not we subscribe to this position, we cannot deny that both the excess and the marginal inevitably fascinate.

We also need to remember that in spite of the fact that the adolescent girl has given rise to these principles, she herself has no actual power. While she may be adored for her physical charm, she is nevertheless confined and dominated, largely forbidden to make her own decisions. It is precisely the fact that her modern consciousness emerged in the context of these restraints that she is the symbol directly representing what we desire. Being forced to act against one's will by family, community, or nation is an unpalatable option. We desire to do only things that interest us and to be the center of attention.

Being this center of attention is what is meant by freedom and arrogance, although how these elements are balanced varies among individuals. Nevertheless, the desire for freedom and arrogance is, in fact, the most basic desire of the modern subject. However, before this self-centeredness can emerge, the girl must be consumed by longing. This is not desire as we know it, for rather than longing to possess the desired object, the girl seeks to become like it. Girl consciousness is contemptuous of the naked desire that demands complete ownership, positing against this a desire that longs to emulate the desired.

The longing for freedom inherent in this mode of desire invokes a form liberated from the restrictions of the individual self of modernity. At times the search for arrogance will be expressed in a trenchant critique of society; at times it may involve a secret contract with phallocentrism. Nevertheless, the girl continues to seek "the fantastic." And through her consciousness of this, she will be astounded to discover a world that permits anything imaginable.

[Last section omitted.]

||| For a Gentle Castration

MATSUURA RIEKO

The Journey from Castration: A New Time-Trip

I want to caress your languid sex, without either foolishly whispering "love" like an incantation or becoming wet with desire. I find this essay a terribly painful one, inspired as it is by the idea of "love" expressed in our individual pores, while we breathe, reeking of fetid hormones, and our thighs are smeared with viscous liquids. I dream silly dreams: that my desire, freed from any sort of purpose, including reproduction, pain, and pleasure, is in awe when it is around your quiet genitals for a moment or an eternity. Although we constantly sell off "time" in our "life" and entrust our world to one person, isn't it lovely to try and appreciate the feeling of reclaiming that "time," suspending it in a state of sweetness rather than in a vacuum?

Our "time" begins to flow when we are born, with our first cry. It is unfortunate that the world's rules prevent us from remembering the moment at which we were wrenched from that Eden that was the womb. The ceremony of birth, which sends us bloody into the world from between our mother's thighs, is perhaps even more profound than that of death. The fact that we can't even remember it thus is all the more regrettable.

The pain of our mothers' birth canals as we struggled to be born had to have been violent and terrible. It has been said that one's body at birth is like a penis, raping the mother from within (whether this can be defined after the fact as a gentle rape, I don't know). Our first experience with our mothers thus is also our first sexual act, and while there is a perverse kind of pleasure in pretending to remember such an unremarkable event, we cannot doubt the pain caused by our bodies-as-penises.

Since I don't know anything for sure, allow me to offer the following lighthearted suggestion: the extreme pain we caused is what keeps us from remembering that profound ceremony.

But what about climaxing? Sure, climaxing is great—the body trembles, and "we" dissolve into nothingness. People who came before us recognized this aspect of climax and discovered that sex allows us to bypass the circuit from life

TRANSLATED BY AMANDA SEAMAN. From Matsuura Rieko, "Yasashii kyosei no tame ni" (For a gentle castration), in *Yasashii kyosei no tame ni* (For a gentle castration) (Chikuma Shobō, 1997), pp. 212–262. The translator would like to thank Ms. Hiromi Kubota of the University of Massachusetts for her gracious assistance. *AS* to death—that is, to escape the flow of "time." How can we help but love and respect those who made this discovery?

Nevertheless, climaxing is a pretty limited means for escaping "time." The sexual process of anticipating climax—in one fell swoop the accumulated time flows like an accelerating piston moving from *adagio* to *allegro,* making climax equivalent to catastrophe—resembles too closely the process in which time stored in the womb is made to flow in one direction. That is to say: because of this fact, it is impossible to have this sex, which is waiting for climax to be swallowed up in a flow of time. The reason for post-sex melancholy is the fact that our attempt to exceed time fails.

Sex is painful.

Sometime in the past, someone (was it you or I?) murmured, "Time is ticking away in the shaft of the penis, the folds of the vagina, and the curves of our genitalia," and "That is the sign of the beginning of time." We responded, either you or I, "Perhaps it's impossible to have sex that exceeds our original sexual experience with our mothers," and "Even if you try to make 'original' time, it's impossible to exceed the original sign."

You and I, fed up with the pain, try and reclaim "time" another way.

It's unrefined to try and escape the flow of time. Our attempts to escape the flow of time sink us deeper in it. Instead, in the beginning we should go with the flow, rather than fight against it.

We mustn't hurry. Hurrying only relieves the body from the nausea caused by the slow motion of time. Even if to some degree the body conceals the rape committed against it by "time," the mind picks out the best moments and attempts to hold its own. *Déjà-vu,* combined with exhaustion, slows down the inner flow of time enough to create a split between "time" in the world and "time" within ourselves.

The fleeting desire both to stop time and restart it merely alters the course of inner and outer "time." If, in comparison with inner "time," outer "time" rocketed along at the speed of light, then you and I would be like astronauts, living in our own separate "time."

Who thinks about a thing like climaxing now? Like acrobats, we flip back and forth between desiring its occurrence and its end, leading ultimately to impotence, frigidity, and foolishness. This is why I just want to gaze upon your tranquil sex.

A Prescription for Desire

Even if you touch me and I slip myself within you, it is only nostalgia that makes me sensitive to the pleasure of sex rather than its pain. Our engorged genitalia usually look forward to pleasure; however, your sexual behavior, and mine, decline into bitterness, just like when you are unable to bear the cold when you ice your burned fingers or when your whole body is chilled. On days when we can't discern the true character of the desire that roils life's smooth surface, I feel that our sex organs are drained of desire. I used to think that desire ends if we rejoice, embrace each other, and mix our spirits together. Yet even when that happens, whatever one might say, although I felt a lack like we are avoiding shared deceits, we indulge our bodies and repeat those actions.

The give and take of our desire is expected to match our mental and physical capacities. In truth, however, we don't really try to absorb our partner's desire in its entirety. Unexpectedly energetic desire is intensely painful and passes straight through us. Somehow, we realize that the desire within us is bigger than our bodies or our minds, and we are left at a loss.

Now we cross words about the origins of desire. "Desire" arises as a protest against the existence of the "individual." That "desire" created in that way is responsible for opening a new path for the imagination that goes from the "individual" to "everyone." Therefore, as soon as this "desire" is born on an individual level, it goes beyond the scale of the "individual." There is no reason for the "individual" who accepts "desire" like this to exist.

We remember our pain at realizing that we both were looking over our shoulders at the "many" while we were making love. How indiscreet—maneuvering to face everyone as our partner is making love to us. Isn't this insulting to us both? To be sure, our desire to deny the "individual" is what reveals our intentions regarding the "many." Yet from the outset, it was sex that provided us with a sense of the "individual." Despite our conviction that the "individual's" importance does not change in spite of the physical change that it undergoes, "desire" leaves a gouge in that very "individual." In light of this, why am I compelled to desire you?

If my partner weren't you, if my partner were a random individual, could I lightheartedly liberate desire? No, it is obvious that I've become impotent. I don't want to have sex with you, but I can't have sex with anyone but you.

Today we find it incredible that once we were able to fuck so innocently. "Passion" was a word that we knew. Perhaps the we of the past could find in climax the key to an undifferentiated "desire" for "everyone," as well as to the individual's feeling of love.

The days of "passion" are gone. Nevertheless, our blood-swollen genitalia remain nostalgic for some reason or another.

"Desire" fills us, oozes out of us, overflows from us. My ridiculous body is contorted with "desire." It swells; it is fevered. Palpitations rise within me. I tremble, and desire rises up within me. The "individual" is purified by desire.

I am pure—filled with desire, I am pure. You and I call this feeling of soaring desire a "bonus climax."

True climaxes—that is, climaxes produced by sex and climaxes that are free of unbearable pain—we want to try to avoid them completely for the time being. We don't want to be forced to flee from the apex of the climax that erupts from the genitals of "desire," so how do we deal with the idea of an "individual" who does not provide an outlet for "desire"? We make the best decision: to get the curious full feeling of the "bonus climax," which unexpectedly appears, to strip away the desire that "desires" "desire," and we try to counteract the far-reaching effects of nostalgia.

If it is normal to guide a climax through our actual sex acts, where "desire" acts as an ignition switch, then it is perverse to have "desire's" maximum satisfaction dependent not on sex but on *coming*. Even though there are all sorts of perversions, climaxing may be the most extreme perversion; for the sake of closing in on "everyone," however, isn't the "individual" unexpectedly effective as a means to overcome the deep-rooted, evil charm of the normal sex act, which needs to use one more "individual"?

When an "extra climax" occurs, "forbidden desire" is assumed to be obscene. This "obscene forbidden desire" is both painful and pleasurable for us.

The Anus: Utopia on the Other Side

On the floor of our dim room, lit only by one small window, you and I crouch and face one another for half a day, although it seems like less than that. If I were to try to break this long silence, this warm air, my words would no doubt be questions. But what would they ask?

Of course, you and I only ponder this question in our waking dreams. The answer is something like this:

"Hey, are you still there? It's evening now—is it still light? Your body is warm—is there any place where it's cool? Do you hurt anywhere? Are you dizzy when you stand up? Since you can still see shadowy and blurred outlines, can you tell how big my body is? Do you remember when we were both naked? Do you know whether the darkness is white or black? Is it true that you can't choose when an orgasm will come? My body embraces your body's sensations—do you find it warm or cold? Can you tell me what you like and dislike, as clearly as you once did? Can you tell whether I'm gay or straight? Can you count how many 'sex organs' are in the body? Do you know what 'you' are? In light of all this, has this room become a pleasurable place?"

Although we've known the answer to these questions for some time, you would playfully pretend to think of the answers—first glancing around the

room, then changing your body's hiding place—start with your hair, move behind your ears, between your fingers and toes, to your armpits, behind your
knees, to your belly button.

Where in this room is the answer, ambiguous yet extremely obvious? Where
are the boundaries of all things blurred?

You laugh and open your anus.

We don't need any practice. Before we notice the existence of our so-called "sex
organs," we begin to take pleasure in feelings arising deep in the bottomless
swamp. The involuntary nervousness of the sphincter produces a sensation that
is ticklish, itchy, and painful all at once. The skin, the tongue, and the lips provide no comparable experience, and the power of such stimulation cannot help
but draw us in.

Simply put, the moment that we discover a value in the anus that goes beyond its practical function as a simple organ of excretion is the first time in our
lives that we begin to understand the notion of "excess." I think that the anus is
really akin to a vibrant, sensitive, perfect marketplace, a shopping mall, a boisterous playground. But while we're playing, do we learn anything?

While doing things like running, talking, laughing, waving our hands, and
crying, our weight increases, and the anus that we love so much isn't regarded
as a thing of value. We try to grow into men and women who fit the shape of
our so-called genitals. Yet even after entering into a time when activity is their
primary mission, the "genitals" are not completely liberated from the anal sensation. In some cases our passion seems drawn from the genitals to the anus,
liberated from its former master.

This is because the "genitals" are a symbol of gender, a mechanism for the
important task of procreation, while the anus is just an unrefined Main Street
where practicality exceeds the sense of surplus. It is simply impossible for the
anus to have an excess of power.

Because you and I have a relationship, the so-called "genitals" are eliminated;
only the anus remains.

Inside us, the anus has a core that has secretly continued from our early years,
and the anus is the "genitals" of a "sexless" *gender.* The anus is never a substitute
for female genitals, nor is it a "third organ" integrating femininity and masculinity. It is an anarchically blessed and utterly freakish organ—one might even
call it "charmed"—emulating those that came before.

How can we help but love the anus's brilliant practicality?

The anus turns back into front.

The anus turns exit into entrance.

The anus turns nadir into zenith.

The anus turns filthy into pure.
The anus turns musician into instrument.
The anus turns past into present.
The anus turns pain into a knife.
The anus is a Klein bottle.[25]
The anus is a fictional place in which to calculate gender.
The anus is sweet intoxication.
The anus is a place where dreams become curiously free from the present.

On the floor of our dark room, we become two anuses.

The Lunatic Dream Women's Genital Collection

You don't have women's genitals.
I can tie a ribbon and hang a hat on your supple organ.
You are good at drawing pictures with your genitals, etching the glass window frozen with white winter frost. Your organ sways like an antenna, like a pendulum.
What I have are women's genitals.
Women's genitals, filled with warm and humid air. Women's genitals, with shaking soft walls that take on many shapes. Women's genitals, able to squeeze tightly and concealing big, strong muscles. Women's genitals, able to have things like jewels set in them, flowers inserted in them, champagne poured in them.
Women's genitals are used to blood. You and I are swept away by a primal passion, and lie facing the ceiling with our clothes stripped off. As our tumbling bodies leave bruises and welts, our genitals collide again and again, and blood flows from between my thighs.
We are both unable to stop laughing, because we are made to hear a persistent joke—the same thing begins to arise. Everything up to our genitals is blood covered, in spite of the marks from nails, lips, and teeth that leave countless marks that ooze salty and iron-tasting bodily fluids, but not from the arms or on the chest, and a delicate red pattern floats in front of our eyes.
What an utterly humorous thing—with the first sex act, women's genitals bleed. It is absurdity that overcomes the fear of incontinence. On that day, we compared body parts covered in blood, pretended to poke fingers in genitals, and laughed a lot.
Women's genitals are used to the moon. My genitals are not dyed red from

25. A Klein bottle is a one sided topologic surface with no inside or outside, formed by inserting the small open end of a taped tube through the side of a tube and making it contiguous with the larger open end. *AS*

sex; instead, blood oozes and pours every twenty-eight days in conjunction with the waxing and waning of the moon. That round organ connected to the upper part of my genitals—here is from whence the blood flows.

This round organ—I can't remember its name. When did this whole thing start? And why?

Just when the time comes each month for clots of blood to fall, my belly suddenly becomes boisterous. My round organ repeatedly expands and contracts, tapping out its own rhythm from within. The tapping rhythm excites me, and I am intoxicated. If menstruation is a festival governed by the moon, then my abdomen must be its drum. Is the organ that emits blood a drum, sounding by itself and answering the moonlight?

You like to stare at my blood-filled genitals. You like them covered in blackish-red. You like genitals that don't look like genitals.

Even for me, it's not a bad feeling when my sex is filled by the crumbling walls of my organ. I bury my genitals in the debris of internal organs. I, who have no genitals, become a drum once a month.

My body is, we might say, elegantly grotesque.

Occasionally in my mind's eye I conjure up women's genitals other than my own:

Yang Guifei's genitals.[26] Nero's mother's genitals. Joan of Arc's genitals. Emily Brontë's genitals. Eva Braun's genitals. Billie Holliday's genitals. Anne Sullivan's genitals. Gertrude Stein's genitals. Graceful genitals. Sturdy genitals. Pure genitals. Cruel genitals. Sluggish genitals. Obsequious genitals. Serious genitals. Scary genitals. Crazy genitals. A lovesick spasm courses through me, and various women's genitals parade before my eyes.

I wonder what would happen if the bodies of all the women in the world were hidden, while their genitals were covered in blood at the same time. You know it's true—menstruation is contagious. If I live with someone having her period and we become intimate, then I start bleeding too. My drum beats in time with one nearby, and I resonate with another person, one with women's genitals.

Let us set aside for a moment girls, crones, and pregnant women. If all the women on the face of the earth with genitals came together in one place, how many days would the noise sound forth? At some point, we would expect blood to trickle from all of them at once.

What would happen at that instant?

For the moon, longtime mistress of the festival of menstruation, this mass of round organs would have the opposite effect of a rhythm pounding in uni-

26. Yang Guifei was a Chinese queen (ca. 719–756) noted for her beauty. *AS*

son. Wouldn't it abrogate the festival's rules and turn it into a madhouse? If you brought together 2 billion women's genitals, could the moon help but reel? Their massive chorus would upset the moon's orderly progress, and the ocean would run roughshod over the face of the earth.

Bringing women's genitals together would be one big carnival, an insurrection against the moon. But my drum, dreaming such pleasant and preposterous dreams, is for now a solo performer.

Pop Navel Poppin'

That sound like a tuba—was that you farting? Or my stomach growling? You can't tell the difference, because both parts of the intestine are empty, and the body is perfectly synchronized. The stomach rumbles on one end, and the intestines immediately convey a message to us on the other; thus both our stomachs rumble at almost the same time.

I'm convinced that we both think our own stomach rumbled, but while we quarrel about it later, we soon realize that it doesn't matter whose stomach rumbled or why, and we exchange a celebratory glass. Our abdominal cavities resonate perfectly. As I just said, uteruses echo one another, but stomachs resonate more directly, provided we cuddle together when they're empty.

It's a plot—an unanticipated, completely inane, natural, instantaneous, and improvised double-bill. Easy like this, pleasant like this—the pleasant discovery that a body and a body are linked. What follows is called "pop." "Pop" cannot simply be described as one second of many seconds—in short, it consists of the smallest unit of pleasure in many instants. The flow of time is cut into particles, and the best way to grab hold of them is called "pop."

During several instants of pop, there is no room for charm or excitement to sprout up. It is totally backwards to maximize pleasure by letting go of such things as desire. In particular, it is shameful to pile up emotions in order to defer time, accumulate mountains of weak phrases, and place the climax in the introduction.

Therefore, sex is boring. Like classical music.

As you and I inspect and compare our bellies, we notice that we both have belly buttons. Once, we were afraid that this closed path, once connecting us to our mothers' wombs, would try to open. Of course, although we realize that the peritoneum, with no reason to open very deeply, has begun to hurt, we carelessly are swept up by an enticing smell, a reserved and unpretentious roundness between the two walls that knocks against our nasal membranes.

In fact, we continue to be entranced by the belly button from an early age, and there is a time when we are compelled to play with our belly buttons more than our genitals. During adolescence we are spurred on by an urge to stick a finger in our belly buttons to our heart's content. I wanted to destroy my peritoneum with my finger and mix up my internal organs. After the belly button loses its role of taking in nourishment in the womb, does this original "mouth" seek to be fed, or does it starve? Is it a screw-like shape pulling in open air, or is it a thing to stimulate the finger?

The belly button is a bit like the anus. Even its shape leads us to a distant and seductive memory.

"It's too bad that it's not as strong as the anus," I murmur, laughing, and you say that there's a charm to the belly button not found in the anus.

"Is it an outie? Isn't the outie shaped like half a globe? Well, if you put an outie into an innie, then you can copulate belly button to belly button. I'm not joking! The belly button has a round shape hidden deep within its folded walls. In the middle of that modest hollow is concealed the simplest, the most refined beautiful shape. You don't find anything like that hidden in the anus."

"Ah, that's so," I say, wanting more. "Moreover, the outie is born in violent tears and wails when one is a baby, and at its most extreme it strongly emphasizes the abdomen. An outie results from great sadness and anger, spurting out from the soft hole before it is closed. The outie is a beautiful anomaly, linked to primitive emotions." As I say this, I notice that the repeated, rolling folds of the intestine begin to bulge in anger, as the belly button's walls slowly expand.

"The belly button is really something," you say, nodding.

The belly button has keen senses.

In the heat of the summer, when drops of sweat fall from the chest and collect in the hollow of the belly button, they appear to jump up.

There are no sphincter muscles in the belly button.

Therefore, the tip of your tongue can't make it tighten.

The belly button doesn't produce any bodily fluids.

Rather, it has a nice smell.

The belly button is quite shallow.

Therefore, it doesn't collect anything extraneous.

The color of the belly button isn't nice.

But the touch of thin skin is seductive and delicate.

The belly button has no expression.

Therefore it isn't necessary to read it.

The belly button makes no sound.

Instead, you must lean your ear closer to it.

The belly button cannot have an orgasm.

Why would you want that?

With the belly button, you don't have to waste many words.

Because it doesn't attract wet words, the belly button stays dry and clean, and the belly button's good point is that it doesn't require an immense number of words in order to love it.

All in all, isn't it more than a bad joke?

All in all, no. Or is it?

When my sister was born and her umbilical cord was cut off, after a little while the torn edge of the flesh, like a plucked stem, joined with her belly. I thought that this was the same organ as the one between her thighs. When the knot of her umbilical cord fell off, I wanted to take it, pestering my parents and wailing bitterly.

This funny story is my gift to you—you, who can't stop loving the cute belly button.

The Song of Sex-Gang-Child

I am nervous in your presence.

My body loses its strength and becomes soft when your body heats up the room, when my lungs take in the air that you exhale, when the noise that you make gently tickles my eardrums.

My blood begins to surge when your shadow falls on my naked skin, when your footsteps echo under my hips as I sit on the floor, when the warm bath-water lapping your body touches mine. Even if we don't touch one another, when I lie next to you, my skin on the side near you becomes warm, and when you roll over, the warmth of your skin goes with you.

Because your sensation is transmitted very strongly, I think that I can feel you naked when you are clothed, and when you are naked, I think that I can touch your nerves directly.

When I am together with you, my threshold of consciousness is low. Small things become a joy, a pleasure.

The I that you know becomes like a shellfish stripped of its shell. Soft, pliant, sensitive—a shellfish that has lost its shell.

Perhaps those who watch you and me, two shell-less creatures rolling on the floor, are nauseated by the sight. When we separate and lie down, other people find it more shameful and obscene than a sex scene.

The pleasure of sex becomes painful due to an excessive decrease in the threshold of consciousness. The greatest pleasure also is deferred, and the sensation that results from sex is described by the formula "too much pleasure = pain."

Now we remember that we are slightly self-conscious. We want to get a little closer, go in a little deeper, know more, embrace more, be more serious, be better. On some days when we meet, both our bodies exude a desire for "more."

At times like these, our bodies probably are somehow harder, more serious, sharper.

While we lament that no matter how serious we are, it isn't serious enough; while no matter how hard we embrace, it isn't hard enough. It is because we drag pleasure from our genitals flowing with desire, and we get sufficient comfort from doing so. The instant we have the thought that it is not that desire has been fulfilled, but that because of desire we are distracted is the instant our unfulfilled desire to take off our clothes and not be completely naked stops our movements.

Even when I am naked, I haven't undressed enough. Is it because we wear something more than clothes—is that why we are suffering from dissatisfaction, as if we are not getting enough embraces? When we think about this, our faces turn red.

We begin to take off . . . what? All sorts of superfluous things, dirty things? Perhaps with celebratory expectations, a spirit of tenacity or biased curiosity. Perhaps somewhere in this world, there exists something that contains the essence of love. Taking off your clothes and throwing them away as you go—this clear, mounting sensation of lightness is a pleasurable thing.

"Genitals," you will notice, also happen to be naked.

You undress your genitals, which cover me from head to toe.

I undress my genitals, which are shaped by your genitals.

You undress your genitals, which put down roots in my genitals.

I undress my genitals, which use your genitals to point to my genitals.

I undress my genitals, which assume the direction of your genitals.

We undress our genitals, which are willing to take a conventional role without getting bored.

We undress our genitals, which await a partner's genitals.

We undress our genitals: annoying genitals, which entice us to put on too many clothes, and our rough genitals, which resolve our genitals into a combination of male and female forms.

In short, the "genitals" that must be stripped and discarded, are always aware of the genitals of the opposite sex, even if they are not in the middle of the sex act. The body gathers the imaginary genitals of the opposite sex, genitals that can be said to be a fiction.

Even if we deal with the "imaginary" genitals, there is no reason for them to feel pain.

This castration is a gentle one.

Even in our castrated bodies, the genitals remain, but as mere organs. When they are at peace, they are not an obstruction. They have no particular value, they don't speak for anything, they aren't a symbol, and they suggest nothing. Perhaps they don't even show sexual difference. You and I stop using genitals as an "expression."

You and I enjoy a pleasure that doesn't depend on genitals.

We call it "sex-gang-child": sex that belongs to us.

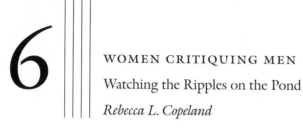

6

WOMEN CRITIQUING MEN

Watching the Ripples on the Pond

Rebecca L. Copeland

On an autumn day in 1989, three women sat down to discuss what would become a topic of literary debate—"the man writer." Their meetings on the subject continued for the next seven months and culminated in the book *Danryū bungakuron* (On men's literature) in 1992, sparking considerable debate. Of course, this was not the first time women had discussed male-authored literature publicly. Women have been critiquing male authors all along. Miyamoto Yuriko published studies of Natsume Sōseki in the 1930s and Kōno Taeko of Tanizaki Jun'ichirō in the 1970s, to cite but two examples. Any woman who wished to receive a degree from a reputable university in modern Japanese literature was expected to write her thesis on a canonical writer; this meant—with the possible exceptions of Higuchi Ichiyō and Yosano Akiko—her work would center on men. Nor was *On Men's Literature* the first time women had discussed men's literary works in a roundtable format. Women had been participants in such exchanges for years. The 1978 dialogue between Tsushima Yūko and Taka-hashi Takako in this volume is but one example.

And yet the discussion among Ueno Chizuko, Tomioka Taeko, and Ogura Chikako in 1989 was different. Their exchange was motivated by a conscious attempt to subject male-authored literature to gender-specific readings. Prior critiques of men's writing had mostly been conducted in what Tomioka would term "male language." In deliberately availing themselves of feminist analyti-cal strategies, the three participants in the "man-style" literature conversations drew attention to the presence of "male language" and the absolutism of the phallocentric approaches to literary criticism that had heretofore been rendered invisible by their very omnipotence. By treating male authors to the same kind of essentialist criticism female authors had been receiving for decades, these critics accentuated the unreasonableness of the exercise, while simultaneously opening the texts considered to new perspectives. It was a bold and calculated act, one that participant Ueno Chizuko likened to casting a stone into a pond: "We have cast the first stone of feminist criticism into the pond of literature. If the subsequent ripples provoke more experiments of greater variety and depth, we will have achieved our goal."[1]

Saitō Minako, a critic clearly inspired by the experiment, describes the importance of the publication of *On Men's Literature* to her own development as a critic by offering an analogy of the "Emperor's New Clothes." She enumerates three reasons why the study was so influential:

> In the first place, of course, it laid bare without remorse the sexually discriminatory concepts that had enshrouded male writers up to now—much like the child who drew attention to the emperor's nakedness. From the very first chapter on Yoshiyuki Jun'nosuke we [women] experienced both surprise and a sense of release. Up to this point, we had felt an unspoken pressure to keep to ourselves the feelings of discomfort that the texts by these men provoked. But now, with a snap, we were freed from that constraint.
>
> Second, not only "man-style" writers, but also "man-style" critics, whose opinions heretofore had been accepted without question, were held up for scrutiny. Needless to say, an emperor (literary masterpiece) cannot exist in a vacuum. He derives his authority from his followers (critics), who will constantly intone, "What fine clothes the emperor wears!"
>
> Third, the charm of the work was found in the style of discussion—in the fact that the participants used the roundtable format to announce, "The emperor is naked."[2]

The style of the discussion was one of the greatest points of contention. Chatty, colloquial, at times pedestrian, it seemed tossed off and insincere. The great canonical writers of Japan, critics complained, should have been afforded more respect. Tsuge Teruhiko, for example, was dismayed that important writers would be waylaid with quips such as "This guy doesn't know squat about women, does he?" or "This fellow's ancient." He compared the three critics to college students and derided their level of research and analysis as "infantile."[3]

The roundtable format, almost by definition, defies sustained analytical criticism, and Saitō notes that it was the fast pace of the discussion that was part of its appeal.[4] On this point, Ogura Chikako, the least experienced in literary criticism of the three, likened her participation in the discussions to that of the ball boy at a Wimbledon tennis match. The interchange between Tomioka and Ueno was so swift, she barely had time to dash in after a stray ball.[5] In reality, the discussions among the three were not carelessly tossed off but involved considerable foresight and planning. The three selected the writers and the works they would discuss in advance of their meetings. Part of the rationale for their discussions in the first place was to question—if not challenge—critical assumptions that had allowed some writers greater recognition than others. They therefore set their sights high, focusing only on those writers who had been honored with the most prestigious literary accolades, and accordingly they chose Yoshiyuki Jun'nosuke, Shimao Toshio, Tanizaki Jun'ichirō, Kojima Nobuo, Murakami Haruki, and Mishima Yukio. After their selections were made, their editor busied herself at the National Diet Library, making copies of the works and the relevant criticism, which she then mailed off to each participant. The material filled the kind of cardboard boxes used to ship fruit, as Ogura describes it. She diligently plowed through the monthly readings and was amazed to find that Ueno always managed to read *beyond* the material assigned.

Despite their careful preparation, detractors questioned the discussants' qualifications to sit in judgment on canonical writers. As has been noted, Ogura is not a literary critic, a fact she is only too ready to concede. She has a doctorate from Waseda University in psychology and is renowned for her research on gender and contemporary culture—particularly the commodification of female sexuality. Ueno Chizuko, while not a literary critic per se, is a prominent public intellectual, weighing in on topics as diverse as labor law and graphic art, appearing regularly on the media circuits in Japan, and headlining conferences both at home and abroad. All of her work is informed by a pointed feminist analysis. Tomioka Taeko, the only writer in the group, had by this time distinguished herself as a poet, screenplay writer, novelist, and essayist. Many of her works have been characterized by an attention to sex as an essentially physical act devoid of social ritual and romantic mythologies. Of the three participants in the roundtable discussions, Ueno noted that Tomioka had the most to lose. "Ogura and I are not invested in literature, and we can walk away from it. But she can't," Ueno observed and then recalled with disgust the "man-style" literary critic who, in keeping with the determination that "feminism is an 'ideology' and not a legitimate approach to literary criticism," complained that Tomioka had been "ruined by feminism."[6]

Not all male critics were as negative, of course. Kitada Sachie summarizes the positive reviews as follows:

Miura Masashi's commentary in the weekly *Shukan asahi* began by characterizing the force of the authors' relentless attack on literary scholars as "equaling the former vigor of male aesthetics." Miura went on to state that the book reflects the recent development of feminist theories of modern literature, a viewpoint that men find quite surprising. The following comments also appeared in other reviews: "it establishes the basic functions of criticism"; "by indicating the limitations of the male perspective, it has the effect of jolting the reader's consciousness"; and "it is not a literary debate limited to literary circles, but a literary debate for all of society."[7]

What made the work so controversial, and equally so valuable, was, as Kitada states, "the application of the perspective and judgment of woman—the 'Other' —to male authors' works, which heretofore had been evaluated only according to masculine value."[8]

The chapter translated here by Maryellen Toman Mori illustrates this very point. In reading Tanizaki Jun'ichirō's texts *Chijin no ai* (Naomi, 1925; tr. 1985); *Manji* (Quicksand, 1930; tr. 1994); and *Kagi* (The key, 1956; tr. 1960) from the subject position of the objectified "Other," the critics push our understanding of Tanizaki's art beyond the standard (comfortable) interpretations of provocative sensuality and eroticism. Their critical gaze—as piercing as it is playful—produces a powerful beam of light that exposes the shadowy corners of his genius with an intensity many find discomforting. Even as their analysis of Tanizaki's portrayal of women as "conceptual allegories" pivots on their own brand of critical essentialism, they nevertheless offer a freshly beguiling approach to reading Tanizaki. The obvious pleasure they derive from their enterprise engulfs his texts with new layers of meaning, enriching his works as a result. And so the ripples grow.

NOTES

1. Ueno, "Ishi wo nageru," p. 402.
2. Saitō, "Kaisetsu," pp. 447–448.
3. Tsuge, "Review of *Danryū bungakuron*," p. 5.
4. Saitō, "Kaisetsu," p. 448.
5. Ogura, "Hanae no higeki," p. 402.
6. Ueno, "Ishi wo nageru," pp. 401–402.
7. Kitada, "Contemporary Japanese Feminist Literary Criticism," p. 75.
8. Ibid.

On Men's Literature

UENO CHIZUKO, OGURA CHIKAKO,

AND TOMIOKA TAEKO

Does Tanizaki's Fiction Really Deal with "Sexuality"?

EDITOR: Well, let's start with *Naomi [Chijin no ai]*.

UENO: This is a novel of manners that's very easy to understand. The story's general context is easy to grasp, and just as Yoshiyuki's *Until Twilight [Yūgure made]* spawned the "twilight tribe," the author's presentation of trends in social behavior is also very clear.[1] The situation fits into a familiar template.

TOMIOKA: That's right. The novel is easy to analyze.

UENO: No matter which of Tanizaki's works I read, it's impossible for me to think of him as a traditional writer. Granted, perhaps, traditional elements can be discerned in his prose style and the surface patterns of his stories. But the subjects that he takes up and the way he arranges his narratives fall within the framework of the twentieth-century literary theme of the pursuit of sexual fulfillment. It's the fate of twentieth-century literature, including this novel, to portray sex in a grotesque way, as a force that dominates every aspect of a person's life. In this respect Tanizaki is almost a Japanese Henry Miller. My impression from reading this novel is that he's an author who treats really modern topics.

TRANSLATED BY MARYELLEN TOMAN MORI. Selections from chapter 3, "Tanizaki Jun'ichirō: *Quicksand* and *Naomi*," in Ueno Chizuko, Ogura Chikako, and Tomioka Taeko, *Danryū bungakuron* (Chikuma shobō, 1992), pp. 136–185.

There are excellent English translations of both of the novels by Tanizaki on which this discussion focuses, as well as others to which brief reference is made. I have thus adopted the titles of those translations, and for the short excerpts from the three novels that the participants have quoted verbatim, I have taken the liberty of quoting from the corresponding English translations. These are as follows: *Chijin no ai* (literally "A fool's love"), translated by Anthony H. Chambers as *Naomi* (New York: Knopf, 1985; reprint, San Francisco: North Point Press, 1990); *Manji*, translated by Howard Hibbett as *Quicksand* (New York: Knopf, 1994); and *Kagi*, translated by Howard Hibbett as *The Key* (New York: Knopf, 1960; reprint, Rutland, Vt., and Tokyo: Charles E. Tuttle, 1971). Parenthetical page references to *Naomi* and *The Key* in the above-translated text are to the reprint editions of those works. *MTM*

1. The expression "twilight tribe" was coined in allusion to Yoshiyuki Jun'nosuke's 1978 novel, *Until Twilight*, shortly after the publication of that novel. It referred to couples composed of young women in their late teens and early twenties and wealthy middle-aged men who were their lovers and patrons. *MTM*

TOMIOKA: I feel that way too.

UENO: Moreover, in this novel the modern theme of sexuality is formulated in a typical way, as a division between spirit and flesh, to put it simply. Hata Kōhei wrote, "This novel is Tanizaki's critique of *The Tale of Genji*."[2] It's the story of how Jōji, hoping to transform Murasaki-Naomi into an ideal woman, tries to harmonize her body and spirit, and how Naomi becomes physically perfect but spiritually corrupt. The very concept of a separation of spirit and flesh isn't a bit imperial or classical; it's a quintessentially modern view of sexuality. Reading this novel made me realize what a thoroughly twentieth-century individual this author was.

TOMIOKA: It's like *My Fair Lady*, isn't it.

UENO: It *is* like a version of *My Fair Lady*. But for the idealized Japanese woman of classical times, body and spirit are one. There's nothing like a conflict between spirit and body among the themes found in Japanese court literature. Tanizaki doesn't write overtly about a division between spirit and flesh, but to bow down in worship to a physically beautiful woman whose spirit is unworthy of respect—that expression of the theme of the separation of body and spirit is terribly modern. Also, the grotesque treatment of sex, as something that takes precedence over all other areas of a person's life, is typical of twentieth-century literature.

TOMIOKA: Ueno-san, you've just said that Tanizaki is a modern author who focused on describing sexuality in his literature. But I had some doubts when I read these novels whether he was really trying to explore human sexuality.

UENO: Why? Why did you feel that way?

TOMIOKA: Well, for example, *Quicksand [Manji]* is a story about an impotent man and a lesbian woman, right? Or take Naomi and Jōji in *Naomi*. A man brings home a girl—fifteen years old by the prewar way of calculating age, so today she'd be considered fourteen—intending for the time being to make her his maid or cleaning girl. His position is clearly that of a master who brings in a servant. He has no affection for her as an equal. Maybe the thought of someday marrying her crosses his mind, but the idea of taking care of her—or, to put it in old-fashioned terms, keeping her as his mistress—is also in the back of his mind. The fantasy of raising this pretty little girl, watching her gradually develop under his care from a bud into a beautiful flower—his attraction to her probably includes various such

---

2. Hata Kōhei (b. 1935) is a novelist and literary critic. The comment that Ueno cites is from his essay "Tanizaki Jun'ichirō ron." *MTM*

desires too. But basically his attitude is that of a person who's employing an underling.

UENO: There's a term, "mistress-servant," so even a mistress has been considered a type of servant.

TOMIOKA: That's right; she's a servant.

UENO: But there's a kind of sex in which a person treats his partner as a servant, you know? When an author portrays that kind of sex, you can't say that he isn't writing about sex. Sex is sex, even when it's not sex between equal partners. In the modern novel, sexual love between equals is seldom depicted.

TOMIOKA: I'm not going so far as to say that. Not yet. But didn't you find Tanizaki's descriptions of female sexuality to be extremely stereotypical?

UENO: Definitely. Is that what you mean when you say that he isn't really writing about sex?

TOMIOKA: Yes.

UENO: In other words, aren't you just saying that his understanding of sex is shallow, and not that he doesn't write about sex? Or else, that his understanding of sex is one-sided?

TOMIOKA: It's not that it's one-sided. How shall I put it? It's not that he doesn't portray sex, but rather that his portrayal of it doesn't go far enough.

UENO: But you don't deny that he treats the topic of sex in his works, right?

TOMIOKA: I wonder if this author was really trying to deal with the subject of sexuality.

UENO: Wasn't Tanizaki in his other works too taking as his theme the idea that among the many different aspects of human life—for example, money, success, relationships between parents and children, family—sex takes precedence, that it exists independently of all the others, and that it influences them all? In *The Key [Kagi]* and *Diary of a Mad Old Man [Fūten rōjin nikki]* too. In every one of these novels the subject of sex is given a grotesquely large degree of significance in relation to others.

TOMIOKA: For example, compare Naomi and Mitsuko. Naomi had been a hostess in a café on the outskirts of Tokyo. In the old days she'd be the equivalent in social class of a woman who was sold into service in a brothel. Mitsuko, on the other hand, is portrayed as a lady of leisure who's cultured and has been educated at good schools. The sexuality of those types of women is taken as a theme in those respective works. But it seems to me that rather than individual women's sexuality, it's merely those categories of sex that are represented.

UENO: Tomioka-san, isn't what you're saying a harsh critique of the literary master, Tanizaki? [Laughter.] He's an author who takes sex as a theme but whose depiction of it is inadequate and unskillful.

TOMIOKA: I'm not saying that he's unskillful. What I meant was that contrary to what everyone says, the things I'm curious to know more about aren't dealt with in his fiction.

OGURA: That's how I felt too. According to established theories, Tanizaki writes about masochism, fetishism, and lesbianism. The two novels that we're discussing in this forum are especially reputed to include those three topics. I read them with that expectation and found that there was nothing in particular about those subjects in them.

TOMIOKA: Back when *Naomi,* for example, was published, for a man to crawl around a room with a girl on his back pretending that he was a horse, or to become ever more enthralled with a woman who was constantly disparaging him, was probably deviant behavior. Descriptions of such behavior must have aroused readers' curiosity about men who had such desires. But now there's nothing especially sensational about such things. In that respect, behavioral standards have really become blurred. So to put it a different way, in certain places in the novel the satire still has vitality, but specific behaviors that are described have lost their shock value.

Woman as Category: Love of a Woman as Love of a Pet

UENO: Why Mishima was so fond of Tanizaki is a mystery to me. Those two writers were so utterly different that you'd think they would have even felt a visceral aversion to each other. Yet Mishima loved Tanizaki as if he were a dear friend, and he regarded his literature as belonging to the same genre as his own. But what I've realized from listening now is that in both of Tanizaki's novels, as you say, women are depicted merely in terms of categories. The female characters in both works are stereotypes. So, as is true of Mishima's fiction, if a writer creates a certain type of character, a certain type of situation, a certain type of relationship, then his characters begin acting allegorically toward each other, and the story proceeds smoothly to a conclusion that pleases the author. Within that framework, there's no unpredictable development. The author doesn't create a process in which the characters, through their relationships with each other, undergo change. The story advances and concludes in a completely allegorical way. In this regard, Mishima and Tanizaki resemble each other, don't they? So you can say that relationships or human beings aren't depicted in Tanizaki's fiction.

OGURA: That's not what I find objectionable about his literature.

UENO: Am I wrong?

OGURA: I agree that female sexuality isn't effectively depicted, but I wonder if this author even understood himself, because I feel that male sexuality isn't represented either.

UENO: For example, the concept of fetishism, the concept of masochism, if you depict them within this kind of context, those aberrations too become types of allegory.

OGURA: I wasn't even at all aware of fetishism as a concept in these works.

UENO: But there are several incidents that symbolize it, right?

TOMIOKA: A little earlier, Ueno-san, you mentioned the separation of body and spirit. In Naomi's case, these seemed at first to be undifferentiated. At the beginning of the novel she's so young that it's not even clear whether or not she's become a woman. Gradually, what has been an amorphous whole separates and acquires nuances. But that process is often treated in literature, even if it isn't described in the context of an extreme situation like this. So I thought, this is really commonplace.

UENO: It's trite, isn't it. The most spiritually base creature captivates a man because of his lust for her physical beauty. A man's mixed feeling of love and contempt for such a woman is the most typical manifestation of Romanticism's view of women. Even if you don't read this novel, its plot is obvious, and how it will develop and conclude are predictable.

TOMIOKA: That's true.

UENO: The novel may be a great achievement because the plot is splendidly fleshed out, or expressed. Still, it's merely a conceptual allegory.

OGURA: Ueno-san, you say that even if you don't read *Naomi* the plot is obvious, and so forth, but I was completely stunned by the conclusion of *Quicksand*.

UENO: I didn't understand *Quicksand*.

OGURA: I felt, this can't possibly happen! [Laughter.] It's amazing that he hit upon this conclusion.

UENO: *Naomi* is immediately understandable. It's the same as Watanabe Jun'ichi's *Metamorphosis [Keshin]*.[3] [Laughter.]

OGURA: But did you really not understand *Quicksand*?

UENO: I was totally baffled by *Quicksand*. Earlier I said that women are represented only in terms of categories in Tanizaki's works. *The Key* is the most

3. Watanabe Jun'ichi (b. 1933) is a prolific, best-selling author of steamy love stories, many of which, including *Metamorphosis*, have been made into successful films. *Metamorphosis* (1986) concerns a wealthy, middle-aged man who tries to transform a young bar hostess into the woman of his dreams. *MTM*

typical example of this. The style in which the wife's diary is written is extremely unnatural for a woman. Itō Sei criticized the author for projecting himself too obviously into the woman's manner of expression in that novel. For example, "In return for being a virtuous, submissive wife, I'm able to gratify my own strong sexual appetite" (65). A woman would never write such a thing in her diary. "I'm the kind of person in whose heart lustfulness and shyness exist side by side" (65) and the like.

TOMIOKA: No woman would write such things.

UENO: It is possible that a *type* of woman, one who has been created as an allegorical figure, might be described from an observer's perspective, in the third-person voice, as "a woman in whose heart lustfulness and shyness exist side by side." But no woman would ever say such a thing about herself—"I'm the kind of person. . . ." Take a similar example: "But my parents brought me up to believe that a woman ought to be quiet and demure, certainly never aggressive toward a man" (12). In this instance too, even if a woman might write this about another woman, she'd never write it about herself. Any woman who's conscious to this degree of her "passivity" is obviously an assertive woman, right? [Laughter.] On top of that, the word "lustfulness" appears over and over. There's a big difference in being referred to in the third person as "lustful" and being aware that "I am lustful." As a woman's style of self-expression, these diary entries are very unnatural. It's blatantly clear that their author is a man who views women in a categorical way, writing in a first-person female voice.

TOMIOKA: I felt that strongly in *Quicksand* too. The married woman Sonoko's intense infatuation with Mitsuko was initially stimulated by seeing a woman standing wrapped in a billowy white gown, posing as the bodhisattva Kannon. That's not very realistic. Didn't you think so? That's a man imagining that if one woman were attracted to another, this is how their affair might begin. Somehow it seems false. But if you can't suspend your disbelief, the ensuing complications are much less enjoyable.

UENO: Can't we assume that Tanizaki deliberately kept the lesbian scenes vague in *Quicksand*?

TOMIOKA: Yes, rather than making them explicit.

UENO: That's right. Concealing was one of Tanizaki's strategies.

TOMIOKA: But if he'd tried looking at women as they really are, rather than as types, even if the descriptions of sex weren't graphic, they wouldn't seem artificial. Because not all novels that deal with sex use realistic techniques to portray sex acts explicitly.

UENO: But if you're talking about graphic sex scenes, even in *The Key*, for example, there are no sex scenes at all. Tanizaki had a kind of ethical code. . . .

TOMIOKA: No, it was because he abided by social mores.

UENO: For instance, something cute in *Naomi* is the expression "Naomi and I were covered with soap" (231). This is really cute, isn't it? Just by that he's hinting at sexual activity. There's not a single description of an actual sex act in the novel. We "were covered with soap" is really cute.

In other works too, there aren't explicit descriptions. For example, in *The Key* there's an allusion to sex when the wife writes in her diary that she's stayed "faithful" to her husband only in the strictest sense of that word. She says that she has engaged in every kind of sex play without having "crossed that last line" (105). In *Quicksand* too, the author goes so far as to write about Sonoko gazing raptly at Mitsuko's body, which is as beautiful as the bodhisattva Kannon's. But he doesn't go beyond such innuendoes. They're sufficient for the reader to understand what he's implying. The male character Watanuki is supposed to be impotent, but Mitsuko often accompanies him to an inn. It's hard to believe that she's just eating meals and chatting with an impotent man; they must be having sex. Even if he can't insert his organ, the reader clearly understands that they must be doing all kinds of other things. Surely no one can think that they are doing only what's written, don't you think?

TOMIOKA: That's right.

OGURA: But Tanizaki wasn't guided by an ethical code.

UENO: If not by an ethical code, then by his tendency to conceal things. In Japanese literature it wasn't until after the war that bed scenes were described in detail.

TOMIOKA: It was after the war, wasn't it.

UENO: Remember? There was that incident.[4] Before the war, an author could go no farther than "They were covered with soap." In *Quicksand* too, even though the activity isn't explicitly described, the implication is clear to the reader from the context and manner of expression isn't it. That the characters must have been engaging in some kind of sex.

TOMIOKA: Another point is that the male characters in Tanizaki's novels subordinate themselves to women, just as the author did to his wife Matsuko. Ordinarily you'd say that they "worship" women, but these men actually

---

4. The "incident" to which Ueno refers is the following. *Naomi* was serialized, beginning in March 1924, in the *Osaka Asahi* newspaper. But in June of that year its publication was discontinued on the grounds that its subject matter was considered by government censors and some general readers to be potentially subversive of public moral standards. (Its publication was resumed several months later in the magazine *Josei*). MTM

prostrate themselves before women. It's because "the rich don't argue," as the saying goes. If you call a rich person a pauper, he's not a bit upset. But if you say that to a poor person, he gets really mad. Similarly, a man's status is inherently high, so it doesn't bother him to grovel. It's all too clear from the start that men have an advantage, so unless they drastically lower themselves, they won't be on the same level as women. On the other hand, these men are modern people, so they have a vague desire to love a woman as an equal. For example, in *Naomi* it comes up that Jōji dislikes the idea of conforming to the traditional Japanese marriage model—encouraging the standard relationship between mother-in-law and bride, and so forth. So by rejecting those conventional roles, he thinks he's come down from his superior position, and yet he remains high. Still, on the surface he acts subserviently to Naomi. That difference between outward behavior and reality is very obvious, I thought, didn't you?

UENO: What's depicted in Tanizaki's literature isn't love for a human being but a pet, and *Naomi* is the epitome of this.

TOMIOKA: That's right. His other works are all like that too. The critics seldom call attention to that.

UENO: In the case of male literary critics, it's not that they just neglect to mention it, but that they're secretly embarrassed by it, don't you think? The commentary in this edition of the book is written by Noguchi Takehiko, isn't it?[5]

TOMIOKA: Oh, really? I haven't read that.

UENO: Here's what Noguchi has to say about Jōji's line at the end of the novel, "If you think that my account is foolish, please go ahead and laugh" (237): "Look at the gracefulness of the concluding sentence, 'Naomi is twenty-three this year and I am thirty-six.' The author tells readers to go ahead and laugh if they find his story foolish. But probably the laughter of male readers will freeze midway." The reason Noguchi says that their laughter will probably freeze is that presumably everyone has secret shameful desires, and so most men must at heart empathize with Jōji. For that very reason, probably no one calls attention to those shameful desires.

TOMIOKA: Oh, I see. Because the point is obvious.

UENO: It's obvious, so it doesn't need to be mentioned.

---

5. Noguchi Takehiko (b. 1937) is a distinguished literary critic who has written extensively on a wide range of Japanese authors and literary topics. The commentary from which Ueno quotes, "*Chijin no ai* ni tsuite" (Concerning *A Fool's Love*), is found in the 1975 paperback edition of the novel published by Shinchō. *MTM*

TOMIOKA: But something that's so obvious it needn't be said, ought to be said, right?

UENO: In short, Tanizaki doesn't think that women are human beings. For him, sex isn't something that takes place between two human beings.

TOMIOKA: That's true.

UENO: For him, a woman is a totally different species, isn't she. She's a totally different species, so he can kneel reverently before her.

TOMIOKA: Oh, I felt that very strongly.

UENO: In a letter that Tanizaki sent to Matsuko in 1932, before they were married, he wrote: "At the mere thought of your noble self, infinite creative energy wells up in me. But I would be dismayed if you were to misunderstand. To me, it's not that you exist for the sake of my art, but that my art exists for your sake. . . . If my devotion to you and to art were to ever become incompatible, I would not hesitate to abandon art." But when Matsuko got pregnant, she wanted the child so badly and she was brooding so much that she even went to consult with the president of the Chūō Kōron Publishing Company. Even so, Tanizaki told her that if she had a child his image of her would be diminished, and so he forced her to have an abortion. Ultimately, his flesh and blood spouse wasn't what was important to him.

TOMIOKA: In Tanizaki's view, if his wife had a child, she'd cease to be a woman—because she'd be a mother. The "supreme female beauty," in quotation marks, that he was searching for would be marred, so he absolutely couldn't allow her to have one.

For Tanizaki, I think that life and fiction weren't that far apart from each other. And yet he doesn't seem at all to be an I-novel writer, does he?

UENO: That's because of his novels' rhetorical power, isn't it.

Naomi *as Satire*

OGURA: Whether it's Matsuko, Mitsuko, or Naomi, all of Tanizaki's women resemble each other, don't they. They all lack the abilities that the ordinary woman normally acquires by the time she's an adult. Tanizaki was incapable of loving any other kind of woman. He could only love a woman who wasn't, as they say, "caged" within her social roles.

UENO: They're all splendid examples of woman-as-category, aren't they? Even though Matsuko was a supreme object of worship for Tanizaki, she gave the impression of having no human competence or distinctive individuality. She just radiated light among the many phantoms that he created, someone like the naked emperor. These women don't decide on a course of action in a practical way; they don't analyze and agonize over various options, and then finally decide which one is the most advantageous for themselves.

OGURA: I wonder about that. Even Naomi complains that while Jōji is away at his company she's bored being alone all day in the house with nothing to do. At those times, you'd expect the idea of giving up this lifestyle and returning to her former hostess job would cross her mind. But when it occurs to her that she's better off now than she was before, she immediately dismisses the thought of any other possibilities.

UENO: Naomi is clearly portrayed as a lower-class young woman, isn't she. She's relieved to have managed to escape from a background that makes it necessary to work in order to survive.

OGURA: These novels don't include middle-class people. The characters are low class or upper class. In other words, the female characters are the kind of women who from the start think that life means playing the part, for their husband or lover, of the woman of that man's dreams. They wouldn't consider trying to live in any other way. There aren't any women who are middle class and are eagerly aspiring to enter the upper class, or who have been deceived by such catch phrases as "self-fulfillment."

UENO: Prewar Japan was that kind of place. People were either high or low; there was no middle range. A woman either was forced to work or she didn't need to work. There was no room for choice.

TOMIOKA: The novel clearly states that Jōji dislikes the kind of married life in which the tasks of husband, wife, and maid are sharply distinguished. If a woman didn't need to work, that meant, in other words, she didn't need to do any housework. In the old days women came to the big cities from nearby farm villages and found employment as maids. So a woman was either a servant or a wife who was a lady of leisure.

UENO: True, she wasn't an ordinary housewife. Tanizaki was a man who loved a woman as a creature of an entirely different species from himself. So he could only treat her as either way below or way above himself, one or the other. That meant she was either a servant or a high-class wife.

TOMIOKA: That's right.

OGURA: To love a maid meant to liberate that woman from the status of servant.

TOMIOKA: Besides that, another idea that appears all over in this novel is "I'll study hard and improve myself." That's interesting, isn't it. I'll study, become a fine woman and a respectable person. In order to rise to the level of a creature that's worthy to be loved by a man, one must study hard, improve oneself, exert efforts. There's this model in *Naomi,* isn't there. It is mentioned any number of times.

UENO: A key idea that appears in those sections of that work is "not to be ashamed to present one's female companion to other people." In other words, a man receives approval from others. It's the same as the current "new breed of youth." A boy wants to choose a girl who'll be attractive to others when he walks around with her.

TOMIOKA: "Not to be ashamed of one's female companion in front of others." And next, "Not to be ashamed to present one's woman to Westerners." That kind of expression appears any number of times. A man wants his co-workers at his company to say that he has a good wife, a pretty wife. That's normal. But the notion of wanting to be proud to show a woman off to Westerners—that's funny, isn't it.

UENO: It's like one of those unequal treaties between Japan and Westerners in the Meiji era. In other words, the West is the public sphere.

TOMIOKA: The West is supreme. In order for Jōji to display Naomi to the West, she must study English diligently, and she must study music too. But traditional Japanese music is no good. It must be opera or other kinds of Western music that she must study devotedly.

UENO: In various senses, the reason I felt this was a typically twentieth-century or typically modern work was because of the value system implied by the fact that Jōji loved Naomi because she resembled Mary Pickford. The original item is in the West, and Naomi has value only as a copy of that. She's the epitome of a culture of imitation.

TOMIOKA: That's right. And another interesting point concerns Naomi's study of English. Jōji is a stickler for grammar, so when Naomi doesn't use the forms of the auxiliary verb "to be" and says things like 'I going, you going,' Jōji has a fit and tries mightily to correct her. But in the end, it's Naomi who becomes fluent in English, and that too is an amusing irony that contemporary people can relate to.

OGURA: At the very beginning, you said that it's interesting to read this as a satirical novel. I don't really understand the author's distance from— in other words, his degree of difference from—this character Jōji. Is he satirizing Jōji too?

TOMIOKA: No, no. He isn't satirizing Jōji, but rather Jōji's expectations of Naomi and also Jōji's obsession with the West, manifested in how he keeps insisting on doing things "like the West, like the West." Not everyone is recommending that the novel be read as a satire of these patterns, but I think that if people read it in that way, they may find it at least somewhat interesting.

EDITOR: No, I think what Ogura-san wanted to ask just now is, did the author create Jōji as a comical character, intending to poke fun at him? Or was the author to some extent unconsciously revealing his own attitudes through Jōji's?

UENO: Ogura-san, do you think it's the latter?

OGURA: Yes. I kept wondering if I was getting glimpses here and there of the author's own real feelings.

UENO: For example?

OGURA: The way of learning English that you were just talking about. In the novel it says that a man's way of learning English and a woman's way are different, right? For a man it's grammar and translation, and the feminine way is through reading. I wonder if the author seriously believed this.

TOMIOKA: He did, don't you think? But he's also being a bit sarcastic about a man's style of learning, it seems to me. I wonder if I'm reading too deeply; maybe he's not being sarcastic.

UENO: As a result of his views, Jōji becomes completely flustered when he's with foreigners, and he can't display his English-speaking ability at all. Yet Naomi joins in conversations with foreigners and chats fluently with them. In that description itself, there's self-criticism. Also, even when Jōji and Naomi play some game, at first he always lets her win, but because she has tremendous fighting spirit, at some point she becomes better at it than he and she begins to win, and so on. I imagine that some of the experiences related in the novel are based on the author's real feelings, and among those, there's some self-criticism, I think.

OGURA: If you read the novel with that idea in mind, it's more enjoyable.

TOMIOKA: If you read it expecting to learn about fetishism and the like, you'll be disappointed.

There's Nothing Frightening about the Erotic Hell That Tanizaki Describes

EDITOR: A while ago you were discussing a kind of woman that a man "wouldn't be ashamed to present to others." Toward the end of *Naomi* it's written that Naomi was being called by an unspeakable nickname. I think she was maybe being called "public toilet" or something. By just one such phrase, something that one finds desirable because it's desirable to others may completely lose its appeal. In other words, no matter how pretty or charming a girl is, if people begin calling her a whore or a public toilet, she becomes worthless. But why doesn't the novel show that this causes grief and disillusionment?

UENO: It's because, conveniently, she has an alternative, right? Naomi becomes a kind of prostitute who abandons Japanese men and caters only to Western men, so she can be tolerated.

TOMIOKA: That's right. If her partners are Westerners, her behavior is acceptable.

UENO: A prostitute who takes Western clients is viewed as desirable by the Japanese.

TOMIOKA: That's true. It's all right if it's the West. "The West" is like a sacred emblem. If one merely displays this sacred icon of "the West," she can get away with anything.

UENO: A prostitute who caters to Westerners is in a privileged class. In the end, that's how Naomi escapes condemnation, right?

EDITOR: Similarly, just at the point when if the couple goes on living extravagantly, they'll also be financially ruined and sink into a bog, Jōji's mother suddenly dies and he inherits a fortune. In the end, that's how they're able to survive. It turns into that kind of situation. So even though you say that grotesque sexuality gradually destroys everything, Jōji and Naomi aren't totally destroyed after all. As long as the situation goes no farther than this, they simply need to change their way of thinking a little. Their lifestyle isn't a bit ruined, it seems to me.

UENO: There's nothing grotesque about the sex depicted in the novel. When I used the word "grotesque" earlier, I only meant that sex is given such a grotesquely large degree of importance that it invades all areas of life. The sex itself isn't at all grotesque. The male protagonists of both *The Key* and *Naomi* seem to be thinking of nothing but sex throughout their waking hours, right?

TOMIOKA: But, surprisingly enough, they're both working, aren't they?

UENO: It's written that they're too distracted to get any work done. They even quit their jobs because they're unable to do any work.

TOMIOKA: Temporarily that happens, but it's not very serious. The husband in *Quicksand* is the same way. He's constantly taking his wife here and there. He's a lawyer, isn't he? They're members of the leisure class. So insofar as their lives proceed as smoothly as a fairy tale, the story *is* conventional.

UENO: But an account of real life doesn't make a good novel, I guess.

TOMIOKA: That's the point. But among the many critical studies of Tanizaki's literature, there's an essay by Noma Hiroshi in which Noma argues that Japanese authors have described male and female sexuality only in the context of categories such as "stylishness" and "refinement."[6]

UENO: His point is well taken. For a man like Tanizaki, sex doesn't signify having a relationship with another person.

TOMIOKA: That's right. He sublimates sex through art, and he portrays it in terms of categories such as stylishness and refinement. But he can't write about it as a way of elucidating human relationships.

UENO: That's right. Sex isn't depicted in the context of a relationship.

TOMIOKA: And I think that's just what's not interesting about his novels. I feel, if only his works had the kind of vitality that comes from understanding human beings in the context of their relationships. When you read a tale that ends neatly and conveniently, like *Naomi,* or else, as in *Quicksand,* the characters die at the end, it's as if you've just been stroking a beautiful silk kimono. You can't slit that open and see what's beneath it, so you're left feeling frustrated.

UENO: It's probably true that Tanizaki doesn't depict relationships or the female partner in a heterosexual relationship. And yet, as Ogura-san pointed out before, I think that a man's reality—for example, a man who's manipulated by his ideas about sex—*is* portrayed. But even if you consider the comical conclusion of *The Key,* although you can say the man is made a fool of, he's only made a fool of by himself, by concepts that he himself has created.

TOMIOKA: I suppose that's a novel of ideas.

UENO: He's almost like a monkey who dies from excessive masturbation. [Laughter.] That's the impression you get, right?

TOMIOKA: Tanizaki generally wrote in such a concrete, realistic way. His prose isn't shallow; it's rich and thickly textured. But as soon as he began describing a woman, he resorted to stereotypes. It's so irritating, isn't it. I really wish that he'd portrayed women in greater depth.

UENO: But if a woman were to break out of the mold he'd created for her, a world like Tanizaki's would collapse.

TOMIOKA: That's probably right. But that doesn't apply only to Tanizaki.

UENO: It's true of Yoshiyuki too.

TOMIOKA: Even the female characters in Nagai Kafū's fiction are like this. There's such a sense of substantiality about them that you feel they're

6. The argument to which Tomioka refers is the subject of Noma Hiroshi's essay, "Nihon bungaku ni okeru iki no mondai" (The question of stylishness in Japanese literature).

going to appear before your eyes. Yet there's something elusive about them, as if they'll vanish when a breeze blows. I wonder if they appeal to male readers.

UENO: If the situation were reversed, I wonder if it would be interesting. If men were completely reduced to categories and women toyed with them, would that be amusing? For example, let's say there's a woman who loves sumo wrestlers. She's a university professor, she can't stand intellectual men, and she's crazy about sumo wrestlers. She says she likes that they barely speak, they're huge, and they hardly reflect on anything. "Puff, puff, puff. . . ." "What was that technique you just used?" the announcer asks. "Everything happened so quickly, I wasn't aware of what I was doing." That sort of thing. They say if a sumo wrestler thinks about the techniques he'll use, one by one, he can't be successful. In sumo, the match is over before the wrestler has time to reflect. So he probably performs the whole sex act before any thought crosses his mind.

TOMIOKA: "Thanks for the feast!" he says afterwards.[7] [Laughter.]

UENO: A sumo wrestler gives the impression of a huge man who's all body and no brain, right?

TOMIOKA: As the wife of a former sumo Grand Champion put it, while he's active, he's hailed as a Grand Champion, but after he retires, he's just some fat ugly guy.

UENO: His face, his physique, his personality, everything about him is like a big baby. He's a person who embodies that metaphor. Our university professor says that she likes that type. If a woman were to reduce a man to a category to that degree and if her partner was a man who was docile enough to go along with that—hardly speaking and not defying that stereotype—I think that would be pretty amusing in and of itself.

OGURA: From now on, more women will probably enter into those kinds of marriages. And not only to sumo wrestlers.

TOMIOKA: In my novels too, the sexy men are usually manual laborers rather than white-collar company workers. I *do* think that real intelligence is erotic, so why is it that intellectual men have no sex appeal?

UENO: Please don't ask such a stupid question! [Laughter.]

OGURA: It's because intelligence itself suppresses the "woman" within a man.

TOMIOKA: That's right. Maybe that's how men feel too.

OGURA: That's why women fetishize construction gang apparel, isn't it? When women create a concept of masculinity to suit themselves and they

7. Tomioka's quip, *"Gotchan desu,"* is an expression used by sumo wrestlers in a variety of situations to convey warm gratitude. *MTM*

force individual men into that model, those men become erotically exciting. So I feel that you can't criticize Tanizaki's works on the grounds that they're terribly conceptual. I say that it doesn't matter if they're conceptual as long as they're enjoyable.

UENO: So when you ask where the eroticism is in Tanizaki's fiction, it's the essence of a culture that has constantly refined the relationship between two artificial categories, male and female, that he's calling eroticism.

OGURA: That's right. That's exactly it.

TOMIOKA: This discussion has become very difficult. It's a culture that men's fantasies have refined, isn't it?

UENO: As such, Tanizaki's literary works are well written. If he were to clumsily insert individuality or personal ego into them, their erotic power would immediately fade.

TOMIOKA: Oh, I get it.

UENO: So what shall we do about it?

OGURA: If Tanizaki was constantly thinking about sex, it wasn't in the sense of what couples actually did in bed or specific sexual techniques. Rather, he was always thinking about the most refined symbolic expression of the essence of "woman."

TOMIOKA: What was it that refined that symbol more for him? I'm saying that's what I want to understand.

OGURA: Eroticism means that for a woman to become a "woman," she kills the part of her female consciousness that's unable to become a "woman." Only after the death of that part of her consciousness can she become a "woman." In a "woman," there's no trace of a flesh-and-blood woman. So probably a depiction of the process of becoming a "woman" would be the ultimate novel of ideas. Mishima's works are like that too. So what's wrong with that?

TOMIOKA: I understand what you're saying. I understand that much very well, but I'm dissatisfied with only that.

UENO: What you're saying, Tomioka-san, is, "The novel *I* want to write is not like this."

TOMIOKA: Please don't say such a bold thing! You're so blunt! I can't stand it!

UENO: Look who's talking! All along you've been saying quite bold things yourself! Why are you suddenly shy at this late stage? "There's not enough sex in his novels," and so on. How bold can you get!

TOMIOKA: Hmmmm. How shall I put it?

EDITOR: It's because his stories are safe, don't you think? They seem risky, but they're strangely safe, aren't they?

OGURA: Oh, is that it? Now I understand very well.

TOMIOKA: They're not a bit scary, are they.

EDITOR: That's right. Satō Haruo said that Tanizaki was a writer who ultimately completely avoided complications. Even though he worshipped women and claimed he was a masochist, fundamentally he was very different from his fictional characters.

Tanizaki Jun'ichirō wasn't afraid of women. We spoke before of how Yoshiyuki Jun'nosuke was in some way afraid of women and so he hated them. For example, in *Plants on the Sand [Suna no ue no shokubutsu-gun]*, the protagonist torments a woman over and over, but his abusive treatment ends up giving her pleasure. That fear, or whatever you'd call it, and the terrible hatred that it produces. The hatred and fear of a creature that goes on betraying one's expectations are completely absent, it seems to me, from Tanizaki's attitude toward women.

UENO: That's right. But the situations Tanizaki describes resemble the one in *Plants on the Sand*. Even in *The Key* he caricatures the man who deteriorates trying to satisfy the lust of a woman who demands "more, more, more." In the end he's murdered by her. Because of his high blood pressure. She leads him on so that his blood pressure rises higher and higher.

EDITOR: But according to Tanizaki, that's pleasure, so in his fiction, in contrast to Yoshiyuki's it's the man who triumphs.

UENO: Yoshiyuki's style of machismo was petty in comparison to Tanizaki's. Tanizaki's machismo was so robust that he experienced his own ruin as blissful.

OGURA: That's absolutely true.

UENO: When the culture of Edo-style sexual love was flourishing, for a man to perish for love was considered the epitome of refinement. Because that didn't mean he was destroyed by a woman, but that he destroyed himself out of devotion to his own concepts. So it was like the ecstasy experienced by the male monkey that dies from excessive masturbation.

TOMIOKA: So what is a woman? For this author.

UENO: At that time of a man's ecstatic death, a woman is a tool of masturbation. As a device of pleasure, she's like a hole in a vast darkness.

TOMIOKA: A hole in. . . . [Laughter.]

Quicksand: *Tanizaki's "Masochistic Personality" and Reverse Triumph*

EDITOR: How about *Quicksand*? At the beginning of this discussion you were talking about the last part of that novel. Please say something about why that surprised you.

UENO: Toward the end, suddenly the tempo of the plot accelerated.

TOMIOKA: All at once it rushes you to the end.

OGURA: As if you're bouncing down a hill.

UENO: Without any explanation.

OGURA: It's like a Chinese poem that presents many variations but lacks the firm conclusion that the genre requires.

UENO: It's written that Mitsuko has died, so I thought it was a lesbian love suicide. But then she revives and the story continues, and I was startled, wondering what was happening. The first half of the novel is written in a subtle, detailed way, but the second half proceeds at a really fast pace to the conclusion.

OGURA: Maybe Tanizaki got sick of it. He may have been manic-depressive.

TOMIOKA: But I wonder what motivated the author to want to write about sex between women, about homosexual love, as it's described in _Quicksand_. Why was he so fixated on lesbian love? Did he really want to describe the love between two women? Maybe he didn't—I'm doubtful.

OGURA: Male authors want to write about lesbians, don't they?

TOMIOKA: But in this work he's expressing the theme especially clearly and directly.

UENO: The situation is unnatural in some ways, but assuming that he intended the novel's main theme to be a love triangle, I think he must have wanted to experiment with a woman-woman-man configuration rather than man-woman-man in order to represent that kind of passion. For example, here's how he expresses Mitsuko's narcissism: " 'I'd much rather be worshipped by someone of my own sex. It's natural for a man to look at a woman and think she's beautiful, but when I realize I can have another woman infatuated with me, I ask myself if I'm really _that_ beautiful! It makes me blissfully happy!' " (107). If a woman is worshipped by a person of her own sex, her value is elevated higher than when she's worshipped by a man. I wonder if he wasn't fascinated by that idea. Moreover, if the triangle is a man-woman-man combination, the two men won't get along well. But if it's a woman-woman-man configuration, one woman and the man will both share in worshipping the other woman without competing against each other. So the sense of complicity among the three will be stronger and the triangle more stable. A love triangle has a certain inevitability; if any of the three elements is deficient, it's impossible for it to exist, right?

TOMIOKA: If he wanted to describe a perfect love triangle, female homoerotic love was absolutely essential, wasn't it.

UENO: I think it was. If it were a man-woman-man arrangement, one member would inevitably be excluded. But if it's a woman-woman-man combination, the triangle can be maintained.

OGURA: Well, if the men were homosexuals, even a man-woman-man triangle would work, wouldn't it?

UENO: Yes, that would be all right. But Tanizaki had no concept of homosexuality. It wasn't in his nature to worship a man.

OGURA: He was homophobic, like Yoshiyuki. A woman is the "Other"; she's an object, so it doesn't matter what she does. But if a man were to do that sort of thing, Tanizaki's internal ethical system would have blown a fuse. [Laughter.]

TOMIOKA: It would have blown a fuse at the mere thought of male homosexuality.

UENO: Even if two men aren't necessarily homosexual, if they share a sense of brotherhood and they allow a woman into their relationship, an isosceles triangle is created. You see this structure in Truffaut's film *Jules et Jim*. But probably for Tanizaki, the idea of male homosexuality was unimaginable.

OGURA: Or else, to embody the supreme form of eros, he needed an amoral personality, just as in *Naomi*. At some level, Tanizaki wasn't able to tolerate an amoral man.

UENO: But didn't he say repeatedly that he thought he might be a pedophile?

OGURA: One of the characters in this novel says that?

UENO: I read in some critical study that Tanizaki himself said that. His kind of sexual love was the love of an inferior, of a pet, wasn't it? Boys or women. It was a love that required an absolute difference in status between the partners. So even if you consider him a kind of pedophile, you could never call him a homosexual.

TOMIOKA: A sexual relationship with a male equal would have been out of the question for him.

OGURA: Even if he could accept immorality, he was afraid of amorality.

UENO: He didn't think that love could exist between himself and a person who had the same personality as his own, don't you think?

OGURA: Like *Naomi*, *Quicksand* has always been stereotyped as a novel that's about masochism. But when I read it, I felt that there was no such thing anywhere in it. There's a man whose wife is unfaithful to him, but you see that sort of thing everywhere. What's described in it isn't "sexual masochism" but a "masochistic personality." Those two are completely different. So the reason that Tanizaki was unable to form close relationships with other men or with social equals, as you've been saying, is that he had within him the strong sense of helplessness or inferiority that's the source of the masochistic personality. I sense that he created this facade of sexual masochism in order to cover up those feelings. Of course, it's not as apparent as in Yoshiyuki's case.

EDITOR: To return to the question of why Tanizaki took up the topic of lesbianism in *Quicksand:* in addition to the reasons that Ueno-san suggested a while ago, I think another has to do with Tanizaki's attitude toward penile insertion. Among his stories that deal with sex, there's rarely any mention of penetration. Of course, this is partly because there are no explicit sex scenes in his literature. But, for example, in *Diary of a Mad Old Man,* the male character's attachment to feet is emphasized. In *Quicksand,* the first three characters to be featured are two women and an impotent man; all of these are individuals who are incapable of penetration. When Sonoko's husband, who's the only character capable of penetration, finally comes on the scene, the author simply pushes him aside. So this makes me think that the author was fixated on kinds of love that didn't involve penetration and wanted to write about one of those.

UENO: At the end of *Quicksand,* when Mitsuko actually has sex with Sonoko's husband, Sonoko says, "For the first time Mitsuko had known a real man" (205). This is a frank reference to penetration, isn't it? Also, even in *The Key,* when the husband, with the help of fantasy, makes love to his wife while she's semiconscious, she writes in her diary that her vagina was suffused with such a sense of pleasure, with such a sense of fulfillment that she'd never before experienced, that she could hardly believe that it was her husband's organ inside her. She means that she wished her husband's organ could make her feel like that.

EDITOR: But still, I'm inclined to think that Tanizaki was a person who wasn't especially fond of insertion. Why he had to make the first male character impotent is a point that I'd like to reflect on a little more.

OGURA: No matter how much the man pleases the woman at the stage of foreplay, when he inserts his penis and consummates the sex act, his desire for domination is satisfied and thus he's rewarded for his initial investment of effort. Any man who engages in sex that doesn't finally yield a return on his investment is a complete masochist.

UENO: Hahaha! That's an excellent definition!

OGURA: It's easy to view sex that doesn't satisfy the desire to dominate as a kind of eroticism that's superior to the sex between normal men and women. The same thing applies to sex between two women.

TOMIOKA: I see.

EDITOR: Well, if Tanizaki intended Watanuki to embody the supreme form of eroticism, that's not suggested anywhere in *Quicksand.*

UENO: *Quicksand* has four structural elements; there are two men and two women. There are two different types of triangle, and the novel is alternating between two different kinds of passion. In the first triangle Mitsuko is in the middle, and Sonoko and Watanuki enter into a contract that establishes their relationship as that of brother- and sister-in-law. One reason they can keep this contract is that Watanuki can't violate a woman. This is a device for ensuring that heterosexual love won't be able to achieve a decisive victory over homosexual love. Sonoko's husband becomes involved in the next triangle, and when sexual love arises between the husband and Mitsuko, Sonoko starts to become suspicious. It dawns on her that her husband and Mitsuko have actually had intercourse. Realizing that "Mitsuko has experienced a real man for the first time," Sonoko rushes to her husband, doesn't she. In the presence of heterosexual love, not a trace of the idea of the sublimity of love between women remains. So the equilibrium that they'd maintained with the impotent Watanuki is shattered. Sonoko has internalized the myth of heterosexual love too, so even though she attempts a love suicide, she can't die because of her suspicions about her husband and Mitsuko. Mitsuko harbors the same kind of suspicions about the other two members of that triangle. Her desperate, ghastly way of coping with them takes the form of forcing Sonoko and her husband to take sleeping pills every night. Mitsuko can't return to her home until she's made sure that the couple has fallen asleep. That three-way deadlock propels the trio into a catastrophe. With regard to heterosexual love, it may be possible for the imperfect original triangle to endure, but the second triangle cannot. I think that's exactly why Tanizaki created two love triangles.

TOMIOKA: If Watanuki were a normal man, suspicion would be a necessary element of the tale from the start, right?

OGURA: I wonder if it's only sexual infidelity that disrupts the power balance. There's a married couple whose names are in the official family register, and a woman who can't have any legally recognized status in the arrangement. You have to consider the family system too, don't you? Isn't there a place in the novel where Mitsuko makes Sonoko and her husband change their way of addressing each other? She wants them to quit calling each other "Dear" and "Sonoko," like a typical married couple, and instead call each other "Kōtarō-san" and "Sonoko-san."

UENO: No, I don't think that's the problem. It says that the reason Sonoko, who's legally married, survives rather than Mitsuko is that she suspects heterosexual love has triumphed over homosexual love. She imagines she'd be treated as a nuisance by the other two in the afterlife if she died with them, and this thought forces her to live on in dishonor. For heterosexual love and homosexual love to maintain equilibrium, tremendous tension is necessary. In the first triangle, that tension is precariously maintained because Watanuki is impotent. But in the second triangle, when Sonoko's husband and Mitsuko begin having sexual intercourse, the balance collapses.

OGURA: But before she met Mitsuko, Sonoko herself was already a person for whom homosexual love and heterosexual love were compatible, right? She had a husband, and she'd already taken that factor into consideration.

UENO: It's because Sonoko isn't the center of the triangle. Mitsuko is always the center.

OGURA: Well then, if the triangle were composed of three women, would the situation drag on and on indefinitely, with no one dying?

UENO: Maybe so.

OGURA: I suspect that the struggle would be more brutal under those circumstances.

UENO: Anyway, it's a sinister, unpleasant novel in which all of the characters are full of paranoid suspicion. Sonoko reflects that when a person is pushed and pulled this way and that by a sneaky man like Watanuki, his or her own personality probably also becomes wily. You see that in *Diary of a Mad Old Man* too. While associating with someone whose personality is twisted by paranoia and who is suspicious, sneaky, and calculating, the originally honest person gradually becomes just the same way. This theme is ubiquitous in Tanizaki's literature, so I think that probably was how the author really felt. I wonder if he himself had always treated the people around him in the same way. He was a very scheming individual, wasn't he.

OGURA: You're saying that Tanizaki's disposition was the same as Watanuki's?

UENO: That's right. Even in *The Key*, the wife keeps a diary with the assumption that her husband is secretly reading it, but the husband insists that he's not. Probably Tanizaki himself had that scheming nature that makes for double and even triple layers of deception. A person who was manipulated by that scheming nature of his gradually turned into a devious individual herself in the course of their relationship—I wonder if this wasn't almost exactly Tanizaki's own actual experience. It says in the novel that even though Mitsuko wasn't originally that way, under the influence of Watanuki's sneaky personality, she turned into a suspicious, scheming person too.

EDITOR: A little while ago Ogura-san mentioned that the masochistic personality is rooted in an inferiority complex.

OGURA: Tanizaki depicts men and women in terms of metaphors such as the West versus Japan or Tokyo versus Osaka. Moreover, he was a man who was a native of Tokyo, but eventually everything he embraced was his opposite. He worshipped women and went to live in the Kansai. Wasn't he a man who was unable to develop an ego that had a masculine, forceful quality about it? Or maybe it wasn't that he was unable to do so, but that he didn't want it to develop in that way. That pulpy, diffuse quality is quintessentially Japanese, and ultimately that triumphs over the West, Tanizaki seems to be saying. In other words, while claiming over and over that Japanese people have an inferiority complex toward the West, it's as if his side wins in the end, just as Naomi winds up completely controlling Jōji. If you read his literature in this way, it's interesting in a completely different way from that of Yoshiyuki's and others'.

TOMIOKA: When I said that his literature was quite satirical, that's just what I meant. When I read these novels from that perspective, I found them appealing in a fresh way. But when I reread them expecting to see the masochism, fetishism, and so forth, for which they're renowned, I was disappointed and I didn't enjoy them. His works are interesting as novels of ideas. Because the author has shaped them in a way that highlights his concept of eros.

Two Reasons Why Tanizaki's Literature Is Timeless:
Its Romantic Underpinning and Its Portrayal of Sexual Love
as a Swamp in a World Lacking an Ethical Vision

TOMIOKA: In that sense, Tanizaki's novels still seem comparatively fresh, don't they? Their luster hasn't faded much.

UENO: If Tanizaki's works haven't lost their glow even now, I think it's for two reasons. One is that he took the classical model of Romanticism's view of women and wrote brilliantly in accordance with that formula. That we haven't yet liberated ourselves from the framework of Romanticism's view of women is a matter for consideration. Another reason is that in Tanizaki's world there isn't a trace of a Western-style ethical code, so it greatly appeals to Japanese lowbrow tastes. Because the swamp of sexual love is neither good nor bad.

TOMIOKA: You may be right. In a way it's similar to how Hasegawa Shin's plays never seem to lose their appeal.

UENO: What I think is interesting is that when Tanizaki treats the subject of sex, if it's within a European context, psychological complications inevitably occur between the physical plane and a metaphysical plane. In other words, the situation induces in the characters a sense of guilt or self-division, it seems. But in these novels that we've been discussing, complications don't arise within the self, only outside the self. There, internalized morality doesn't intervene at all. I felt, how splendidly Japanese this is! In a realm where morality doesn't intrude at all, if a man feels attachment or yearning, it's understandable that he'd probably behave as described here. In *Naomi,* there's a scene where Naomi brings home Kumagai and two other youths, and the four of them sleep together under a mosquito net, remember? Even though she's flirting with other men, Jōji can't offer a bit of resistance; he just spends the night among them. In a kind of world where there's no morality, only attachments, situations like this are bound to occur, I thought. I was struck by how skillfully the author evoked that swamp-like context of human relationships. My response when I read this was, oh, this truly is an erotic world that's unaffected by morality. Once morality enters the picture, there are always internal complications. Here, there are external complications but no internal ones. So it can't be a psychological novel. Because it lacks any interior drama. So the reason why *Naomi* is an excellent novel is that it isn't a psychological novel. Precisely because it's not, it's excellent. Only external events are described: what happens to Naomi, and in relation to that, what happens to "me," Jōji.

TOMIOKA: But what you've said doesn't apply to only that novel, right?

UENO: That's right. If there were such a thing as transcendence, a dialogue would begin between the physical plane and whatever transcends the physical. But in these novels, there's no such psychological drama.

TOMIOKA: In that sense, they're traditional.

UENO: Yes. Ah, Japan. This is Japan. Japan is a place that lacks any notion of transcendence; it's an amoral world, I thought as I read these works. That swamp-like atmosphere is really skillfully evoked. The complications that are portrayed in *Quicksand* too aren't the kind that occur in so-called psychological drama. Even when one character becomes suspicious of another, he or she doesn't experience inner turmoil. The only thing that plunges the main characters into their peculiar predicament is concern for "respectability." It's interesting that respectability should play a role in the novel. Mitsuko can't openly have a relationship with Watanuki, and so forth.

TOMIOKA: By "concern for respectability," do you mean because the family system in those days had so much authority?

UENO: In a broad sense it was probably because of the family system. For example, in *Quicksand,* Mitsuko is a young woman who's still unmarried. And Sonoko and her husband must worry about giving others the impression that the husband fails to adequately supervise his wife. If it weren't for that, it wouldn't matter what Sonoko did. "As long as you're not caught, it doesn't matter what you do" is an awfully Japanese attitude. People have no internal ethical code; they only have concern for what others think of them.

Here's another thing I admired. You know that Tanizaki published an essay in 1931 called "Love and Lust." In it he writes: "People complain that the personalities of women in novels of the past, since the time of *The Tale of Genji,* all seem to be the same; their individual traits aren't described. But men of the old days didn't fall in love with a woman's unique personality. They weren't captivated by a particular woman's lovely face or her attractive body. For them, just as the moon is always the same moon, 'woman' was probably eternally one and the same 'woman.'" In other words, he's saying she was all women, as a category. "In the darkness, he would hear the faint murmur of her voice, smell the fragrance of her silken garments, stroke her hair, caress with his fingertips her dewy skin, and then, when dawn came, all those sensations would vanish somewhere. Men of the past must have thought of all those attributes together as 'woman.'" This is very clear. It's not necessary to distinguish women as separate individuals.

TOMIOKA: Besides, they can't be distinguished, right?

UENO: Individual women all melt together in the category called "woman." Now and then the touch of her skin, or some other physical sensation, is all there is.

TOMIOKA: In general, this man was fond of shadows.

UENO: There's darkness on the other side of a curtain, and within that darkness, occasionally a hole opens up. Clutching at that darkness, a man thrusts in his organ—it's that kind of image. Woman-as-category blends into that darkness; there's very little difference from one woman to another. The fragrance that lingers after she's gone is just slightly different from one woman to another; that's the impression you get, isn't it. It's as if the man is embracing the darkness.

TOMIOKA: But that was more or less the sensibility of Japanese people before the present age, wasn't it?

UENO: Probably so.

TOMIOKA: To put it differently, it was probably because Tanizaki could see things from the opposite perspective that he was able to write these kinds of novels.

GLOSSARY OF NAMES AND TERMS

REIGN YEARS AND HISTORICAL ERAS

Readers of this volume will frequently encounter reference to particular reign years and historical eras. The following are the reign years mentioned most consistently in this volume and the calendar years to which they refer.

Meiji—1868–1912
Taishō—1912–1926
Shōwa—1926–1989
Heisei—1989–present

The period prior to the Meiji is termed either the Tokugawa era—in reference to the fact that the period was dominated by the rule of the Tokugawa shogun— or the Edo period—because the shogun's power base was in the city of Edo (now known as Tokyo). This era covers the period 1600–1868. The Heian era, when the aristocratic women Ono no Komachi, Murasaki Shikibu, Sei Shōnagon, and others wrote their great works, covers the years 794–1185.

WRITERS AND CRITICS

The authors of the critical essays translated in this volume assume their readers will be familiar with writers either currently in the news or well known by their collective readership. The following identification of the names cited in these essays is intended to assist readers of this volume. When writers are introduced, the titles of a few of their works are offered, and the availability of a coinciding English translation is noted when applicable.

Akiyama Shun (b. 1930) studied French at Waseda University. Akiyama is known as a literary critic and professor of literature at Tokyo University of Agriculture and Technology and Musashino University. *TA*

Akutagawa Ryūnosuke (1892–1927) was a short story writer, essayist, and critic. Many of his stories are taken from traditional tales but feature elegance and psychological insights. Citing a feeling of "vague unease," he took his own life. Among works in translation are "Rashōmon" (1915; tr. 1920) and "Yabu no naka" (In a Grove, 1921; tr. 1952). *BH*

Arai Motoko (b. 1960) is a popular author of science fiction. While she was still a high school student, her *Atashi no naka no* (That within me) was awarded an honorable mention for the *Kisō tengai* magazine's first Newcomers to Science Fiction Award in 1977 and was released as a book the following year. A few of her novels are available in English translation, such as *Gurīn rekuiem* (Green requiem, 1981; tr. 1984). *RLC*

Arishima Takeo (1878–1923) was a novelist and essayist whose writings reflect his wide-ranging familiarity with Western literature and culture, including Christianity. Notable in English translation is *Aru onna* (A certain woman, 1919; tr. 1978). He died in a double suicide with his lover. *MTM*

Ariyoshi Sawako (1931–1984), novelist, playwright, translator, and essayist, spent the first ten years of her life in Java. Her books have great popular appeal but nevertheless engage controversial social issues. Notable is *Kōkotsu no hito* (The twilight years, 1972; tr. 1984), which deals with senility and the problems that caring for the elderly poses on women. *RLC*

Asada Akira (b. 1957) is an economist and cultural critic who deals with a variety of literary, political, and intellectual topics. An associate professor of economics at Kyoto University, he co-edited *Critical Space* with Karatani Kōjin. *ES*

Chikamatsu Shūkō (Tokuda Shūkō, 1876–1944) was a writer of confessional fiction in the style of the Naturalist School. *RLC*

Dazai Osamu (1909–1948) was noted for a bohemian lifestyle marked by drug and alcohol problems. His fiction drew on his own life experiences, which he presented with ironic humor. Something of a cult figure representing the anguish and displacement of modernity in Japan, he took his own life in a double suicide with his lover, leaving behind a wife and three children. Representative works in translation include *Shayō* (The setting sun, 1947; tr. 1956) and *Ningen shikkaku* (No longer human, 1948; tr. 1958). *BH*

Egusa Mitsuko (b. 1941) graduated from Ochanomizu Women's University with a degree in Japanese literature. A professor at Bunkyō University specializing in modern Japanese literature and women's studies, her works include a study of Arishima Takeo and *Onna ga yomu kindai bungaku* (Women reading modern literature), which she co-edited with Urushida Kazuyo. *RLC*

Enchi Fumiko (1905–1986), the daughter of a famed philologist, began her literary debut as a playwright before switching to fiction in the 1950s. Her work drew praise from literary heavyweights such as Mishima Yukio and Tanizaki Jun'ichirō. She completed modern translations of *The Tale of Genji* in addition to short and long works of fiction and essays. Works in translation include *Onnazaka* (The waiting years, 1957; tr. 1971) and *Onnamen* (Masks, 1958; tr. 1985). *BH*

Fukuda Shōji (Shōji Kaoru, b. 1937) was awarded the Akutagawa Prize in 1969 for *Akazukin-chan ki o tsukete* (Take care, Red Riding Hood). He was extremely popular among young people in the 1970s. *BH*

Fukuzawa Yukichi (1835–1901), samurai-born, was a member of the first delegation to the United States. An ardent supporter of "civilization and enlightenment," Fukuzawa was an educator, author, and journalist. He published his seventeen-volume *Gakumon no susume* (An encouragement of learning) between 1872 and 1876. *RLC*

Furui Yoshikichi (b. 1937) is associated with fiction that focuses on the inner lives of its characters. Often his female characters are embodiments of primitive energy and mystery, as perceived through the eyes of male characters in search of spiritual rejuvenation. Representative works in translation include *Yōko* (1971; tr. 1997). *MTM*

Futabatei Shimei (1864–1909), novelist and translator, is credited with writing Japan's first "modern novel," *Ukigumo* (Floating clouds, 1889; tr. 1967). His extensive translations of Russian literature into Japanese were said to have contributed to the development of *genbun itchi,* a writing style that rejected the ornamentation of the classics in favor of a written language closer to spoken Japanese. *BH*

Gō Shizuko (b. 1929), a novelist, was awarded the Akutagawa Prize in 1973 for *Rekuiemu* (Requiem; tr. 1985), her semi-autobiographical account of her childhood wartime experiences. *BH*

Hagiwara Yōko (b. 1920) was the eldest daughter of the renowned poet Hagiwara Sakutarō (1886–1942). She made a relatively late literary debut with *Chichi Hagiwara Sakutarō* (My father Hagiwara Sakutarō, 1959), which was awarded the Japan Essayist Club Prize. *Tenjō no hana* (The heavenly flower) won the Tamura Toshiko Prize in 1966. She is best known for her autobiographical trilogy: *Irakusa no ie* (The house of nettles, 1976, winner of the Women's Literature Prize); *Tozasareta niwa* (The closed garden, 1984); and *Rinne no koyomi* (The calendar of transmigration, 1997). *TA*

Hara Shirō (b. 1924) is a poet and literary scholar born in Nagasaki Prefecture. He taught Japanese literature at Waseda University for many years. In 1963 he published a collection of poetry and remained active as a poet and critic in the decades that followed. In 1994 Hara was the author of a text dealing with rhetoric in Japan, *Shūjigaku no shiteki kenkyū* (A historical study of rhetoric). *TA*

Harada Yasuko (b. 1928) is best known for *Banka* (Elegy, 1956), which heralded a new era for women freed from the sexual repression of the prewar era. An immense best seller, the book made its way to the film and television screens. *RLC*

Hasegawa Izumi (b. 1918) is a prolific literary critic who has written extensively on modern and contemporary Japanese literature. Although he began publishing in the late 1940s, Hasegawa first came to notice with a series of articles published in the mid-1950s in which he discussed the work of novelist Yokomitsu Riichi. He has continued actively publishing into the twenty-first century and was made a life member of the Japan Pen Club. Hasegawa has recently released an autobiography entitled *Hasegawa Izumi jiden* (Hasegawa Izumi: My life). *BH/TA*

Hasegawa Shigure (1879–1941) is now known, along with her friend Okada Yachiyo, as the founder and editor of *Nyonin geijutsu* (Women and the arts), a feminist journal that began in 1928. Shigure was at this time a rising playwright. Although written for the kabuki stage, her plays, such as *Chōji midare* (Wavering traces, 1911; tr. 1996), resisted clichéd tragic endings and featured heroines who strove for self-fulfillment and independence. *RLC*

Hasegawa Shin (1884–1963) was a novelist and playwright whose works were infused with his empathy for the hardships of common people and his espousal of traditional Japanese values. *MTM*

Hashimoto Osamu (b. 1948), novelist and critic, is best known for his comic-satirical fiction such as the *Momojiri musume* (Peach-bottomed girl) series and for his critical works on a wide range of topics, including girls' comics. With Saitō Minako, he was the joint recipient in 2002 of the inaugural Kobayashi Hideo Prize, sponsored by Shinchōsha, for the work *Mishima Yukio wa nani mono datta no?* (Who was this person called Mishima Yukio?). *TA*

Hayashi Fumiko (1903–1951) was the child of itinerate peddlers. Her writing—both poetry and fiction—drew on her own experiences and those of lower-class working women. She would rival Higuchi Ichiyō as Japan's most beloved woman writer. Representative works in translation include *Hōrōki* (Diary of a vagabond, 1928–1930; tr. 1997). *RLC*

Hieda no Are was a late seventh-century court attendant whose sex has been disputed since the early nineteenth century. Hieda no Are had extraordinary memory capacity and recited the texts that were then transcribed by Ō no Yasumaro (d. 723) and compiled as the *Kojiki* (Record of ancient matters). *BH*

Higuchi Ichiyō (1872–1896) lost her father and brothers while still young. Unmarried, lacking any male support, she struggled to provide for her mother and younger sister with the meager income she received from writing and from a variety of odd jobs—such as serving as scrivener and seamstress for the denizens of the local licensed quarter. She is known for her short stories, many of them depicting the hardships women face in a patriarchal society, and for her diary. Representative works in translation include "Takekurabe" (Child's play, 1896; tr. 1956, 1981). *RLC*

Himuro Saeko (b. 1957) won an honorable mention in the tenth Shūeisha New Writers' Award in 1977 with her debut piece, *Sayōnara Arurukan,* which she wrote while still a college student. Subsequently she has produced numerous best sellers for Cobalt Library and is very popular with fans of girls' comics. *RLC*

Hirabayashi Taiko (1905–1972) was a highly respected proletarian novelist and critic whose work, often based on her own experiences, depicts the lives of working-class people in Japan. Subject to police persecution for her activities in prewar Japan, she suffered serious health problems. She recommended literary activity after the war and remained active until her death. Notable among her works in translation are "Azakeru" (Self-mockery, 1927; tr. 1987). *BH*

Hiraiwa Yumie (b. 1932), a prolific novelist and essayist, was awarded the 1959 Naoki Prize for "Taganeshi" (The chisel master). Although this story is set in contemporary Tokyo, much of her work conforms to historical fiction. *BH*

Hirano Ken (1907–1978), a professor at Meiji University, was an influential literary critic credited with "discovering" Ōe Kenzaburō, Kurahashi Yumiko, and others. *RLC*

Ikuta Chōkō (1882–1936), recognized for his prominence as a translator of Western works (Nietzsche, D'Annunzio, Marx), was the driving force behind an early twentieth-century salon for women's writing. He also encouraged the founding of the feminist journal *Seitō*. *RLC*

Inagaki Taruho (1900–1977) had a unique combination of interests, including "love for the boy," astronomy, aviation, poetry, aestheticism, and fantasy. For a collection of his short surrealist works, see *One Thousand and One-Second Stories*. *TA*

Inoue Mitsuharu (1926–1992) was a Marxist writer whose fiction contains a strong vein of social commentary. *MTM*

Ishihara Shintarō (b. 1932), a novelist and politician, was awarded the Akutagawa Prize in 1955 for a story of rebellion and violence among postwar youth. For representative works in English, see the story collection *Season of Violence: The Punish Room, The Yacht and the Boy* (1966). He continued to write fiction until his election to the Diet in 1968. Author of *The Japan That Can Say "No,"* he is currently the mayor of Tokyo and noted for antiforeigner and conservative views. *BH*

Ishikawa Jun (1899–1987), writer and translator, was noted for his antiwar stance. Well read in the literature of modern Europe, Edo-period Japan, and ancient China, he won the Akutagawa Prize in 1936. For a translation of his stories, see *The Legend of Gold: And Other Stories* (1998). *RLC*

Ishimure Michiko (b. 1927). Shortly after her birth in Kumamoto Prefecture, her family moved to Minamata City, site of one of Japan's earliest and most bitterly fought pollution scandals. Her extensive coverage of the suffering of victims of so-called "Minamata disease" was used in the legal battle for compensation. See her *Kugai jōdo: Waga Minamata byō* (Paradise in the sea of sorrow: Our Minamata disease, 1969; tr. 2003). *BH*

Itagaki Naoko (1896–1977) was a pioneer woman literary critic. A graduate of Japan Women's University, her significance lies in her role in foregrounding the otherwise overlooked writing of women in the early and mid-Shōwa period. In addition to her overview of women's writing in modern Japan, entitled *Meiji shōwa taishō no joryū bungaku* (Women's writing in Meiji, Taishō, and Shōwa, 1967), her contribution to Natsume Sōseki scholarship is considerable. *TA*

Itō Sei (1905–1969) was a distinguished critic, novelist, and translator. Firmly declaring himself antiproletarian, he advocated instead the modern psychological approach to writing seen in James Joyce and Virginia Woolf, whose work he translated into Japanese. Itō's analysis of the "I-novel" had a strong influence on later postwar critical thought. *BH*

Iwamoto Yoshiharu (1863–1942), journalist and Christian educator, was the co-founder in 1885 of *Jogaku zasshi* (Women's education magazine) and the Meiji Jogakkō (Meiji School for Women). He was influential in encouraging women's writing.

Izumi Kyōka (1873–1939), often described as a romanticist, is known for his exquisite use of language and his often fantastic plots, many of which feature ghosts, spirits, and beautiful women. "Kōya hijiri" (The holy man of Mount Kōya, 1900; tr. 1996) is perhaps his best known work. *RLC*

Izumi Shikibu (fl. ca. 1000) is known for her poetic diary, *Izumi Shikibu nikki* (The Izumi Shikibu diary; tr. 1969); for her private poetry collection; and for her love affair with a prince. *RLC*

Kamei Katsuichirō (1907–1966) was a co-founder of the Nihon Rōmanha (Japanese Romanticists). An erudite scholar of Japanese literature, he wrote extensively on Shimazaki Tōson and modern Japanese love poetry, Arishima Takeo, and Dazai Osamu, among others. *RLC*

Kanai Mieko (b. 1947), a novelist and essayist, was awarded the Akutagawa Prize in 1970. A prolific writer and recipient of many literary accolades since that time, her best-known work in English translation is "Usagi" (Rabbits, 1976; tr. 1982). *BH*

Karatani Kōjin (b. 1941) was the most influential literary critic of the 1970s and 1980s. He was an editor of a cutting-edge intellectual journal, *Critical Space,* in the 1980s and 1990s. Currently he is a professor at Kinki University and a visiting full professor at Columbia University. *ES*

Katō Norihiro (b. 1948) is a literary critic from the baby boomer generation and former student activist of the late 1960s. A professor of literature at Waseda University, he is one of the current leaders of traditional (mainstream) criticism of modern Japanese literature. *ES*

Kawabata Yasunari (1899–1972) was the recipient of the Nobel Prize for literature in 1968. A founding member of Shinkankakuha (New Sensualist Group), which advocated writing in a manner that evoked the senses, he combined European avant garde literary influence with a deep love for the traditions of Japan. His works, such as *Yukiguni* (Snow country, 1948; tr. 1957), *Yama no oto* (The sound of the mountain, 1954; tr. 1970), and *Nemureru bijo* (The house of sleeping beauties, 1960; tr. 1969), emphasize the fragility of existence, marked by a strain of oppressive perverseness. *BH*

Kawamura Jirō (b. 1928) is a scholar of French literature, professor emeritus at Tokyo Metropolitan University, and a celebrated literary critic whose works have won numerous awards, including the Kamei Katsuichirō Prize. *RLC*

Ki no Tsurayuki (ca. 868–945), a poet and scholar, wrote the first *kana* diary, *Tosa nikki* (The Tosa diary; tr. 1978) and the *kana* preface to the first imperially authorized collection of Japanese poetry, *Kokinshū* (Collection of old and new verses; tr. 1984), which he also co-edited. *BH*

Kikuda Ippu (1908–1973) was a playwright. He received a Tony in 1973 for lifetime achievement. *RLC*

Kirishima Yōko (b. 1937) is a popular nonfiction writer whose subjects vary from cross-cultural experience to cooking. *BH*

Kitada Sachie, a scholar and critic, completed her doctoral work at Hokkaido University and is currently a professor of Japanese literature and women's studies at Jōsai International University. She has been instrumental in the recovery of women's writing of the Meiji period, producing studies on Shimizu Shikin, Nakajima Shōen, and Kimura Akebono. *RLC*

Kitada Usurai (1876–1900), a protégé of Ozaki Kōyō, in 1895 wrote an essay, "Asamashi no sugata" (Wretched sights; tr. 2006), from the perspective of a licensed prostitute. Her *Aki no sora* (Autumn sky, 1896) described the plight of a woman sold into prostitution by her husband. The didactic tone of her works and her obvious indictment of men as the source of women's woes earned her scathing reviews from men who were affronted by her display of "superficial knowledge." Also available in translation is her short story "Shiragazome" (Hiding the grey, 1897; tr. 2006). *RLC*

Kobayashi Hideo (1902–1983) is variously described as a literary critic, an art critic, and a cultural critic. While studying French literature at Tokyo Imperial University, he began to write short fiction. In 1929, when he won second place in a magazine contest for amateur critics, he found a new niche. His writing style, displaying at once his strong personality and his shrewd intellect, became immensely popular. Kobayashi was not only dubbed the first "modern" literary critic in Japan, but for many years he was also the most influential. For a collection of his critical essays in English, see *Literature of the Lost Home: Kobayashi Hideo Literary Criticism, 1924–1939* (1995). *KP*

Kōda Aya (1904–1990) began her writing career in 1947 as a memoirist, penning pieces about her late father, the highly regarded writer Kōda Rohan (1867–1947). She turned to fiction in 1956 with her novella *Nagareru* (Flowing). A number of her short stories are available in English translation, among them "Kuroi suso" (Black hems, 1955; tr. 1993; Black skirt, 1956). *RLC*

Koganei Kimiko (1871–1956) was, along with Wakamatsu Shizuko, one of the first recognized female translators. Younger sister of Mori Ōgai, she was known for her graceful rendering of German and English into classical Japanese. *RLC*

Komashaku Kimi (b. 1925) was one of the founders of the Women's School in Osaka. Formerly a professor at Hosei University, she is the author of *Majo no ronri* (Theories of the witch, 1978) and *Murasaki Shikibu no meseeji* (Murasaki Shikibu's message, 1991), and she is also recognized for her incisive studies of Natsume Sōseki, Takamura Kōtarō, and other canonical male writers. *RLC*

Kōno Taeko (b. 1926) was awarded the Akutagawa Prize in 1963. She was one of the first writers to address taboo areas such as child hatred and sadomasochism, subjects that figure in her translated collection *Toddler Hunting and Other Stories* (1991). Now a revered figure in the Japanese literary community, she serves on numerous prize committees and is the recipient of many literary accolades. *BH*

Kōra Rumiko (b. 1932) attended Tokyo University of Fine Arts and Keio University. Since 1958, she has published poetry, criticism, personal essays, translations, and novels. She is known as a feminist and as a translator and critic of Asian and African literature. *Kōra Rumiko jisen hyōronshū* (Kōra Rumiko: Self-selected collected criticism, 1992) is the third volume of a six-volume compilation of her critical works. *JBE*

Kubo Sakae (1900–1958) was a dramatist and fiction writer. *RLC*

Kunikida Doppo (1871–1908) was a poet, essayist, and fiction writer. Considered a member of the Naturalist School, he is known for his simple yet evocative depictions of natural beauty and commonplace events, after the fashion of Wordsworth, whom he greatly admired. For a collection of his stories in English, see *River Mist and Other Stories* (1983). *RLC*

Kunikida Haruko (1879–1962) had a brief writing career and a meager output. She is known primarily as the long-suffering wife of Kunikida Doppo. *RLC*

Kurahashi Yumiko (1935–2005), known for her experimental style, fantasy fiction, and essays, was awarded the 1961 Women's Literature Prize. Her work is represented in English by the short story collection *The Woman with the Flying Head* (1997). *BH*

Masamune Hakuchō (1878–1962) was a novelist, playwright, critic, and essayist. Associated with the Naturalist literary movement, his work spanned the three eras of modern Japan. *BH*

Matsuura Rieko (b. 1958) is a writer, critic, and essayist known for her interest in moving beyond male-centered, heterosexual paradigms. *Nachuraru ūman* (Natural woman, 1991) openly and graphically explores lesbianism, while *Oyayubi P no shukugyō jidai* (The apprenticeship of Big Toe P, 1995) is about a woman whose toe transforms into a penis. *RLC*

Mayama Seika (1878–1948) began as a fiction writer in the Naturalist style but by 1907 had turned his attention to the theater. He is best known as a *shin-kabuki,* or new kabuki playwright, and for his modern version of the Forty-Seven Rōnin story. *RLC*

Mishima Yukio (1925–1970) was a prolific writer in a variety of genres—prose, drama, film, poetry. Noted for his postwar nihilistic writing, his self-acclaimed right-wing politics, and his sensational suicide, a large number of his works are available in English translation. *Kamen no kokuhaku* (Confessions of a mask, 1948; tr. 1958) and *Kinkakuji* (1956; tr. 1959) are but two. *RLC*

Miwata Masako (1843–1927), the daughter of a Confucian scholar, received a thorough education in the Japanese and Chinese classics. After being widowed in her midthirties, she began a school that ultimately became Miwata Kasei Jogakuin and then, after the war, Miwata Gakuen. It is now a junior-senior high school for girls in Chiyoda-ku, Tokyo. Miwata was active in several national organizations for women and was the first woman educator to be decorated by the Japanese government. *JBE*

Miyamoto Yuriko (1899–1951) was a novelist, essayist, and critic. Raised in a well-to-do family and enjoying a privileged education that included a year at Columbia University in New York, Miyamoto's work is marked by independence, intelligence, and the social/political causes she embraced, most notably communism. Portions of her novels *Nobuko* (1926), *Banshū heiya* (The Banshū Plain, 1946; tr. 1984–1985), and *Fūchisō* (The weathervane plant, 1946; tr. 1984) are available in English translation. *RLC*

Miyao Tomiko (b. 1926), a prolific novelist of primarily historical fiction, was awarded the 1962 New Woman Writer Award and the 1972 Dazai Osamu Award. *BH*

Miyoshi Tatsuji (1900–1964) was one of the more influential poets of the twentieth century. He had a tempestuous relationship with Hagiwara Sakutarō's younger sister (the bullying aunt in *The House of Nettles*). Hagiwara Yōko's *Tenjō no hana* (The heavenly flower, 1966, winner of the Tamura Toshiko Prize) includes a semifictional account of this relationship. *TA*

Mizuta Noriko, a leading feminist critic, took her Ph.D. in American Literature at Yale University. Subsequently she taught comparative literature at the University of Southern California for ten years before assuming a post at Josai University. She is the co-editor and co-translator, with Kyoko Iriye Selden, of *Japanese Women Authors: Short Fiction* (1991) and the author and editor of numerous studies of feminist literary criticism in Japanese. Currently she serves as the president of Josai International University. *RLC*

Mori Atsushi (1912–1989) was one of the oldest recipients of the Akutagawa Prize— typically given to promising new writers—which he was awarded in 1973 at the age of sixty-one. *BH*

Mori Makiko (1934–1992) wrote "Kiiroi shōfu" (The yellow prostitute, 1971), which was nominated for the Akutagawa Prize. Her *Yuki onna* (Snow woman) won the Izumi Kyōka Prize in 1980. *BH*

Mori Mari (1903–1987) began publishing translations of French literature, essays, and reviews in 1929. However, she did not become a professional writer until the publication of her first collection of essays and memoirs about her renowned writer father, Mori Ōgai; the work won an Essayist Club Award. In the following three decades she produced both essays and fiction exploring unique styles and themes, including male homosexual romance and father-daughter romance. An example of the latter is her 1975 novel, *Amai mitsu no heya* (A room as sweet as honey). *TA*

Mori Ōgai (1862–1922) was a high-ranking military doctor whose medical study in Germany inspired him to pursue an additional career as a writer. Novelist, critic, and translator, his works had a profound influence on the development of the modern Japanese canon. Among his works in translation are "Maihime" (The dancing girl, 1890; tr. 1975); *Gan* (*Wild geese*, 1913; tr. 1959); and *Vita Sexualis* (1909; tr. 1972). *RLC*

Morita Shiken was the pen name of Morita Bunzō (1861–1897), a journalist who dominated the world of translation in the 1890s, becoming known as the "translation king." *JW*

Moto Kukiko has been nominated three times for the Naoki Award since 1974–1975. A number of her novels have been made into films. *BH*

Murakami Haruki (b. 1949) is a popular novelist whose 1979 debut novella, *Kaze no uta wo kike* (Hear the wind sing; tr. 1987), set a drastically new, postmodern style of narration. His light, cool, casual, and mildly sentimental tone has become the overwhelmingly dominant one today, adopted by a subsequent generation of novelists. Among his many works in translation are *Hitsuji wo meguru bōken* (The wild-sheep chase, 1982; tr. 1989) and *Nejimakidori kuronikuru* (The wind-up bird chronicle, 1995; tr. 1998). *ES*

Murakami Ryū (b. 1952) is a prolific author of fiction and nonfiction and is known for depictions of gritty urban violence. His first novel *Kagirinaki tōmei ni chikai burū* (Almost-transparent blue, 1976; tr. 1977), won the Akutagawa Prize in 1976. *RLC*

Murasaki Shikibu (d. 1014?), best known as the author of the early eleventh-century *The Tale of Genji,* also left a diary in which she describes aspects of her upbringing and her years at the Heian court in the service of Empress Shōshi. Murasaki evidently showed an early talent for literature, including Chinese poetry, which she learned more quickly than the brother her father was actually tutoring. Knowledge of Chinese was at that time a skill demanded of male courtiers and bureaucrats but discouraged in women. *LRR*

Murō Saisei (1889–1962), poet, novelist, and essayist, is noted for his portrayal of women, which reflects overt traces of patriarchal desire. Nevertheless, his literary prowess is acknowledged even by some feminist critics. *TA*

Mushanokōji Saneatsu (1885–1976) was an influential novelist, playwright, poet, essayist, and critic. He was the leading figure in Shirakabaha (White Birch Society), which advocated a discourse of universal cosmopolitanism while remaining unmoved by imperial expansionist policies of the time. Among his works in English translation are *Yūjō* (Friendship, 1919; tr. 1958). *BH*

Nagai Kafū (1879–1957), novelist, essayist, and critic, was a scholar of kabuki and Edo culture, as well as a professor of French at Keio University. Influenced by writers such as Maupassant and Zola, his works retain a strong sense of Japanese aesthetics. For works in English translation, see *A Strange Tale from East of the River and Other Stories* (1971). *BH*

Nakamori Akio (b. 1960), fiction writer, critic, editor, and commentator of popular culture, is said to be responsible for coining the term *otaku* (geek; nerdish fan of digital technology, especially anime and computers). *TA*

Nakayama Kazuko (b. 1931) is a professor of Japanese literature at Meiji University. Nakayama brought a scholarly commitment to advancing feminist literary analysis. Her most recent study is *Nakayama Kazuko korekushon: Natsume Sōseki, josei, jendaa* (Nakayama Kazuko's collected works: Natsume Sōseki, women, and gender, 2003). *JE*

Nakazato Tsuneko (1909–1987) was a writer whose 1938 story, "Noriai basha" (The carriage), won the Akutagawa Prize—the first time the prize was awarded to a woman. The story concerned the lives of foreign wives in Japan. Her 1959 "Kusari" (Chains) describes a mother's concern over her daughter's mixed-race marriage. *RLC*

Natsume Sōseki (1986–1916) is one of the most revered figures in modern Japanese literature. He resigned his position of professor of English at Tokyo University to become a full-time writer. Advocating a neo-romanticism that eschewed both romantic ideals and bohemian excess, much of his work is marked by an oppressive sense of guilt and a desire for self-sacrifice. Among his many works in translation are *Wagahai wa neko de aru* (I am a cat, 1906; tr. 1921); *Kokoro* (1914; tr. 1957); *Sore kara* (And then, 1909; tr. 1978); and *Michikusa* (Grass on the wayside, 1915; tr. 1969). *BH*

Nogami Yaeko (1885–1985) was a prolific and successful novelist, essayist, and translator from her twenties until her death. Well-known works include *Kaijinmaru* (The Neptune, 1922; tr. 1961), *Machiko* (1931), and *Mori* (The forest, 1985). Stories in translation include "Kata-ashi no mondai" (A story of a missing leg, 1931; tr. 1987) and "Subako" (Birdhouses, 1970; tr. 1993). *BH*

Noma Hiroshi (1915–1991) was a novelist and essayist who demonstrated an unwavering commitment to examining serious social problems and political issues. Traumatized by his military experiences during World War II, his postwar novels contain powerful descriptions of wartime brutality, as well as the demoralized atmosphere of occupied Japan. A lifelong Communist sympathizer, Noma is also admired for his literary treatment of victims of various forms of prejudice and oppression. Available in English translation is *Dark Pictures and Other Stories* (tr. 2000). *MTM*

Nomizo Naoko (1897–1987), professor of literature at Tōyō University, wrote *Kuchinashi* (The gardenia, winner of the 1924 *Fukuoka nichinichi shinbun* Prize) and many other novels and short stories, as well as scholarly and critical works. Thanks to the efforts of critics such as Yagawa Sumiko, Kuze Teruhiko, and Takahara Eiri, her works and her extraordinary life have begun to attract attention in the last two decades. *TA*

Ōba Minako. See Ohba Minako.

Ōe Kenzaburō (b. 1935) was awarded the Akutagawa Prize in 1955 and the Nobel Prize for literature in 1994. Now considered the doyen of Japanese letters, he writes with a strong sense of social justice against what he sees as the excesses of an affluent and apathetic contemporary Japan. Works in English translation include *Kojinteki na taiken* (A personal matter, 1964; tr. 1968); *Man'en gannen no futto bōru* (The silent cry, 1967; tr. 1974) and *Pinchirannaa chōsho* (The pinchrunner memorandum, 1976; tr. 1994). *BH*

Oguri Fūyō (1875–1926) was a disciple of Ozaki Kōyō. His sensational story, "Neoshiroi" (Bedtime makeup, 1896), about incest in a *buraku* community, was banned upon publication. *RLC*

Ōhara Mariko (b. 1959) is a multi-award winning science fiction writer. One of her most well-known works is *Hybrid Child*. *TA*

Ōhara Tomie (1912–2000) published "Ane no purezento" (My older sister's present) in 1938. She won the Noma Prize in 1960 for her novel *En to iu onna* (A woman to call En; tr. 1986). *BH*

Ohba Minako (b. 1930), a novelist and essayist, spent several years in the United States, where she began writing fiction. Awarded the Akutagawa Prize in 1968, she has received many literary accolades since that time. Available in English translation are "Rōsoku uo" (Candle fish, 1986; tr. 1991); "Yamauba no bishō" (The smile of the mountain witch, 1976; tr. 1982); "San biki no kani" (The three crabs, 1968; tr. 1982); and other stories. *BH*

Okada Yachiyo (1883–1962), fiction writer, playwright, and drama critic, was the younger sister of Naturalist writer Osanai Kaoru (1881–1928). She used fiction as an opportunity to criticize patriarchal systems that oppressed women. *RLC*

Okamoto Kanoko (1899–1939) was a poet, essayist, and fiction writer of extraordinary breadth and vitality. Her husband, Ippei (1886–1948), was a famous illustrator for the *Asahi Newspaper*. Kanoko's works are notable for the lush and evocative avowal of female sexuality and strength. *Rōgi shō* (The tale of the old geisha, 1938; tr. 1985), "Hana wa tsuyoshi" (A floral pageant, 1937; tr. 1963), and other stories are available in English translation. *RLC*

Okuno Takeo (1926–1997) was one of postwar Japan's most prominent and influential literary critics. He was born in Tokyo and originally trained in the sciences at the Tokyo Institute of Technology. Okuno's seminal work was a discussion of the critical role of setting in modern literature: *Bungaku ni okeru genfūkei* (The primal landscape in literature, 1972). He also wrote widely on women's literature and played a role in advocating for the acceptance of many young postwar women writers. The excerpt given in this collection, however, clearly indicates the conditional nature of that advocacy. *TA*

Ono no Komachi (dates unknown; active mid-ninth century), was the leading female poet of the early Heian period and the only woman among the Six Immortals of Poetry. *JBE*

Orihara Mito (b. 1964) made her debut as a *manga* artist in 1985. Two years later she became an author of girls' stories. Having close to 150 volumes to her credit, she is also known for her collections of essays, poems, translations, and recipes and is extremely popular with female readers between the ages of ten and thirty. *RLC*

Orikuchi Shinobu (1887–1953) is best known as a scholar of Japanese literature and a *tanka* poet (under the name Shaku Chōkū). He also wrote fiction, among which is *Kuchibue* (The whistle, 1914), which deals with two boys yearning for each other. *TA*

Ōshima Yumiko (b. 1947), together with Hagio Moto, Takemiya Keiko, and others, established the genre of girl comic fantasy in the 1970s. Ōshima-style illustrations are characterized by fine, flowery-line heroines with large dreamy eyes, and her stories deal with such topics as a sensitive and lonely girl protagonist's search for love; complex family situations; supernatural elements; and the beautification of male-male love. *ES*

Ōtsuka Eiji (b. 1958) is a literary and cultural critic known for his analyses of the subcultures developed by Generation Xers in the 1980s and 1990s. *ES*

Ōtsuka Kusuoko (1875–1910), poet, essayist, and fiction writer, was known for creating middle-to-upper-class female characters who uninhibitedly give voice to their own desires. Her 1908 novella, *Sora daki* (Incense burner), for example, depicts the lust a married woman has for her attractive stepson. *RLC*

Ozaki Kōyō (1867–1903), novelist and poet, was the leading figure of the literary coterie Ken'yūsha (Friends of the Inkstone Society). Highly influential in his time, he mentored young novelists, such as Izumi Kyōka, and early women writers. *BH*

Ozaki Midori (1896–1971) published modernist fiction in the early 1930s. In spite of a positive reception from leading critics, her career was short-lived. Pressured by her brother to return to her home in Tottori, she spent the next few decades in literary oblivion until 1969, when her work was included in an anthology of black humor. The reevaluation of her texts continues with posthumous publications. *TA*

Ryūtanji Yū (1901–1992) began his career as a writer of modernist fiction in the late 1920s. He was briefly ostracized by mainstream literary journalism following his criticism in 1934 of the cliquish nature of the Japanese literary establishment. *TA*

Saegusa Kazuko (1929–2003), a brilliant intellectual, began her literary career in the 1960s with dreamlike stories dominated by images of death and destruction. From the 1980s she dedicated herself to writing fiction on feminist themes, but those works too tend to be bleak in tone and stylistically difficult. Saegusa was also a pioneering feminist literary critic. She is represented in English by the story "Rokudō no tsuji" (Rain at Rokudō Crossing, 1987; tr. 1991). *MTM*

Saitō Minako (b. 1956) is one of the few professional female literary critics in Japan, with such studies as *Ninshin shōsetsu* (Pregnancy literature, 1994) and *Bundan aidoru ron* (Idols of literary journalism, 2002). She has urged women to adopt new methods of reading Japanese literature as a fundamental protest against male writers, male readers, and patriarchy itself. *AS*

Sasazawa Saho (b. 1930) is a writer of detective fiction whose stories often provide as much romantic adventure as mystery. *RLC*

Sata Ineko (1904–1998) was at one time a member of the Japan Communist Party and active in the proletarian movement before its suppression in the early 1930s. Later she distanced herself from overt political literature, although her work continued to depict hardships in the lives of everyday people. In English she is represented by short stories such as "Yuki no mau yado" (The inn of dancing snow, 1972; tr. 1988); "Yoru no kioku" (Memory of a night, 1955; tr. 1982); and a portion of her 1936 novel, *Kurenai* (Crimson; tr. 1987). *BH*

Satō Aiko (b. 1923) was awarded the Naoki Prize in 1964 for her short story "Kanō tai'i fujin" (The wife of Captain Kanō). The daughter of popular writer Satō Kōroku (1874–1949), she continues to produce novels and humorous essays. *BH*

Satō Haruo (1892–1964), a long-time close acquaintance of Tanizaki Jun'ichirō's, wrote poetry and prose fiction with a romantic cast. Tanizaki divorced his first wife in 1930 so that he and Satō, who had been in love for many years, would be free to marry. The highly publicized incident and the events that surrounded it created a sensation at the time. *MTM*

Seki Reiko (b. 1949) is a scholar and critic. Professor of modern Japanese literature at Asia University, her research and publications have contributed significantly to the re-visioning of Meiji women's writings. *RLC*

Setouchi Harumi (now known by her Buddhist name, Setouchi Jakuchō; b. 1922) is a novelist, critic, and social and religious commentator. She was awarded the inaugural Tamura Toshiko Prize in 1960 for that writer's biography. In 1973 she became a Buddhist nun. Recently she completed a modern translation of *The Tale of Genji*. Translations of her works include *Bi wa ranchō ni ari* (Beauty in disarray, 1966; tr. 1993) and *Natsu no owari* (The end of summer, 1963; tr. 1989). *BH*

Shibaki Yoshiko (1914–1991) as a nineteen-year-old attended lectures in literature given by Yokomitsu Riichi and Kobayashi Hideo. She was awarded the Akutagawa Prize in 1942 and subsequently received a range of literary honors. Translations of her work in English include "Kazahana" (Snow flurry, 1984; tr. 1986) and "Hamon" (Ripples, 1970; tr. 1985) *BH*

Shibusawa Tatsuhiko (1928–1987) is widely recognized as the translator and scholar of the Marquis de Sade and other French writers. His critical essays on topics ranging from ancient Greek to contemporary Japanese literature, and to a lesser extent his fiction, have also had a great impact upon many readers and writers. *TA*

Shiga Naoya (1883–1971), though not prolific, was regarded as "the god of the 'I'-novel," the autobiographical fiction that has been a feature of Japanese narrative throughout much of the twentieth century and that focuses on character psychology to the exclusion of social factors. Shiga was prominent in Shirakabaha (the White Birch Society). Among his works in translation are the novel *An'ya kōro* (A dark night's passing, 1937; tr. 1976) and numerous short stories. *BH*

Shima Sachiko (b. 1928) was awarded the Women's Literature Newcomer Award in 1969. *BH*

Shimamoto Hisae was born in Tokyo in 1893. Her death date is unknown. A journalist for nine years before assisting her husband with the editorship of a literary journal, she wrote fiction for girls and later novels for an adult market. *BH*

Shimao Toshio (1917–1986) is best known for his stories based on his harrowing life with his wife after she suffered a mental breakdown upon discovering her husband's infidelity. *The Sting of Death* (1977; tr. 1985) is a collection of these stories. *MTM*

Shimazaki Tōson (1872–1943), novelist and poet, was known for the romantic yearnings expressed in his poetry and the autobiographical nature of his prose. Among his works in translation are *Hakai* (The broken commandment, 1906; tr. 1974); *Ie* (The family, 1911; tr. 1976); and *Yoake mae* (Before the dawn, 1935; tr. 1987). *RLC*

Sono Ayako (b. 1931) emerged in the 1950s as a "female genius." She was an

Akutagawa Prize nominee in 1954 for one of the first works critical of the American occupation forces. Her works, often informed by Christian doctrine, reveal a deep concern for social issues—from the ostracizing of the destitute and the mentally ill to the performing of abortions. She is represented in English translation by *Kami no yogoreta te* (Watcher from the shore, 1979; tr. 1990), in addition to selected short stories. *RLC/BH*

Takahara Eiri (b. 1959; alias Katō Mikiya) has written two important book-length studies of neglected areas of modern Japanese literature: *Shōjo ryōiki* (The territory of the girl, 1999) and *Muku no chikara: "Shōnen" bungaku hyōshōron* (The power of innocence: A study of representations of the boy, 2003). He has also published numerous critical essays, as well as works of fiction and poetry. Takahara was awarded the first Fantasy Literature New Writers' Award and the thirty-ninth Gunzō Literary Criticism Award. He was awarded a Ph.D. by the Tokyo Institute of Technology for his study based on *Muku no chikara*. Takahara teaches part-time at Waseda University. *TA*

Takahashi Takako (b. 1932), an essayist, novelist, and translator, began her career with a degree in French literature from Kyoto University. Her dark, often brooding works explore the toll patriarchal society takes on bright, sensitive women. Converting to Catholicism in 1975, Takahashi has lived in convents in France and Japan and became a nun in 1985. She is represented in English by numerous short stories, including *Ronrii ūman* (Lonely woman, 1977; tr. 2004), a collection of five linked stories. *RLC*

Takami Jun (1907–1965), a writer, poet, and critic, was initially affiliated with proletarian literature before being forced to renounce his political interests. He wrote *Shōwa bungaku seisuiki* (A history of the rise and fall of Shōwa literature, 1952–1957). *RLC*

Takenishi Hiroko (b. 1929), essayist, critic, and novelist, is also a specialist in the classics. She was awarded the Noma Prize in 2003. In English, see "Gishiki" (The rite, 1963; tr. 1985). *BH*

Tamura Toshiko (1884–1945) attended the newly founded Japan Women's College before financial pressure forced her to withdraw. She aspired to become an actress but was more successful as a writer. She was a member of the Seitō (Bluestocking) group whose early works explore a woman's struggle to find her voice. Married twice, she traveled to Canada and subsequently to China, where she died. A literary award for women writers was established in her name in 1961. She is represented in English by the short stories "Onna sakusha" (A woman writer, 1913; tr. 1987); "Eiga" (Glory, 1916; tr. 1987); "Ikichi" (Lifeblood, 1911; tr. 2006); and "Seigon" (The oath, 1912; tr. 2006). *RLC*

Tanaka Miyoko (b. 1936) was a graduate of Waseda University and a literary critic. Her major publications include *Romanshugisha wa akutō ka* (Is the romanticist a villain?) and *Tanshi no kikagaku* (Geometry of the angel). *TA*

Tanizaki Jun'ichirō (1886–1965) is an eminent twentieth-century novelist noted for his ability to create sensuously evocative and complex fictional scenarios, often based on historical material, in which masculine desire is given full reign. The inspiration of his third wife, Matsuko, provided some of the most exquisitely written texts of modern Japanese literature. He completed modern translations of *The Tale of Genji*. Among his works in English translation are *Chijin no ai* (A fool's love, 1924; tr. as Naomi, 1985); "Shunkin-shō" (A portrait of Shunkin, 1933; tr. 1963); and *Fūten rōjin nikki* (The diary of a mad old man, 1962; tr. 1965). *BH*

Tawara Machi (b. 1962) is a popular *tanka* poet who fills the traditional *tanka* form with contemporary topics. Tawara's 1988 debut anthology of *tanka* poems, *Sarada kinenbi* (Salad anniversary; tr. 1990) sold 2 million copies within the year. *ES.*

Tazawa Inabune (1874–1896), painter, poet, and aspiring writer, wrote gothic-laced pieces that warned of the dangers awaiting innocent women who placed their trust in sweet-talking men. Married briefly and unhappily to Yamada Bimyō (1868–1910), who had been her mentor, Inabune's final work, "Godaidō" (The Temple Godai, 1896; tr. 2006), was published posthumously. *RLC*

Togawa Masako (b. 1933) was originally a singer who began writing between acts in her dressing room. Awarded the 1962 Edogawa Ranpo Prize for mystery, she is a prolific writer of short stories, novels, and essays. Recently she has been prominent as a daytime television talk show commentator. Among her novels translated in English are *Hi no seppun* (Kiss of fire, 1984; tr. 1989). *BH*

Tokuda Shūkō. See Chikamatsu Shūkō.

Tokuda Shūsei (1871–1943) was initially a member of Ozaki Kōyō's literary coterie. After Kōyō's death he made a name for himself as a Naturalist writer. In his later years, he brought a new direction to I-novels and psychological stories. His best-known works, many of which treat the women in his life, include *Ashi ato* (Footprints, 1910); *Kabi* (Mold, 1911); *Tadare* (Sore, 1913); and *Arakure* (Rough living, 1915; tr. 2001). *KP*

Tomioka Taeko (b. 1935), novelist, poet, essayist, scriptwriter, literary critic, and commentator, is highly critical of discursively ascribed gender roles. A native of Ōsaka, she has rejected standard Japanese in favor of the Osaka dialect as a writing medium. A number of her poems and stories are available in the English collections *The Funeral of a Giraffe: Seven Stories by Tomioka Taeko* (2000) and *See You Soon: Poems of Tomioka Taeko* (1979). *BH*

Tsuboi Sakae (1899–1967) was an essayist, television dramatist, children's story writer, and fiction writer. She grew up in a poor village on a tiny island in the Inland Sea, and many of her works describe the travails of women struggling to survive unfair and untenable conditions. She is best known for *Nijūshi no hitomi* (Twenty-four eyes, 1954; tr. 1957). *RLC*

Tsushima Yūko (b. 1947) was born in Tokyo shortly before her father, writer Dazai Osamu, died in a love suicide. Her stories frequently feature single and often unwed mothers whose bouts with social ostracism and uncertainty are balanced by the exhilaration of independence. For a collection of short stories in English translation, see *The Shooting Gallery and Other Stories.* Among her novels are *Chōji* (Child of fortune, 1978; tr. 1983) and *Yama wo hashiru onna* (Woman running in the mountains, 1980; tr. 1991). *RLC*

Ueno Chizuko (b. 1948) is a professor of sociology at Tokyo University and one of the most publicly recognized feminists. She is a prolific critic whose essays span the gamut from contemporary social issues in Japan to historical surveys of the image of women and women's language in Japanese literature. Ueno participated with Tomioka Taeko and Ogura Chikako in the controversial *danryū bungaku* (male literature) discussions. Her *Nationalism and Gender* is available in English translation. *RLC*

Uno Chiyo (1897–1996), fiction writer, essayist, magazine editor and publisher, kimono designer, and entrepreneur, was known for her sensational love life and her narratives that detailed it with seemingly little hesitation. In English translation, see *Irozange* (Confessions of love, 1935; tr. 1989); *Aru hitori no onna no hanashi* (The story of a single woman, 1971; tr. 1993); and *Ohan* (1957; tr. 1961), among others. *RLC*

Wakamatsu Shizuko (1864–1896) contributed articles in Japanese to *Jogaku zasshi* (Women's education magazine) and in English to the *Japanese Evangelist.* Recognized for her promotion of both translation and children's literature, she is best known today for her translation of Frances Burnett's *Little Lord Fauntleroy. RLC*

Watanabe Sumiko (b. 1930), formerly a professor of Japanese literature and women's studies at Daitō Bunka University, has written extensively on modern women's writing, most recently a biography of Otake Kōkichi (1893–1966), a member of the Seitō (Bluestockings) group. *RLC*

Yagawa Sumiko (1930–2002) was an acclaimed translator of German and English literature. She is also known for her witty and playful poems; critical and biographical works on writers such as Mori Mari, Anaïs Nin, and Nomizo Naoko; and autobiographical fiction, some of which deals with her relationship with Shibusawa Tatsuhiko (whose essay on Okamoto Kanoko is included in chapter 3 above). *TA*

Yamamoto Michiko (b. 1936) is a poet and novelist who has spent time in Australia. She was awarded the Akutagawa Prize in 1972 for *Betei-san no niwa* (Betty-san's garden, 1972; tr. as Betty-san, 1983), an account of difficulties encountered by a Japanese woman overseas. *BH*

Yamamoto Shūgorō (1903–1967), was a popular and prolific novelist whose heroes often represented traditional moral values of self-sacrificing love, diligence, and perseverance. Some of the Kurosawa Akira movies, such as *Dodeskaden* and *Red Beard,* were adaptations of Yamamoto stories. A literary prize was created in his honor in 1988. *ES*

Yamazaki Tomoko (b. 1931) is a historian whose works explore the lives of exploited and marginalized women in Japan and other Asian countries. Her first major work, *Sandakan hachiban shokan* (Sandakan Brothel No. 8, 1972; tr. 1998), which was awarded the Ōya Sōichi Prize for Nonfiction Literature, became a national best seller and established Yamazaki as a leading feminist writer. In 1974, Kumai Kei directed a film version of *Sandakan Brothel No. 8* and its sequel, *The Graves of Sandakan* (*Sandakan no haka*, 1974), which was nominated for an academy award in the foreign film category. *RLC*

Yamazaki Toyoko (b. 1924), whose name is sometimes romanized "Yamasaki," began as a journalist before shifting to fiction. Her better known works, such as *Fumō chitai* (The barren zone, 1978; tr. 1985), feature individuals stranded between national identities. *RLC*

Yanagawa Shun'yō (1877–1918) wrote domestic fiction *(katei shōsetsu)* for newspapers. One of his better known serialized stories is *Nasanu naka* (No blood relation, 1912–1913), a melodramatic account of the turmoil that befalls a once tranquil family. *RLC*

Yonaha Keiko is a Japanese literature professor at Tōyō Eiwa University with a focus on the literature of Okinawa and women's writing. Among her published works is *Gendai joryū sakka ron* (On contemporary women's writing, 1986). *RLC*

Yosano Akiko (1878–1942) was a poet, essayist, translator, and writer whose *Midaregami* (Tangled hair, 1902; tr. 1971) combined a modern female sensibility with the earlier *tanka* form. She would continue to make a name for herself as a writer of free verse and a translator (into modern Japanese) of *The Tale of Genji*. In her time she was also recognized as a formidable social critic. *RLC*

Yoshimoto Banana (b. 1964) has been one of the most popular and contested female writers in Japan since her debut in the late 1980s, publishing a prodigious number of books with sales in the millions of copies. This level of popularity also has subjected her to attacks from many literary critics in Japan and elsewhere, who have derided her as a mass producer of "mass" literature. For representative works, see *Kitchin* (Kitchen, 1987; tr. 1993); *NP* (1990; tr. 1994), *Amrita* (1994; tr. 1998); and others. *ES*

Yoshimoto Takaaki (b. 1924) is a poet, literary critic, and intellectual. He was the most influential leftist thinker and respected literary critic during the 1950s and 1960s. *ES*

Yoshiya Nobuko (1896–1973) was known for her popular serialized novels, which appealed to a readership of primarily adolescent girls. *Hana monogatari* (Flower stories) and *Yaneura no ni shōjo* (Two virgins in the attic) are typical of her prewar works. *Atakake no hitobito* (The people of the Ataka family) was a postwar best seller. To date none of Yoshiya's novels are in translation. *RLC*

Yoshiyuki Jun'nosuke (1924–1994) wrote stories set in the pleasure quarters about men who seek respite from their tedious lives in liaisons with prostitutes. His elegant prose and ironic tone are imbued with a delicate pathos. He is the author of *Anshitsu* (Dark room, 1970; tr. 1994). *MTM*

Yoshiyuki Rie (b. 1939) was awarded the 1968 Tamura Toshiko Prize and the 1981 Akutagawa Prize for "Chiisana kifujin" (The little lady; tr. 1982). She is the sister of prominent postwar novelist Yoshiyuki Jun'nosuke. *BH*

BIBLIOGRAPHY

English

Ariga, Chieko. "Dephallicizing Women in *Ryūkyō shinshi:* A Critique of Gender
Ideology in Japanese Literature." *Journal of Asian Studies* 51 (3) (August 1992):
565–586.

———. "Text versus Commentary: Struggles over the Cultural Meanings of
'Woman.'" In Schalow and Walker, *The Woman's Hand,* pp. 352–381.

Beichman, Janine. *Embracing the Firebird: Yosano Akiko and the Birth of the Female
Voice in Modern Japanese Poetry.* Honolulu: University of Hawai'i Press, 2002.

———. "Yosano Akiko: Return to the Female." *Japan Quarterly* 37 (2) (April–June
1990): 204–228.

Benjamin, Walter. "The Task of the Translator." Translated by Harry Zohn in *The
Translation Studies Reader.* Ed. Lawrence Venuti. London and New York:
Routledge, 2000. Originally published 1923.

Bernstein, Gail Lee, ed. *Recreating Japanese Women, 1600–1945.* Berkeley: University
of California Press, 1991.

Bowring, Richard. *Murasaki Shikibu: Her Diary and Poetic Memoirs.* Princeton,
N.J.: Princeton University Press, 1982.

Buckley, Sandra. "Altered States: The Body Politics of 'Being-Woman.'" In *Postwar
Japan as History.* Ed. Andrew Gordon, pp. 347–372 . Berkeley and Los Angeles:
University of California Press, 1993.

Copeland, Rebecca L. *Lost Leaves: Women Writers of Meiji Japan.* Honolulu:
University of Hawai'i Press, 2000.

———. "The Made-Up Author: Writer as Woman in the Works of Uno Chiyo."
Journal of the Association of Teachers of Japanese 29 (1) (April 1995): 3–25.

———. "Setouchi Harumi." In *Dictionary of Literary Biography,* vol. 182: *Japanese
Fiction Writers since World War II.* Ed. Van Gessel, pp. 196–203. Detroit: Gale
Research, 1997. A Bruccoli Clark Layman Book.

Ericson, Joan E. *Be a Woman: Hayashi Fumiko and Modern Japanese Women's
Literature.* Honolulu: University of Hawai'i Press, 1997.

———. "The Origins of the Concept of 'Women's Literature.'" In Schalow and
Walker, *The Woman's Hand,* pp. 74–115.

Hurley, Adrienne. "Demons, Transnational Subjects, and the Fiction of Ohba
Minako." In *Ōe and Beyond: Fiction in Contemporary Japan.* Ed. Stephen Snyder
and Philip Gabriel, pp. 89–103. Honolulu: University of Hawai'i Press, 1999.

Kitada, Sachie. "Contemporary Japanese Feminist Literary Criticism." *U.S.-Japan
Women's Journal, English Supplement* 7 (1994): 72–97.

Kiyooka, Eiichi, trans. and ed. *Fukuzawa Yukichi on Japanese Women: Selected Works.*
Tokyo: University of Tokyo Press, 1988.

Lermontov, Mikhail Yurievich. *A Hero of Our Time.* Trans. J. H. Wisdom and Marr Murray. New York: Alfred A. Knopf, 1916.

Lippit, Noriko Mizuta, and Kyoko Iriye Selden, eds. and trans. *Stories by Contemporary Japanese Women Writers.* New York: M. E. Sharpe, 1982.

Mackie, Vera. *Feminism in Modern Japan: Citizenship, Embodiment and Sexuality.* Cambridge: Cambridge University Press, 2003.

McCullough, Helen, trans. *"Tosa Nikki:* A Tosa Journal." In Helen McCullough, *Kokin Wakashū: The First Imperial Anthology of Japanese Poetry with "Tosa Nikki" and "Shinsen Waka,"* pp. 263–291. Stanford, Calif.: Stanford University Press, 1985.

Miyake, Lynne K. *"The Tosa Diary:* In the Interstices of Gender and Criticism." In Schalow and Walker, *The Woman's Hand,* pp. 41–73.

Miyoshi, Masao. "Gathering Voices: Japanese Women and Women Writers." In Miyoshi, *Off Center,* pp. 189–216.

———. *Off Center: Power and Culture Relations between Japan and the United States.* Cambridge, Mass.: Harvard University Press, 1991.

Mori, Maryellen T. "The Splendor of Self-Exaltation: The Life and Fiction of Okamoto Kanoko." *Monumenta Nipponica* 50 (1) (Spring 1995): 67–102.

Nolte, Sharon H., and Sally Ann Hastings. "The Meiji State's Policy toward Women." In Bernstein, *Recreating Japanese Women,* pp. 151–174.

Orbaugh, Sharalyn. "The Body in Contemporary Japanese Women's Fiction." In Schalow and Walker, *The Woman's Hand,* pp. 119–164.

Ozaki Shirō. "Japanese Women Novelists Today." *Contemporary Japan: A Review of East Asiatic Affairs* 10 (2) (February 1941): 214–220.

Rich, Adrienne. *On Lies, Secrets, and Silence: Selected Prose 1966–1978.* New York: W. W. Norton, 1979.

Robertson, Jennifer. "The Shingaku Woman." In Bernstein, *Recreating Japanese Women,* pp. 88–107.

Rodd, Laurel Rasplica. "Yosano Akiko and the Taishō Debate of the 'New Woman.' " In Bernstein, *Recreating Japanese Women,* pp. 175–198.

Saegusa, Kazuko. "The Narcissism of Female Representation and the Professional Writer." Trans. Nina Blake. *Review of Japanese Culture and Society* 4 (December 1991): 18–21.

Sakaki, Atsuko. "Sliding Door: Women in the Heterosocial Literary Field of Early Modern Japan." *U.S.-Japan Women's Journal, English Supplement* 17 (1999): 3–38.

Schalow, Paul Gordon, and Janet A. Walker, eds. The Woman's Hand: Gender and Theory in Japanese Women's Writing. Stanford, Calif.: Stanford University Press, 1996.

Takahashi Takako. *Lonely Woman.* Trans. Maryellen Toman Mori. New York: Columbia University Press, 2004.

Tamura, Toshiko. "A Woman Writer." In Y. Tanaka, *To Live and to Write,* pp. 11–18.

Tanaka, Yukiko. "Introduction." In Y. Tanaka and E. Hanson, *This Kind of Woman.*

————, ed. and trans. *To Live and to Write: Selections by Japanese Women Writers 1913–1938.* Seattle: Seal Press, 1987.

Tanaka, Yukiko, and Elizabeth Hanson, eds. *This Kind of Woman: Ten Stories by Japanese Women Writers, 1960–1976.* Stanford, Calif.: Stanford University Press, 1982.

Torrance, Richard. "Translator's Introduction." In Tokuda Shūsei, *Rough Living,* pp. 1–19. Honolulu: University of Hawai'i Press, 2001.

Uno Chiyo. "A Genius of Imitation" (Mohō no tensai). In Y. Tanaka, *To Live and to Write,* pp.189–196.

Uno, Kathleen. "The Death of 'Good Wife, Wise Mother'?" In *Postwar Japan as History,* ed. Andrew Gordon, pp. 293–324. Berkeley and Los Angeles: University of California Press, 1993.

Upham, Frank K. "Unplaced Persons and Movements for Place." In *Postwar Japan as History.* Ed. Andrew Gordon, pp. 325–346. Berkeley and Los Angeles: University of California Press, 1993.

Vernon, Victoria V. *Daughters of the Moon: Wish, Will, and Social Constraint in Fiction by Modern Japanese Women.* Berkeley: Institute of East Asian Studies, 1988. Japan Research Monograph 9.

Woolf, Virginia. "Professions for Women." In *Collected Essays of Virginia Woolf,* vol. 2. Ed. Leonard Woolf. London: Chatto and Windus, 1972.

Yoshida, Sanroku. "Setouchi Harumi." In *Japanese Women Writers: A Bio-Critical Sourcebook.* Ed. Chieko I. Mulhern, pp. 345–353. Westport, Conn.: Greenwood Press, 1994.

Japanese

(All publications in Tokyo unless indicated otherwise. Asterisk indicates work translated in this volume.)

*Akiyama Shun. "Joryū bungaku no tōwaku" (Confessions of a women's literature convert). *Kokubungaku kaishaku to kyōzai no kenkyū,* July 1976: 14–17.

Egusa Mitsuko and Urushida Kazuyo, eds. *Onna ga yomu nihon kindai bungaku* (Modern Japanese literature as read by women). Shin'yōsha, 1992.

Fukuzawa Yukichi. "On Japanese Women, Part 2." In *Fukuzawa Yukichi on Japanese Women: Selected Works.* Ed. and trans. Eiichi Kiyooka. University of Tokyo Press, 1988.

Gotō Chūgai. "Keishū shōsetsu wo yomu." *Waseda bungaku,* January 1896: 30–33.

Government of Japan, Ministry of Education. *Gakkō kihon chōsa hōkoku sho (Kōtō kyōiku kikan)* (Report on the basic survey of schools, vol. 2: Higher education). 1985.

*Hara Shirō. "Buntai ni okeru ratai to sōshoku" (Nakedness and decoration in women's writing). *Kokubungaku kaishaku to kyōzai no kenkyū,* July 1976: 98–104.

*Hasegawa Izumi. "Gendai joryū bungaku no yōsō" (Contemporary women's literature). *Kokubungaku kaishaku to kanshō,* September 1976: 6–14.

Hata Kōhei. "Tanizaki Jun'ichirō ron" (On Tanizaki Jun'ichirō). In Hata Kōhei, *Hana to kaze* (Flowers and wind). Chikuma shobō, 1972.

Itagaki Naoko. "Shōwa no joryū sakka" (Women writers of the Shōwa era). *Kokubungaku kaishaku to kanshō,* September 1962: 29–33.

Kawabata Yasunari. "Joryū sakka" (Women writers). *Tokyo nichi nichi shinbun,* August 1, 1934.

———. "Joryū sakka" (Women writers). In *Kawabata Yasunari zenshū,* vol. 31. Ed. Kawabata Hideko, pp. 230–242. Shinchōsha, 1982.

*Kobayashi Hideo. "Joryū sakka" (Women writers). In *Kindai bungaku shisō taikei, 29: Kobayashi Hideo shū* (Major collection of modern literary thought, vol. 29: The Kobayashi Hideo collection). Ed. Yoshimoto Takaaki, pp. 46–50. Chikuma shobō, 1977.

*———. "Joryū sakka" (Women writers). *Shinjoen,* January 1938: 140–143.

*Kunikida Doppo. "Joshi to hon'yaku no koto" (Women and translation). In *Kunikida Doppo zenshū* 1 (The collected works of Kunikida Doppo, vol. 1), pp. 364–366. Gakushū ken'yūsha, 1965.

*Matsuura Rieko. "Yasashii kyosei no tame ni" (For a gentle castration). In *Yasashii kyosei no tame ni* (For a gentle castration), pp. 212–262. Chikuma shobō, 1997.

*Mishima Yukio. "Narushishizumu ron" (On narcissism). In *Mishima Yukio zenshū* 32, pp. 375–389. Shinchōsha, 1973–1976.

*Miwata Masako. "Shisō to joshi" (Women and poetic thought). In *Kōtō saienbunshū* (Essays for higher school women). Comp. Fujinami Shimako, pp. 98–100. Bungaku dōshi kai, 1903.

*Mizuta Noriko. "Hon'yaku to jendā: Trans/gender/lation" (Translation and gender: Trans/gender/lation). *Gunzō* 46 (8) (August 1991): 216–223.

Nakamura Mitsuo. "Hayashi Fumiko ron" (On Hayashi Fumiko). In *Gendai sakka ron sōsho: Shōwa no sakkatachi,* 2 (On modern authors: The authors of the Shōwa, vol. 2). Ed. Nakajima Kenzō et al., pp. 94–112. Eiōsha, 1955.

*Nakayama Kazuko. "Joryū bungaku to sono ishiki henkaku no shudai" (The subject of women's literature and the transformation of its consciousness). *Kokubungaku kaishaku to kyōzai no kenkyū* 31 (5) (May 1986): 37–43.

———. *Nakayama Kazuko korekushon: Natsume Sōseki, josei, jendaa* (Nakayama Kazuko's collected works: Natsume Sōseki, women, and gender). Kanrin shobō, 2003.

Noma Hiroshi. "Nihon bungaku ni okeru iki no mondai" (The question of stylishness in Japanese literature). *Shisō,* September 1956.

Ogura Chikako. "Hanae no higeki" (The tragedy of Hanae). In *Danryū bungakuron* (On men's literature). Chikuma shobō, 1992.

*Oguri Fūyō et al. "Joryū sakkaron" (On women writers). *Shinchō,* May 1908: 6–11.

*Okuno Takeo. "Shōsetsu wa honshitsuteki ni josei no mono ka?" (Is fiction inherently the realm of women?) In *Joryū sakka ron* (On women writers), pp. 9–15. Daisan bunmeisha, 1974.

Saegusa Kazuko. *Sayonara otoko no jidai* (Farewell to the age of men). Jinbun shoin, 1984.

Saitō Minako. "Kaisetsu: Idobata kaigi no suriru to kōyō" (Commentary: The thrill and benefit of the well-curb chat). In *Danryū bungakuron* (On men's literature), pp. 447–448. Chikuma shobō, 1997.

———. *Kōitten ron: Anime, tokusatsu, denki no hiroinzō* (On the single red drop: The image of the heroine in anime, montages, and biographies). Village Center shuppankyoku, 1998.

*———. "Yoshimoto Banana shōjo karuchā no suimyaku" (Yoshimoto Banana and girl culture). In *Bundan aidoru ron* (Idols of literary journalism), pp. 60–90. Iwanami shoten, 2002.

Seki Reiko. *Ane no chikara: Higuchi Ichiyō* (Higuchi Ichiyō: The strength of an elder sister). Chikuma shobō, Chikuma raiburari, 1993.

———. *Higuchi Ichiyō wo yomu* (Reading Ichiyō). Iwanami shoten, 1992.

*Setouchi Harumi. "Joryū sakka ni naru jōken" (Requirements for becoming a woman writer). In *Shukke suru mae no watashi kaku koto* (What I wrote before I took Buddhist vows), pp. 20–26. Kawade bunko, 1990.

*Shibusawa Tatsuhiko. "Okamoto Kanoko aruiwa onna no narushishizumu" (Women, narcissism, and Okamoto Kanoko). In *Hen'aiteki sakkaron* (On the writers I'm partial to), pp. 310–321. Kawade shobō shinsha, 1997.

Takahara Eiri. *Shōjo ryōiki* (The territory of the girl). Kokusho kankōkai, 1999.

*———. "Shōjogata ishiki: Jiyū to kōman" (The consciousness of the girl: freedom and arrogance). In Takahara, *Shōjo ryōiki*, pp. 6–20.

Takahashi Takako. "Furui Yoshikichi-san no hisseki" (On Furui Yoshikichi's handwriting). In *Shin-ei sakka sōsho: Furui Yoshikichi—shū geppō* (Promising new authors' series: Furui Yoshikichi collection—monthly report). Kawade shobō shinsha, 1971. Reprint in Takahashi Takako, *Tamashii no inu* (Soul dogs), pp. 137–139. Kōdansha 1975.

*Takahashi Takako and Tsushima Yūko. "Onna no sei to otoko no me" (Female sexuality and the male gaze). *Waseda bungaku* 30 (11) (November 1978): 4–14.

*Tanaka Miyoko. "Hyōgen ni miru narushishizumu to shinishizumu" (Narcissism, cynicism, and the writing of women). *Kokubungaku kaishaku to kyōzai no kenkyū,* July 1976: 88–92.

Tazawa Inafune. "Godaidō" (The Temple Godai). In *Meiji joryū bungakushū* (Collection of Meiji women's literature), pt. 1. *Meiji bungaku zenshū* 81 (Collection of Meiji literature, vol. 81). Chikuma Shobō, 1966.

Tomioka Taeko. *Fuji no koromo ni asa no fusuma* (Wisteria clothing and linen quilts). Chūō kōron sha, 1984.

*———. " 'Onna no kotoba' to 'kuni no kotoba' " (Women's language and the national language). In *Tomioka Taeko shū* 8 (The collected works of Tomioka Taeko, vol. 8), pp. 85–97. Chikuma shobō, 1999.

Tsuge Teruhiko. *"Danryū bungakuron"* (On men's literature [a review]). *Shūkan dokushojin,* April 13, 1992: 5.

Ueno Chizuko. *Hatsujō sōchi* (The erotic apparatus). Chikuma shobō, 1998.

———. "Ishi wo nageru" (Throwing stones). In *Danryū bungakuron* (On men's literature). Chikuma shobō, 1992.

———. *Onna wa sekai wo sukueru ka?* (Can women save the world?) Keisō shobō, 1986.

*Ueno Chizuko, Ogura Chikako, and Tomioka Taeko. "Tanizaki Jun'ichirō: *Quicksand* and *Naomi*." In *Danryū bungakuron* (On men's literature), pp. 136–185. Chikuma shobō, 1992.

*Yosano Akiko. "'Onna rashisa' to wa nani ka" (What is 'Womanliness'?) In *Yosano Akiko hyōron*. Ed. Kano Masanao and Kōuchi Nobuko, pp. 334–345. Iwanami, 1985.

Yoshiya Nobuko, ed. *Joryū sakka jikkasen* (Ten masterworks by women writers). Tokyo: Kōa Nipponsha, 1940. Reprinted in Hasegawa Kei. *"Senjika" no josei bungaku* (Women writing "under" war), vol. 4. Yumani shobō, 2002.

RECOMMENDED FURTHER READING

English

The list below is intended to suggest the diversity of recent research in English related to writing by women in Japan.

BIBLIOGRAPHIES

Ericson, Joan E., and Midori McKeon. "Selected Bibliography of Japanese Women's Writing." In Schalow and Walker, *The Woman's Hand*, pp. 461–493. (See bibliography above.)

Mamola, Claire Zebroski. *Japanese Women's Writings in English Translation: An Annotated Bibliography*. 2 vols. New York: Garland, 1989, 1992.

Alvis, Andra. "Fantasies of Maternal Ambivalence in Takahashi Takako's 'Congruent Figures.'" In Kuribayashi and Terasawa, *The Outsider Within*, pp. 131–152.

Aoyama, Tomoko. "Food and Gender in Contemporary Japanese Women's Literature." *U.S.-Japan Women's Journal, English Supplement* 17 (1999): 111–136.

———. "Literary Daughters' Recipes: Food and Female Subjectivity in the Writings of Mori Mari and Kōda Aya." *Deutsches Institut für Japanstudien Yearbook Japanstudien* 12 (2000): 91–116.

———. "Male Homosexuality as Treated by Japanese Women Writers." In *The Japanese Trajectory: Modernization and Beyond*. Ed. Gavan McCormack and Yoshio Sugimoto, pp. 186–204. Cambridge: Cambridge University Press, 1988.

———. "A Room as Sweet as Honey: Father-Daughter Love in Mori Mari." In Copeland and Ramirez-Christensen, *The Father-Daughter Plot*, pp. 167–193.

Ariga Chieko. "Destabilization of Gender in New Age Japanese Women's Literature: Yoshimoto Banana and Arai Motoko." In Kuribayashi and Terasawa, *The Outsider Within*, pp. 191–206.

———. "Politicizing Gender: Amino Kiku and the Literary Canon in Japanese Literature." In *Japanese Women: New Feminist Perspectives on Past, Present, and Future*. Ed. Kumiko Fujimura-Fanselow and Atsuko Kameda, pp. 43–60. New York: Feminist Press, 1995.

———. "Who's Afraid of Amino Kiku? Gender Conflict and the Literary Canon in Japanese Literature." *International Journal of Social Education* 6 (1) (Spring 1991): 95–113.

Bardsley, Jan. *The Bluestockings of Japan: New Women Fiction and Essays from Seitō, 1911–1916*. Ann Arbor, Mich.: Center for Japanese Studies, 2006.

———. "Seitō and the Resurgence of Writing by Women." In Mostow et al., *The Columbia Companion to Modern East Asian Literature*, pp. 93–98.

Beichman, Janine. "Akiko Goes to Paris: The European Poems." *Journal of the Association of Teachers of Japanese* 25 (1) (April 1991): 123–145. Special issue: "Yosano Akiko (1878–1942)." Ed. Laurel Rasplica Rodd.

———. "Yosano Akiko." In *Reference Guide to World Literature*, 3rd ed. Ed. Sara Pendergast and Tom Pendergast. Vol. 1: *Authors*, pp. 1107–1110. Detroit: St. James Press, 2003.

———. "Yosano Akiko in Heaven and Earth." In *Currents in Japanese Culture: Translations and Transformations.* Ed. Amy Vladeck Heinrich, pp. 135–154. New York: Columbia University Press, 1997.

Bhowmik, Davinder L. "Kōno Taeko." In Rubin, *Modern Japanese Writers*, pp. 169–184.

Bolles, Marilyn. "Enchi Fumiko." In Mostow et al., *The Columbia Companion to Modern East Asian Literature*, pp. 212–215.

Brown, Janice. "De-siring the Center: Hayashi Fumiko's Hungry Heroines and the Male Literary Canon." In Copeland and Ramirez-Christensen, *The Father-Daughter Plot*, pp. 143–166.

———. "Hayashi Fumiko: Voice from the Margin." *Japan Quarterly* 43 (1) (1996): 85–99.

———. *I Saw a Pale Horse and Selections from Diary of a Vagabond.* Ithaca, N.Y.: Cornell University, Cornell East Asia Series 86, 1997.

———. "Ōba Minako." In Mostow et al., *The Columbia Companion to Modern East Asian Literature*, pp. 230–232.

———. "Ōba Minako: Telling the Untellable." *Japan Quarterly* 45 (3) (July–September 1998): 50–59.

———. "Reconstructing the Female Subject: Japanese Women Writers and the 'Shishōsetsu.'" *B.C. Asian Review* 7 (Winter 1993–1994): 16–35.

Brown, Janice, Sonja Arntzen, and Brad Ambury, eds. *Across Time and Genre: Reading and Writing Japanese Women's Texts; Conference Proceedings.* University of Alberta, 2002.

Bullock, Julia C. "Barely There: Language and Narrative Strategy in Takahashi Takako's 'Kirameki.'" *U.S.-Japan Women's Journal, English Supplement* 26 (2004): 3–17.

Burns, Robert Alan. "The Novels of Ariyoshi Sawako." In McGreal, *Great Literature of the Eastern World*, pp. 401–408.

Carpenter, Juliet Winters. "Enchi Fumiko: 'A Writer of Tales.'" *Japan Quarterly* 37 (3) (July–September 1990): 343–355.

Cavanaugh, Carole. "Wavering Traces/Hasegawa Shigure." In *Modern Drama by Women, 1880s–1930s: An International Anthology.* Ed. Katherine E. Kelly, pp. 254–268. London and New York: Routledge, 1996.

Chambers, Marian E. "Ōba Minako: Rebirth in Alaska." *Japan Quarterly* 38 (4) (October–December 1991): 474–483.

Copeland, Rebecca L. "The Meiji Woman Writer 'Amidst a Forest of Beards.'" *Harvard Journal of Asiatic Studies* 57 (2) (1997): 383–418.

———. "Motherhood as Institution." *Japan Quarterly* 39 (1) (January–March 1992): 101–110.

———. *The Sound of the Wind: The Life and Works of Uno Chiyo.* Honolulu: University of Hawai'i Press, 1992.

———. "Woman Uncovered: Pornography and Power in the Detective Fiction of Kirino Natsuo." *Japan Forum* 16 (2) (2004): 249–269.

Copeland, Rebecca L., and Esperanza Ramirez-Christensen, eds. *The Father-Daughter Plot: Japanese Literary Women and the Law of the Father.* Honolulu: University of Hawai'i Press, 2001.

Cornyetz, Nina. "Bound by Blood: Female Pollution, Divinity, and Community in Enchi Fumiko's *Masks.*" *U.S.-Japan Women's Journal, English Supplement* 9 (1995): 29–58.

———. "The Fictional Works of Enchi Fumiko." In McGreal, *Great Literature of the Eastern World,* pp. 392–396.

———. "Power and Gender in the Narratives of Yamada Eimi." In Schalow and Walker, *The Woman's Hand,* pp. 425–457. (See bibliography above.)

Danly, Robert Lyons. *In the Shade of Spring Leaves: The Life and Writings of Higuchi Ichiyō, a Woman of Letters in Meiji Japan.* New Haven, Conn.: Yale University Press, 1981.

Dollase, Hiromi Tsuchiya. "Reading Yoshiya Nobuko's 'Yaneura no Nishōjo': In Search of Literary Possibilities in Shōjo Narratives." *U.S.-Japan Women's Journal, English Supplement* 20–21 (2001): 151–178.

Enomoto, Yoshiko. "The Reality of Pregnancy and Motherhood for Women: Tsushima Yūko's *Chōji* and Margaret Drabble's *The Millstone.*" *Comparative Literature Studies* 35 (2) (1998): 116–124.

Ericson, Joan. "Hayashi Fumiko." In Mostow et al., *The Columbia Companion to Modern East Asian Literature,* pp. 158–163.

Fairbanks, Carol. *Japanese Women Fiction Writers: Their Culture and Society, 1890's to 1990's.* Lanham, Md.: Scarecrow Press, 2002.

Fessler, Susanna. *Wandering Heart: The Work and Method of Hayashi Fumiko.* Albany: State University of New York Press, 1998.

Field, Norma. "Somehow: The Postmodern as Atmosphere." In *Postmodernism and Japan.* Ed. Masao Miyoshi and H. D. Harootunian, pp. 169–188. Durham, N.C.: Duke University Press, 1991.

Frederick, Sarah. "Women of the Setting Sun and Men from the Moon: Yoshiya Nobuko's Ataka Family as Postwar Romance." *U.S.-Japan Women's Journal, English Supplement* 23 (2003): 10–38.

Gardner, William O. "Mongrel Modernism: Hayashi Fumiko's *Hōrōki* and Mass Culture." *Journal of Japanese Studies* 29 (1) (Winter 2003): 69–101.

Gessel, Van C., ed. *Dictionary of Literary Biography,* vol. 182: *Japanese Fiction Writers since World War II.* Detroit: Gale Research, 1997. A Bruccoli Clark Layman Book.

———. "The 'Medium' of Fiction: Fumiko Enchi as Narrator." *World Literature Today* 62 (3) (Summer 1988): 380–385. Special issue: "Contemporary Japanese Literature."

Gossmann, Hilaria. "The Emancipation of Women as Shown in the Novels of Sata Ineko." In Nish, *Contemporary European Writing on Japan,* pp. 231–235.

———. "The Quest for Emancipation: The Autobiographical Novels of Miyamoto Yuriko and Sata Ineko." *Japan Quarterly* 42 (3) (July–September 1995): 332–342.

Hartley, Barbara. "The Mother, the Daughter, and the Sexed Body in Enchi Fumiko's 'Fuyu momiji.'" In Sekine, *Love and Sexuality in Japanese Literature,* pp. 250–262.

———. "Writing the Body of the Mother: Narrative Moments in Tsushima Yūko, Ariyoshi Sawako, and Enchi Fumiko." *Japanese Studies* 23 (3) (2003): 293–305.

Heinrich, Amy. "Double Weave: The Fabric of Japanese Women's Literature." *World Literature Today* 62 (3) (Summer 1988): 408–414. Special issue: "Contemporary Japanese Literature."

Hirota, Aki. "Image-Makers and Victims: The Croissant Syndrome and Yellow Cabs." *U.S.-Japan Women's Journal, English Supplement* 19 (2000): 83–121.

———. "Kirishima Yōko and the Age of Non-Marriage." *Women's Studies* 33 (4) (June 2004): 399–421.

Hogan, Eleanor Joan. "When Art Does Not Represent Life: Nogami Yaeko and the Marriage Question." *Women's Studies* 33 (4) (June 2004): 381–398.

———. "Beyond Influence: The Literary Sisterhood of Nogami Yaeko and Jane Austen." *U.S.-Japan Women's Journal, English Supplement* 28, forthcoming.

Hulvey, S. Yumiko. "Enchi Fumiko's Portal to Desire." *Japan Studies Review* 2 (1998): 37–55.

———. "The Intertextual Fabric of Narratives by Enchi Fumiko." In *Japan in Traditional and Postmodern Perspectives.* Ed. Charles Wei-hsun Fu and Steven Heine, pp. 169–224. Albany: State University of New York Press, 1995.

Jones, Gretchen. "The 1960s and 1970s Boom in Women's Writing." In Mostow et al., *The Columbia Companion to Modern East Asian Literature,* pp. 221–229.

———. "Subversive Strategies: Masochism, Gender and Power in Kōno Taeko's 'Toddler-Hunting.'" *East Asia: An International Quarterly* 18 (4) (Winter 2000): 79–107.

Kaneko, Masayo. "Setouchi Jakuchō: Female Subjectivity in the Exploration of 'Self,' Sexuality, and Spirituality." In Kuribayashi and Terasawa, *The Outsider Within,* pp. 63–88.

Keene, Donald. "The Revival of Writing by Women." In *Dawn to the West,* vol. 1: *Fiction,* pp. 1113–1166. New York: Holt, Rinehart and Winston, 1984.

Kimura-Steven, Chigusa. "Reclaiming the Critical Voice in Enchi Fumiko's *The Waiting Years.*" In Kuribayashi and Terasawa, *The Outsider Within,* pp. 39–62.

Kleeman, Faye Yuan. "A House of Their Own: Constructing the Gynocentric Family in Modern Japan." *Japan Studies Review* 2 (1998): 1–15.

——. "Sexual Politics and Sexual Poetics in Kurahashi Yumiko's *Cruel Fairy Tales for Adults.*" In *Constructions and Confrontations: Changing Representations of Women and Feminisms East and West.* Ed. Cristina Bacchilega and Cornelia N. Moore. *Literary Studies East and West* 12 (1996): 150–158.

Knighton, Mary A. "Kanai Mieko." In Mostow et al., *The Columbia Companion to Modern East Asian Literature,* pp. 242–245.

——. "Tracing the Body of the Question Mark: Kanai Mieko's Ai Aru Kagiri." In Sekine, pp. 286–299. *Love and Sexuality in Japanese Literature.*

Kobayashi, Fukuko. "Killing Motherhood as Institution and Reclaiming Motherhood as Experience: Japanese Women Writers, 1970s–90s." In *Transnational Asia Pacific: Gender, Culture, and the Public Sphere.* Ed. Shirley Geok-lin Lim, Larry E. Smith, and Wimal Dissanayake, with the assistance of Laura Scott Holliday, pp. 145–158. Urbana: University of Illinois Press, 1999.

Komashaku, Kimi. "Murasaki's Message: A Reinterpretation of *The Tale of Genji.*" Trans. Tomiko Yoda. *U.S.-Japan Women's Journal, English Supplement* 5 (July 1993): 28–51.

Kuribayashi, Tomoko. "Flower Power: Nature, Art, and Woman in Okamoto Kanoko's 'A Floral Pageant.'" In Kuribayashi and Terasawa, *The Outsider Within,* pp. 19–36.

Kuribayashi, Tomoko, and Mizuho Terasawa, eds. *The Outsider Within: Ten Essays on Modern Japanese Women Writers.* Lanham, Md.: University Press of America, 2002.

Langton, Nina. "On the Edge: Mother and Child in the Works of Kōno Taeko." In Tsuruta, *Mothers in Japanese Literature,* pp. 291–317.

Larson, Phyllis Hyland. "Re-reading Tamura Toshiko: A Failed New Woman?" In *Revisionism in Japanese Literary Studies: Proceedings of the Midwest Association for Japanese Literary Studies* 2. Ed. Eiji Sekine, pp. 253–267. West Lafayette, Ind.: Midwest Association for Japanese Literary Studies, 1996.

——. "Yosano Akiko and the Re-Creation of the Female Self: An Autogynography." *Journal of the Association of Teachers of Japanese* 25 (1) (April 1991): 11–26. Special issue: "Yosano Akiko (1878–1942)." Ed. Laurel Rasplica Rodd.

Lewell, John. *Modern Japanese Novelists: A Biographical Dictionary.* [Entries on Ariyoshi Sawako, Enchi Fumiko, Hayashi Fumiko, Higuchi Ichiyō, Hirabayashi Taiko, Miyamoto Yuriko, Nogami Yaeko, Ōba Minako, Tsushima Yūko, and Uno Chiyo.] New York, Tokyo, and London: Kodansha International, 1993.

Lippit, Noriko Mizuta. *Reality and Fiction in Modern Japanese Literature.* White Plains, N.Y.: M. E. Sharpe, 1980.

Loftus, Ronald. *Telling Lives: Women's Self-Writing in Modern Japan.* Honolulu: University of Hawai'i Press, 2004.

McClain, Yoko. "Ariyoshi Sawako: Creative Social Critic." *Journal of the Association of Teachers of Japanese* 12 (2 and 3) (May and September 1977): 211–228.

———. "Eroticism and the Writings of Enchi Fumiko." *Journal of the Association of Teachers of Japanese* 15 (1) (April 1980): 32–46.

McGreal, Ian P., ed. *Great Literature of the Eastern World: The Major Works of Prose, Poetry and Drama from China, India, Japan, Korea and the Middle East.* New York: HarperCollins, 1996.

McKeon, Midori. "Ogino Anna's Gargantuan Play in *Tales of Peaches.*" In Copeland and Ramirez-Christensen, *The Father-Daughter Plot*, pp. 327–367.

Mikals-Adachi, Eileen. "Enchi Fumiko: Female Sexuality and the Absent Father." In Copeland and Ramirez-Christensen, *The Father-Daughter Plot*, pp. 194–214.

———. "Nonami Asa's Family Mysteries and the Novel as Social Commentary." *Japan Forum* 16 (2) (2004): 231–248.

Mitsutani, Margaret. "Higuchi Ichiyō: A Literature of Her Own." *Comparative Literature Studies* 22 (1) (Spring 1985): 53–66.

———. "Renaissance in Women's Literature." *Japan Quarterly* 33 (3) (1986): 313–319.

Miyoshi Masao. "Women's Short Stories in Japan." *Mānoa: A Pacific Journal of International Writing* 3 (2) (Fall 1991): 33–39.

Mizuta, Noriko. "In Search of a Lost Paradise: The Wandering Woman in Hayashi Fumiko's Drifting Clouds." In Schalow and Walker, *The Woman's Hand*, pp. 329–351. (See bibliography above.)

———. "Madonna as Self-Begetting Mountain Witch: Ohba Minako's Mythmaking." In *The Force of Vision: Proceedings of the XIIIth Congress of the International Comparative Literature Association* 6. Ed. Koji Kawamoto, Heh-Hsiang Yuan, and Yoshihiro Ohsawa, pp. 441–447. Tokyo: University of Tokyo Press, 1995.

———. "Symbiosis and Renewal: Transformation of the Forest World of Ōba Minako." Trans. Julianne Komori Dvorak, *Review of Japanese Culture and Society* 5 (1993): 59–66.

———. " 'Unconventional Women': From the Body as the Site of Domination to the Body as the Site of Expression." *U.S.-Japan Women's Journal, English Supplement* 20–21 (2001): 3–16.

Monnet, Livia. " 'Child of Wrath': The Literature of Takahashi Takako." *Transactions of the Asiatic Society of Japan*, 4th series, 5 (1990): 87–122.

———. "Connaissance délicieuse, or the Science of Jealousy: Tsushima Yūko's 'The Chrysanthemum Beetle.' " In Schalow and Walker, *The Woman's Hand*, pp. 382–424.

———. "In the Beginning Woman Was the Sun: Autobiographies of Modern Japanese Women Writers." *Japan Forum* 1 (1–2) (1989): 55–57, 197–223.

———. "Montage, Cinematic Subjectivity and Feminism in Ozaki Midori's Drifting in the World of the Seventh Sense." *Japan Forum* 11 (1) (1999): 57–82.

———. "Not Only Minamata: An Approach to Ishimure Michiko's Work." In Nish, *Contemporary European Writing on Japan*, pp. 225–231.

———. "The Politics of Miscegenation: The Discourse of Fantasy in 'Fusehime' by Tsushima Yūko." *Japan Forum* 5 (1) (April 1993): 53–74.

Mori, Maryellen T. "Cross-Cultural Patterns in the Quest Fiction of Okamoto Kanoko." *The Comparatist* 20 (1996): 153–178.

———. "Introduction." In Takahashi Takako, *Lonely Woman*, pp. ix–xl. New York: Columbia University Press, 2004.

———. "The Liminal Male as Liberatory Figure in Japanese Women's Fiction." *Harvard Journal of Asiatic Studies* 60 (2) (December 2000): 537–594.

———. "The Quest for *Jouissance* in Takahashi Takako's Texts." In Schalow and Walker, *The Woman's Hand*, pp. 205–235.

———. "The Rhetoric of Reversal in Three Texts of Bliss by Takahashi Takako." *Journal of the Association for the Interdisciplinary Study of the Arts* 7 (1–2) (Autumn 2001–Spring 2002): 143–170.

———. "The Subversive Role of Fantasy in the Fiction of Takahashi Takako." *Journal of the Association of Teachers of Japanese* 28 (1) (April 1994): 29–56.

Morton, Leith. "The Canonization of Yosano Akiko's *Midaregami*." *Japanese Studies* 20 (3) (December 2000): 237–254.

———. "Feminist Strategies in Contemporary Japanese Women's Poetry." *Journal of the Association of Teachers of Japanese* 31 (2) (October 1997): 73–108.

Mostow, Joshua S., et al., eds. *The Columbia Companion to Modern East Asian Literature*. New York: Columbia University Press, 2003.

Mulhern, Chieko I., ed. *Heroic with Grace: Legendary Women of Japan*. New York: M. E. Sharpe, 1991.

———. "Japanese Harlequin Romances as Transcultural Woman's Fiction." *Journal of Asian Studies* 48 (1) (February 1989): 50–70.

———. *Japanese Women Writers: A Bio-Critical Sourcebook*. Westport, Conn.: Greenwood Press, 1994.

Nakagawa, Shigemi. "What's Happening to Sexuality: Corporeal Sensations in Matsuura Rieko's *Oyayubi P no shugyō jidai*." In Sekine, *Love and Sexuality in Japanese Literature*, pp. 339–352.

Napier, Susan. "The Woman Lost: The Dead, Damaged, or Absent Female in Postwar Fantasy." In Susan Napier, *Fantastic in Modern Japanese Literature: The Subversion of Modernity*, pp. 53–92. London and New York: Routledge, 1996.

Nish, Ian, ed. *Contemporary European Writing on Japan: Scholarly Views from Eastern and Western Europe*. Woodchurch, Ashford, Kent: Paul Norbury, 1988.

North, Lucy. "Enchi Fumiko." In Rubin, *Modern Japanese Writers*, pp. 89–105.

Ōba, Minako. "Special Address: Without Beginning, Without End." In Schalow and Walker, *The Woman's Hand*, pp. 19–40. (See bibliography above.)

Orbaugh, Sharalyn. "Arguing with the Real Kanai Mieko." In Snyder and Gabriel, *Ōe and Beyond*, pp. 245–277.

————. "Ōba Minako and the Paternity of Maternalism." In Copeland and Ramirez-Christensen, *The Father-Daughter Plot,* pp. 265–291.

Pounds, Wayne. "Enchi Fumiko and the Hidden Energy of the Supernatural." *Journal of the Association of Teachers of Japanese* 24 (2) (November 1990): 167–183.

Rodd, Laurel Rasplica. "The Prose and Poetry of Yosano Akiko." In McGreal, *Great Literature of the Eastern World,* pp. 356–359.

————. "Yosano Akiko and the Bunkagakuin: 'Educating Free Individuals.'" *Journal of the Association of Teachers of Japanese* 25 (1) (April 1991): 75–89. Special issue: "Yosano Akiko (1878–1942)." Ed. Laurel Rasplica Rodd.

————. "Yosano Akiko and Nationalism." In *Modern Japan: An Encyclopedia of History, Culture, and Nationalism.* Ed. James L. Huffman, pp. 296–297. New York: Garland Publications, 1998.

————. "Yosano Akiko on Poetic Inspiration." In *The Distant Isle: Studies and Translations of Japanese Literature in Honor of Robert H. Brower.* Ed. Thomas Hare, Robert Borgen, and Sharalyn Orbaugh, pp. 409–425. Ann Arbor, Mich.: Center for Japanese Studies, 1996.

————. "Yosano Akiko's 'On Poetry'" in *New Leaves: Studies and Translations of Japanese Literature in Honor of Edward Seidensticker.* Ed. Aileen Gatten and Anthony Hood Chambers, pp. 235–246. Ann Arbor, Mich.: Center for Japanese Studies, 1993.

Rowley, G. G. *Yosano Akiko and the Tale of Genji.* Ann Arbor, Mich.: Center for Japanese Studies, 2000.

Rubin, Jay, ed. *Modern Japanese Writers.* New York: Charles Scribner's Sons, 2001.

Ruch, Barbara. "Beyond Absolution: Enchi Fumiko's *The Waiting Years* and *Masks.*" In *Masterworks of Asian Literature in Comparative Perspective: A Guide for Teaching.* Ed. Barbara Stoler Miller, pp. 439–456. Armonk, N.Y.: M. E. Sharpe, 1994.

Ryu, Catherine. "A Golden Needle, a Rabbit's Tail, and the Density of Female Body Fat: An Analysis of Murō Saisei's Metaphors for Enchi Fumiko's Writing Libido." In Sekine, *Love and Sexuality in Japanese Literature,* pp. 264–273.

Sakaki, Atsuko. "Kurahashi Yumiko." In Rubin, *Modern Japanese Writers,* pp. 185–197.

————. "Kurahashi Yumiko's Negotiations with the Fathers." In Copeland and Rameriz-Christensen, *The Father-Daughter Plot,* pp. 292–326.

————. "(Re) Canonizing Kurahashi Yumiko: Toward Alternative Perspectives for 'Modern' 'Japanese' Literature." In Snyder and Gabriel, *Ōe and Beyond,* pp. 153–176.

————. "Re-Configuring the Dyad: Mother-Daughter Relationships in Kurahashi Yumiko's Fiction." In Tsuruta, *Mothers in Japanese Literature,* pp. 397–443.

————. "With Traces: The Iterability of Memory and Narration in Kanai Mieko's 'Yawarakai tsuchi o funde.'" In *Japanese Poeticity and Narrativity Revisited:*

Proceedings of the Association for Japanese Literary Studies 4. Ed. Eiji Sekine, pp. 296–310. West Lafayette, Ind.: Association for Japanese Literary Studies, Purdue University, 2003.

Sakamoto, Kiyo. "The Ordinary and the Marginal: The Significance of Mother in Tomioka Taeko's Works." In Kuribayashi and Terasawa, *The Outsider Within*, pp. 113–130.

Schierbeck, Sachiko Shibata. *Japanese Women Novelists in the 20th Century: 104 Biographies, 1900–1993*. Copenhagen: University of Copenhagen, 1994.

Seaman, Amanda C. *Bodies of Evidence: Women, Society, and Detective Fiction in 1990s Japan*. Honolulu: University of Hawai'i Press. 2004.

———. "Introduction: Cherchez la Femme: Detective Fiction, Women, and Japan." *Japan Forum* 16 (2) (2004): 185–190.

———. "There Goes the Neighbourhood: Community and Family in Miyabe Miyuki's *Riyu*." *Japan Forum* 16 (2) (2004): 271–287.

Sekine, Eiji, ed. *Love and Sexuality in Japanese Literature: Proceedings of the Midwest Association for Japanese Literary Studies* 5. West Lafayette, Ind.: Midwest Association for Japanese Literary Studies, Purdue University, 1999.

———. "Writing the Limits of Sexuality: Tomioka Taeko's 'Straw Dogs' and Nakagami Kenji's 'The Immortal.'" In *Acts of Writing: Proceedings of the Association for Japanese Literary Studies* 2. Ed. Rebecca Copeland, Elizabeth Oyler, and Marvin Marcus, pp. 338–352. West Lafayette, Ind.: Association for Japanese Literary Studies, Purdue University, 2001.

Sherif, Ann. "Ichiyō (Higuchi Ichiyō)." In Rubin, *Modern Japanese Writers*, pp. 121–133.

———. "Japanese Without Apology: Yoshimoto Banana and Healing." In Snyder and Gabriel, *Ōe and Beyond*, pp. 278–301.

———. *Mirror: The Fiction and Essays of Kōda Aya*. Honolulu: University of Hawai'i Press, 1999.

———. "Yoshimoto Banana." In Mostow et al., *The Columbia Companion to Modern East Asian Literature*, pp. 256–258.

Snyder, Stephen, and Philip Gabriel, eds. *Ōe and Beyond: Fiction in Contemporary Japan*. Honolulu: University of Hawai'i Press, 1999.

Sokolsky, Anne. "Miyamoto Yuriko and Socialist Writers." In Mostow et al., *The Columbia Companion to Modern East Asian Literature*, pp. 164–169.

Storey, Donna. "Yamamoto Michiko's *Betei-San no Niwa*: Anxiety Displaced." In Kuribayashi and Terasawa, *The Outsider Within*, pp. 153–172.

Sugisaki, Kazuko. "A Writer's Life: A Biographical Sketch." In *The House Spirit and Other Stories*, pp. 7–30. Santa Barbara, Calif.: Capra Press, 1995.

Tahara, Mildred. "Ariyoshi Sawako: The Novelist." In Mulhern, *Heroic With Grace, Women of Japan*, pp. 297–322.

Tanaka, Yukiko. *Women Writers of Meiji and Taisho Japan: Their Lives, Works and Critical Reception, 1868–1926*. Jefferson, N.C.: McFarland, 2000.

Tansman, Alan M. *The Writings of Kōda Aya: A Japanese Literary Daughter.* New Haven, Conn.: Yale University Press, 1993.

Tatsumi, Takayuki. "Matsuura Rieko's Oyayubi P no shugyō jidai (The Apprenticeship of Big Toe P)." Trans. James Koetting. *Japanese Literature Today* 20 (1995): 68–73.

Terasawa, Mizuho. "Sharing Sex, Sharing Meals: A Discussion of Hayashi Mariko's Works." In Kuribayashi and Terasawa, *The Outsider Within*, pp. 175–190.

Tsuruta, Kin'ya, ed. *Mothers in Japanese Literature.* Vancouver: University of British Columbia Press, 1997.

Tsushima, Michiko. "In Search of Lost Language: Kōra Rumiko and the Aphasic Experience." *Nichibunken Japan Review: Journal of the International Research Center for Japanese Studies* 15 (2003): 153–173.

Treat, John Whittier. "Yoshimoto Banana's *Kitchen*, or the Cultural Logic of Japanese Consumerism." In *Women, Media and Consumption in Japan.* Ed. Lise Skov and Brian Moeran, pp. 274–298. Honolulu: University of Hawai'i Press, 1995.

———. "Yoshimoto Banana Writes Home: *Shōjo* Culture and the Nostalgic Subject." *Journal of Japanese Studies* 19 (2) (Summer 1993): 353–387.

Ueno, Chizuko. "In the Feminine Guise: A Trap of Reverse Orientalism." *U.S.-Japan Women's Journal, English Supplement* 13 (1997): 3–25.

———. "Vernacularism and the Construction of Gender in Modern Japanese Language." In *Ga/Zoku Dynamics in Japanese Literature: Proceedings of the Midwest Association for Japanese Literary Studies* 3. Ed. Eiji Sekine, pp. 2–37. West Lafayette, Ind.: Midwest Association for Japanese Literary Studies, 1997.

Viswanathan, Meera. "In Pursuit of the Yamamba: The Question of Female Resistance." In Schalow and Walker, *The Woman's Hand*, pp. 239–261. (See bibliography above.)

Williams, Mark. "Double Vision: Divided Narrative Focus in Takahashi Takako's Yosōi seyo, waga tamashii yo." In Snyder and Gabriel, *Ōe and Beyond*, pp. 104–129.

Wilson, Michiko. "Becoming or (Un)Becoming: The Female Destiny Reconsidered in Ōba Minako's Narratives." In Schalow and Walker, *The Woman's Hand*, pp. 293–326. (See bibliography above.)

———. "Misreading and Un-Reading the Male Text, Finding the Female Text: Miyamoto Yuriko's Autobiographical Fiction." *U.S.-Japan Women's Journal, English Supplement* 13 (1997): 26–55.

Yonogi, Reiko. "Desire for Autonomy and Connection: Tamura Toshiko's Female Characters." In Kuribayashi and Terasawa, *The Outsider Within*, pp. 3–18.

Zimmerman, Eve. "'Curling Up Tight': Tsushima Yūko finds the Shōjo." In Sekine, *Love and Sexuality in Japanese Literature*, pp. 300–309.

———. "Not a Geisha: Visions of Girlhood in Contemporary Japanese Women's Fiction." *Harvard Asia Pacific Review* 4 (1) (Winter 2000): 78–80.

Japanese

(All publications in Tokyo unless indicated otherwise.)

Egusa Mitsuko. *Ohba Minako no sekai: Arasuka, Hiroshima, Niigata* (Ohba Minako's world: Alaska, Hiroshima, Niigata). Shin'yōsha, 2001.

Egusa Mitsuko, Seki Reiko, Kanai Keiko, et al. *Danshi sakka wo yomu: Feminizumu hihyō no seijuku e* (Women reading male Japanese writers). Shin'yōsha, 1994.

Imai Yasuko, Yabu Teiko, and Watanabe Sumiko, eds. *Tanpen josei bungaku gendai* (Contemporary women's short stories). Ōfūsha, 1993.

———. *Tanpen josei bungaku kindai* (Modern women's short stories). Ōfūsha, 1987.

Iwabuchi Hiroko, Kitada Sachie, and Kōra Rumiko, eds. *Feminizumu hihyō e no shōtai: Kindai josei bungaku wo yomu* (An invitation to feminist criticism: Reading modern women's literature). Gakugei shorin, 1995.

Kumakura Takaaki and Chino Kaori, eds. *Onna? Nihon? Bi?* (Woman? Japan? Beauty?). Keiō gijuku aigaku shuppankai, 1999.

Matsuura Rieko and Shōno Yoriko. *Okaruto dokumi teishoku.* (A poison-taster's magic menu). Kawade shobō shinsha, 1994.

Mizuta Noriko. *Feminizumu no kanata* (The way of feminism). Kōdansha, 1991.

———. *Hiroin kara hiro e: Josei to jiga no hyōgen* (From heroine to hero: Women and the expression of self). Tabata shoten, 1982.

———, ed. *Josei gaku to no deai* (Meeting women's studies). Shūeisha shinsho, 2004.

———, ed. *Josei no jiko hyōgen to bunka* (Women's self-expression and culture). Tabata shoten, 1993.

———. *Monogatari to hanmonogatari no fūkei* (The landscape of romance and anti-romance). Tabata shoten, 1993.

———. *Nijusseiki no josei hyōgen* (Twentieth-century women's expressions). Gakugei shorin, 2003.

———, ed. *Nyū feminizumu rebyū 2: Onna to hyōgen* (New feminism review 2: Women and expression). Gakuyō shobō, 1991.

Mizuta Noriko and Kitada Sachie, eds. *Yamanbatachi no monogatari* (Stories of mountain witches). Gakugei shorin, 2002.

Murō Saisei. *Ōgon no hari* (Golden needles). Chūō kōron sha, 1961.

Saegusa Kazuko. *Ren'ai shōsetsu no kansei* (Pitfalls of modern love stories). Seidosha, 1991.

Saeki Junko. *'Iro' to 'ai' no hikaku bunkashi* (A comparative cultural history of *iro* and *ai*). Iwanami shoten, 1998.

Saitō Minako. *Modan gāru ron* (Modern girls). Magazine House, 2000.

———. *Ninshin shōsetsu* (Pregnancy novels). Chikuma shobō, 1994.

Seki Reiko. *Kataru onnatachi no jidai: Ichiyō to Meiji josei hyōgen* (Ichiyō and Meiji women's expression: The age of women storytellers). Shin'yōsha, 1997.

Setouchi Jakuchō, Donald Keene, and Tsurumi Shunsuke. *Dō-jidai wo ikite: Wasureenu hitobito* (Living through the same era: People we can't forget). Iwanami shoten, 2004.

Shin Feminizumu Hihyō no Kai (New Feminist Criticism Society), ed. *Higuchi Ichiyō wo yominaosu* (Rereading Higuchi Ichiyō). Gakugei shorin, 1994.

Tanaka Yūko. *Higuchi ichiyō 'iyada!' to iu* (Higuchi Ichiyō says, "No way!"). Shūeisha shinsho, 2004.

Watanabe Kazuko. *Feminizu shōsetsuron* (On feminist literature). Tsuge shobō, 1993.

Yonaha Keiko. *Gendai joryū sakkaron* (Contemporary women's writing). Shinbisha, 1986.

Select Special Issues on Women's Writing in Japanese Journals

"Gendai joryū sakka no himitsu" (The secrets of contemporary women writers). *Kokubungaku kaishaku to kanshō*, September 1962.

"Kindai joryū no bungaku" (Modern women's literature). *Kokubungaku kaishaku to kanshō*, March 1972.

"Joryū bungaku no genzai" (Women's literature today). *Kokubungaku kaishaku to kyōzai no kenkyū*, July 1976.

"Joryū sakka to aidenchichi" (Women writers and identity). *Kokubungaku kaishaku to kanshō*, September 1976.

"Joryū no zensen: Higuchi Ichiyō kara 80-nendai no sakka made" (From Higuchi Ichiyō to the writers of the 1980s: On the front lines of writing women). *Kokubungaku kaishaku to kyōzai no kenkyū* 25 (15) (December 1980).

"Onna to wa nani ka: Josei sakka no sekai (What do we mean by 'woman'?: The world of the woman writer). *Kokubungaku kaishaku to kanshō*, February 1981.

"Joryū sakka" (Woman writer). *Kokubungaku kaishaku to kanshō*, September 1985.

"Josei: Sono henkaku no ekurichūru" (Women and the écriture of transition). *Kokubungaku kaishaku to kanshō*, May 1986.

"Sekushuaritii to sōzōryoku" (Sexuality and the power of imagination). *Gunzō*, November 1990.

"Josei sakka no shinryū" (New stream of women writers). *Kokubungaku kaishaku to kanshō*, May 1991.

"Kotoba to josei" (Women and language). *Kokubungaku kaishaku to kanshō*, July 1991.

"Feminizumu no shinpuku" (Feminism's pendulum). *Gunzō*, October 1991.

"Feminizumu no gengo: Josei bungaku" (The language of feminism: Women's literature). *Kokubungaku kaishaku to kyōzai no kenkyū*, November 1992.

"Dansei to iu seidō" (The 'male' institution). *Nihon bungaku*, November 1992.

"Masei to bosei: Onna no me de bungaku wo yominaosu" (Witches and mothers: Rereading literature through women's eyes). *Shin Nihon bungaku*, Winter 1992.

"Josei bungaku no shinsō wo yomu" (Reading the depths of women's literature). *Shin Nihon bungaku*, October 1993.

"Josei no 'chi' no saizensen: Onna no disukūru" (At the forefront of women's knowledge: Female discourse). *Kokubungaku kaishaku to kyōzai no kenkyū*, March 2000.

"Higuchi Ichiyō: Kore made no, soshite kore kare no" (Higuchi Ichiyō: What came before, what follows). *Kokubungaku kaishaku to kanshō*, May 2003.

"Josei sakka 'genzai' " (Women writers 'today'). *Kokubungaku kaishaku to kanshō*, March 2004.

ABOUT THE CONTRIBUTORS

Tomoko Aoyama is a senior lecturer at the University of Queensland, Australia.
Her publications include "The Cooking Man in Modern Japanese Literature," in
Asian Masculinities: The Meaning and Practice of Manhood in China and Japan
(2003); "Childhood Reimagined: The Memoirs of Ōgai's Children," *Monumenta
Nipponica* (Winter 2003); "A Room Sweet as Honey: Father-Daughter Love in
Mori Mari," in *Father-Daughter Plots: Japanese Literary Women and the Law of the
Father* (2001); and "The Love That Poisons: Japanese Parody and the New
Literacy," *Japan Forum* (April 1994).

Jan Bardsley is an associate professor of Japanese humanities at the University of
North Carolina at Chapel Hill. She is author of *The Bluestockings of Japan: New
Women Fiction and Essays from Seitō, 1911–1916* (2006). In 2001, she and Joanne
Hershfield produced and directed the video documentary *Women in Japan*.

Janine Beichman is a professor at Daitō Bunka University in Tokyo. She has
published two critical biographies, *Masaoka Shiki: His Life and Works* (2002) and
*Embracing the Firebird: Yosano Akiko and the Birth of the Female Voice in Modern
Japanese Poetry* (2002); an original *nō* play, *Drifting Fires* (1986); and several
translations of modern writers, including *The End of Summer* (1993), by the
novelist Setouchi Harumi, and two books by the poet and critic Makoto Ooka.

Rebecca L. Copeland is an associate professor of Japanese literature at Washington
University in St. Louis, Missouri. Her published works include *The Sound of the
Wind: The Life and Works of Uno Chiyo* (1992); *Lost Leaves: Women Writers of
Meiji Japan* (2000); and *The Father-Daughter Plot: Japanese Literary Women and
the Law of the Father* (2001), which she co-edited with Dr. Esperanza Ramirez-
Christensen of the University of Michigan. She is currently completing an
anthology of translations of Meiji women's writings in collaboration with
Dr. Melek Ortabasi.

Mika Endo is a graduate student in the Department of East Asian Languages and
Civilizations at the University of Chicago. Her interest is in fiction written for
children in Taishō and early Shōwa Japan.

Joan E. Ericson is an associate professor of Japanese and also chair of the
Department of German, Russian, and East Asian Languages at Colorado
College. Author of *Be a Woman: Hayashi Fumiko and Modern Japanese Women's
Literature* (1997), she is currently working on a history of children's literature
in Japan.

Barbara Hartley is a lecturer in Asian Studies and Japanese Studies at the University
of Queensland, Australia. Her research focus is twentieth-century Japan, with
particular interest in the study of nation and gender. Current projects include
representations of the mother in modern Japan and the body in the writing of

colonial subjects. She has written recently on the subversion of national discourse in the narratives of the early modern women writers Mizuno Senko and Shiraki Shizu.

Maryellen Toman Mori was a university professor of Japanese language and literature for fifteen years. She has published numerous essays on and translations of Japanese literature. Among her current projects are a translation of Takahashi Takako's novel *Ikari no ko* (Child of wrath) and a study of the boy androgyne in the literature of several Japanese women writers.

Yoshiko Nagaoka is an assistant professor at the University of Evansville, where she teaches language, culture, and literature and is responsible for the development of the Japanese program. Her research focuses on language education, features of Japanese language, educational and cultural globalization, and minority issues. She is currently researching Japanese cultural globalization and its impact on South Korean culture in Japan.

Kathryn Pierce received her M.A. in East Asian studies from Washington University in St. Louis. She is working towards a Ph.D. at the University of Chicago.

Laurel Rasplica Rodd is a professor of Japanese and comparative literature at the University of Colorado at Boulder. In addition to publications and translations of classical Japanese *waka*, she has published numerous articles on the twentieth-century poet Yosano Akiko, including "Yosano Akiko and Nationalism," in *Modern Japan: An Encyclopedia of History, Culture, and Nationalism* (1998); "Yosano Akiko on Poetic Inspiration," in *The Distant Isle* (1996); "Yosano Akiko's 'On Poetry,'" in *New Leaves* (1993); "Yosano Akiko and the Bunkagakuin: 'Creating Free Individuals,'" in the *Journal of the Association of Teachers of Japanese* (1991); and "Yosano Akiko and the Japanese Women's Movement in the Taishō Era," in *Recreating Japanese Women* (1991).

Amanda Seaman is an assistant professor of Japanese language and literature at the University of Massachusetts at Amherst. She is the author of *Bodies of Evidence: Women, Society, and Detective Fiction in 1990s Japan* (2004) and guest editor of a *Japan Forum* special issue (July 2004) on women and detective fiction.

Eiji Sekine is associate professor of Japanese at Purdue University. He is the author of *"Tasha" no shōkyo: Yoshiyuki Jun'nosuke to kindai bungaku* (Erasure of the other: Yoshiyuki Jun'nosuke and modern literature, 1993) and the editor of *Uta no hibiki, monogatari no yokubō* (Echo of poetry and desire for narrative, 1996). He has also edited the proceedings of both the Midwest Association for Japanese Literary Studies and the Association for Japanese Literary Studies.

Judy Wakabayashi is an associate professor at Kent State University, where she currently teaches Japanese-English translation and translation theory in the M.A. in Japanese Translation program. She has published various articles relating to the theory and practice of translation and also translates professionally. Her main research interests are the history of translation in Japan and the development of a Japanese-English translation textbook.

INDEX